The Collingridge Guide to

Garden Plants in Colour

Adrian Bloom

Alan Bloom

Jack Harkness

Royton E. Heath

Arthur Hellyer

Frances Perry

Percy Thrower

Dennis Woodland

The Collingridge Guide to

Garden

Hamlyn

LONDON · NEW YORK · SYDNEY · TORONTO

Plants in Colour

Published by The Hamlyn Publishing Group Ltd.,
London · New York · Sydney · Toronto
Astronaut House, Feltham, Middlesex, England

Copyright © The Hamlyn Publishing Group Ltd., 1975

Printed and bound by Litografia A. Romero, S.A.
Santa Cruz de Tenerife, Canary Islands (Spain)

Filmset in England by Keyspools Limited,
Golborne, Lancashire, England
Set in 9 on 11 pt. Monophoto Times

ISBN 0 600 38673 2

ACKNOWLEDGEMENTS

The Editor would like to thank the following for the
photographs used in this book:

Bernard Alfieri, *Amateur Gardening*, Alan Bloom, Pat
Brindley, *Country Life*, Ernest Crowson, Jack Harkness, Royton
E. Heath, Anthony Huxley, Elsa Megson, Kenneth Scowen,
The Harry Smith Horticultural Photographic Collection,
Michael Warren and Dennis Woodland.

Line drawings by Colin Gray
D. L. TF. 759 - 1975

Contents

Introduction

To walk into a well-stocked nursery or garden centre these days, as an enthusiastic gardener, is to be put rather in the position of a small boy given a handful of money and let loose in a sweet shop to help himself. The choice is wide to the point of embarrassment.

I'm not suggesting that is a bad thing, indeed quite the reverse; but it does raise problems and that is where this book comes in. How often have you, for instance, mulled over the question of which plants to give precious garden space to, or wondered which really are the best forms of familiar – and, sometimes, not so familiar – plants? What the team of distinguished contributors to this excellent compilation provide is the answer to just such questions of plant evaluation and assessment, and by so doing narrow down your options to manageable proportions.

They would be the last to suggest, I'm quite sure, as indeed would I, that their recommendations include all the best plants available. With the vast mass of plant material they have had to choose from, that would clearly be impossible, and even the most fair-minded and knowledgeable of plantsmen have their likes and dislikes which must, to some extent, colour their views. What can be said, though, is that the glittering parade of fine plants which are described, and in many cases illustrated, here will give a great deal of enjoyment. They are out of the top drawer, whether they are trees or shrubs, conifers, heathers, roses, herbaceous perennial or bulbous plants, rock plants, annuals, biennials or the increasingly popular pool plants which grace so many a terrace and patio setting these days, not to mention more expansive garden scenes.

What I would like to think is that *The Collingridge Guide to Garden Plants in Colour* will become your passport to garden enjoyment, that it will be a book you will turn to without hestitation every time you are making up an order for a nursery or are treating yourself to a spending spree at your local garden centre. A book, too, which you will get down off the shelf whenever some new decorative garden feature is planned – for inspiration and a comforting helping hand.

For it is a helping hand which we all need in gardening. The subject's so vast that nobody can claim to be an absolute master of all its highways and byways. Therein lies its fascination. You can garden for pleasure for a lifetime, and still, in all humility, recognize that you still don't know the half of it.

As a reference book this has everything to commend it – it is a survey of plants from the four corners of the world, as well as from the plant breeders' skilful hands and from gardens, for it should not be forgotten that many a good plant has arisen naturally in this way. All the plants described can bring to your garden increased beauty and interest. And that, after all, is what decorative gardening is all about.

Robert Pearson
EDITOR

Shrubs and Climbers

Arthur Hellyer, M.B.E., V.M.H., F.L.S., one of Britain's leading gardening writers, has been intimately connected with horticulture since he left Dulwich College, London, where he was educated. He spent eleven years on the staff of various commercial nurseries before becoming assistant editor of *Amateur Gardening* in 1929, and he became editor of that magazine in 1946, a post he held with distinction until he retired in 1967. He was also editor of *Gardening Illustrated* from 1947 to 1956 and has been gardening correspondent of the *Financial Times* since 1959.

He combines his many journalistic activities with running his large garden in East Sussex and his other, smaller garden in Jersey, this last made from what was once a stone quarry. He is the author of many books on all aspects of gardening and has brought pleasure and increased understanding of their hobby to countless gardeners through his writings.

Mr Hellyer has travelled extensively abroad, and is in close touch with developments and trends in horticulture throughout the world. This, together with his highly developed critical facilities and his unrivalled knowledge of practical gardening and the problems of amateur gardeners make his writings of exceptional value. He also has the gift, given to few, of making the more technical aspects of gardening easily understandable to the layman.

Mr Hellyer was awarded the M.B.E. in 1967 and The Royal Horticultural Society's coveted Victoria Medal of Honour – there can be only sixty-three holders at any one time, one for each year of Queen Victoria's reign – in the same year. He is also a Fellow of the Linnean Society.

American gardeners, who are very good at inventing names that are highly descriptive, often refer to the trees and shrubs used in gardens as foundation planting. This expresses perfectly one of the major roles which these plants perform in providing the permanent framework into which other plants with a shorter life or a greater need for renewal can be fitted. Because they are the foundation of the whole planting scheme, one grasps immediately why they must be considered with the greatest care and why also, as a rule, this must be done at the beginning of every new planting scheme or, if this is quite impossible, a very clear picture of where these foundation plants are to go must be in mind before anything else is put in.

However, though this foundation role is immensely important, it is not the only part that shrubs have to play in the garden. They provide some of the shade and shelter that can be so much appreciated by other plants, they assist in preserving privacy and they can also cut out much of the noise of the outside world. Their roots can be very valuable in binding the soil on steep slopes or in other places subject to erosion, though it must not be overlooked that the roots of some species can be so numerous, so near to the surface and so hungry that they can make life difficult for close neighbours.

Shrubs can be divided into evergreen and deciduous kinds, the former retaining leaf cover throughout the year, the latter dropping all their leaves each autumn and producing a new lot the following spring. Both types have their value and the proportions in which they are used need to be considered carefully.

Evergreens tend to dominate in winter when their solid shapes stand out conspicuously amid the tracery of bare branches of deciduous trees and shrubs, and at this season they provide much of the shelter, which can be very important for plants growing close to them. However, deciduous shrubs offer the advantages of constantly changing patterns, textures and colours which can be entrancing. It is broadly true to say that a garden with too many evergreens can be heavy and dull and that a garden with too many deciduous trees and shrubs can seem bare and bleak for five or six months each year. The ideal is one in which there is a constantly changing pattern with new combinations of colour and form emerging all the time and never a dull moment from January to December.

Into this scheme of permanent planting, perennial or shrubby climbers fit perfectly.

They too may be evergreen or deciduous, and they too are there all the time, though it is fair to observe that deciduous climbers in general have considerably less to offer in winter than deciduous trees and shrubs since most of them are then reduced to a more or less meaningless tangle of growth and may even, in some cases, need to be cut back almost to ground level. Yet by summer these same plants can have shot up to 15 or 20 ft. and be draping walls, screens, buildings and even trees and shrubs with their leaves and flowers.

If one thinks of garden planting in terms of interior decor (and for very small gardens it is by no means an inappropriate comparison), shrubs may be regarded as major objects of furniture and climbers as wall coverings, curtains and other drapes. Where the comparison breaks down is that a room remains much the same at all seasons, whereas a garden is in a state of constant change which is one reason why making a garden and then living with it can be so very exciting and satisfying.

This raises another point that must be carefully considered. Shrubs may continue to increase in size for many years. If they are planted sufficiently close to give a well-furnished appearance almost from the start, they are certain to be overcrowded after a few years, yet if they are spaced at the outset to accommodate their ultimate proportions, the garden may well appear thin and poorly balanced for a long time.

There are several ways in which these difficulties may be overcome. One is deliberately to overplant at the beginning in such a way that there can be a progressive thinning out of plants over the years without materially upsetting the balance. Another is to use some swift-growing shrubs to give a quick effect with the knowledge that they will be too big, and so will have to be removed, after a few years, and at the same time to plant slower-growing kinds which will be ready to take over when that time arrives. Yet a third way is to plant the trees and shrubs thinly and to fill in during the early years with herbaceous and bedding plants which by their nature must be frequently renewed. All three methods have their merits and drawbacks and which is chosen must depend upon personal preference and circumstances.

Preparation of the Soil

Shrubs and climbers are always planted for years and often for permanency so the preparation of the ground should be thorough. In particular difficult weeds such as nettle, docks, ground elder, couch grass and bindweed should be removed, for though it is possible to deal with these later on with herbicides, it is much more time consuming and expensive then than making a clean sweep at the outset. If the sites for the shrubs are dug about 18 in. deep, it will be possible to pick out most of the weed roots, but to make doubly sure the weeds can be treated with a suitable herbicide a few weeks before digging commences, so that they are already more or less dead when cultivation starts. If you do choose this course, be sure to use a herbicide with a wide spectrum of effectiveness, since some kinds only kill weeds of a particular type, and also one that leaves no harmful residues in the soil. Paraquat is very suitable for this purpose, but since it operates through the leaves it is most effective in fairly warm, sunny weather when growth is active.

If well-rotted manure or garden compost is available, this can be mixed with the soil while it is being prepared at the rate of 5 to 6 lb. per sq. yd. Peat at 2 to 4 lb. per sq. yd. will improve the texture of both heavy and light soils, and bonemeal (applied while wearing gloves) at 4 oz. per sq. yd. will provide a steady source of plant food for the first few months.

Selection of Plants

Plants may be sold as 'bare root', 'balled' or 'container grown'. Bare root means that they are lifted from a nursery bed and that all, or most, of the soil adhering to the roots is shaken off so that the plants are as light as possible to transport. Transplanting bare root can be done only in autumn and winter when plants are dormant or nearly so. It is the cheapest way of buying plants, but many kinds, particularly evergreens, cannot be transplanted safely in this way, even at the most favourable periods.

Balled plants are also lifted from nursery beds but with as much soil as practicable and this soil is then held around the roots with hessian or polythene so that it does not fall off during transplantation. Balled plants weigh a great deal more than bare root plants and so cost more to transport, but provided the work of balling and replanting is well done they have a better chance of survival. The planting season is a little more extended, balled evergreens often being moved in early spring or early autumn.

Container-grown plants are those that are really well established in pots, polythene bags or anything else which will ensure that all the roots and the soil around them can be transported and planted with the minimum of disturbance. Well-grown

container plants can be put in at any time of the year when the soil is in good working condition, but they weigh more and usually cost more than comparable bare root or balled plants. Most of the shrubs and climbers offered for sale in garden centres are container grown and this is an ideal method for the cash and carry trade. Even for mail order many climbing plants are pot grown since some do not transplant well in any other way, and it is a method used for many other plants that resent root breakage, such as brooms, romneya and perowskia.

Some plants refuse to grow in alkaline soils unless regularly fed with iron and manganese in specially prepared (chelated or sequestrated) forms. Rhododendrons and azaleas are two of the most important groups of plants in this category and unless one is prepared to make special acid soil beds for them it is really unwise to attempt to grow them on soils containing much chalk or limestone. Other lime-hating plants are mentioned in the individual notes on plants.

Planting

If container-grown or balled plants are obtained, it is only necessary to prepare a hole just a little larger than the container and slip the plant into this with as little root disturbance as possible. Pot-grown plants can usually be tapped out quite safely by turning them upside down and rapping the rim of the pot sharply on something firm, such as the handle of a spade thrust well into the soil. Of course the plant itself must be carefully held while this is done so that it does not fall to the ground and possibly snap off. In the case of balled plants and those grown in polythene bags, the covering material can usually be cut and then stripped off with the plant on the edge of, or actually in, the hole it is to occupy. But whatever the precise method used, the covering must come off unless it is only of paper or compressed peat or some other substance that will rot away in the soil.

With bare root plants a little more thought and care are necessary. The hole made must be large enough to ensure that there is space for all the roots to be naturally disposed, with room at the top for a covering of 1 or 2 in. of soil over the uppermost roots. Another way to determine depth is to look for the dark soil mark on the stem or stems, indicating where the soil came to in the nursery bed, and to replant so that this is just beneath the surface. With bare root plants it is also necessary to work soil around and between the roots and to make this easy it

Firm the soil well around the roots and plant to the soil mark on the stem; this indicates the level at which the shrub was planted in the nursery

often pays to prepare in advance a planting mixture of well-broken soil mixed with about a third its bulk of peat and containing a sprinkling of bonemeal.

Whatever type of plant is being used, once the soil has been returned around and over the roots it should be made thoroughly firm by pressing all round with the foot, after which a little loose soil or peat can be scattered over the soil to leave everything tidy.

Shelter

Some shrubs, particularly evergreens, may require some shelter from wind or sun for a few months after planting until they are well established and able to look after themselves. Large plastic bags of the type used for fertilizers, composts and peat make excellent shelters if slit top and bottom and then slipped over the shrub and held open with three or four canes. Hessian screens can be made in a similar way or quite effective temporary shelter can be given by thrusting evergreen boughs into the soil around the newly planted shrubs.

Pruning

Not many shrubs require pruning immediately after planting, though it always pays to cut out damaged stems or any that appear so badly placed as to upset the balance of the specimen. Some hedge shrubs, notably privet and lonicera, will repay immediate shortening to ensure that they branch freely right from the base, but it is not until later years that pruning becomes a serious problem.

9

A plastic fertilizer bag supported by canes will provide shelter for a newly planted shrub

Basically pruning has four aims: the first to prevent plants from growing too large; the second to get rid of diseased or decrepit growth; the third to improve the natural appearance of the plant by removing badly placed or overcrowded stems and the fourth to improve the quality of the flowers or leaves.

Often the steps taken to achieve one of these ends also look after some of the others as well. Thus it is always wise to start by removing obviously diseased, damaged or weak growth, because when this has been done the specimen may look very different and require little further pruning. If it does appear that something more is needed, thinning out overcrowded, crossing branches may put things right.

A few shrubs, particularly those that flower in summer such as the purple buddleia, the varieties of *Hydrangea pani-*culata, fuchsia and caryopteris, can be cut hard back each spring with considerable benefit to the quality of their flowers and without destroying their natural habit. Some spring and early summer-flowering kinds, such as forsythia, weigela, philadelphus and cytisus, can have most of their flowering growth removed immediately the flowers fade, and this can be a convenient way of restricting their size and improving the quality of their flowers at one and the same time. Details are given in the list which follows.

Selected Shrubs and Climbers

Acer

Most species are trees but some varieties of *Acer palmatum*, the Japanese maple, are shrubby and very useful for planting as isolated specimens because of their usually picturesque shape and attractive foliage. Specially recommended are the *dissectum* varieties with deeply divided almost fern-like leaves, green in *dissectum* itself, beetroot red in *dissectum atropurpureum*, yellowish in *dissectum flavescens*, bronzy in *dissectum ornatum*. These all grow 5 or 6 ft. high and maybe more in diameter. All forms of *A. palmatum* like soil that is fairly moist in spring and summer but not wet in winter when the bushes are leafless. Pruning is undesirable, except to remove any badly placed stems, which can be done in winter.

When pruning deciduous shrubs, dead, diseased and weak wood should always be removed, the aim being to produce a good open framework of branches. It is also advisable to remove a portion of old wood each year

Actinidia

Two kinds are grown, both twiners but very different in appearance. *Actinidia chinensis* is very vigorous, capable of covering a whole outbuilding or a large wall with its red-haired stems and large heart-shaped leaves. Its clusters of creamy flowers are followed by edible, gooseberry-like fruits, and since it comes from China it is sometimes called the Chinese gooseberry. It is as a tropical looking, yet quite hardy, foliage plant that it is most valued.

A. kolomikta is much less vigorous and more fussy, needing good soil and a sheltered place, and it is valued for its green, cream and pink leaves. These colours are best developed when the plant is grown against a warm sunny wall. Both kinds lose their leaves in winter, and both can be pruned by shortening side growths to about 6 in. in summer and taking out the tips of any stems that threaten to grow too far.

Aucuba

The kind cultivated is *Aucuba japonica*, a vigorous evergreen with large, shining green, laurel-like leaves. It is often used as a hedge or screen plant because of its dense growth and the ease with which it can be grown in almost any soil and place. But there are several handsome forms which can be used in more decorative ways, notably *crotonifolia*, 6 to 8 ft. high, with leaves heavily splashed with yellow, and *nana rotundifolia*, only 2 to 3 ft. high, a female plant which will produce good crops of scarlet berries if planted near a male such as *crotonifolia*. All aucubas can be pruned hard in spring or can be trimmed more lightly at any time during the summer, though with fruiting bushes it is best to leave this until after the berries are set when care can be taken not to cut them off.

Azalea

From a botanical standpoint all azaleas are rhododendrons, but in nursery catalogues they are usually listed separately. Some varieties are evergreen and some are deciduous, and these differ greatly in appearance. The evergreens mostly have small leaves and a rather twiggy, densely branched habit and small to medium-sized flowers in shades of pink and lavender to scarlet and crimson, plus white, whereas the deciduous azaleas have larger leaves, often turning crimson in autumn, a more open habit and larger flowers in shades of yellow, orange, coppery red, crimson and white. The flowers of some deciduous kinds, particularly the common yellow, are spicily scented.

All flower in spring or early summer and grow best in lime-free, moderately acid soils and half-shaded places, but the deciduous varieties will also grow well in full sun provided that the soil is not dry. It pays to work in plenty of peat or leaf-mould before planting and to topdress with either or both each spring. Pruning is usually undesirable, but badly placed branches can be cut out in spring, immediately after flowering.

Berberis

This is one of the big families of shrubs, containing both deciduous and evergreen species, the former grown mainly for their heavy crops of small scarlet or crimson berries, the latter for their yellow flowers and attractive foliage. Most are very spiny, which makes them suitable for use as outer protective hedges or screens, and most are also very hardy and easy to grow in almost any soil.

Specially recommended deciduous kinds are Buccaneer, 4 to 6 ft., red berries; *thunbergii atropurpurea*, 5 to 7 ft., beetroot-purple leaves, and if there is room for a really big bush, *jamesiana*, 8 to 10 ft., with arching, coral-red stems and berries which change from coral to crimson.

Fine evergreen kinds are *darwinii*, 8 to 10 ft., with small holly-like leaves and orange flowers in spring, followed by grape-purple berries; *stenophylla*, 8 to 10 ft., with arching stems wreathed in spring in sweet-scented, yellow flowers, and *verruculosa*, which has much the effect of *darwinii* reduced to half its size. There are also dwarf forms of *Berberis stenophylla*, such as *corallina*, red buds opening to yellow flowers, and *gracilis*, yellow, which can be very useful in small gardens.

The dense growth of most barberries tends to kill the stems beneath and so dead wood needs to be cut out in winter, and at the same time unwanted or overgrown stems of deciduous kinds can be removed. Pruning of evergreen varieties is best done after flowering.

Buddleia

Most familiar are the numerous varieties of *Buddleia davidii*, a normally rather tall, shuttlecock-shaped shrub with small, honey-scented flowers packed into conical spikes in late summer. Of this fine shrub there are lavender, purple, deep blue and white varieties. There are also other good species that are quite different in appearance, such as *B. alternifolia*, a big shrub

Above: *Actinidia kolomikta*
Below: **Azaleas and hostas**

Above: *Buddleia davidii* **Peace**
Below: *Camellia japonica elegans*

with long, slender, arching stems wreathed in early summer with lavender-blue flowers, and *B. globosa*, open and rather gaunt in habit, with orange flowers in globose clusters which suggested its common name, orange ball tree. There is a hybrid between this and *B. davidii*, named *B. weyeriana*, but since the chief effect of the cross is to change the bright colour of the orange balls to a dirty mauve it is more

of a curiosity than a decorative asset.

All buddleias thrive on chalk and limestone soils and grow well wherever the soil is well drained and the situation warm and sunny. All varieties of *B. davidii* can be cut back hard early each spring if desired, which somewhat reduces their size, though they can still reach 8 ft. in a season, and this improves the size of the flower spikes. *B. alternifolia* is best pruned in summer immediately after flowering, when the old flowering stems can be cut back to side shoots. With *B. globosa* it is usually sufficient to cut out weak and dead growth in early spring, but if bushes are too big they can be cut back, though with loss of flower that year.

Buxus

This is the common box or boxwood, an evergreen that is much used for making topiary specimens and also for forming small hedges and the elaborate clipped patterns in knots and parterres. Its little rounded leaves have a pungent scent which some people like and others find disagreeable.

There are numerous forms of *Buxus sempervirens*, of which the most useful are Gold Tip, young leaves yellowish; *handsworthensis*, a sturdy variety specially recommended for hedges, and *suffruticosa*, the edging box, a dwarf form that has become scarce, but is particularly good for clipping to a maximum height of 18 in. There is also a highly attractive variety named *elegantissima* in which each leaf is edged with white.

All varieties grow well in most soils, including chalk. They can be clipped at any time in summer, but any hard pruning necessary is best done in spring. *Suffruticosa*, when obtainable, is usually sold by the 'yard' which means sufficient rooted pieces to plant a yard length of edging.

Callicarpa

Not many shrubs have violet or lilac-blue berries, but callicarpas have, and this is their special contribution to the garden. They are not the hardiest of plants and should be given a warm, sunny place in good fertile soil. The best kind is *Callicarpa bodinieri*, or the form of it known as *giraldii*, both of which usually grow 5 or 6 ft. high, though in favourable places they can be taller. As plants age some of the older or less well-placed stems can be cut out annually in early spring.

Camellia

Handsome evergreen foliage and abundant flowers make the camellia a valuable garden shrub wherever conditions are

suitable. It requires an acid or neutral soil, unless it is regularly fed with specially prepared iron and manganese, and, although fairly hardy, its flowers are produced so early in the year that these are subject to severe damage by frost unless planted in fairly sheltered places. They succeed well in thin woodland, especially in the south and west, and also do well in many town gardens since they do not mind shade and benefit from the slight extra warmth that comes from many closely packed buildings.

Two races are of major importance, one composed of the almost innumerable varieties of *Camellia japonica*, the other of hybrids between this species and *C. saluenensis*. The colour range is similar in both races from white and palest pink to scarlet and crimson, and flowers may be single, semi-double or fully double.

Camellias transplant easily and it is best to buy them in flower so that the colours and flower shapes that appeal most to the purchaser can be selected. Most will make big bushes in time, but are fairly slow growing. Regular pruning is undesirable, but bushes can be cut hard back in spring after flowering, though with loss of flower the following year. A few misplaced or overlong branches can be removed without this danger and if this is done while the bushes are in bloom these branches may be useful for floral decoration indoors.

Campsis

This is the botanical name of the trumpet vines, twining or self-clinging climbers with clusters of trumpet-shaped flowers in late summer or early autumn. In warm, sunny, sheltered places they can be spectacular, but they are unsuitable for cold gardens, partly because much growth may be killed by frost, but even more because flower buds may form so late in the season that they have no chance to open. The best place for them is against a wall facing south or west. Each spring most of the old stems should be cut out or shortened as the best flowers are borne on young growth.

The hardiest and most self-clinging kind is *Campsis radicans*, with orange-scarlet flowers. *C. grandiflora* has larger orange and red flowers but is only partially self-clinging and this is also true of Madame Galen, the fine salmon-red hybrid between these two species.

Carpenteria

There is only one species, *Carpenteria californica*, a lovely but slightly tender evergreen for a warm, sunny, sheltered place in fertile, well-drained soil. It grows 5 or 6 ft. high and produces its white flowers, each with a golden boss of anthers in the centre, in July. Little pruning is necessary, but worn-out stems that are producing little new growth can be cut out in spring.

Caryopteris

This sun-loving shrub is often killed almost to ground level in winter, but sprouts up again strongly in the spring to produce 2-ft. stems set with small greyish leaves and producing, in late summer and early autumn, rather fluffy-looking clusters of lavender-blue flowers. The best kind to plant is a hybrid named *Caryopteris clandonensis*, and of this there are several forms with extra deep blue flowers, such as Ferndown and Kew Blue. All can be pruned to within a few inches of ground level early each spring and all succeed best in rather light well-drained soils.

Ceanothus

There are both deciduous and evergreen species and they require different treatment in the garden. Most of the evergreen kinds flower in spring and many are best grown against sunny walls as they are not fully hardy. If they are pruned at all it should be immediately after flowering when unwanted stems can be cut out and side shoots shortened a little. By contrast the most useful deciduous varieties flower in late summer and early autumn and can, with advantage, be pruned hard each spring when they will make long stems terminated by sprays of the typical thimble-shaped clusters of small flowers. All like good, well-drained soil and a warm, sunny position.

Ceanothus impressus, 4 ft. high by 6 ft. wide, with deep blue flowers and a densely branched habit, and *C. thyrsiflorus*, with light blue flowers, are two of the hardiest evergreen kinds. *C. thyrsiflorus* is variable in habit, tall with arching growths in the variety Cascade, but making low, wide-spreading mounds of growth in the variety *repens*. Typical deciduous varieties are Gloire de Versailles, light blue; Topaz, deep blue, and Perle Rose, rose pink.

Chaenomeles

Some catalogues still list these shrubs under their old name cydonia, and gardeners often refer to them simply as Japanese quinces or japonicas. They are deciduous shrubs with apple-like blossom, scarlet, crimson, pink or white, according to variety, produced in late winter or early spring, usually followed by large, hard,

Cistus purpureus

fragrant fruits which can be used to flavour apple pies and make quince preserves. Grown naturally the various varieties of chaenomeles make densely branched, spiny bushes, but they are often trained against walls, when they should be pruned after flowering to get rid of any stems that cannot conveniently be tied in and to shorten forward-pointing side growths to a few inches so that everything is tidy. Bushes in the open need not be pruned unless they need to be reduced in size or density.

All kinds are very hardy and easy to grow in almost any soil, in sun or semishade. Good varieties are *cardinalis*, scarlet; *moerloosii* (Apple Blossom), pink; *nivalis*, white, and *simonii*, crimson.

Chimonanthus

This is the winter sweet, a name which perfectly describes its chief attraction, that of scenting the air in winter for many yards around. There is only one species, *Chimonanthus praecox* (also sometimes called *C. fragrans*) and its pale yellow, purple-centred flowers are not in the least spectacular, but they make up in perfume what they lack in colour. It is deciduous, makes a large, rather open-branched bush which is best left unpruned, though this may not be possible if it is trained against a sunny wall, as it often is. Then forward-growing stems that cannot readily be

trained in can be cut out or be shortened in late winter. The winter sweet thrives in most well-drained soils, including chalk.

Choisya

The popular name of *Choisya ternata*, Mexican orange blossom, describes both the appearance and the scent of its white flowers, most freely produced in late spring, though usually there are some more to follow in summer. The leaves are evergreen, divided and bright shining green, making this a very decorative shrub even in winter. Unfortunately, though it will withstand quite a lot of frost, it is not completely hardy, so it should be given a sunny place sheltered from north and east winds. It is not fussy about soil, does well in town gardens and can be pruned in early summer when the first blossoming is over, at which time stems can be shortened by up to 1 ft.

Cistus

No doubt these would be much more widely planted if they were just a little more reliably hardy, for they have many good qualities including evergreen foliage and tremendous flowering capacity in early and mid-summer. There are no better shrubs for hot, dry places in reasonably good soil, but they are not really

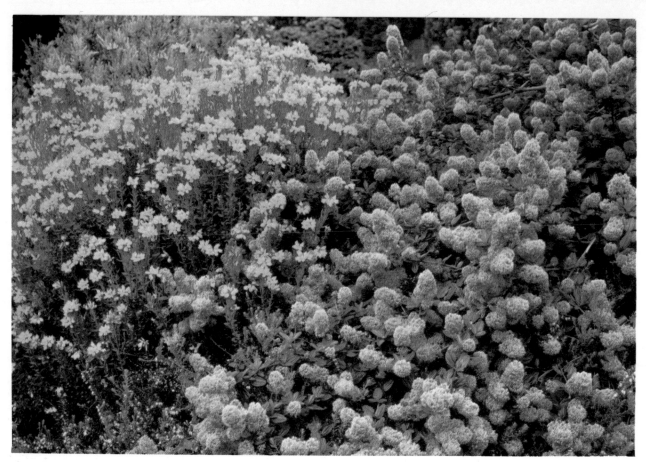

suitable for cold districts or poorly drained soils. The hardiest kinds are *Cistus corbariensis*, white, 2 to 3 ft.; *crispus*, magenta, 2 ft.; *cyprius*, white blotched crimson, 6 ft.; *ladaniferus*, very large white flowers blotched with maroon in most forms but sometimes pure white, 4 to 5 ft.; *laurifolius*, white, 6 to 7 ft.; *pulverulentus* (Sunset), magenta, 2 to 3 ft., and Silver Pink, light pink, 2 ft. One of the most beautiful kinds is *C. purpureus*, deep rose, maroon blotched, 3 to 4 ft., but it is less hardy than those just listed.

Cistus do not transplant easily and so are best purchased in containers. They need little pruning, but frost-damaged stems should be cut out in spring. As a rule bushes are not long lived so replacements must be made from time to time.

Clematis

There are herbaceous species of clematis, but the kinds we are concerned with here are all climbers with slender stems and tendrils with which to cling to twigs, wires, trellises or other not too stout supports. There are a great many different kinds and varieties, ranging from plants of quite modest size which can be trained up pillars, to sturdy climbers that will ascend tall trees or cover large outbuildings. Some have small flowers, some large, there are single, semi-double and fully

double-flowered varieties; the colour range is from white, pink and lavender to crimson and deep violet purple and there are varieties to bloom from early spring until autumn. Small wonder that clematis is the most popular of all climbing plants.

Clematis will thrive in most fertile soils and are particularly happy on chalk and limestone provided they are well fed. They do not transplant particularly well and so are best purchased in containers. They enjoy having their roots in the shade and their leaves in the sun which can be achieved by planting small shrubs or herbaceous plants around or in front of them to shade the soil. Some varieties, particularly some of the large-flowered hybrids, suffer from wilt disease which causes whole stems or even complete plants to collapse suddenly. The best preventative is to spray every fortnight each April and May with a copper fungicide.

Most kinds benefit from pruning and this may be essential if clematis have to be fitted to a particular area, but the pruning time and methods differ according to variety. Those that have finished flowering by the end of May can be pruned immediately after that as there will still be time for them to make good new growth for the following year. All the shoots that have just flowered can be removed, also some

Genista hispanica (yellow) and *Ceanothus thyrsiflorus repens* (blue)

of the older growth if there is too much of it. Varieties that flower in May and June, often with some more flowers in the summer, are pruned in February when thin stems and side growths are shortened to strong growth buds or to the new shoots that will then be starting. Again some of the old stems can be removed if there are too many of them, but a good framework of 'vines' must be retained as the flowers are produced on short stems from these.

Varieties that do not start to bloom until mid-summer or later are also pruned in February in the same way if they still have a lot of space to cover, but much harder if they have already filled their space, since they flower on long young shoots. It is quite safe to cut these varieties to within about 1 ft. of ground level if available space is limited.

Good small-flowered species are *Clematis armandii*, white, early spring, one of the few evergreen kinds, to 20 ft.; *flammula*, white, scented, August–September, to 15 ft.; *montana*, white, and *montana rubens*, purplish pink, both May flowering, to 30 ft.; *tangutica*, yellow, July–October, to 15 ft.

Good large-flowered hybrids are Barbara Dibley, violet purple, May–August;

Comtesse de Bouchard, pink, June–August; Countess of Lovelace, pale blue, double, June–September; Daniel Deronda, purplish blue, semi-double in May–June, but single from July–September; Ernest Markham, petunia purple, July–September; Hagley Hybrid, pink, June–September; *henryi*, white, May–June and again August–September; *jackmanii*, violet purple, July–September, and *jackmanii superba* similar but wider sepals; Lasurstern, lavender blue, May–June and again August–September; Nelly Moser, mauve and carmine, May–June and again August–September; Perle d'Azur, blue, June–August and Ville de Lyon, carmine, July–October.

Colutea

These are the bladder sennas, deciduous shrubs with clusters of yellow pea-type flowers followed by inflated seedpods which are distinctive and decorative. They will thrive in dry, hot places where many other plants would fail. *Colutea arborescens* will grow 10 or 12 ft. high if unrestricted, but can be kept to half that height by cutting back most or all the previous year's growth each February or March. *C. orientalis* is naturally smaller and *C. media* is a hybrid between the two and intermediate in size.

Cornus

These are the dogwoods, some of which are grown primarily for their coloured stems, some for their ornamental leaves and some for their flowers, or the showy, petal-like bracts that surround the true flowers. Since these different effects entail different treatment in the garden the groups need to be treated separately.

The dogwoods with coloured stems or variegated leaves all thrive in most soils and places, including those that are very wet. The best bark effects are produced by cutting all stems back to within a few inches of the base in early spring and the same treatment can be given to the foliage varieties or they can simply be thinned out a little, some of the older stems being removed where overcrowded. *Cornus alba sibirica*, the Westonbirt dogwood, has crimson stems and *C. stolonifera flaviramea* has greenish-yellow stems. *C. alba elegantissima* has white-variegated leaves and *C. alba spaethii*, yellow-variegated leaves.

The best dogwood to grow for true flowers is *Cornus mas*, the Cornelian

Above: *Cornus alba* Westonbirt
Below: *Cotoneaster frigida cornubia*

cherry, a tall, loosely branched shrub with clusters of small yellow flowers in February, but more spectacular are the bract-bearing kinds such as *C. kousa* with big white bracts in June, and *C. florida rubra* with pink bracts in May. Both make big bushes or small, widely branched trees and do best in good, loamy soil, preferably moderately acid and without lime or chalk. They need no pruning.

Corylopsis

Some kinds make small trees, but *Corylopsis pauciflora* is a shrub, 4 to 6 ft. high, with clusters of primrose-yellow, pleasantly scented flowers in March. It does best on lime-free soils and as a rule requires no pruning. Larger kinds are *C. glabrescens*, *C. spicata* and *C. willmottiae*, all with primrose-yellow flowers produced in little dangling chains along the bare stems in early spring.

Cotinus

This is a new name for a handsome shrub which many gardeners know as *Rhus cotinus*, the smoke tree or wig tree. The popular names refer to the tangle of hair-like filaments which carry the small flowers and which turn smoky grey in late summer. The rounded leaves become coppery red in autumn before they fall and in some varieties such as *purpureus* and Royal Purple are reddish purple all the summer. *Cotinus coggygria* is a big shrub, often 10 ft. high and considerably more, but if grown for foliage effect only it can be pruned annually in early spring, each stem made the previous year being shortened to a few inches. Plants thrive best in a warm sunny place and well-drained soil.

Cotoneaster

All the cotoneasters are capable of producing showy crops of berries, scarlet or crimson in most varieties, but many are also first-rate foliage shrubs with an interesting diversity of habit and leaf shape. *Cotoneaster dammeri* is completely prostrate, making a carpet of evergreen leaves ideal as covering for a bank or under other shrubs. *C. horizontalis* has a curious fishbone habit of branching and will make a wide low bush in the open or spread itself flat like a climber against a wall or fence. Its small leaves turn orange and scarlet before they fall in autumn.

C. microphyllus has small, dark green, evergreen leaves and its branches will mould themselves to any solid object or mound themselves into low, wide bushes. *C. conspicuus decorus*, making a bigger, dome-shaped bush, is also evergreen and notably free fruiting. *C. franchetii sterni-*

anus is semi-evergreen, of open shuttlecock habit and *C. salicifolius* is fully evergreen and has a number of forms, some spreading, some erect. Finally there are large, almost tree-like kinds, such as *C. frigidus*, which is deciduous and has a yellow-fruited variety named *fructu-luteo*, and scarlet-fruited hybrids such as *cornubia* and *watereri* which can reach 15 ft. or more.

All are very adaptable as to soil and position and, though pruning is not essential, stems or branches can be shortened or removed in spring if bushes occupy too much room, and when used as hedges they can in addition be trimmed lightly in summer.

Cytisus

This is one genus (the other two being genista and spartium) of the trio collectively known as brooms. Nearly all species of cytisus have the small pea-type flowers typical of the family, but in other respects they differ widely. There are prostrate kinds with creeping underground stems such as pale purple *Cytisus purpureus*; low, wide-spreading kinds such as cream-coloured *C. kewensis*; 12 to 18-in. small bushes such as bright yellow *C. beanii*; medium-sized bushes such as 3-ft. sulphur-yellow *C. praecox*, and tall bushes such as 6 to 8-ft. *C. multiflorus*, better known as the white Spanish broom. All these are April or May flowering as are the numerous varieties and hybrids of the common broom, *C. scoparius*, available in yellow, yellow and crimson, cream, pink, cerise and crimson varieties and all making bushes 5 to 6 ft. high. By contrast *C. battandieri*, 6 ft. or more, does not commence to produce its erect spikes of yellow, pineapple-scented flowers until June and its silky grey leaves are quite large. All the foregoing are deciduous.

C. monspessulanus and *C.* Porlock are evergreen, 6 to 8 ft. high, with yellow flowers in spring and early summer, sweet scented in Porlock. Unfortunately they are less hardy and therefore most suitable for southern, western and maritime gardens.

All brooms succeed best in sunny places and well-drained, moderately acid or neutral soils. Most can be pruned moderately immediately after flowering and *C. battandieri* can have old stems cut back to young side growth in spring.

Danae

There is only one species, *Danae racemosa*, the Alexandrian laurel, grown for its slender stems closely set with narrow evergreen leaves. It will grow in most soils

and places, even in dense shade, and is excellent for cut foliage at any time of the year as well as making an attractive 3-ft. high bush.

Daphne

Many kinds have richly scented flowers but by no means all are easy to grow and some have a tendency to die suddenly without obvious cause. When planting daphnes, therefore, it is usually wise to have some spares and to be prepared to replace or thin out from time to time. Most do not transplant well and so are best purchased in containers from which they can be moved with a minimum of root disturbance. All succeed best in open, sunny places and in soils that remain moist in summer but do not become waterlogged in winter.

Daphne mezereum, which is deciduous and produces its purple or white flowers on leafless stems in February and March, likes limestone or chalk soils. It has scarlet berries containing seeds that germinate readily when ripe to produce replacement plants. Other good kinds are *D. blagayana*, creamy white, March–April, prostrate; *burkwoodii*, pink, May–June, 3 ft., deciduous; *cneorum*, rose pink, May–June, evergreen, prostrate; *collina*, reddish purple, May, evergreen, 2 to 3 ft., and *odora*, reddish purple, February–March, evergreen, 3 to 6 ft., and variety *marginata*, hardier and with yellow-edged leaves. None requires regular pruning.

Deutzia

These are most attractive deciduous shrubs with small flowers freely produced in spring and early summer. They succeed in all reasonably fertile soils, prefer sunny positions and can have most of the flowering stems removed immediately the flowers fade, provided there is plenty of young growth coming along to flower the following year.

Good kinds are *Deutzia elegantissima*, rose pink, June, 4 ft.; *gracilis*, white, April–May, 3 to 5 ft., needs sheltered place as flowers are liable to be injured by spring frosts; *magnifica*, white, double, June–July, 6 to 8 ft.; Mont Rose, purplish pink, May–June, 3 ft.; *scabra flore pleno*, white and purple, double, June–July, 8 to 10 ft.

Elaeagnus

Sturdy evergreen and deciduous shrubs of which the former, grown mainly for their foliage, are the most useful in gardens.

Elaeagnus pungens maculata, with dark green leaves heavily splashed with yellow, is one of the brightest of all golden-

Left: *Cytisus praecox*
Right: *Daphne burkwoodii*

variegated shrubs and a good bush catching the sun is a heartwarming sight in winter. It will make a bush 10 ft. or more high and through, but can be kept much smaller by annual pruning in May. Its small silvery-white flowers, produced in autumn, often pass unnoticed but are delightfully scented. *E. macrophylla* has similar flowers, makes a wide-spreading bush 8 ft. or more high and has large leaves, silvery all over at first but becoming green on the upper surface as they age. It can be pruned in the same way as *E. pungens*.

Both kinds prefer neutral or moderately acid and fairly fertile soils, can be grown in sun or shade and make useful windbreaks near the sea. There is also a quick-growing hybrid between the two species named *E. ebbingei*, a useful shrub where shelter is required.

Enkianthus

The best kind, *Enkianthus campanulatus*, is grown for its little bell-like flowers in spring, buff or reddish bronze in colour and freely produced, and also for its fine autumn colour before the leaves fall. It makes a bush 6 to 9 ft. high and succeeds best in a lightly shaded place in lime-free, moderately acid soil – the same conditions as those which suit azaleas and rhododendrons, to which it is related.

Escallonia

There are deciduous escallonias but the most useful garden varieties are all evergreen or semi-evergreen with rather small shining green leaves and small bell-shaped flowers freely produced in summer. They have a reputation for tenderness but there are plenty of good kinds that will stand a lot of frost, notably *Escallonia langleyensis* with arching stems and rose-pink flowers and the numerous varieties associated with it. These include Apple Blossom, pink and white; Donard Radiance, rose red, and *edinensis*, red buds, pale pink flowers. All will make big bushes up to 8 ft. high.

E. rubra can grow even taller and is frequently used as a hedge or screen plant near the sea, but is not so reliable inland. Crimson Spire is a fast-growing, erect form of it with crimson flowers. All these varieties will grow in any reasonably fertile soil, but *E. virgata*, which is deciduous, white flowered and notably hardy, dislikes lime and chalk and needs an acid soil. All can be thinned in spring or even cut back severely at the sacrifice of a season's flowering. When grown as hedges they should be trimmed in summer after flowering.

Euonymus

There are evergreen and deciduous kinds and they serve quite different purposes in the garden; the evergreens being grown for their ornamental foliage and as hedges and screens, particularly in maritime districts, since they withstand salt spray; the deciduous kinds (known as spindle trees) for their highly ornamental fruits and autumn leaf colour. All grow freely in most soils including chalk and limestone, and they will also succeed in sun or shade, though the deciduous kinds colour and fruit best in light places. Evergreen kinds can be pruned in spring as necessary to keep them in bounds and can be clipped in summer if this seems desirable. Deciduous kinds are best pruned in March when old stems can be cut out or shortened to younger replacement stems.

Euonymus fortunei is an evergreen, trailing or climbing according to situation and able to cling to tree trunks, walls, etc. with aerial roots. It has several varieties such as *coloratus*, green leaved in summer, purple in winter; *radicans*, with small green leaves; Silver Queen, bushy in habit, with a wide cream edge to every leaf, and *variegatus*, leaves grey green, edged with white and often splashed with pink.

E. japonicus is the kind commonly used for hedges and screens, a bushy evergreen which can reach 20 ft. but can be kept to a quarter of that height by pruning. Typically dark shining green, it also has variegated varieties such as *aureopictus* (sometimes called *aureus*) with a splash of gold in the centre of each leaf, and *ovatus aureus* (also called *aureo-variegatus*) with a cream margin to each leaf. *Microphyllus* (also known as *myrtifolius*) is very slow growing, compact and has small green leaves.

Good deciduous kinds are *E. europaeus* and *E. latifolius*, both with scarlet fruits, and *E. yedoensis* with rose-pink fruits. Most have orange seeds which show prominently as the fruits ripen, and all can grow to 10 ft. or more. *E. alatus* has the most brilliantly coloured autumn foliage and will reach 8 ft.

17

Fatsia

There is only one species, *Fatsia japonica*, an evergreen 6 to 8 ft. high, with large, deeply lobed, rather thick-textured leaves which have a fine architectural look enhanced by the cream-coloured flowers produced in globular heads on stiffly branched sprays in autumn. It grows in most soils, in sun or shade, and is first rate both in city gardens and near the sea. It is related to ivy, though it does not climb, and there is an interesting hybrid between it and ivy named *Fatshedera lizei*, which has long lax (not climbing) stems and leaves intermediate in size and shape.

Forsythia

These are among the first shrubs to make a massive display in early spring when covered in their yellow blossom, provided the buds have not been picked out in winter by birds. This can be a serious difficulty in country gardens, but in towns and near roads there is usually little trouble. All will grow in any reasonably fertile soil in sun or partial shade. They can be pruned immediately after flowering when the old flower stems can be cut out but strong young stems, particularly those from near the base, should be retained to flower the following year.

Recommended kinds are *Forsythia intermedia* and its varieties Lynwood and *spectabilis*, deep yellow, 6 to 8 ft., and *F. suspensa* with paler flowers and long arching stems which can be trained against a wall or fence. There is an attractive variety of this named *atrocaulis* with purplish-black young stems.

Fuchsia

Even the hardiest fuchsias are liable to be killed to ground level in very cold winters, but they usually shoot up again strongly from the roots in spring. Since the flowers of fuchsias are highly attractive and are produced more or less continuously all summer and well on into the autumn, until stopped by frost, they must be considered valuable garden plants despite this risk of winter damage.

To reduce losses to a minimum the following precautions should be observed. Choice of varieties should be restricted to those proved to be suitable for growing out of doors. Young plants should be obtained in containers in mid or late spring and planted in saucer-like hollows, the lowest point about 2 in. below soil level. These hollows will serve to hold water when the plants are watered in summer, which they should be whenever the soil is dry, and then in autumn they can be filled in with soil, peat and sand and

a little more mounded on top to protect the basal buds in winter. In February or March all dead, weak or unwanted growth should be cut off 1 in. or so above soil level. Further pruning can be done when the new shoots are 4 in. or more long and it can be seen where the best growth is.

Recommended varieties are Alice Hoffman, rose and white, 18 in.; Chillerton Beauty, pink and violet, 2 ft.; Corallina, scarlet and purple, wide-spreading habit, 18 in.; Howlett's Hardy, scarlet and violet, 3 ft.; Lady Thumb, carmine and white, 1 ft.; Lena, pink and purple, 2 ft.; *magellanica gracilis*, scarlet and violet, 3 ft.; *magellanica versicolor*, scarlet and violet, leaves grey green, pink and white, 3 ft.; Margaret, scarlet and violet purple, 3 ft.; Margaret Brown, carmine and rose, 2 ft.; Mme Cornelissen, scarlet and white, 2 ft.; Mrs Popple, scarlet and violet purple, 3 ft.; Mrs W. P. Wood, pale pink, 3 ft.; *riccartonii*, scarlet and purple, 4 to 6 ft.; Tennessee Waltz, rose and mauve, 2½ ft., and Tom Thumb, scarlet and mauve, 1 ft.

Garrya

The best kind is *Garrya elliptica*, a vigorous evergreen with long narrow grey-green catkins freely produced in winter. Male and female catkins are produced on separate bushes and though the males are most handsome in flower, the females will produce pendant clusters of small purple fruits if there is a male nearby to effect pollination. Garrya is a little tender and should be given a sunny sheltered place or may be trained against a wall, in which case forward-growing stems can be shortened in spring when the catkins fade.

Genista

This is the second of the genera which are commonly known as brooms (see also cystisus and spartium). Like the other two genistas enjoy sunny, warm places and prefer neutral or acid soils, though they will grow where there is lime or chalk. They can also be cut back lightly after flowering, but not into hard, old wood, which usually refuses to produce new growth.

There are many different kinds varying greatly in size and habit. *Genista aethnensis*. the Mount Etna broom, is almost a tree, often 15 ft. or more high with slender, whip-like, hanging stems covered with small yellow flowers in summer. It needs secure staking as it is very easily blown over.

By contrast *G. hispanica* is a dwarf plant, like a 2-ft. gorse bush, spiny and stiff and spreading gradually to cover quite a lot of ground in time. Its light

Fatsia japonica

yellow flowers appear in May–June. *G. lydia* is also a small plant but quite smooth and spineless with arching stems and yellow flowers in May–June. It looks well on a rock garden or terrace wall.

Genista tinctoria, the dyer's greenweed, creeps and is best planted in its double-flowered variety *plena*, with showy yellow blooms from June to September.

Genista tenera (also known as *G. virgata*) and *G. cinerea* are both vigorous, erect-growing shrubs, 8 ft. or more high, with yellow flowers in June and July.

Hamamelis

These are the witch hazels, valuable because they flower in mid-winter. They look rather like nut bushes until the spidery flowers begin to unfurl their narrow petals along the bare branches in December and January. By far the best for general planting are *Hamamelis mollis*, daffodil yellow, and its primrose-yellow variety *pallida*. Both can make big bushes, 10 ft. high and through, but overlong branches can be removed or shortened either for forcing into flower from bud or after flowering. All kinds thrive best in good, loamy, lime-free soil in sun or partial shade.

18

Hebe

These used to be known as veronica, a name which now applies only to the herbaceous species. Hebes are all evergreen shrubs, mostly rather tender though they usually thrive well by the sea and can be grown in many gardens that are sunny, warm and sheltered. They are not at all fussy about soil and transplant safely even when quite large. They can be pruned hard in spring or be trimmed in summer if used as hedges, though some loss of flower that year will occur. The hardiest species are *Hebe brachysiphon* (often wrongly called *H. traversii*) and *H. salicifolia*. The first is 5 to 6 ft. high with neat, box-like leaves and white flowers in small spikes in July, the second 6 to 12 ft. high with narrow leaves and white flowers in slender trails from June to August.

H. hulkeana is one of the most graceful kinds, normally a couple of feet high but twice as much if trained against a wall, with rather loose stems bearing sprays of lavender-blue flowers in May–June, but it is distinctly tender.

Hebe pinguifolia pagei has grey leaves, white flowers in June, is semi-prostrate and makes excellent ground cover, and *H. armstrongii* is grown for its foliage, the whole 2-ft. plant looking rather like a windswept coppery-bronze cypress.

There are also a great many garden hybrids since hebes cross freely and seed germinates readily. The most handsome but also the most tender are the *speciosa* hybrids with stout leaves and showy spikes of flowers in late summer, such as Alicia Amherst, violet purple; La Seduisante, carmine; Simon Delaux, crimson, and *andersonii variegata*, purplish blue, leaves heavily variegated with cream. All are about 3 ft. high.

A little hardier is Midsummer Beauty, with long lavender trails from July to November and growing to 6 ft. Still hardier are Autumn Glory, 2 ft., purplish blue, July to November; Carl Teschner, sprawling, violet, July; *carnea* and Great Orme, both 3 ft., white and pink, flowering from May to September; Margery Fish, 2 to 3 ft., violet blue and white, July to September, and Marjorie, 2 to 3 ft., light blue, July to September.

Hedera

These are the ivies which many people fear in gardens because they believe that they will damage the masonry of their houses or kill their trees. In fact it is only old-fashioned lime mortar that may be shrunk and dragged out by ivy and only very old trees that are already dying that are likely to be overrun by it. Ivy can actually pro-

tect walls and keep them dry, but it can be a nuisance if it is allowed to fill gutters or grow beneath roofing tiles. There is, however, no reason why ivy should not be cut back drastically in spring or be clipped or pruned at any time of the year. It will grow in any soil and situation, in sun or shade, and all forms of the common ivy are completely hardy, though this is not true of all the other species.

There are also, in addition to the normal climbing ivies which support themselves by aerial roots, bush ivies with no ability to climb and the habit of flowering freely and producing abundant crops of black berries. These are produced by rooting cuttings from the flowering stems of ordinary ivies and they resemble their parents in every respect except habit.

The common ivy, *Hedera helix*, has a great many varieties differing in leaf size, leaf colour and habit. Representative examples are *arborescens*, green leaved, non-climbing; Buttercup, leaves yellow; *cavendishii*, leaves edged cream and pink; *conglomerata*, dwarf, non-climbing, with crowded wavy-edged leaves; *cristata*, leaves round, crimped at the edge; Glacier, leaves grey, white edged; Gold Heart (also known as Golden Jubilee), leaves dark green with central yellow blotch; *hibernica*, the Irish ivy, leaves to 6 in. across; *marginata elegantissima* (Silver Queen and *tricolor* are the same or very similar), leaves edged white with some pink as well

Right: *Garrya elliptica*
Below: *Hebe andersonii variegata*

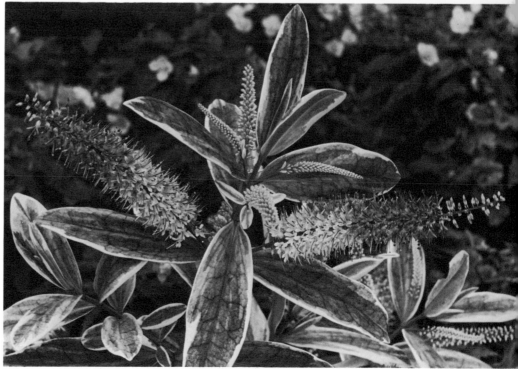

19

in winter; *sagittifolia*, leaf arrow shaped, lobes very narrow.

Hedera colchica has much larger leaves, up to 7 in. across, and in variety *dentata variegata* they are dark green, grey green and cream. This is one of the most handsome of all variegated climbing plants. There is also a fine green, grey and cream-variegated form of *H. canariensis*, the Canary Island ivy, named *variegata* or Gloire de Marengo, but this is a little less hardy.

Hibiscus

Many kinds of hibiscus are so tender that they can only be grown in warm greenhouses, but *Hibiscus syriacus* is hardy in all but the coldest parts of Britain, and is a handsome deciduous shrub which can reach 10 ft. but is more usually about 6 ft., with showy, mallow-type flowers in late summer and early autumn. It likes a warm sunny place, will thrive in all reasonably fertile, well-drained soils, including those containing chalk or limestone, and can be pruned in late winter if it grows too large. It transplants badly so should be purchased in containers while still small and plants should also be staked securely for the first few years to prevent roots being damaged by wind rocking.

Hydrangea

This is one of the big and important families from the garden standpoint and one which contains climbing as well as bushy plants. All are deciduous and all thrive best in fairly fertile soil that does not dry out severely in summer. All will grow in sun or shade.

Hydrangea macrophylla is the species that has produced the greatest number of garden varieties and these have variously coloured flowers in summer and early autumn. In some all the flowers are sterile and have large sepals so that the flower head is ball shaped. These are often known as Hortensias. In other varieties the flowers are arranged in a flat, more or less circular cluster with small fertile flowers in the centre and sterile flowers with showy sepals forming a ring outside. These are often known as Lacecaps. In both types, if the sepals are coloured, the colour will be changed by the character of the soil, tending towards pink and crimson in alkaline soil and to blue or violet purple in acid soil. White sepals remain the same whatever the soil.

All forms of *macrophylla* are a little tender, some more so than others. They do best in warm, sheltered gardens, particularly in towns, near the sea and in thin woodland which provides some protec-

tion from frost. Old flower heads should be removed in winter or early spring and at the same time weak stems can be removed. As a rule this is all the pruning required, but if bushes get too large stems can be cut back in early spring but with loss of flower.

Hydrangea paniculata and *H. arborescens grandiflora* can be hard pruned each March without loss of flower since they bloom on strong young stems. Both are fully hardy. *H. paniculata* has white flowers fading reddish, in large conical heads in August–September. Variety *praecox* starts to flower in July, and variety *grandiflora* has larger flower trusses. *H. arborescens grandiflora* has white flowers in ball-shaped clusters from July to September.

Hydrangea petiolaris climbs by aerial roots and can reach the tops of tall trees. Its white flowers are produced in June in flat, lacecap trusses. It can be pruned in spring, but only with some loss of flower that summer.

Hypericum

Easily grown shrubs thriving in most soils, including chalk and limestone. All have yellow flowers, some have evergreen leaves, some are semi-evergreen and some are fully deciduous. Most do best in sunny or at any rate fairly light places, but *Hypericum calycinum*, the rose of Sharon, will grow equally well on hot, sunny banks and under trees. It is prostrate, fast spreading, has large flowers from July to September and makes excellent ground cover where there is room for its rather invasive growth. It can be cut back or sheared off a few inches above soil level in April.

Hypericum Hidcote, semi-evergreen 4 to 5 ft. high, flowering in summer and autumn, is one of the best kinds for general planting. *H. forrestii* is similar but deciduous and has a shorter flowering season, but can give pleasant autumn colour of leaf and bronze-red fruits. Even better in this respect is *H. inodorum* Elstead, with abundant small yellow flowers followed by shining orange-red fruits.

Jasminum

There are shrubby jasmines, most notably *Jasminum humile revolutum*, 5 to 6 ft. high, with more or less evergreen leaves and good yellow flowers in summer. But it is the climbing or rambling jasmines that are most popular with gardeners, such as *J. officinale*, the common jasmine, a vigorous deciduous twiner with white, sweetly scented flowers in summer and early autumn, and *J. nudiflorum*, the

winter jasmine, with long green stems and yellow flowers from November until February.

J. officinale simply wants a trellis, wires or something similar to climb over; *J. nudiflorum* has no means of holding itself up and so must be tied to whatever support is provided. The common jasmine likes a warm sunny place, does not need any regular pruning, and can be cut back or thinned out in late winter if overcrowded. The winter jasmine will grow in sun or shade and is improved in habit if each of the old flowering stems is shortened to 1 in. or so after flowering. All jasmines will thrive in any reasonably fertile soil.

Kalmia

These beautiful evergreen shrubs thrive in acid, lime-free soils in similar conditions to rhododendrons. The highly distinctive flowers, produced in May or June, look like little Chinese lanterns. The most showy species is *Kalmia latifolia*, the calico bush, with pink flowers. It grows slowly but can eventually make a big, rounded bush 8 to 10 ft. high. *K. angustifolia* seldom exceeds 3 ft. and has smaller deep rose or red flowers.

Kerria

It is a curious fact that the double-flowered form of *Kerria japonica* is markedly different in habit from the single form, with much longer stems which can readily be trained against a wall or over a screen, whereas the single variety forms a 4 to 5-ft. high thicket of growth, constantly spreading by suckers. Both are useful but it is the double form, *pleniflora* (or *flore pleno*), which is most popular. Its little, buttercup-yellow, pompon flowers are freely produced in late spring. Both kinds will grow well in any reasonably good, not too dry soil and can be pruned after flowering, when some of the older stems can be cut out and those that are too long can be shortened.

Kolkwitzia

American gardeners call *Kolkwitzia amabilis* the beauty bush, and a good specimen in full bloom in June is certainly a lovely sight. The flowers are similar in shape to those of weigela, but smaller, downy, very freely produced and clear pink with a splash of yellow. It is deciduous and will make a big bush to 8 ft. high with arching stems. It is quite hardy, will grow in all reasonably fertile soils and flowers best in sunny places. Old and weak branches can be cut out immediately after flowering, but care should be taken not to spoil the naturally graceful habit of the bush.

Lavandula

This is the botanical name for lavender, a genus of small shrubs which succeed best in warm sunny places and on well-drained soils, particularly those that are neutral or alkaline. All are improved in habit by moderate clipping after flowering.

The most popular kind is the common or Old English lavender, which has narrow grey leaves and flowers in spikes in June–July. It is usually known as *Lavandula spica* though it is probably a hybrid between that species and *L. angustifolia*. There are numerous varieties such as *alba*, white, 2 ft.; Grappenhall, lavender blue, 2 to 3 ft.; Hidcote, violet purple, 18 to 24 in.; Munstead, bluish purple, 18 to 24 in.; *rosea*, lilac pink, 18 to 24 in., and Twickel Purple, purple, 18 to 24 in.

Lavandula stoechas, the French lavender, has its purple flowers crowded into cylindrical heads with a few purple bracts on top. It grows about 18 in. high and is in flower for a very long time in summer and early autumn, but it is considerably less hardy than the common lavender.

Lavatera

The best shrubby species, *Lavatera olbia*, makes a loosely branched bush 6 or 7 ft. high with mallow-like leaves and rose-pink flowers, freely produced all summer. It likes warm sunny places and well-drained soils and is first class near the sea. The rather soft stems often die back in winter and should be pruned in early spring to good live wood near the main branches or the base of the bush.

Leycesteria

The kind commonly grown, *Leycesteria formosa*, makes long, green, cane-like growths carrying, in summer, drooping sprays of white flowers enclosed in maroon bracts. These are followed by quite large and decorative reddish-purple berries which contain seeds that are distributed by birds and often produce seedlings in all manner of unlikely places. In severe winters the rather soft stems can be damaged by frost but new growth generally comes freely from the roots in spring. Leycesteria succeeds best in fairly good soil and a sunny place, though it will grow in shade. Dead or damaged stems should be cut out each spring, also those that are weak or old.

Ligustrum

This is the botanical name of privet, an invaluable shrub for screens and hedges, but there are also other species, some more decorative. *Ligustrum lucidum* is one of the best of these, a big evergreen shrub or even a small tree in favourable places, with shining green leaves and sprays of flowers, rather like a small white lilac, in August and September.

The best hedge-making kind is *Ligustrum ovalifolium*, which is semi-evergreen and can reach 15 ft., but can be pruned to 3 ft. without harm. Its yellow-leaved variety, *aureum*, is the popular golden privet and it also has an attractive variety named *argenteum* with a creamy-white border to each leaf.

All privets grow best in fairly fertile

Top left: *Hydrangea petiolaris*
Top right: *Lavandula spica*
Above: *Leycesteria formosa*

21

soil and the variegated varieties colour best in the sun, but there are few soils or places in which privet cannot be grown. When planted as hedges the tops should be cut out immediately to ensure branching from the base. Privet can be pruned hard in spring, if this is necessary, and can be trimmed at any time in summer.

Lonicera

These are the honeysuckles of which there are shrubby as well as climbing varieties. One of the bushy kinds, *Lonicera nitida*, is a popular hedge-making shrub with little rounded evergreen leaves giving some-what the appearance of box. It stands clipping well, but because of its rather thin, flexible stems is not suitable for hedges above 5 ft. in height. There is also an excellent yellow-leaved variety named Baggessen's Gold.

Also useful are the winter-flowering shrubby honeysuckles, such as *Lonicera fragrantissima*, *L. standishii* and the hybrid between them, *L. purpusii*, all of which make medium-sized, open-branched

Right: *Lonicera periclymenum*
Below: *Hydrangea macrophylla* Westfalen

shrubs with small, sweetly scented, white or cream flowers from December to March.

The climbing honeysuckles are all vigorous twiners, suitable for growing over arches, pergolas and screens. All like fairly rich soils that do not dry out seriously in summer, and most will grow in sun or shade, but the scarlet trumpet honeysuckle, *Lonicera sempervirens*, is best in a sunny, warm place. Its orange-scarlet flowers are very showy but not scented, and it is semi-evergreen. So is *L. japonica*, usually planted in one or other of two varieties, *halliana*, with creamy, intensely scented flowers in summer, and *aureo-reticulata*, grown primarily for its gold-netted leaves.

The most popular climbing honeysuckle is the woodbine, *Lonicera periclymenum*, though again it is one of its varieties rather than the true species that is usually planted. The two best are *belgica*, known as Dutch honeysuckle, and *serotina*, known as late red honeysuckle. Both have handsome, reddish-purple and yellow

Left: *Hypericum calycinum*
Below: *Hibiscus syriacus*

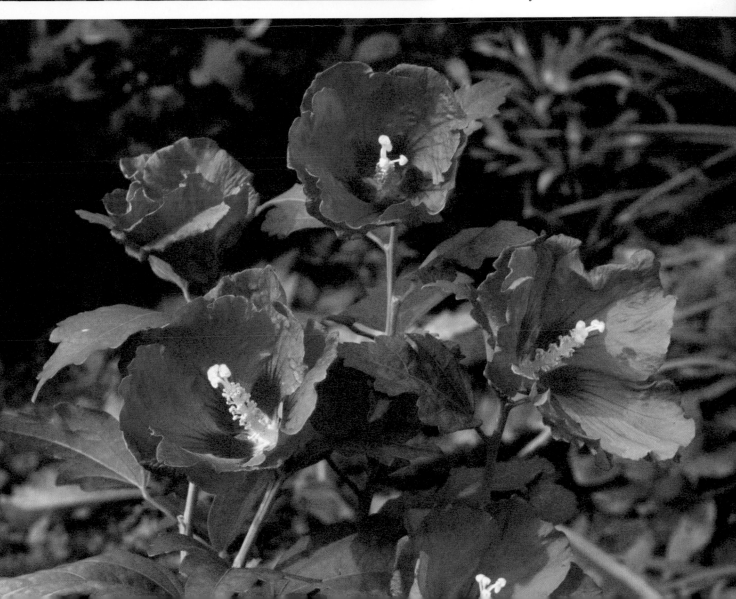

flowers in summer, but *serotina* is to be preferred because of its longer flowering season.

Growth of the climbing honeysuckles is usually so intertwined that pruning is difficult, but excessive growth can be clipped after flowering or some of the older stems can be cut out.

Magnolia

Most magnolias are trees, but *Magnolia stellata* is a shrub growing slowly to about 9 ft. It is an exceptionally beautiful plant, with rather narrow-petalled white flowers, very freely produced in March and April. There are also pink varieties, one very pale in colour named *rosea*, another, a little deeper, named *rubra*. All succeed best in neutral or moderately acid soil and a rather sheltered position as the flowers are apt to be spoiled by frost or cold winds. Pruning is undesirable. It is advisable to purchase young plants in containers as, like most magnolias, this species resents root injury.

Mahonia

Handsome evergreen shrubs with holly-like leaflets arranged in some varieties in long, compound leaves that are very distinctive and decorative. All will grow in any reasonably good, well-drained soil and in sun or shade, but the winter-flowering kinds should be given a fairly sheltered position, and a few kinds are distinctively tender. *Mahonia aquifolium*, with clusters of yellow flowers in March–April, followed by grape-purple berries, is one of the easiest and hardiest, thriving in sun or shade, usually 3 or 4 ft. high and spreading slowly by suckers.

M. japonica and *M.* Charity make stiff, erect stems, can reach 8 to 10 ft., and have big leaves and yellow flowers in slender spikes arranged like the spokes of a wheel in the first named, clustered into a sheaf in Charity. The flowers of *M. japonica* are also very sweetly scented. Both these handsome shrubs need a warm, sheltered but not necessarily sunny position. Neither is improved by pruning, but *M. aquifolium* can be cut back after flowering or trimmed lightly in summer and is sometimes used as a low hedge.

Neillia

The most decorative kind, *Neillia longiracemosa*, makes cane-like stems up to 7 ft. high and spreads indefinitely by suckers. It is deciduous and the pink flowers are produced in slender trails in May–June. This is an attractive shrub for a semi-wild place where there is room for it, and it can be pruned by cutting out the old canes

either immediately after flowering or in the autumn. It does best in fairly fertile, loamy soil.

Olearia

These are the daisy bushes, so called because of their numerous, daisy-like flowers. All are evergreen and all will grow in most adequately drained soils, including chalk and limestone. They will withstand salt-laden wind, which makes them good shrubs for seaside gardens, and *Olearia haastii* is also an excellent town shrub. But not all are fully hardy so selection must be determined by the kind of temperatures likely to be experienced in winter.

O. haastii, 5 to 6 ft. high, with small, rounded leaves and a dense habit which makes it suitable for use as a screen or hedge, is probably the hardiest, but its white flowers in July–August are not so pure a white as those of *O. scilloniensis*, 3 to 4 ft. high, with small grey leaves and flowering in May–June. *O. gunniana* and *O. stellulata* are similar to the last named, but the latter also has blue and pink-flowered forms, distinguished as variety *splendens*. *O. macrodonta* has the largest leaves, resembling those of a holly. It has big flattish clusters of scented white flowers in June, can reach 10 ft. and is a very handsome shrub often used as a windbreak in maritime gardens.

Most kinds prefer warm sunny places, but *O. haastii* will grow in semi-shade. All can be cut back in spring, if necessary, but with some loss of flower that summer. They can also be trimmed after flowering.

Osmanthus

The most popular kind is *Osmanthus delavayi*, a densely branched evergreen, eventually 6 ft. high and more through, with small rounded leaves and sweetly scented white flowers in April–May. Though it usually flowers freely the tubular flowers are too small to make much display and it is for its perfume and as a foliage shrub that it is most admired.

Osmanthus ilicifolius (also known as *heterophyllus* and *aquifolium*) is also a fine foliage shrub, but very different in appearance. It grows slowly to 10 ft. or more, could easily be mistaken for a holly and has small white scented flowers in October. It is best planted in one of its variegated forms, such as *aureomarginatus*, leaves edged with yellow, and *variegatus*, leaves edged with white.

All kinds thrive in any reasonably fertile soil, in sun or partial shade, but *O. delavayi* is a little tender and may need to be grown against a sunny sheltered wall

in cold districts. Both species can be pruned in spring, *O. delavayi* immediately after flowering.

Osmarea

There is only one kind, *Osmarea burkwoodii*, a hybrid between *Osmanthus delavayi* and *Phillyrea decora*. It is rather like the former in appearance with similar flowers, not perhaps either quite so freely produced or so sweetly scented, but it is stiffer in growth and hardier which makes it suitable for use as a hedge or screen and it also makes an attractive specimen bush, eventually 7 or 8 ft. high. It grows well in most soils, including those on chalk or limestone, and it can be pruned quite hard in spring after flowering, or it can be trimmed any time in summer.

Paeonia

This is the botanical name for peony and in addition to the familiar herbaceous kinds it covers several useful shrubs. Easiest to grow are *Paeonia delavayi* with single deep crimson flowers and *P. lutea* with single yellow flowers which are larger and better displayed in variety *ludlowii*.

All make quite large bushes 5 or 6 ft. high and flower in May, and all will grow freely in any reasonably fertile soil and sunny place. But they are not so spectacular as the varieties of *P. suffruticosa*, which are usually only 3 or 4 ft. high and have much bigger, often fully double flowers in a range of colours including pink, scarlet and crimson. There are also hybrids between *P. suffruticosa* and *P. lutea* with double yellow or yellow and red flowers.

All these need a rather sheltered position, not subject to severe spring frosts as they start to grow early and the young shoots are rather tender. They enjoy rather rich soil, not liable to dry out badly in summer but never waterlogged in winter.

Parthenocissus

These are the climbers that gardeners often call ampelopsis or Virginia creeper, though the latter name properly belongs to one kind only, *Parthenocissus quinquifolia*, which has extra large vine-like leaves that colour brilliantly before they fall in autumn. It is partially self-clinging and excellent for covering sheds, screens, fences etc. or for running up into old, not very valuable trees.

Better as a wall covering, because it is entirely self-clinging by little adhesive pads, is *P. tricuspidata*, popularly known as Boston ivy. It also colours well but is more variable in leaf than the Virginia

Above: *Magnolia stellata*
Right: *Passiflora caerulea*

creeper, one of the most popular forms being *veitchii* with relatively small leaves.

P. *henryana* has deeply lobed leaves that combine dark green and bronzy purple with white veins. It is exceptionally decorative since the colour is there all summer and it is completely self-clinging but it needs a sheltered wall as it is a little tender.

All kinds will grow well in most soils, in sun or shade, though autumn colour is best in a light place. No regular pruning is necessary but shoots that grow too far can be cut back in the autumn.

Passiflora

All the passion flowers are more or less tender, but *Passiflora caerulea* is near enough hardy to be worth planting out of doors in sunny, sheltered places. It is a very vigorous climber which is capable of growing 15 ft. even after it has been cut to ground level by winter frost. The bluish-white flowers look a little like those of a clematis, but with a central corona of filaments which are in three concentric zones of blue, white and purple in the common variety but are all white in variety Constance Elliott. Both plants climb by tendrils so require wires, trellises or something similar to which to cling.

They succeed best in fertile, well-drained soils. Frost-damaged growth should be cut out in spring at which time any stems that threaten to grow too far can also be shortened.

Pernettya

Evergreen shrubs grown primarily for their marble-like berries which may be scarlet, crimson, purple, pink, lilac, mauve or white according to variety. *Pernettya mucronata* is the best kind, usually about 3 ft. high, spreading into a dense thicket by means of suckers, and with small, white, heather-like flowers in May–June. Sometimes the flowers on a bush are all of one sex, and since only the female flowers can produce berries and then only if fertilized with pollen from male flowers, it may be necessary to plant several bushes to be certain of a display. But there are also hermaphrodite varieties (i.e. varieties producing both male and female sex organs) and these will both produce berries on their own and fertilize purely female bushes. Bell's Seedling, with deep red berries, is such an hermaphrodite form.

All varieties require acid soil, dislike chalk and limestone, and fruit freely in sunny places though they grow quite well in shade. Pruning in the ordinary sense is not usually necessary or desirable, but if plants threaten to spread too far they can be chopped back with a sharp spade in spring. Many of the rooted pieces dug out in this way can be grown on into good bushes if desired.

Perovskia

The best kind, *Perovskia atriplicifolia*, looks rather like a tall unusually spiky lavender, with grey leaves and stems and lavender-blue flowers in late summer. It grows well in warm, sunny places and well-drained soils, but is only semi-shrubby and the 3-ft. stems are usually partly killed each winter. This matters little as the best results are obtained by shortening all stems to a few inches each spring.

Perovskia (sometimes spelled perowskia) transplants badly and plants should always be purchased in containers from which they should be planted with a minimum of root disturbance.

Philadelphus

The correct popular name for these easily grown shrubs is mock orange from the resemblance in appearance and scent of the flowers of some varieties to orange blossom. It is a pity that they are sometimes called syringa, the botanical name of lilac, a totally unrelated shrub.

All the popular varieties of philadelphus are completely hardy and will grow in all reasonably fertile soils preferably in a sunny, or at least light, and open position where they flower most freely. All flower in June and nearly all are white, though often with some suffusion of purple and with yellow stamens which show clearly in the single-flowered varieties. Varieties differ greatly in size and habit, a few reaching a height of 10 or 12 ft., but all can be reduced in size by cutting out the old flowering stems as soon as the flowers fade. The young, non-flowering stems should be retained to flower the following year.

Good varieties are Beauclerk, ivory white and purple, 7 ft.; Belle Etoile, white and purple, 6 ft.; *coronarius*, creamy white, 6 ft., and its variety *aureus*, not very free flowering but with yellow foliage; *delavayi*, white and purple, 10 ft.; Manteau d'Hermine, creamy white, double, 3 ft.; *microphyllus*, white, small flowers and leaves, 3 ft.; Sybille, white and purple, 4 ft.; Virginal, white, double, 8 ft.

Phlomis

The kind most commonly planted is *Phlomis fruticosa*, the Jerusalem sage,

Paeonia lutea L'Esperance

which grows about 3 ft. high, has grey sage-like leaves and whorls of large yellow sage-type flowers in summer. It is handsome in foliage and flower but also worthy of attention is another less familiar species, *P. chrysophylla*, which is similar in habit and appearance, but has yellowish-grey leaves which are very distinctive. Both are shrubs for warm places and well-drained, even rather dry soils, just the plants in fact for a difficult sun-baked situation. Sometimes their rather soft stems are damaged by frost in which case they should be cut back to live growth in spring.

Pieris

These evergreens are sometimes called lily-of-the-valley bushes because of the slight resemblance of their sprays of white, urn-shaped flowers, produced in spring, to those of the lily-of-the-valley. All like rather acid soils and are not really suitable for chalk or limestone where special beds of lime-free loam and peat must be prepared for them. They also appreciate the shelter of fairly widely spaced trees though they will grow right out in the open.

The young growth of *Pieris formosa*

Pieris formosa forrestii

forrestii is bright red and it is often grown primarily as a foliage shrub, especially in forms selected for this leaf colour, such as Wakehurst. However, it is less hardy than some of the others and so in cold gardens or exposed places it would be better to plant Forest Flame, a hybrid between it and the hardier, green-leaved *P. japonica*. All these and also *P. taiwanensis*, another handsome species, will eventually grow to 7 or 8 ft. high, but *P. floribunda* grows more slowly and may take years to reach 6 ft. Pruning is as a rule unnecessary, but if plants get too big they can be cut back in spring after flowering.

Pileostegia

Another of the climbing hydrangeas, this time an evergreen one with dense clusters of small ivory-white flowers in autumn. *Pileostegia viburnoides* is a vigorous climber adhering by roots on the stems, like ivy, and can be grown over a tree stump or up a wall. It likes fertile soil and will grow in sun or shade. It can be cut back in spring as necessary to keep it in bounds or the tips of straying stems can be pinched out in summer.

Polygonum

Most polygonums are herbaceous plants but one, *Polygonum baldschuanicum*, is a very vigorous climber capable of ascending to the top of a tall tree or completely covering a sizeable outbuilding with its twining stems which erupt into foaming cascades of creamy-white or pinkish-white blossom in late summer and early autumn. It will grow in most soils in sun or semi-shade and is very useful for quick cover of an unsightly building, though it loses its effectiveness as a screen in winter as it is deciduous. If it strays too far, as it often does, it can be cut back in winter.

Potentilla

The shrubby potentillas are particularly valuable because of their long flowering season, often from May to October. They are mostly small shrubs with dense twiggy growth, small divided leaves and yellow or white flowers. All will grow in semi-shade, but flower most freely in sunny, rather warm places and they thrive in all reasonably well-drained soils. The naturally rather dense habit can be improved if some of the older stems are cut out each March and the previous year's growth is shortened by a third or even more.

Good kinds are *Potentilla arbuscula*, yellow, 2 ft.; Elizabeth, light yellow, 3 ft.; and varieties of *P. fruticosa* such as Katherine Dykes, light yellow, 6 ft.; *grandiflora* (or Jackman's Variety), canary yellow, 4 ft.; *mandschurica*, white, 1 ft.; Tangerine, orange yellow, 2 ft., and *vilmoriniana*, silvery leaves, cream flowers, 4 to 6 ft.

Prunus

This is the great genus to which the cherries, plums, almonds and peaches belong, most of which are trees, but there are valuable shrubby kinds as well. Among the best known of them are the cherry laurel or common laurel, *Prunus laurocerasus*, and the Portugal laurel, *P. lusitanica*, both of which are vigorous evergreens capable of reaching 15 ft. or more and much planted as hedges or screens. Both will grow in all reasonably fertile, not too dry soil, in sun or shade, the common laurel being particularly well able to survive in very shady places and in cities, though grime does spoil the appearance of its large glossy green leaves. Both plants have spikes of white flowers, those of the common laurel appearing in April, those of the Portugal laurel in June. Both also have useful varieties, *azorica* being a particularly large-leaved, handsome-flowered form of Portugal laurel, and Otto Luyken, a short (4 ft.) free-flowering form of the common laurel. All can be pruned in May as necessary to keep them in bounds, or can be lightly trimmed any time in summer.

Prunus glandulosa albiplena is a small bushy cherry, 4 ft. high, with double white flowers in April. *P. cistena* looks like a dwarf version of the purple-leaved plum, has similar white flowers in spring and reddish-purple leaves and makes an excellent 3 to 5-ft. hedge. *P. incisa* can also be used as a hedge and covers itself in March with small white flowers as freely as a sloe. *P. tenella* Fire Hill is a dwarf almond with small deep rose flowers in March. *P. triloba* needs a warm sunny place to ripen its wood and produce its very beautiful double pink flowers in spring. All these are deciduous and succeed best in good, fertile, neutral or alkaline soil and a sunny place.

Pyracantha

The firethorns are often planted against walls and they can be trained in such places very effectively, but they are not climbers, they will make big bushes in the open and are perfectly hardy. They have clusters of white flowers in early summer followed by red, orange or yellow berries in autumn and winter and all are evergreen. They will grow in sun or shade, but flower and fruit best with plenty of light. They are not fussy about soil and do especially well on chalk and limestone. All can be pruned in spring or summer, the most convenient time for doing this usually being immediately after flowering when it can be seen where the berries are forming and care be taken not to cut them off.

Good kinds are *Pyracantha atalantioides*, scarlet berries; *coccinea lalandei*, orange-red berries; Orange Glow, similar to *lalandei* but more resistant to disease; *rogersiana flava*, yellow berries, and *watereri*, red berries.

Rhododendron

There are so many different rhododendrons, varying in height from ground cover to trees, some with minute leaves and some with very large leaves, with an equally wide range in flower sizes, forms and colours and a flowering season from January to July, that it would be possible to stock a garden with this remarkable genus alone and still have plenty of variety. All kinds thrive best in rather acid soils and are not happy on chalk or limestone unless regularly fed with specially

Pyracantha rogersiana flava

formulated iron and manganese. Most succeed best in soil that contains plenty of peat or leafmould so that it retains moisture well in summer without becoming waterlogged in winter, and most also like to grow in the dappled shade provided by fairly widely spaced trees. However, the varieties collectively known as Hardy Hybrids, all of which make fairly big evergreen bushes carrying flowers in May and June in dome-shaped clusters, are extremely adaptable and will succeed quite well in full sun. They are also the best rhododendrons for town gardens since they put up with a chemically polluted atmosphere better than most of the species and pedigree hybrids.

Rhododendrons transplant well and can be moved in autumn or late winter, even when quite large, which makes them specially useful where quick results are essential. They will submit to quite hard pruning in spring, but this results in the loss of at least one year's flowering.

Varieties are so numerous that it is impossible to do justice to them in any short list. Because they transplant so readily and are usually available either balled or in containers, there is much to be said for purchasing them in flower, but since most start to flower while still very young, the size of nursery plants does not give any indication of ultimate dimensions which should therefore be ascertained.

Ribes

The currants and gooseberries that are grown in the fruit garden are species of ribes, but there are also purely ornamental kinds, none more useful in the garden than the flowering currant, *Ribes sanguineum*.

This quickly makes a big bush up to 8 ft. high, with currant-like leaves and clusters of rose-pink flowers in April. There are several varieties including two with much deeper coloured flowers, King Edward VII, crimson, and Pulborough Scarlet, magenta red. All forms flower on year-old stems and the quality of the flowers can be improved and the bushes reduced in size by cutting out the old stems immediately after flowering. They will grow in all soils, in sun or shade.

Other useful kinds are *Ribes odoratum*, sometimes wrongly called *R. aureum*, rather shorter than the flowering currant with richly scented yellow flowers in April and *R. speciosum*, often called the fuchsia-flowered gooseberry because of the resemblance of its crimson flowers to very small fuchsias. It flowers in April and May, grows about 5 ft. high and, unlike the others, is evergreen, but it is less hardy and should be given a warm sunny place.

Rosmarinus

Charming evergreen shrubs with narrow, aromatic leaves and small blue flowers, freely produced in spring or even earlier in warm, sheltered places. They grow best in well-drained soils and will withstand a good deal of heat and drought. All are a little tender, some more so than others, but the common rosemary, *Rosmarinus officinalis*, can be grown successfully in all but the coldest parts of the British Isles. Typically bushy, 3 or 4 ft. high, it has numerous varieties including white flowered, pink flowered, deeper blue flowered and narrowly erect forms.

R. lavandulaceus (also known as *R. officinalis prostratus*) is prostrate or semi-weeping, a lovely shrub for the top of a sunny terrace wall, but decidedly more tender than the common rosemary. All kinds can be pruned in spring, immediately after flowering, but frost-damaged growth should be removed as soon as noted.

Rubus

These are the brambles, the genus to which the blackberry and loganberry belong, but there are also several decorative species well worth planting where there is room for them. They will grow in almost any soil, in sun or partial shade. Those grown for their white stems (often known as whitewash brambles) can be pruned almost to ground level early each spring just before they re-start into growth; those grown for their flowers are best pruned immediately after flowering when the old flowering stems can be cut out.

Rubus deliciosus, *R. trilobus* and the

beautiful hybrid between them, Tridel, all make long arching stems bearing big white flowers rather like single roses in May and June. *R. spectabilis* is shorter, 4 to 5 ft., spreading by suckers and with magenta flowers in April. *R. ulmifolius bellidiflorus* is semi-climbing or rambling with little double pink pompon flowers in summer. One of the best whitewash brambles is *R. cockburnianus* (also known as *R. giraldianus*) making a wide spreading bush 6 or 7 ft. high and even more through.

Sambucus

This is the genus to which the elder or elderberry belongs, and although the handsome British species, *Sambucus nigra*, is only worth planting in the wilder parts of the garden, it has several useful varieties, the most popular of which are *aurea*, the golden elder, with yellow leaves, and *laciniata*, with finely divided leaves. It thrives in most soils, including those overlying chalk or limestone, colours best in light places and can be pruned to within a few inches of the main stems every spring. For flowers the best kind is *S. canadensis*, the Canadian elderberry, which has very large flat heads of small white flowers in summer followed by black berries.

Santolina

These small evergreen shrubs, collectively known as lavender cotton, are ideal for edging borders or for grouping in hot, rather dry places where they grow especially well. They have narrow, finely divided leaves, grey in *Santolina chamaecyparissus* and its shorter variety *corsica* (also known as *nana*), bright green in *S. virens*. All forms have small button-shaped yellow flowers like the central disc of a daisy. They succeed best in well-drained soils and can be made even more bushy and compact by being trimmed with shears in summer as soon as the flowers fade or before if the flowers are not regarded as attractive.

Sarcococca

These are useful evergreen shrubs for shady places and though their white flowers are small and partly hidden by the leaves they are very welcome because they are so sweetly scented and come in late winter or early spring. The best kinds are *Sarcococca confusa* and *S. hookeriana digyna*, both about 3 ft. high and both excellent for cutting as foliage.

Schizophragma

This is yet another genus of self-clinging

Rubus cockburnianus

climbing hydrangeas. Soil, aspect and pruning are exactly the same as for *Hydrangea petiolaris* which these plants resemble except that the showy sepals round the sterile flowers are larger. The most spectacular kind is *Schizophragma integrifolia* with creamy-white flowers. *S. hydrangeoides* is similar but the sepals are a little smaller and are tinged with pink in variety *roseum*.

Senecio

The best-known shrubby member of this very large and varied genus is *Senecio greyii*, a grey-leaved evergreen about 3 ft. high and becoming considerably broader than this with age. In summer it produces showy clusters of yellow daisy flowers and it is a fine plant for a warm sunny place, though like most shrubby senecios it is not completely hardy. If it does get damaged by winter frost, it can be pruned back to live wood in spring. *S. laxifolius* is similar and much confused with *S. greyii* but has narrower, less rounded leaves.

Senecio rotundifolius (also known as *S. reinoldii*) is useful near the sea since it will withstand salty gales better than most shrubs. It has large round leathery leaves, green above and grey beneath, and it can reach 8 ft. or so but is usually considerably less.

Skimmia

These useful shrubs are attractive in leaf, flower and fruit and will grow well in all reasonably fertile soils, in sun or in shade. The most popular kind, *Skimmia japonica*, grows 3 to 5 ft. high, has small white flowers in spike-like clusters and segregates male and female flowers on separate

Frost on the leaves of *Senecio greyii*

bushes. Only the females produce crops of berries and then only if fertilized with pollen from a male so it is wise to plant both sexes. However, this is no hardship since the males are most effective in flower, especially such varieties as *fragrans*, in which the flowers are scented, or *rubella*, in which the flower buds are red. *Foremannii* is a good female variety and usually the berries remain so long that they are still there the following spring when the plants start to flower again or even when the next crop of berries has set.

Skimmia reevesiana (also known as *S. fortunei*) has flowers of both sexes on the same bush so if there is only room for one plant this is the kind to choose provided the soil does not contain chalk, to which it objects. It is shorter than *S. japonica* and has narrower leaves, but otherwise the effect is similar.

Solanum

The two most useful shrubby kinds, both deciduous, are *Solanum jasminoides* and *S. crispum*. The first is a true climber supporting itself by twining around branches, posts, trellis work, wires etc. In the common form the flowers, produced in late summer and autumn, are a rather slaty blue, but it is usually the pure white variety *album* that is planted and this is very attractive. Both blue and white forms are distinctly tender and require a warm sunny place where winter frosts are not likely to be severe, though even if stems are damaged new growth is usually produced in spring from lower down.

The other popular kind, *Solanum crispum*, is usually grown as a climber but is really a sprawling shrub and if used to cover a wall or fence its long flexible stems need to be tied to some kind of support. The flowers, also produced in late summer and autumn, are larger than those of *S. jasminoides* and a good violet blue with a raised yellow centre. This species is a little hardier but still in need of a warm, sunny, sheltered place. It can be hard pruned in spring if desired and frost-damaged growth should certainly be removed then.

Sorbaria
These handsome, suckering shrubs are closely allied to spiraea and their large plumy clusters of small white or cream flowers, produced freely in summer, closely resemble those of some of the herbaceous astilbes. *Sorbaria aitchisonii*, 8 to 10 ft. high, is one of the best. *S. arborea* and *S. tomentosa* will easily reach 15 ft. and *S. sorbifolia* is the shortest at 4 or 5 ft. They succeed best in fairly fertile, rather moist soils, but are not really fussy and provided there is room for them, there are few places in which they could not be grown. Left unpruned vigorous kinds will reach 10 or 12 ft. and be as much or more through, but most of the old stems can be cut out each winter, leaving the young ones to grow up and produce even finer heads of bloom.

Spartium
The Spanish broom, *Spartium junceum*, is invaluable in the garden because it continues to produce its bright yellow, sweetly scented flowers throughout the latter half of summer and even into the autumn when they are a splendid foil for purple buddleia and blue or red hydrangeas. Though deciduous, spartium has an evergreen look because of its light green, rush-like stems and though in good soil and sheltered places it may grow too tall for convenience it can be kept to 5 or 6 ft. by shortening each spring all or most of the previous year's growth. In rather poor sandy soils or in windswept places near the sea, conditions for which it is well suited, it remains naturally compact. Unlike most brooms its flowers last well in water.

Spiraea
From a garden standpoint there are two very distinct groups of spiraea, one which makes rounded or shuttlecock-shaped bushes from a compact stool, the other which makes a thicket of erect stems spreading ever wider by suckers. The latter, though excellent in semi-wild places where there is plenty of room, can be a nuisance in small gardens or more formal situations where they must be constantly kept in place by chopping through their tough stolons in winter. All these suckering spiraeas produce their flowers in fluffy bottle-brush spikes in late summer, and the least overpowering and most beautiful of them is *Spiraea billiardii triumphans* (also known as *S. menziesii triumphans*), 6 to 8 ft., with rose-pink flowers, but it is not suitable for markedly alkaline chalk or limestone soils.

In the other group there are numerous fine garden shrubs. *Spiraea arguta*, popularly known as bridal wreath, crowds its thin, twiggy stems with snowy bloom in April and May. It is 5 to 6 ft. high. *S. thunbergii* is similar, 3 to 4 ft. high, and a week or so earlier. *S. bumalda* grows 3 ft. high and has flattish heads of rose-pink flowers (crimson in variety Anthony Waterer) all summer. *S. prunifolia* is 5 or 6 ft. high with arching stems loaded with double white flowers in April and May. *S. vanhouttei* is similar in habit but has clusters of single flowers in June. *S. veitchii* is a larger shrub, 8 to 9 ft. high, with white flowers all along the arching stems in June–July. There are many more.

Symphoricarpos
The snowberry is the most popular species of this genus, a twiggy bush 4 or 5 ft. high with small pink flowers followed by white, marble-like berries. There is considerable confusion regarding its name and it may appear in catalogues as *Symphoricarpos albus*, *laevigatus*, *racemosus* or *rivularis*, but the last appears to be correct. It will grow in all soils, in sun or shade, can be used as a hedge or as game cover and its berries are very useful for winter decorations. There are several other useful kinds, equally easy to grow, including the coral berry, *S. orbiculatus*, similar in appearance but with rose-pink berries, and numerous hybrids such as Magic Berry, purple; Mother of Pearl, pink, and White Hedge, white. All kinds can be pruned in spring as necessary to keep them in shape.

Syringa
These are the lilacs, some of which will grow almost to tree size in time. They are beautiful shrubs thriving in all reasonably fertile soils and succeeding particularly well on chalk and limestone. They will grow in shade but flower most freely in warm, sunny places. Pruning is not essential but, if bushes must be restricted in size, old flowering stems can be cut back to young growths immediately after flowering. When lilacs are cut for flower decoration they automatically receive this kind of pruning.

The common lilac, *Syringa vulgaris*, is available in numerous varieties, both single and double flowered. Typical single varieties are Blue Hyacinth, mauve and blue; Charles X, purple; Clarke's Giant, lavender and mauve; Congo, deep reddish purple; Maud Notcutt, white; Primrose, pale primrose yellow, and Souvenir de Louis Spaeth, wine red.

Typical double varieties are Charles Joly, purplish red; Kathleen Havemayer, purple and lilac pink; Madame Antoine Buchner, rosy mauve; Madame Lemoine, white; Michael Buchner, lilac, and Mrs Edward Harding, wine red. All these varieties are scented and all flower in May or early June.

A little later are the Canadian hybrids (*Syringa prestoniae*) such as Bellicent, rose pink, and Elinor, purplish red.

The Persian lilac, *Syringa persica*, is a smaller bush, to 7 ft. high, with sweetly scented pink flowers (white in variety *alba*) in May, and the Rouen lilac, *S. chinensis*, is a hybrid between this and the common lilac, similar in size to the Persian lilac and with white, pink or reddish-purple flowers according to variety.

Tamarix
The tamarisks are splendid shrubs to plant as a windbreak in exposed gardens near the sea and some kinds, such as *Tamarix pentandra*, with plumes of pink flowers in August and September, and *T. tetrandra*, with small pink flowers wreathing the long slender branches in May, make beautiful specimen bushes. All grow best in open sunny places and well-drained, preferably acid or neutral soils. The spring-flowering varieties are best if cut back moderately immediately after flowering and the late summer-flowering varieties in early spring.

Viburnum
There are a great many useful species of viburnum and from a decorative point of view they can be divided into kinds grown primarily for their flowers, or for their fruits, or for their foliage. Some are evergreen and some deciduous, and though most will grow well in any fairly fertile soil and are hardy in all parts of the British Isles, a few have special requirements or are just a little tender.

A few species have flowers of two kinds, as in hydrangea, small fertile flowers gathered into a flattish cluster and showy sterile flowers surrounding them. The British native guelder rose, *Viburnum opulus*, is of this kind and the fertile flowers are followed by shining currant-red fruits (yellow in variety *fructuluteo*). Normally 8 or 9 ft. high, it has a shorter variety, *compactum*, only 4 to 5 ft. high. It also has a variety, *sterile*, in which all the flowers are sterile, forming large white balls, hence it is known as the snow-ball tree. All forms flower in June as does the Japanese snowball, *V. plicatum*, which has smaller but equally effective flower clusters. A form of this with some sterile.

Above: Shrubs used to good effect in a mixed border (see key)

(a) *Coreopsis verticillata*
(b) *Elaeagnus pungens maculata*
(c) *Hosta ventricosa variegata*
(d) *Rhododendron* **Britannia**
(e) *Cotinus coggygria* **Royal Purple**
(f) *Thuja occidentalis* **Rheingold**
(g) *Cotoneaster frigidus cornubia*
(h) *Salix chrysocoma*

some fertile flowers is known as *V. plicatum tomentosum*. The flat flower clusters are carried all along more or less horizontal branches and it is a notably decorative shrub but one which needs a fair amount of space to do itself justice.

Other kinds with the ball-like type of flower head are *V. macrocephalum*, which is just a little tender and needs a warm, sunny place, and *V. carlcephalum*, a hybrid between it and *V. carlesii*, quite hardy with scented flowers.

Then there are numerous species with quite normal flower clusters entirely composed of fertile flowers. Most of these are sweetly scented and they include *V. fragrans* (also known as *V. farreri*), white, to 8 ft., flowering in winter; *bodnantense*, pink, to 9 ft., also flowering in winter;

Wisteria chinensis

big bush with arching stems, red becoming black in *lantana* which is stiffer in habit and thrives particularly well on chalk.

Viburnum tinus, the laurustinus, is a big bushy evergreen, to 8 ft. high with clusters of white flowers in winter and spring. It will thrive in sun or shade and can be used as a hedge or windbreak. It does well in town gardens and by the sea.

Viburnum rhytidophyllum has the largest leaves, evergreen, wrinkled and dark green above, covered with rusty coloured down beneath. It can reach 10 ft. and is a very handsome foliage shrub. In the common form the flower clusters, which come in May, are a rather dull white, but there is a variety *roseum* with rose-tinted flowers which are more decorative. Another evergreen species, *V. davidii*, is also grown primarily for its foliage, but it is very different in appearance, only 2 or 3 ft. high, wide spreading with ribbed dark green leaves. The small white flowers are sometimes followed by good crops of small turquoise berries.

Vitis

The grape vine belongs here, its name being *Vitis vinifera*, and a few varieties are worth planting for ornament. Particularly recommended are Brandt, with blackish-purple fruits and leaves which turn crimson before they fall in the autumn, and *purpurea*, similar in fruit and with leaves that are purple throughout the summer. Both are vigorous climbers clinging by tendrils and capable of covering a fairly large house front, but the tips of the shoots can be pinched out at any time in summer and all the year's growth can be cut to within 1 in. or so of the main stems in winter if it needs to be restricted. Vines succeed best in warm sunny places and fertile, neutral or alkaline soils.

Even more rampant in growth is *Vitis coignetiae* which is grown solely for its very large rounded leaves which colour brilliantly in the autumn. This is a handsome climber to run up into an old tree or to cover an outhouse or large wall. Treatment is the same as for the varieties of grape vine.

Weigela

Sometimes these easily grown shrubs are known as diervilla. They grow well in almost all soils and reasonably open places and produce their funnel-shaped flowers freely in May and June. Most kinds grow 5 or 6 ft. high and can spread fairly widely, but they can be kept smaller by cutting out most of the old flowering stems as soon as the flowers fade. Most of the varieties grown are garden hybrids such as Abel

Carrière, rose; Bristol Ruby, ruby red, and Newport Red, bright red, but there is a very good variety of a species, *Weigela florida*, named *variegata*, with pale pink flowers and cream-variegated leaves.

Wisteria

There are two species of particular value in the garden, both twiners with trails of scented, pea-type flowers in spring, but differing in vigour and flower character. The Chinese wisteria, *Wisteria chinensis*, is the kind usually seen covering house fronts or climbing high into trees. It is a very vigorous plant capable of reaching 50 ft. or even more and its flowers, blue mauve in the common form, are in trails 9 to 12 in. long. There are also white and double-flowered varieties. The Japanese wisteria, *W. floribunda*, is less vigorous, usually about 12 ft. high and often trained as a kind of small weeping 'tree'. In general the flower trails are a little shorter, but one remarkable variety, *macrobotrys*, has trails up to 3 ft. long. This variety is the typical blue purple of the species, but there are also white, pink and violet-blue varieties.

All wisterias grow best in warm, sunny places and fertile, well-drained soils. They transplant badly and should be purchased young in containers, moved from these without root breakage and watered and syringed frequently in hot dry weather until established. They can be pruned in summer when all young growths not required for extension can be shortened to five leaves and again, if desired, in winter when the same growths can be cut back to two dormant buds. When the plants have filled their allotted space all surplus growth can be cut out each winter.

Yucca

These are shrubs that give the garden a really exotic, sub-tropical appearance, yet several of them are surprisingly hardy and all succeed well in a wide variety of places from seaside to city gardens. They make large rosettes of stiff, sword-shaped leaves and the large, bell-shaped flowers are carried in broad, upstanding spikes. Some kinds, such as *Yucca gloriosa*, the Adam's needle, and *Y. recurvifolia*, gradually form a stout trunk several feet high, but the hardiest and most easily grown kinds, *Y. filamentosa* and *Y. flaccida* sit more closely to the soil and only produce short basal stems. All flower in late summer or autumn. There are also varieties of *Y. gloriosa* and *Y. filamentosa* with yellow-striped leaves. All grow best in full sun and well-drained soil. No pruning is desirable.

burkwoodii, white, evergreen, 5 ft., flowering in late winter and spring; *carlesii*, similar to the last but deciduous and spring flowering; *juddii*, yet another in the same style, also deciduous, and by many considered easier to grow than *carlesii*, and *V. utile*, white, evergreen, flowering in May.

Viburnum betulifolium and *V. lantana*, the latter the British wayfaring tree, are grown primarily for their berries, small and currant red in the first which makes a

Roses

Jack Harkness, one of the most respected and successful rosarians of the present time, is managing director of the famous rose nursery which bears his surname. The word successful is used advisedly for since he began breeding roses in 1962 – as distinct from growing them, which began much earlier – he has won sixty-seven awards from The Royal National Rose Society and from foreign trials. His best varieties he would consider to include Escapade, Alexander, Elizabeth Harkness, Kim, Southampton, King Arthur, Compassion and Yesterday – a galaxy of talent by any reckoning. In addition, he either assisted in, or directed, the staging of the exhibits which won for his company the R.N.R.S.'s Championship Trophy on no less than twenty-three occasions. (Harkness's have won it forty times overall, nearly half the total number of times it has been awarded – a remarkable achievement considering the competition).

Born in Shropshire and educated at Whitgift School, Croydon, he was apprenticed to the Slieve Donard Nursery Co., Newcastle, Co. Down, where he spent the years from 1934 to 1937. He then joined the family firm of R. Harkness and Co., of Hitchin, Hertfordshire, and apart from six years war service in the Army – he ended up as a major in the Far East – he has been immersed in rose growing and breeding ever since.

Mr Harkness has served, and indeed still serves, on numerous committees of The Royal National Rose Society and in 1969 he was elected a vice-president of the society. He has written a book on roses and is a frequent contributor to the gardening press.

Roses are deciduous shrubs and climbers of great diversity in habit, foliage, fruit and flower. These differences arise from their far flung natural distribution, all around the temperate zones of the northern hemisphere.

Popular practice puts the Queen of flowers in a bed. Whether so used, or as a flowering shrub, hedging plant, climber or standard, she is valued by many as the most desirable of garden plants.

Roses are normally grown in the open, being so hardy as to render winter protection uncustomary in Britain, but they also grow well in greenhouses, and in pots. Their great advantages are beauty, ease of cultivation, cheapness and long life.

Conditions

Roses require a soil which retains moisture but permits drainage. The more fertile the soil the better because roses grow readily in response to fertility. Tolerant of alkalinity or acidity, they are unhappy only at the further ends of the scale, more particularly at the acid extreme. They are not shade plants; they prefer to grow in the sun. Roses usually endure exposed places well, with some inhibition of growth.

Soil Preparation

The three objects are to feed the plants, to give them anchorage and to drain the soil. Deep digging attains all three, preferably by trenching, at the same time thoroughly mixing organic substances with the soil. But preparation must be adapted to the soil, of which here follow four instances.

A **soil impervious to water** (which may be tested by filling a hole with water to see if it drains in forty-eight hours) demands the lower spits be broken, and if necessary a soakaway provided, to prevent the bed becoming a sump for the surrounding area. Render heavy clay more porous with gypsum (calcium sulphate) at about 3 lb. to the sq. yd. in the bottom of the trench.

A **soil with a high water table** will only grow roses if the beds are raised.

A **shallow soil** which drains well needs to be dug only for the purpose of adding food, particularly substances to hold moisture. The lower spit may be replaced with better soil. Beds must not be raised on such soil because in the summer they dry out.

A **fertile, well-drained soil** need only be cleaned, levelled and planted.

Planting

Buy good strong plants, and be suspicious of cheap offers. Plant October to April when the soil is crumbly. The ground is the place for roses, but if they cannot enter it at once, keep them in a cool place, not in a heated room, for the briefest possible time. If the soil is not crumbly, plant them temporarily elsewhere, close together and firmly, with the roots wet. Do not plant in prepared ground until it has re-settled.

The average planting distances to create a close array are: miniatures 12 in.; dwarf floribundas 15 in.; floribundas and hybrid teas 21 in.; shrub roses 42 in.; climbers at least 10 ft. apart, and standards 4 ft. But all may be grown individually at optional distances, and standards in particular do not really need to be closely set.

Use a good seed and potting medium as a planting mixture; or enthusiasts can make their own by mixing two handfuls of sterilized bonemeal (use gloves) and one of hoof and horn to a large bucketful of peat. Do not let other fertilizers or manure touch the roots.

Trim off snags, suckers and damaged or immature growth before planting, and wet the roots. Dig a shallow hole, and place the plant to one side of it, with the roots spread out on the bottom, towards the horizontal. Place at soil level the point where thorny stems and smooth rootstock join. If the plant does not sit comfortably, deepen the hole – 6 or 7 in. is usually deep enough. Cover the roots first with planting mixture, then half fill the hole with soil, and tread very firmly for rose roots must be tight to the ground. Fill the hole, tread lightly and level off. The plant should resist a firm tug. When filling up, take the soil from the next planting position, and the next hole is ready dug.

Put the stake in before the standard, the top of it just below the lowest graft.

When the soil is dry in April to June,

The container should be removed and the plant inserted with as little disturbance to the roots as possible. Ensure that the soil in the container is moist and that the plant is well firmed

tread again, especially any slow starters, which will also benefit from a bucketful of water.

Roses grown in containers must be planted (after removing the container) with the soil closely firmed to the sides and bottom of the container soil, which should be moist. Planting time, obviously, is optional for container plants.

Pruning

A rose shoot normally grows to its terminal point in one season. It exists in the future by means of side shoots, which are usually incapable of girth greater than the parent shoot. By pruning, only the strongest wood is left, and new growth is therefore obliged to arise from it.

Such, in a nutshell, are the reasons and methods, to which we add one fact: after a few years, rose stems resist sap flow, which is forced into new growth elsewhere on the plant, whereupon the old growth system can be cut away.

Efficient secateurs and a narrow-bladed saw are the tools. The time is winter or spring, before growth is far advanced, but it is well to shorten the plants in November or December to reduce wind damage. Cuts are made just above an eye, without injuring it, and on a slant of which the eye side is the higher. Unless the plant's development demands otherwise, an outward-facing eye is chosen. All weak, unripe, damaged or dead wood is removed.

Prune new plants hard: bedding roses being left about finger length out of the ground; flowering shrubs up to 1 ft.; climbers 2 to 3 ft., and standards about 6 in. from the grafts. When the plants are mature, strong growths can be retained to any length; they will develop into a considerable system, which may be encouraged and retained, with suitable shorten-

Dead, diseased and a certain amount of old wood is removed from hybrid teas, leaving an open framework about one third the height of the original bush

ing of the side shoots, or of the whole system if the top of it is becoming unproductive.

Exceptions are many belonging to the group known as the old garden roses, which grow one year, and flower the next. Unless adequate length is retained, the flowers will have been pruned away. Wild roses look more graceful if the long shoots are not shortened. Standard roses do not replace growth as easily as the others, and caution is needed in removing large parts of them.

The long growths of climbers are trained to fit their position, and in future years their side shoots shortened; or the best may be trained. The main stem is kept until it is not satisfactorily productive, when it may be removed entirely, or shortened to a point where it is productive.

Cultivation

After pruning, shallow cultivation by spade or fork will tidy the beds; but only an inch or two deep – the roots hate being disturbed. Weeds may be controlled by the hoe, or by weedkillers or suppressants, first ensuring the herbicide may safely be used among roses.

Fertility is increased by the proper use of mulches, soil fertilizers or foliar feeding; it is better not to use fertilizers in the first year after planting.

The best mulch is good farmyard manure, applied to the surface in May. Alternatives are compost, leafmould or peat.

Fertilizers for roses are so carefully prepared by the leading manufacturers that most people can safely buy them, and

apply once after pruning. It goes down more quickly if spread on a frosty morning. A second dressing can be applied in June when the buds have formed, preferably in a rainy spell. Ideally, fertilizers should answer the needs of the soil, which can only be discovered by expert analysis, and in cases of difficulty this is a sensible procedure.

Never use any fertilizer containing muriate of potash; Nitro-chalk is unsuitable for chalky soils; sulphate of magnesium should be a constituent of a good rose fertilizer, for magnesium in a small amount is an essential rose food. Lime must be used with caution, only on a soil proved to be too acid without it, and preferably in the form of calcium carbonate.

Foliar feeding is especially useful if the soil is alkaline or chalky.

Suckers should be pulled or cut off, as

Suckers, which arise from the stock on to which the rose variety was budded, should be removed as close to the plant as possible

Pruning cuts:
(a) Too far away from the bud
(b) Too close to the bud
(c) Sloping the wrong way
(d) Correct

Blackspot can be controlled by removing infected leaves and by spraying with maneb or captan

soon as noticed. They are recognized by their different leaves and by their point of origin being separate from the grafting union. It is not true that they can be detected by counting their leaflets.

Fading flowers should be dead-headed before they set seed to induce new flowering shoots; ideally, trim them down to the next sound eye, but failing that, trim them off quickly.

Pests and Diseases
Be prepared with efficient sprayers and remedies because troubles spread very swiftly. The chief enemies are greenfly, mildew, blackspot and rust. The leading companies have good remedies for each, and regularly introduce new products.

Greenfly killers should be applied when the greenfly become obvious.

Mildew is a light greyish mould; look just under the flower buds for early warning, and spray when seen. Current remedies include those based on dinocap, dodemorph, benomyl and chlorani-formethan.

Blackspot and rust are the most damaging diseases. Blackspot shows as irregular black spots on the leaf, and rust as orange (later, black) pustules underneath it. Current remedies are maneb for both, captan for blackspot and thiram for rust. These two diseases need preventive spraying, from pruning time until flower buds form, if there has been any sign of them in the previous year; and remedial spraying after flowering should the diseases appear. Prevention is more effective than cure, and the undersides of the leaves must be sprayed as well as the tops.

The choice of varieties resistant to fungal diseases is also a sensible precaution.

Lesser pests are thunderflies (thrips) and leafhoppers, which are controlled by greenfly killer; caterpillars and sawflies, which make the leaves curl up, for which trichlorphon is effective, and red spider mites, like miniature spiders, slightly mobile, on the undersides, for which white oil may be used, although new products are now being tested.

Classification
In 1971, The Royal National Rose Society produced a framework of classification, which we simplify here as follows:

MODERN GARDEN ROSES
Large-flowered bush roses (Hybrid Tea)
Cluster-flowered bush roses (Floribunda)
Shrub roses
Miniature roses
Climbing roses

OLD GARDEN ROSES
Shrubs and climbers

WILD ROSES
Shrubs and climbers, either wild, or hybrids resembling wild roses.

With which preamble, we can now explore the best and most beautiful roses which cover the whole range of the genus at this present time. The more unusual and diverse types have received the longer descriptions.

Selected Roses

Large-flowered Bush Roses (Hybrid Teas)
Average height is 2½ to 3 ft., or as varied by conditions and cultivation.

Adolf Horstmann Orange yellow marked red. Here is a stately bloom, full of petals, initially yellow but opening more orange, especially when the blooms are cut. Average height. Raised by Kordes (Germany) 1971.

Alec's Red Crimson to cherry red. A large flower with strong sweet scent it has collected four international awards for fragrance. Average height. Raised by Cocker (Scotland) 1970.

Alexander Vermilion. A breath-catching colour, especially vibrant in the sunlight. Good form, without a lot of petals, but plenty of flowers on long straight stems. Above average height. Raised by Harkness (England) 1972.

Baccara Deep vermilion. For growing under glass, or in a plot adjoining a greenhouse. It is no good in the open. Provider of long-stemmed, long-lasting cut flowers, the florist's dream. Young leaves, bronze. Average height. Raised by Meilland (France) 1956.

Alexander (Hybrid tea)

35

Beaute Orange yellow. Modesty itself: few petals, but broad, high-centred flowers; dull foliage and low growth, but a pleasing bush. Below average height. Raised by Mallerin (France) 1954.

Blessings Rose pink, slightly salmon. An excellent bedding rose, very free flowering, of even growth. Medium-sized flowers, well formed. Average height. Raised by Gregory (England) 1968.

Blue Moon Lilac pink. The best of the hopefully blue roses, and very fragrant. Handsome flowers (better still under glass) but watch it for blackspot. Average height. Raised by Tantau (Germany) 1964.

Bonsoir Pink, pretty peach-blossom colour. A beauty for large, well-formed flowers, pleasantly fragrant. Handsome leaves. Average height. Raised by Dickson (Ireland) 1968.

Chicago Peace Phlox pink and yellow. Excepting colour, it has the characteristics of Peace, large flowers and all. Above average height. Raised by Johnston (USA) 1962.

Colour Wonder Orange red, yellow reverse. Scintillating colour, well-formed blooms, thorny plant. Wonderful when it settles in, but does not always do so. Try a few plants rather than a bed. Average height. Raised by Kordes (Germany) 1964.

Curiosity Red, yellow reverse. The flowers are not so marvellous, but the leaves are brightly variegated with light marks. An interesting curiosity. Below average height. Raised by Cocker (Scotland) 1971.

Diorama Yellow marked red. One of the best yellow roses; mainly the outer petals have the red marks. Average height. Raised by De Ruiter (Holland) 1965.

Elizabeth Harkness Ivory shaded buff or pink. Most handsome and consistent in flower form. Free flowering, fragrant; and beautiful beyond words. Average height. Raised by Harkness (England) 1969.

Ena Harkness Bright crimson. The most famous red rose. The form of flowers and rich colour have made it a household name. Does not like dry conditions in which it hangs its head. Average height. Raised by Norman (England) 1946.

Ernest H. Morse Deep crimson. Has an excellent habit of growth for a bed, and produces well-formed flowers without a great many petals. Average height. Raised by Kordes (Germany) 1964.

Eroica Dark crimson. Large flowers, perhaps a little dull in colour, but richly scented. Average height. Raised by Tantau (Germany) 1968.

Evensong Deep rosy salmon. A real beauty, not known as well as it deserves. The flowers are fragrant, well formed,

attractive and kind in colour. Average height. Raised by Arnot (Scotland) 1963.

Fragrant Cloud Dusky scarlet. Wonderful scent has made it a best seller, but the colour fades. Good habit for a bed. Some risk of blackspot. Average height. Raised by Tantau (Germany) 1963.

Grandpa Dickson Lemon yellow; takes some red flushes especially on later blooms. An excellent rose, from which flowers of supreme quality in size and form can be obtained. Average height. Raised by Dickson (Ireland) 1966.

Harlow Salmon, indeed almost smoked salmon, and strangely very suitable among surroundings of concrete; a common but unaesthetic substance which does little to help most colours. Average height. Raised by Cocker (Scotland) 1969.

Honey Favourite Buff yellow shaded pink. Has the beautiful, disease-resistant foliage of Pink Favourite, of which it is a sport. Average height. Raised by Von Abrams (USA) 1962.

John Waterer Deep crimson. The colour is deep and bright, set off well against lustrous foliage. Not much scent, unfortunately, but a very handsome rose for a bed. Average height. Raised by McGredy (Ireland) 1970.

Josephine Bruce Dark crimson. The darkest of them all, stunning on its first flower, a bit ragged later, and apt to mildew. Below average height. Raised by Bees (England) 1949.

Just Joey Salmon flushed coppery orange. No ordinary colour, it sometimes looks between fawn and orange, and invites pleased notice. Below average height. Raised by Cants (England) 1973.

King's Ransom Deep yellow. The clear yellow colour agrees well with the glossy green of the foliage. Average height. Raised by Morey (USA) 1961.

Kronenbourg Purple red, reverse yellow. A sport from Peace, in a colour some may call daring, others ugly. It is unique at least. Above average height. Raised by McGredy (Ireland) 1965.

Lady Seton Rose pink. A fragrant pink rose, producing medium-sized flowers on good stems abundantly. Upright, well-leafed bush. Average height or a bit more. Raised by McGredy (Ireland) 1966.

Meinatac Rose pink. Large fragrant flowers of pleasing colourful pink. Average height. Raised by Meilland (France) 1974.

Mischief Salmon pink; the September flowers have a hint of orange. Popular, fragrant, well formed and free flowering, but it may get rust. Average height. Raised by McGredy (Ireland) 1961.

Mullard Jubilee Deep pink. A big plant in

every way; growth, foliage and flowers are all exuberant. Colour approaching light red. Above average height. Raised by McGredy (Ireland) 1970.

National Trust Bright crimson. The flowers are smaller than most, not fragrant, but for a blaze of red in the garden it is superb. Below average height. Raised by McGredy (Ireland) 1970.

Pascali White. The best white hybrid tea, and one of the best of all garden roses for cutting. A most satisfactory rose to grow. Average height. Raised by Lens (Belgium) 1963.

Peace Yellow flushed pink. One of the easiest to grow, provided blackspot is controlled. Famous for the beauty, size and delicate colouring of its flowers. Above average height. Raised by Meilland (France) 1942.

Peer Gynt Bright yellow flushed red. One of the boldest yellow colours, capable of producing blooms both exquisite and substantial. May need mildew control. Average height. Raised by Kordes (Germany) 1968.

Perfecta Cream shaded and marked pink. The great blooms are indeed perfection, but so heavy the wind can snap them off. Given shelter, and forgiven its ugly buds, Perfecta offers great enjoyment. Average height. Raised by Kordes (Germany) 1957.

Pharaoh Rich scarlet. Spectacular flowers, large and bright, stand above thick, leathery leaves, which nonetheless need watching for blackspot. Average height. Raised by Meilland (France) 1967.

Piccadilly Scarlet and yellow. A brilliant bedding rose, not only in flower, but in glistening dark foliage too. Keep an eye on it for blackspot. Average height or less. Raised by McGredy (Ireland) 1960.

Pink Favourite Bright pink. Wonderful foliage, very resistant to disease. The flowers grow large and shapely. Good habit for a bed. Average height. Raised by Von Abrams (USA) 1956.

Prima Ballerina Deep rose pink. The fragrance is delightful, the colour kind, and the flowers handsome without many petals. Strong growth, some chance of mildew. Above average height. Raised by Tantau (Germany) 1957.

Red Devil Light crimson. Famous for the enormous size its flowers can grow to, this is the best variety to put its owner in the exhibitor's class without really trying. Fragrant, and a handsome plant. Above average height. Raised by Dickson (Ireland) 1967.

Red Planet Deep bright crimson. Health and colour are superb, but fragrance is lacking. The autumn flowers are usually the best. Average height. Raised by Dickson (Ireland) 1970.

Rose Gaujard Carmine rose and white. Usually proves one of the easiest to grow, with attractive slim buds, opening to show a twisted centre. Average height. Raised by Gaujard (France) 1959.

Stella Creamy pink and carmine. For maximum pleasure, leave only one flower bud per shoot, by removing the side buds when young. A glorious, stately flower is then given, instead of a somewhat untidy head. Average height. Raised by Tantau (Germany) 1958.

Super Star Light vermilion. A famous rose, with beautifully formed flowers, in attractive colour. Apt to mildew. Above average height. Raised by Tantau (Germany) 1960.

Sutter's Gold Yellow flushed pink. Ruddy gold buds open to well-formed flowers, without many petals. Elegant, fragrant, free flowering. Average height. Raised by Swim (USA) 1950.

Sweet Promise Salmon pink. The flowers are on the small side, most beautifully formed. Lots of Sweet Promise go to the flower shops. Average height. Raised by Meilland (France) 1972.

Troika Orange and red. Attractive in colour and form when young, but discolours with age. The orange colour is one of the best in roses. Average height. Raised by Poulsen (Denmark) 1972.

Truly Yours Salmon pink shaded orange. Delightfully fragrant, well-formed blooms. Average height. Raised by Robinson (England) 1974.

Typhoon Salmon pink shaded orange. Fragrant and easy to grow. Colour is variable, which can give pleasant surprises. Average height. Raised by Kordes (Germany) 1972.

Wendy Cussons Deep pink, near to light red. A splendid English rose, easy to grow, usually well behaved and fragrant. Above average height. Raised by Gregory (England) 1959.

Whisky Mac Amber yellow. One of the most beautiful colours in roses, with elegant, fragrant flowers to set it off. But watch out for mildew. Average height. Raised by Tantau (Germany) 1967.

Yellow Pages Deep yellow. A very bold yellow, like glittering gold against its shining foliage. Average height. Raised by McGredy (Ireland) 1973.

Cluster-flowered Bush Roses (Floribundas)

Average height is 2½ to 3 ft., or as varied by conditions and cultivation.

Allgold Bright yellow. Clusters of well-formed buds open to clear yellow blooms,

Typhoon (Hybrid tea)

holding the colour well. Deep green, shiny foliage provides a lovely backing. Below average height. Raised by Le Grice (England) 1958.

Anne Cocker Glowing vermilion. Flowers the size of overcoat buttons, double, long lasting, one to a stem in mighty inflorescences. May need anti-mildew precautions. Above average height. Raised by Cocker (Scotland) 1971.

Apricot Nectar Light apricot. Wide, semi-double flowers, charming pale colour, with fragrance. Average height. Raised by Boerner (USA) 1965.

Arakan Blush pink. High-centred flowers, crammed in profusely, and looking straight up from the clusters. Below average height. Raised by Harkness (England) 1968.

Arthur Bell Bright yellow, fading cream. Grows upright, with handsome bright green leaves, and is one of the most

fragrant of its class. Above average height. Raised by McGredy (Ireland) 1965.

Bonfire Night Brilliant orange red with a touch of yellow. The crowded semi-double flowers and dark sparkling foliage provide a deep glow of colour. Average height or more. Raised by McGredy (Ireland) 1971.

Busy Lizzie Soft light pink. Remarkable explosion of bloom covers the plants. Semi-double, unsophisticated. Average height. Raised by Harkness (England) 1971.

Charles Dickens Salmon to orange pink. A most pleasing colour, in blooms opening semi-double from well-formed buds. Average height. Raised by McGredy (Ireland) 1970.

City of Belfast Bright scarlet. An aggressive display of colour from quite a modest plant. Colour is held very well. Below average height. Raised by McGredy (Ireland) 1968.

City of Leeds Salmon pink. Rather a plain

37

Escapade (Floribunda)

colour, but a splendid performer, giving quantities of well-formed flowers. Makes an excellent bed. Average height. Raised by McGredy (Ireland) 1966.

Dearest Soft rose pink. Gains a subtle touch of salmon, especially as a cut flower. Fragrant and well loved, although it gets in a mess in rain, and needs a watch for disease. Average height. Raised by Dickson (Ireland) 1960.

Dr Barnardo Crimson. A safe red variety as a rule, with large flowers for the class, and commendable foliage and vigour. Average height. Raised by Harkness (England) 1969.

Elizabeth of Glamis Salmon shaded apricot. Included here for the supreme beauty of elegant flowers in glorious colour – and with fragrance too. But watch it like a hawk for rust. Average height. Raised by McGredy (Ireland) 1964.

Escapade Rosy violet, white centre. Has about nine petals, which it opens to show its stamens, and to diffuse its perfume. Unconventional, very charming, and a gem to cut – take it when the buds show colour. Above average height. Raised by Harkness (England) 1967.

Evelyn Fison Bright deep scarlet. One of the most generally used modern varieties for bedding. A good, satisfying red colour. Average height. Raised by McGredy (Ireland) 1962.

Gardeners' Sunday Bright yellow. Has the desirable quality of holding the colour fast, on a tallish plant with flowers of good form and fragrance. Above average height. Raised by Harkness (England) 1975.

Hakuun White tinted buff. This compact provider of summer snowdrifts suffers the injustice of almost totally being ignored. Below average height. Raised by Poulsen (Denmark) 1966.

Iceberg White. The flowers are of lovely formation, and borne abundantly on a plant which lends itself both to bedding and to being grown as a shrub. The supreme white rose; it can get mildew and blackspot, but is responsive to a helping spray. Average height or more. Raised by Kordes (Germany) 1958.

Irish Mist Orange salmon. Colour and flower form have strong appeal. The plants branch well for bedding purposes. Glossy leaves. Average height or less. Raised by McGredy (Ireland) 1966.

Kerryman Pink. The unusual rose-pink colour is warm and lively, the flowers large and well formed. May need watching for blackspot. Average height. Raised by McGredy (Ireland) 1970.

Kim Yellow flushed red. One of the dwarf floribundas, making cushion plants 15 in. or so high. The flowers are full and well formed. Well below average height. Raised by Harkness (England) 1973.

Lagoon Pale lilac. The five-petalled flowers open to show a fluffy centre of yellow stamens against the pastel lilac petals. Unusual. Average height. Raised by Harkness (England) 1973.

Lilli Marlene Bright crimson. A workman-like producer of brilliant red by the yard. A good bedding rose, semi-double, to be found in most parks. Average height. Raised by Kordes (Germany) 1959. ,

Lively Lady Rosy vermilion. Handsome double flowers, in a colour both lively and out of the ordinary. Average height. Raised by Cocker (Scotland) 1969.

Living Fire Orange red. Grows upright, with a mantle of fairly large semi-double flowers to justify the name. Above average height. Raised by Gregory (England) 1973.

Manx Queen Orange (actually orange yellow and red). Carries its smallish flowers very densely, has some scent, makes a bold show. Average height. Raised by Dickson (Ireland) 1963.

Margo Koster Coppery salmon, but may revert to red. A short grower, with clusters of small cup-shaped flowers; quite an individual rose, comes from an old polyantha line. Well below average height. Raised by Koster (Holland) 1931.

Marlena Deep crimson. The best dwarf floribunda, making extremely neat rounded plants 1 ft. or so high. Very good looking and free flowering. Well below average height. Raised by Kordes (Germany) 1964.

Masquerade Yellow, turning pink and finally red. The rose which showed the world at large the chameleon ability in the genus. Semi-double flowers, well formed. Unfortunately is generally infected with rose mosaic virus. Average height. Raised by Boerner (USA) 1949.

Maud Cole Slate purple. A strange colour, reflected to some extent in the purplish foliage; an off-beat colour for floral artists. Average height. Raised by Harkness (England) 1968.

Megiddo Scarlet. Large semi-double flowers provide a great blaze of red. May get blackspot. Average height. Raised by Gandy (England) 1970.

Meteor Vermilion red. Dwarf floribunda, up to 18 in. usually, with well-formed flowers of apt size for a little plant. Well below average height. Raised by Kordes (Germany) 1958.

Michelle Salmon pink. Attractive double flowers, fragrant. A good rose, which unfortunately has failed to gain general favour. Average height. Raised by De Ruiter (Holland) 1968.

Molly McGredy Rose red, whitish reverse. Double flowers of good size and form. This is a dependable variety to produce plenty of blooms and abundant dark green leaves, but not everyone's colour. Above average height. Raised by McGredy (Ireland) 1969.

Moonmaiden Light primrose. The flowers

cluster in all the open space they can find about the plant, not crowded, but abundantly and full of life. Below average height. Raised by Mattock (England) 1970.

News Reddish purple. A bold beetroot kind of colour, which goes well with Moonmaiden, and shows the interesting range of rose hues. Average height. Raised by Le Grice (England) 1969.

Orangeade Vermilion red. Large clusters of flowers open to show the stamens, and thus present a bold show of colour. Some liability to blackspot. Average height. Raised by McGredy (Ireland) 1959.

Orange Sensation Light vermilion red. Small double flowers, of pleasant formation and fragrance, and excellent lively colour. Average height. Raised by De Ruiter (Holland) 1961.

Orange Silk Orange vermilion. Well-formed flowers in a clear bright colour. The leaves are bright and glossy. Average height or a little less. Raised by McGredy (Ireland) 1965.

Paddy McGredy Carmine. Although lowly in stature, it bears large double flowers in spreading inflorescences, giving an impression of quality en masse. May blackspot. Below average height. Raised by McGredy (Ireland) 1962.

Picasso Design of red upon whitish eye, rims and reverse. 'Hand painted' is the raiser's way of putting it. Unique and beautiful, needs fine weather to show itself off. Below average height. Raised by McGredy (Ireland) 1971.

Pineapple Poll Orange yellow flushed red. Small flowers, very neatly formed, with delicious pineapple scent. Usually better in summer than autumn. Below average height. Raised by Cocker (Scotland) 1970.

Pink Elizabeth Arden Rose pink. One of the most agreeable pink colours, soft and warm. Enough petals to make a flower of very pleasant formation. The leaves are deep green, a good foil. Average height. Raised by Tantau (Germany) 1964.

Pink Parfait Pink with creamy shading. Elegant and free flowering, with long flowers of much beauty and grace. Average height. Raised by Swim (USA) 1960.

Princess Michiko Deep orange red. One to commend notice in all the glaring colours of modern roses; vivid without being vulgar. Average height. Raised by Dickson (Ireland) 1966.

Queen Elizabeth Rose pink. Tall and easy growing, the best rose for a hedge, and also one of the best for cutting; its clusters of well-formed pink flowers are compact, on pleasant straight stems. Well above average height. Raised by Lammerts (USA) 1954.

Redgold Yellow marked red. The blooms are shapely, of good size, and the colours bright and pleasing. Average height. Raised by Dickson (Ireland) 1966.

Rob Roy Brilliant crimson. About as fine a shade of red as one could wish to see. The flowers are large, the foliage abundant. Average height. Raised by Cocker (Scotland) 1971.

Sarabande Bright red. Not so easy to procure as it should be; the flowers have five petals, and fairly cover the spreading plants in red. Below average height. Raised by Meilland (France) 1957.

Scented Air Rosy salmon. Large semi-double flowers, rather loosely formed. This is a handsome plant to grow as a

Southampton (Floribunda)

single specimen, and pleasantly fragrant. Above average height. Raised by Dickson (Ireland) 1965.

Southampton Apricot orange. Those who want another orange floribunda cannot do better than plant this healthy rose. Fragrant. Above average height. Raised by Harkness (England) 1972.

Stephen Langdon Deep crimson. A splendid bright red, with well-formed flowers in abundance. Average height. Raised by Sanday (England) 1971.

Tony Jacklin Coral pink shaded orange. Bright in colour, a reliable bedding rose with well-formed blooms. Average height.

Raised by McGredy (Ireland) 1972.

Topsi Vermilion. A dwarf floribunda, with clusters of closely set flowers borne not only in profusion, but in quick succession. Well below average height. Raised by Tantau (Germany) 1972.

Vera Dalton Rose pink. The buds are well formed, high centred, and the flowers are still charming when fully open. Average height. Raised by Norman (England) 1961.

Yvonne Rabier White. A sweetly scented white, with small double flowers on neat bush plants. Not widely grown, unfortunately. Average height or less. Raised by Turbat (France) 1910.

Modern Shrub Roses

Some of these are to be found as floribundas in the rose catalogues, and they may be grown in beds, or as shrubs, or as hedges. Average height is 4 ft. or as varied by conditions and cultivation. The origin and old classes are shown at the end of each. Except where stated, they flower in summer and autumn.

Ballerina Light pink, white eye. Tiny single flowers crammed dozens together in mop heads. Impression of a solid square plant nothing will harm. Easy to grow, and rewarding. Average height. Raised by Bentall (England) 1937. Hybrid musk.

Bonn Vermilion. Semi-double flowers, in rather scattered clusters, but of brilliant effect against bright green leaves. Above average height. Raised by Kordes (Germany) 1949. Hybrid musk (alleged).

Buff Beauty Creamy buff. Double flowers, apt to nod; nothing special but somehow the charm is there. Fragrant. Below average height. Origin unsure, introduced 1939. Hybrid musk.

Chinatown Bright yellow. Such lush green foliage and rich yellow flowers, there is no chance of overlooking this. Fragrant into the bargain. Average height or more, grows fairly wide. Raised by Poulsen (Denmark) 1963. Floribunda.

Cornelia Light pink, touch of strawberry pink. Semi-double, small flowers in large clusters; the stems usually grow up and outwards, and have attractive dark bark. Fragrant. Average height or more, grows fairly wide. Raised by Pemberton (England) 1925. Hybrid musk.

Dorothy Wheatcroft Scarlet. Large heads of closely set semi-double flowers, very bright. Apt to grow tall and thin. Above average height. Raised by Tantau (Germany) 1960. Floribunda.

Felicia Light pink, touch of yellow. Small flowers, well formed and fragrant; unobtrusive. Average height. Raised by

Pemberton (England) 1928. Hybrid musk.

Fountain Bright crimson. A multitude of wide-petalled flowers wave their glorious red colour for all to see. Growth is quick, foliage ample, and Fountain wastes no time before flowering again. Average height. Raised by Tantau (Germany) 1972. Floribunda.

Fred Loads Vermilion. An upright plant, with large heads of vivid semi-double flowers, showing stamens; the colour is bright and pure. Very effective. Above average height. Raised by Holmes (England) 1967. Floribunda.

Fritz Nobis Rich, beautiful pink. One of the few roses in this section which is summer flowering only (in June usually). Also one of the most glorious shrubs in existence. The flowers are fairly large,

Topsi (Floribunda)

with firm petals and a form that invites close inspection. They are carried evenly on the plant. Grows fairly wide. Well above average height. Raised by Kordes (Germany) 1940. Has sweet briar breeding.

Frühlingsgold Creamy yellow. Summer flowering only (in May usually). Very fragrant, semi-double flowers. A large shrub, very spectacular in its two or three weeks of glory. About twice average height. Raised by Kordes (Germany) 1937. Has *spinosissima* breeding.

Frühlingsmorgen Pink with yellow centre and maroon stamens showing against the yellow. Large single flowers, worth a long look for their simple and lovely construction. Strong scent, rather mealy. Mainly early summer flowering, but some appear in autumn too. Above average height. Raised by Kordes (Germany) 1942. Has *spinosissima* breeding.

Golden Wings Light primrose. Wide single flowers, each an essay on how to be fragile and beautiful. Average height. Raised by Shepherd (USA) 1956. Has *spinosissima* breeding.

Heidelberg Bright crimson. The double flowers are augmented by the bronze tint in the foliage. This can be a splendid sight, but is apt to get blackspot. Above average height. Raised by Kordes (Germany) 1958. Floribunda.

Herbstfeuer Crimson. Not easy to find. It has unique, large, pear-shaped seedpods, very decorative. Semi-double flowers. Above average height. Raised by Kordes (Germany) 1961. Parentage not stated.

Joseph's Coat Yellow and various shades of red. A brilliant and versatile rose, may be grown in a bed, as a shrub or persuaded to climb. Semi-double flowers; the name conveys the effect very well. Average height. Raised by Swim (USA) 1964. Floribunda.

Marguerite Hilling Rosy pink, looks as if brushed on a white base. Large single flowers. Branches tend to arch, have soft dull leaves, and are festooned with flowers coming on very short stems direct from the branch. A most agreeable sight. Above average height. Raised by Hilling (England) 1959. Sport of Nevada.

Nevada White. The twin of the foregoing in all but colour. Raised by Dot (Spain) 1927. Has *moyesii* breeding.

Penelope Blush. Semi-double flowers, small and fragrant. Not much in themselves, but there is something satisfying in their abundant appearance. Average height (may be less). Raised by Pemberton (England) 1924. Hybrid musk.

Pink Grootendorst Rose pink. This is the one with small double flowers frilled at the edges. Interesting, although one may feel bush and flowers are out of scale. Above average height. Raised by Grootendorst (Holland) 1923. Has *rugosa* breeding.

Saga White, with buff tints. Extremely free blooming, with medium-sized semi-double flowers borne simultaneously at many levels. Average height. Raised by Harkness (England) 1974. Floribunda.

Schneezwerg White. Very hardy and trouble free, with smallish foliage, and a long succession of flat, well-formed, semi-double blooms. Average height. Raised by Lambert (Germany) 1912. Has *rugosa* breeding.

The Fairy Pink. Masses of little double flowers, like those of the old ramblers,

from July onwards; the smother of blooms is soft against the small dark shiny leaves. Apt to stay short; below average height. Raised by Bentall (England) 1932. Has *wichuraiana* origin.

Yesterday Rose to lilac pink. Very small flowers and leaves. Blooms in large heads, opening on a programme that ensures long continuity. The flowers are semi-double, open from rose red to pink with a touch of lilac, beautiful in conjunction. Sweetly fragrant. Has power to exert a very strong charm. Average height or less. Raised by Harkness (England) 1974. Highly complicated origin.

Miniature Roses
Average height is 12 in.

Baby Faurax Amethyst. The most re-

Yesterday (Modern shrub)

markable 'blue' colour in roses. Small, flat, double flowers, on a stumpy plant that can really do with protection. Not strictly speaking a miniature, but the height fits. Average height. Raised by Lille (France) 1924.

Baby Masquerade Yellow marked pink. The easiest miniature to grow, with plenty of shoots, tiny leaves and narrow-petalled flowers similar in effect to Masquerade. Average height or more. Raised by Tantau (Germany) 1956.

Coralin Coral red. Flowers are well formed, double, and a trifle larger than most miniatures. Small leaves with a bronze tint. Average height. Raised by Dot (Spain) 1955.

Easter Morning Cream. Well-shaped buds, true miniature roses. Average height. Raised by Moore (USA) 1960.

Humpty Dumpty Pink. May not be easy to find. Very short, with little flowers of fifty petals or more. Below average height. Raised by De Vink (Holland) 1950.

Little Buckaroo Crimson. Pretty miniature buds, opening semi-double. The plant, however, manages quite a lot of growth, up to twice average height, but with miniature leaves. Raised by Moore (USA) 1956.

Little Flirt Orange pink touched yellow. The leaves a trifle larger than most, the flowers more open. But it certainly gives a shameless performance. Above average height. Raised by Moore (USA) 1961.

New Penny Salmon red. Flowers, growth and leaves are all that one expects a miniature should be. Glossy foliage. Average height. Raised by Moore (USA) 1962.

Perla de Alcanada Light crimson. Double flowers, opening flat, the colour not particularly bright. The plant makes a little thicket, and this admirable habit has enabled it to survive for no other miniature grows into such a good little plant. Above average height. Raised by Dot (Spain) 1945.

Pour Toi White touched yellow at base. Small neat flowers and leaves on a bushy little plant. Average height. Raised by Dot (Spain) 1946.

Rosina Yellow. Pretty buds, opening semi-double. Well known under its English name, Josephine Wheatcroft. Watch it for blackspot. Above average height. Raised by Dot (Spain) 1951.

Sweet Fairy Pink. A tiny plant with double flowers. Below average height. Raised by De Vink (Holland) 1946.

Modern Climbing Roses

Height of climbing roses is extremely variable, according to the conditions and cultivation.

Albéric Barbier Cream. Small flowers open semi-double from elegant buds. Glossy leaves stay on late in winter. One of the best to grow on a north or east wall, or in other difficult positions. Flowers in summer with a fair scattering again in autumn. Well above average height. Raised by Barbier (France) 1900.

Albertine Salmon and light rose. Attractive buds, the flowers pale as they open. A rose famous for its fantastic abundance of summer flower. Does not repeat in autumn. Some liability to mildew. Best allowed some freedom, that is by a tree

Above: Nevada (Modern shrub)
Right: Easter Morning (Miniature)

stump, or over a shed or shelter, not tied to walls or posts. Well above average height. Raised by Barbier (France) 1921.

Altissimo Bright crimson. Handbreadth single flowers, spectacular. Repeat flowering, and adaptable for most uses. Above average height. Raised by Delbard-Chabert (France) 1967.

Bantry Bay Pink. Well-formed flowers, opening semi-double, pleasant colour. Repeat flowering and adaptable for most uses. Average height. Raised by McGredy (Ireland) 1967.

Casino Deep yellow. Double flowers quite large and very well formed. One of the best for freedom of flower through the season, but is choosy about its position, and likes some warmth and shelter. A warm place on a wall would seem ideal. Average height. Raised by McGredy (Ireland) 1963.

Compassion Light salmon pink shaded apricot. Double flowers, well formed and very fragrant. Abundant dark foliage. Repeats well and is adaptable for most uses. Average height or more. Raised by Harkness (England) 1973.

Crimson Shower Deep crimson. A rambler, that is to say the shoots would be more or less prostrate unless tied up. Consequently ideal to tie to a post for a waterfall effect of bloom. Small flowers in close clusters, mid-July and August. Average height. Raised by Norman (England) 1951.

Danse des Sylphes Light red. Small flowers, not immediately impressive, but the plant is a useful one for difficult positions, and the later blooms are apt to flower when other climbers are off. Above average height. Raised by Mallerin (France) 1959.

Danse du Feu Scarlet. Double flowers, well formed, and very spectacular until the colour fades, at which stage it can scarcely be termed pleasing. Repeats its bloom exceptionally well, and is suitable for most uses. Average height. Raised by Mallerin (France) 1954.

Ena Harkness, Climbing Bright crimson. Best grown on a wall or fence; the large red flowers are likely to be even better than on the bush form. Some scattered repeat bloom. Average height. Raised by Murrell (England) 1954.

Etoile de Hollande, Climbing Deep crimson. Very fragrant; a fine red climber for the wall, but flowers early, and is not very generous in repeating. Above average

Above: Climbing Cécile Brunner (Old garden rose)
Right: *Rosa gallica versicolor* **(Old garden rose)**

height, often after a slow start. Raised by Leenders (Holland) 1931.

Golden Showers Bright yellow. Attractive buds open semi-double, at times with very attractive spread of petals around stamens. Extremely free flowering, repeats like a bush, has good foliage. Can be grown as a shrub or trained on a smallish area of fence or wall. Below average height. Raised by Germain (USA) 1957.

Handel Cream flushed rose particularly at petal edges. Handsome flowers. Very free flowering, repeats well, and could be regarded as the finest climber of all, but for some risk of blackspot. Average height. Raised by McGredy (Ireland) 1965.

Maigold Bronzy yellow. Rich colour, mealy scent, beautiful leaves; the stems are handsome, closely set with bristles. Quite an individual character, its rather untidily formed semi-double flowers are a riot in early summer, sparse later. Adaptable, easy to grow. Average height, but variable. Raised by Kordes (Germany) 1953.

Mermaid Light primrose. Great moonlike single flowers, with handsome amber stamens. Very continuous in bloom and holds its smooth cut foliage late in winter. Awkward to train because the shoots are brittle and thorns viciously hooked, nevertheless a wall is the place for it. May be killed in hardest winter. Above average height, after a slow start usually. Raised by Paul (England) 1918.

Morning Jewel Bright pink. The semi-double flowers and bright foliage make a delightful glowing plant. Repeats well and adaptable for most uses. Below average height. Raised by Cocker (Scotland) 1968.

New Dawn Pearl pink. Very light colour; small flowers of admirable form and fragrant. Adaptable to most uses, can also be grown as a large shrub, and is best not too strictly confined. Useful cut flower for mixed arrangements. Repeats, but not generously. Average height. Raised by Somerset Nurseries (USA) 1930.

Parkdirektor Riggers Bright red. Semi-double flowers, not very large, show a brilliant deep colour against glossy dark leaves. Flowers in summer, with a scattering later. Adaptable for most uses. Above average height. Raised by Kordes (Germany) 1957.

Paul's Scarlet Climber Brilliant scarlet. Has only a summer-flowering period, in which the semi-double, smallish flowers present a vivid sight. Adaptable to most uses, except walls, where mildew is likely. Average height or more. Raised by Paul (England) 1916.

Phyllis Bide Light yellow shaded pink.

Small double flowers with narrow petals are matched by small deep green leaves. Flowers in summer and autumn, generously. Not easy to get, as few nurseries grow it. Adaptable for most uses, especially good as a pillar. Below average height. Raised by Bide (England) 1923.

Pink Perpetue Pink, with deeper reverse. Well-formed flowers, and plenty of them both in summer and autumn. Reliable and adaptable to most uses. Average height. Raised by Gregory (England) 1965.

Rosy Mantle Rose pink. Flowers of good size, double, fragrant. Adaptable to most uses and repeats well. Average height. Raised by Cocker (Scotland) 1968.

Sanders' White Rambler White. Cascades of small double flowers, sweetly scented, shown well against small dark leaves. See Crimson Shower for comments on ramblers. This flowers for several weeks in summer, and it is a beauty. Average height or more. Raised by Sanders (England) 1912.

Schoolgirl Apricot pink, towards orange. Large double flowers, well formed. Useful as the only climber in this colour. Flowering is usually intermittent through the season rather than in a spectacular flush. Adaptable to most uses. Average height or more. Raised by McGredy (Ireland) 1964.

Sympathie Crimson. Double flowers, small to medium size, in clusters. Good bright green foliage. Repeats well, and adaptable to most uses. Average height. Raised by Kordes (Germany) 1964.

Veilchenblau Greyish lilac pink. Perhaps the best of the climbers showing a touch of violet colour; small semi-double flowers, abundantly produced in summer only. Adaptable to most uses, but preferably not on a wall. Above average height. Raised by Schmidt (Germany) 1909.

White Cockade White. Well-formed double flowers, small to medium size. Repeats very well, adaptable to most uses. Can also be grown as a shrub. Below average height. Raised by Cocker (Scotland) 1969.

Old Garden Roses

Some of the old roses are charming, and others are mildewy old wrecks. This list of the choicest rejects sentiment in favour of performance. The average height is around 4 ft. and the traditional class follows each description.

Blanche Moreau Creamy white. Calyx has brown mossy covering, flowers are double, confused, appear summer only. Upright grower, likely to mildew; flower stems arise from last year's wood so do not prune it all off. Above average height.

Raised by Moreau-Robert (France) 1880. Moss.

Camaieux Purple pink with white marks, fades grey and white, the white marks prominent. Double flowers, in summer only, arising from previous year's wood. Fragrant. Some mildew. Below average height. Raised by Vibert (France) 1830. *Gallica.*

Capitaine John Ingram Dark crimson. Only slightly mossed calyx. Flowers small, very double, with button eye which is paler. Blooms summer only, from previous year's wood. Some mildew likely. Average height. Raised by Laffay (France) 1855. Moss.

Cardinal de Richelieu Purple. Double flowers, small, colour nicely varied in flower. Blooms in summer only, from previous year's wood. Average height. Raised by Laffay (France) 1840. *Gallica*

Cécile Brunner Light pink. Clusters of miniature rose buds; a young flower would go in a thimble, most appealing; flowers summer to autumn, either from old or current season's wood. About half average height. Raised by Ducher (France) 1880. China.

Cécile Brunner, Climbing Light pink. Vigorous climbing form of the foregoing, good to cover 20 ft. or so once it gets going. Some repeat bloom, abundant foliage. Raised by Hosp (USA) 1894. China.

Celestial Soft pale rose. The flowers are fairly large, of delicately lovely form, and set a perfect picture against grey-green leaves. Fragrant. Flowers in summer only, from previous year's wood. Average height or more. Origin unknown, probably France 1780–1836. *Alba.*

Charles de Mills Crimson purple. The buds look as if their tops were cut off, but open to full, fragrant blooms, in red, purple and maroon shades. Flowers in summer only, from previous year's wood. Mildew likely. Average height or more. Origin unknown, probably France 1820–1840. *Gallica.*

Commandant Beaurepaire Pink with red and purple stripes, all splashed together and marbled white. Large double flowers in summer, and perhaps a few later, mainly from wood of previous years; fragrant. Keep an eye on it for rust. Fairly spreading habit. Average height. Raised by Moreau-Robert (France) 1874. Bourbon.

Common Moss Pink. Calyx bears green mossy covering. Smallish double pink flowers, fragrant, in summer only, from previous year's wood. Upright habit, liable to mildew. Average height. Origin unknown, possibly Holland early 1700s. Moss.

Charles de Mills (Old garden rose)

Crested Moss Pink. Calyx has a wavy frill, hence its popular name Chapeau de Napoleon. Small double pink flowers, summer only, from previous year's wood. Average height. Found growing in a convent in Fribourg, introduced in France 1827. *Centifolia.*

De Meaux Rose pink. Small flat flowers, ring upon ring of little petals. Fragrant. Flowers in summer only, from previous year's wood. Blackspot likely. Below average height. Raised by Sweet (England) 1814. *Centifolia.*

Félicité et Perpétue Creamy white. An old climber, with pink buds, opening to white pompon flowers, small, but perfectly formed by many tiny petals. Foliage stays on late in winter. Flowers in summer, may be a few later; good wall plant, better still if it can be given its head. Vigorous climber. Raised by Jacques (France) 1827. *Sempervirens.*

Gallica Versicolor Red striped blush white. The semi-double flowers open wide and flat, thus showing the stripes clearly. The traditional name is *Rosa mundi.* May revert to its all-red original. Flowers summer only, on wood of previous years. Usually gets mildew after flowering. Compact growth. Below average height. Origin unknown. *Gallica.*

Lady Penzance Coppery pink, yellow centre. The flowers are small and fleeting; the sweet briar scent from the foliage is the object of growing this, and the small dark leaves provide it beautifully on a still summer evening. Some blackspot risk, however. Above average height. Raised by Lord Penzance (England) 1894. Sweet briar.

Laneii Purple. Large flowers, flat, with many petals and a remarkable rich colour. Flowers summer only, from wood of previous years. Although called a moss rose, there is next to no moss to be seen. Average height. Raised by Laffay (France) 1846. Moss. (Alleged to be William Lobb which came from the same raiser in 1855. But Laneii appears to be more compact in growth and richer in colour.)

La Reine Victoria Pink. The petals open out into the shape of a bowl. Fragrant. Upright grower, flowering in summer, with some in autumn, mainly from wood of previous years. May get blackspot. Average height or a little over. Raised by Schwartz (France) 1872. Bourbon.

Little White Pet White. Rare and difficult to get. Double flowers, just like those of Félicité et Perpétue, except that on this little bush they keep flowering into the autumn. Half average size. Raised by Henderson (USA) 1879. *Sempervirens.*

Lord Penzance Fawn yellow; apart from which all that is said for Lady Penzance applies.

Maiden's Blush Light blush. A handsome shrub, with grey-green leaves, and lovely unsophisticated flowers which are pale yet colourful, and very fragrant. Blooms in summer only, from wood of previous years. Above average height. The only difference between the great and small forms of this rose is a relatively minor one of growth. The origin of the former is unknown, and the latter is attributed to Kew Gardens (England) 1797. *Alba.*

Mme Hardy White. Pale green leaves, untidy sort of plant, but the flowers are marvellous. They open wide and flat, with what appear to be hundreds of small petals in meticulous array, with old-fashioned quartering and green centre. Flowers in summer only, from wood of previous years. Fragrant. Above average height. Raised by Hardy (France) 1832. Damask.

Mme Pierre Oger Cream, heavily shaded rose pink. Has the same fascinating bowl shape as La Reine Victoria, and the colour is perhaps more interesting. The description of La Reine Victoria otherwise fits this. Raised by Oger (France) 1878. Bourbon.

Nuits de Young Dark purplish red. Small, flat flowers, double, but showing golden stamens. Not much mossy growth. Flowers in summer only, from wood of previous years. Average height. Raised by Laffay (France) 1845. Moss.

Old Blush Cheerful pink. This is the old Monthly Rose, with small, bright pink, semi-double flowers on an open bush. Flowers from new and old wood, summer to late autumn intermittently. Small bright leaves. Below average height. Origin uncertain, recorded in Europe in 18th century. China.

Petite de Hollande Pink. Small double flowers, of attractive pompon form. Flowers in summer only, from wood of previous years. Likely to get mildew. Average height. Origin unknown, said to be Holland before 1800. *Centifolia.*

Pompon de Paris, Climbing Pink. This is in effect a climbing miniature rose, with small bright pink flowers and tiny leaves. Very charming, but not easy to find. Flowers in summer, with a few odd blooms later. Grows 4 to 6ft., ideal for a terrace wall. Origin unknown. China.

Président de Sèze Purple red with tinted white areas mostly at the petal tips. Double, quartered flowers in summer only, from wood of the previous years. Apt to get mildew. Average height. Origin unknown; was grown in France in 1836. *Gallica.*

Souvenir de la Malmaison Blush. Has something of the delicacy of the *alba* roses about its large, pale, quartered flowers. Blooms in summer, with a few later, mainly from wood of previous years. Fragrant. Average height. Raised by Béluze (France) 1843. Bourbon.

Spong Pink. Small pompon flowers in generous clusters on a compact plant. Attractive neat flower form, pleasant scent. Blooms from wood of previous years, and in summer only. Apt to get mildew. Below average height. Origin unknown, introduced 1805. *Centifolia.*

Stanwell Perpetual White shaded blush. Double, fragrant flowers in early summer, and intermittently afterwards. Useful in floral arrangements to give an informal, old-fashioned effect. Growth rather lax, plants thorny, leaves small. Below average

Rosa banksiae lutea (Wild rose)

height usually. Raised by Lee (England) 1838. Scotch.

Tuscany Superb Dark crimson purple. Double flowers, opening flat, a telling deep colour. (The original Tuscany has fewer petals, and therefore shows more of its stamens). Flowers in summer only, from wood of previous years. Growth upright, rather a narrow plant, with large leaves. Average height. Origin unknown, before 1848. *Gallica*.

Zéphirine Drouhin Deep pink. Flowers of medium size, quartered, fragrant; produced in summer and quite a few later, from both new and old wood. Usually grown as a climber, but suitable also as a shrub or hedge. Some mildew susceptibility. Well known as the thornless rose, which it is – almost. Above average height. Raised by Bizot (France) 1868. Bourbon.

Wild Roses

The wild roses and their hybrids teach us that the genus has beauties to offer unseen by those who know only the conventional bedding roses. Height is variable according to conditions and cultivation, but may be taken as 6 ft., except for the climbers. The common names are used, with proper botanical name or source in brackets. Note that many flower on short stems along the branches made in previous years.

Altaica (*R. spinosissima altaica*) Ivory white. Single flowers, borne along the branches, in early summer. Flowers are large in relation to the thin stems. Looks very fresh and pure. Has round, black seedpods, small leaves. Below average height. Introduced from northern Asia, about 1820.

Austrian Copper (*R. foetida bicolor*) Brilliant orange red with yellow reverse. Single flowers on the small side fairly set the bushes ablaze in early summer. Rarely, it may revert to its yellow progenitor. Likely to get blackspot. Below average height. Introduced from Asia Minor, prior to 1590.

Banksian Yellow (*R. banksiae lutea*) Yellow climber. Small flowers of unusual formation for a rose – more like double primroses. They grow closely in clusters, are fragrant, and the foliage behind them is smooth cut and handsome. Flowers best from sub-laterals, so prune very cautiously. Only hardy enough for favoured localities. Can grow 25 ft. easily. Introduced from China 1824.

Blanc Double de Coubert (variety of *R. rugosa*) White. Large, semi-double flowers, with petals like thin paper, sweetly fragrant; blooms summer to autumn, from both old and new growths. Large, thick leaves, rather open growth. Below average height. Raised by Cochet-Cochet (France) 1892.

Californica Pink, with suggestion of lilac. Small single flowers with bright yellow stamens are produced in large untidy inflorescences. Flowers intermittently summer to autumn, and has small bright red seedpods. Foliage is dull, small, and looks rough cut, but it makes a good thicket. There is also a double form. Average height. Introduced from North America 1878.

Canary Bird (*R. xanthina* Canary Bird) Yellow. Single flowers with numerous stamens are borne along and very close to the branches, causing them to bow under the beautiful load. The blooms are medium size, fragrant, and appear in early summer. The leaves are small, divided (fern-like) on the average into eleven little leaflets. Amazingly beautiful. A little below average height usually. Introduced from China, probably about 1907, but its history is unclear.

Cantabrigiensis (Hybrid from *R. hugonis*) Primrose. Pale single flowers in early summer, borne along and close to the branches. Small leaves, divided into eleven little leaflets or so. Average height, or a bit over. Raised at Cambridge Botanic Garden (England) 1931.

Complicata (Hybrid from a *gallica* rose) Pink. Very large single blooms of bright colour, lighter centres, are borne along the branches. Grows wider than its height, into other plants if in its way. Flowers in summer. Average height, or just under. Origin unknown.

Dupontii (Hybrid possibly from a *gallica* and *R. moschata*) White tinted blush. Fragrant single flowers showing yellow stamens agreeably and covering the bush in summer. Foliage light greyish green, fairly large. Average height or less. Origin unknown, was before 1817.

Farreri Persetosa Bright pink. Although the bush is quite lusty, the flowers are just about the smallest of any rose, single, with pretty yellow stamens. They appear in early summer. Hair-like thorns bristle the stems; the leaves are subdivided into tiny leaflets. Average height. Introduced from China 1914.

Frau Dagmar Hartopp (Hybrid of a *rugosa* rose; also known as Frau Dagmar Hastrup). Light rose pink. Large and

Top right: *Rosa moyesii* **fruits (Wild rose)**
Right: *Rosa sericea pteracantha* **(Wild rose)**
Above: *Rosa californica plena* **(Wild rose)**

Rosa filipes Kiftsgate (Wild rose hybrid)

luminous single flowers with creamy stamens and sweet scent. Blooms in summer and repeats into autumn from new and old wood. Large thick leaves, and big round red seedpods. Compact growth, below average height. Origin not known.

Golden Chersonese (Hybrid of *R. ecae* × Canary Bird) Bright yellow. Single flowers are borne along and close to the branches in early summer; fragrant and very richly coloured. This lovely plant holds its flowering branches reaching handsomely upwards. Dark bark, small leaves subdivided into many leaflets. Average height or a little more. Raised by Allen (England) 1967.

Hardii (Hybrid of *R. persica*) Yellow with a bold red eye. A rarity, best grown under glass with anti-mildew precautions. It is unique and beautiful, having single flowers, quite large, produced for a long period in summer. About half average height. Raised by Hardy (France) 1836.

Kiftsgate (*R. filipes* Kiftsgate) Creamy white. A mighty climber, used for scrambling into trees. Single flowers after mid-summer, very fragrant and profuse in enormous clusters. Handsome foliage. Can grow 30 ft. easily. Found in Gloucestershire (it is a sport from the Chinese species, *R. filipes*) and introduced 1954.

Longicuspis White. A vigorous climber, with large clusters of fragrant single flowers after mid-summer; has particularly handsome shiny leaves. Used for growing through trees, or on spacious pergolas. Can easily grow 20 ft. Introduced from China before 1915.

Mirifica (*R. stellata mirifica*) Bright pink. A rare and interesting rose, whose leaves are like those of gooseberries; the flowers are single, with bright stamens, appearing intermittently for a long period in summer. Likes a hot sunny spot. Below half average height. Introduced from New Mexico 1916.

Moyesii Geranium Crimson. The *moyesii* crimson has its own distinct character. The flowers are single, with effective light stamens. Blooms in summer only, but that is only half the story, because long seedpods of gorgeous red hang like lanterns on the plants in the autumn. Above average height. A form of *moyesii* found by The Royal Horticultural Society 1938. *Moyesii* itself is a Chinese species.

Multibracteata Pink. Very small, single flowers in summer only. The leaves are subdivided into tiny leaflets, and are a regular work of art in themselves. It is quite a big shrub, hung with a cloud of fairy scale foliage and bloom. Average height. Introduced from China 1910.

Mutabilis (*R. chinensis mutabilis*) Quickly changing its colours from buff yellow to pink to salmon red to crimson. A rare plant, not perfectly hardy, with large single flowers produced early summer to late autumn. Half average height, unless you are lucky. Origin doubtful; came from China, who knows when?

Paulii Rosea Silky pink. Large single blooms, fragrant and very beautiful, in summer only. The habit of growth is to trail several feet along the ground in all directions, the plant itself 3 ft. or less high. Therefore advocated for ground cover, but is so prickly that weeding will be painful. Sport from *paulii*, which is white, and a *rugosa* hybrid.

Roseraie de L'Hay Purple red. A blatant nobility guides this outrageous colour into favour. The touch of purple is royal, on strong plants with thick bright green leaves, and in flowers which are fairly full, with the petals worn carelessly. Fragrant; flowers freely in summer and repeats generously. Makes a splendid hedge. Average height. Raised by Cochet-Cochet (France) 1901.

Rubrifolia Pink. The flowers are small and fleeting; the foliage is the joy – soft grey with a sheen of reddish purple over it. The smooth stems are purplish when young, maturing red brown. Generous supply of round red seedpods in autumn. A lovely garden plant. Average height. Introduced from central Europe, long ago.

Rugosa Alba White. Single white flowers, fairly large, fragrant, and suitable as purity's emblem. Blooms summer, and repeats later. Orange-red seedpods, thick *rugosa* foliage. Below average height. A sport from *R. rugosa*, which is a Japanese species; origin uncertain.

Rugosa Scabrosa Mauve pink. Very large single blooms, the colour fortified by dusty yellow stamens. Blooms early summer to autumn, commendably continuous. Bright red seedpods, round and big; thick *rugosa* foliage. Average height or less. Origin obscure, but close to *R. rugosa*.

Sericea Pteracantha (Name recently changed from *R. omeiensis pteracantha*) White. The flowers are small and fleeting. This is grown for its extraordinary thorns, whose juncture with the stem can be an inch long; on the young growths, they are red and translucent. They narrow to an extremely sharp point. Average height or a bit more. Introduced from China 1890.

Viridiflora (*R. chinensis viridiflora*) Green. A sterile oddity, in which the flower parts are imperfectly modified leaves. Quite small plant, blooming (if that is the right word) summer and autumn. Less than half average height. Raised by Bambridge and Harrison (England) 1855.

Trees

Dennis Woodland could hardly have had a better grounding for his future career than student training at The Royal Botanic Gardens, Kew and The Royal Horticultural Society's Wisley Gardens, near Ripley, Surrey. After leaving Wisley he gained experience on several well-known nurseries before joining Hillier and Sons of Winchester in 1950, the firm for which he has worked ever since.

As Hillier's horticultural consultant he spends his time visiting gardens all over Britain and overseas advising owners on such matters as design and planting problems.

He lives in a quiet Hampshire village in a cottage which has, not surprisingly, a very interesting garden where his ideas are put into practice and where there is always something of special interest to see whatever the time of year. Photography – naturally with a horticultural bent, although landscape is another of his interests – is his main leisure pursuit, with listening to good music his first choice for relaxation.

He has also made botanical and plant hunting trips to the eastern Mediterranean and other parts of Europe, and lectures widely on travel, gardening and botanical subjects.

I think most would agree that the garden scene is incomplete without the inclusion of a tree or, if space permits, a number of trees. Perhaps the most noble of all nature's creations, trees add stature and grace to the garden as well as remarkable interest and variation of both colour and form in foliage and flower and often berry. Furthermore, trees are indispensable to frame and balance the garden; to provide permanent and satisfying focal points of interest; to cast shade where required and often, at the same time, to perform some necessary screening function.

A number of notable garden trees give two seasons of spectacular effect. Spring flower is often followed by a grand display of berry or autumn tint; others are noted for their unique winter bark as well as for autumn colour of leaf. Striking effects can be produced in the garden by the use of trees with brightly coloured foliage, a feature often retained throughout the growing season. Leaves may be red, purple, grey, yellow and there are many examples of attractive variegation; such colours effectively contrasting with the many shades of green of the other trees and shrubs.

A considerable variety of shape, form and size is to be found among trees suitable for planting even in the smallest of gardens. They may be of narrow, upright growth (columnar or fastigiate), and therefore ideal for confined areas even near buildings; or their shape may be pyramidal, broadly pyramidal, ball headed, mushroom headed, wide spreading, upright spreading or weeping.

With the great range of small or medium-sized trees available today, I feel it is a mistake to plant forest trees, ultimately of large size, in small gardens. While recognizing the noble stature of oak, beech, lime or ash, I consider such trees are best suited to parkland or more spacious circumstances and should be used where there is room for them to grow unrestricted to their full height and spread.

However, owners of small new gardens often inherit large forest trees. Although such trees are valued for their undoubted beauty and for the exclusive air of grandure and maturity they add to the scene, they can be rather a mixed blessing. Their large canopies cast deep shade and darken windows and it is usually difficult, if not impossible, to grow other trees, shrubs and plants satisfactorily under the overhanging branches and in competition with the hungry feeding roots of such large trees which invariably invade the entire area of a small garden. This situation usually has to be accepted and a compromise reached by lopping branches or thinning the head of the tree – work which in these days should be carried out only by a skilled tree surgeon or reliable tree surgery company. However, I feel that the lesson to be drawn from this state of affairs is the advisability of planting, wherever possible, only small trees (ultimate height 12 to 30 ft.) or, at the most, medium-sized trees (ultimate height 30 to 50 ft.) in small gardens and particularly near buildings.

It is worth a study of the ultimate height, spread and shape of the trees you choose and to bear this knowledge carefully in mind when considering their sites. Where there is room for a number of garden trees, sensible spacing, again with due regard for mature growth, is equally vital. It is better to remove every other tree in later years where initial spacing has been too close rather than to indulge in heavy pruning or lopping thus ruining the natural form and beauty of the individual tree. Most garden trees – Japanese cherries (prunus), ornamental crabs (malus), mountain ashes and whitebeams (sorbus) and thorns (crataegus) – allowing for mature growth, should be initially spaced at least 18 to 25 ft. apart – some varieties considerably more – unless it is proposed to remove every other tree after six or eight years. However, it is becoming the custom today to treat the small garden as one might a room, refurnishing it after eight or ten years – a task often carried out anyway if the property changes hands.

I appreciate also that closely planted trees may perform a necessary screening function. Nevertheless, it is important that thinning is attended to before such trees ruin or suppress one another. It is better to plant cypresses (Lawson's or Leyland) or *Thuja plicata* (western red cedar) or one of their forms or tall-growing evergreen cotoneasters as a screen perhaps along the appropriate boundary of your garden. Your deciduous garden trees are best sited as lawn specimens with their heads well clear of other plantings and where their beauty and form can be enjoyed to the full.

Soils vary widely from district to district: some people are blessed with a good, rich loam; others have the doubtful blessing of heavy clay; some have to contend with a poor thin soil overlying chalk, gravel or rock, while others must garden in very acid, peaty and often boggy conditions. With a few exceptions most garden trees will grow reasonably well on most of these soils although their ultimate

a   *b*   *c*   *d*

Tree planting:
(a) The hole should be large enough to accommodate all the roots and deep enough to plant the tree to the correct level. The stake is inserted before planting

(b) The tree is inserted and the hole checked for size. The stick laid over the hole should align with the soil mark on the stem of the tree
(c) The soil, which may be mixed with

well-rotted manure, is replaced and firmed with the heel as planting progresses
(d) Finally, the tree is fastened with the stake most conveniently with purpose-made tree ties

sizes may vary according to the poverty of the ground. Some leading nurserymen give details of anticipated ultimate growths in their catalogues and in the alphabetical list which follows this introduction, I shall be describing a wide range of trees for small gardens and giving details of their size and shape under average conditions.

I think it will be helpful to detail here the various forms of tree usually available from nurserymen.

A bush form tree may branch into a number of stems a little above ground level; such trees are useful for their multi-stemmed bark effects.

A feathered tree is a young specimen, usually 4 to 6 ft. high, without a formed head of branches. Lateral growths may still be retained from near the ground upwards. A standard or half standard may be formed from a feathered specimen by correctly stopping the leading shoot and pruning or thinning the lateral branches formed as a result to form a head; ultimately lateral twigs are removed flush to the stem below the head to form the standard or half standard. Alternatively, a feathered tree may be allowed to develop naturally if a specimen is required 'furnished to the ground' whereupon most side branches are retained.

A half standard usually has a 3½ to 4½-ft. and a standard tree a 5 to 6-ft. clear stem before branching commences; varying somewhat according to species; the overall height of a standard may be between 7 and 10 ft.

In recent years, primarily to counter vandalism to trees planted in public places, an extra heavy standard has appeared. This form may be 12 to 15 ft. with a 7 to 9-ft. clear stem and a good head of branches. Trees of this size are also useful in providing more immediate effects in gardens and particularly where screening is required.

Although confined advisedly to a restricted variety of trees which transplant easily, finally there is the semi-mature or instant tree which should be especially prepared for lifting by the vendor in order to ensure an adequate ball of fibrous roots. A crane or specialized lifting gear may be necessary to lift and transport such trees which may vary in height from 15 to 35 ft. or more and weigh one or two tons. The value of semi-mature trees for immediate effects in gardens (or elsewhere) is considerable but I stress that such specimens must be adequately prepared and competently lifted, handled and replanted to be successful. Before ordering ensure there is adequate access to the proposed site for both tree and handling gear.

Nurserymen lift and despatch deciduous trees in open weather between the end of October and about mid-March. Occasionally, dry conditions in early autumn may delay commencement of lifting. Evergreens may be moved from early October until about mid-April. Where available, pot or container-grown specimens may be planted at any time.

Preparation of Sites and Planting
To ensure rapid establishment and satisfactory growth it is essential to prepare each site by taking out a hole for each tree (of normal nursery size) at least 3 ft. in diameter and 1½ ft. deep. If in the course of this preparation, chalk, gravel, sand, clay or poor subsoil is encountered, this should be excavated and replaced by good topsoil imported if necessary for the purpose. On poor soils a bucketful of well-rotted farm-yard manure dug into the bottom of the hole is a worthwhile addition. Ideally this work should be done well in advance of planting, the holes being temporarily filled back. At planting time remove the loose soil to the depth of about 1 ft. and thoroughly firm the soil remaining in the hole. Before attempting to plant, position

a stout stake (2 to 3-in. diameter), driving the pointed and preserved end 1½ to 2 ft. into the ground. Position the tree against the stake, well spreading the root system. Fill back with a mixture of topsoil and moist peat, shaking the tree gently to work the soil among the root fibres, leaving no air spaces. It is most important to firm the tree very thoroughly using the full weight of the body behind the heel. Ensure that the finished level of planting corresponds with the previous soil mark near the base of the stem.

Finally, secure the tree to the stake using purpose-made tree ties, one at the very top of the stake where it should terminate immediately below the head and one half way down the stem, in the case of standard trees. Lighter stakes and ties may be sufficient for smaller feathered trees while extra heavy standards may require a stake either side of the trunk, the tree being secured between them with a wooden cross-piece or rubber belting. Large-headed, semi-mature trees need guying, using galvanized wire hausers and wooden plugs driven into the ground.

Maintenance and Aftercare
Intelligent maintenance and attention to watering is very necessary and need not be arduous and time consuming.

If there is a drought in the spring or early summer, when a newly moved tree is in greatest need of moisture at the roots, then it is certainly worth the application of at least two bucketfuls of water per standard tree per week. Those trees set in grass are at greater risk as they have to compete with the grass for all available food and moisture. A cultivation area at least 3 ft. in diameter should be maintained free of grass or weeds for the first three years following planting. A mulch of peat, strawy manure, well-rotted leaves or

Right: *Acer japonicum aureum*

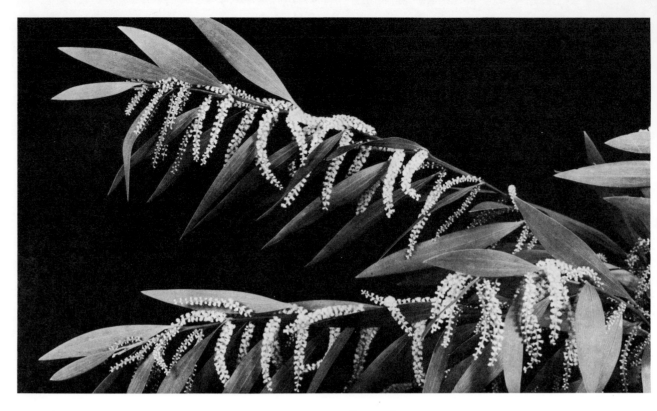

Acacia longifolia

pulverized bark-fibre, applied to moist ground, is a useful means of both conserving essential moisture and maintaining the cultivation area in a clean condition.

Once the tree is fully established, bulbs – winter aconites (eranthis), grape hyacinths (muscari), snowdrops (galanthus) etc. – may be added or one of the many ground-cover plants – lesser periwinkle (*Vinca minor*), green and variegated forms of ivy (hedera), hardy geranium, or ladies' mantle (alchemilla) – may be installed in the cultivated area. Not only is this an additional attraction, but such a planting helps to ensure that the base of the tree is not subjected to repeated wounding by the lawn mower – a distressing complaint I see all too often in both private gardens and public plantings!

If the bottom 2½ ft. of the stake has been stripped of bark and dipped in a preservative such as Green Cuprinol (not creosote please), the stake should last until the tree is firmly anchored and is growing well; but the tree ties will require annual adjustment as the stem expands. This amounts to the loosening of a buckle or the refixing of rubber belting to allow the stem to grow without restriction.

Pruning

As the newly planted tree develops, some pruning is usually necessary to maintain a balanced and well-spaced head of branches with the leading shoot carefully preserved. This generally involves the removal or shortening back of badly placed or crossing branches and superfluous growth. When the trunk has developed to reasonable proportions, the tree should begin to assume the shape and outline characteristic of its species or variety. In later years, some further thinning of superfluous growth from the head may be necessary periodically.

The trees described are considered suitable for a wide range of conditions in European and North American gardens. Most are also appropriate for South African and Australasian conditions. Attention is drawn in the text to those subjects succeeding only in mild or maritime conditions, otherwise most can be considered hardy in all but the most extreme climates involving cold and exposure.

Ultimate Sizes

The mature height of a tree will vary according to the soil, degree of shading, amount of rainfall etc. However, in the British Isles and in countries with similar climates, the following measurements may serve as a guide to the range of anticipated eventual growth of trees growing under average garden conditions: small trees, 12 to 30 ft.; medium trees, 30 to 50 ft.; large trees, over 60 ft. Some indication is given in the following descriptions of expected shape or spread of head of the trees listed which should assist in the selection of a tree for a particular site.

Selected Trees

Acacia

The acacias, also commonly known as the wattles or mimosas, comprise a large genus of Australasian trees and shrubs. There are a few species which in mild coastal areas of the northern hemisphere will make small garden trees, interesting in their variable evergreen foliage and often spectacular in their early spring flower. The hardiest species are successful in warm sheltered coastal districts especially when grown against south or west-facing walls. In their native Australia and in the Mediterranean countries, they may make bushy-headed trees of medium or large size. The acacias grow well in most well-drained soils but will be short lived with yellowing foliage on shallow chalky soils.

The best-known and most widely planted species is *Acacia dealbata*, the silver wattle, with its finely divided fern-like leaves and young shoots, both covered with a silvery down against which are seen myriads of ball-like, fragrant, yellow flowers – a perfect association. Forms of this species are the popular florists' mimosa.

The Sydney golden wattle, *A. longifolia*, is quite distinct with its long lance-like leaves or phyllodes. Cylindrical spikes of bright yellow flowers are produced in the axils of the leaves. This is one of the hardiest and also one of the most lime-tolerant species.

Acer

The maples provide us with a wide range of mostly hardy deciduous and easily cultivated trees. Many are notable for their elegance and for the spectacular effect of their autumn foliage. The tree-like forms of *Acer japonicum* and *A. palmatum* are particularly significant in this respect. Garden forms of sycamore (*A. pseudoplatanus*), Norway maple (*A. platanoides*) and the box maple (*A. negundo*) can be useful for screening and for garden effect, while several other species are grown as much for their unusual bark effects as for the autumn colour of their leaves.

Acer campestre, the common, field or hedge maple, is often grown and clipped as a hedge plant but this hardy European species if unpruned will make a pictur-esque, round-headed, small or medium-sized tree. It is notable for the clear, bright yellow in autumn of its attractively lobed leaves and will show up well as a hedgerow tree or as a specimen near the perimeter of a larger garden. There is also a variety *schwerinii* with leaves which are purple tinted in the spring.

A. cappadocicum is a medium to large-sized hardy tree from the Caucasus, having large five or seven-lobed leaves which colour well in the autumn. It is usually represented in cultivation by its garden varieties which are both vigorous, fast-growing trees as useful for screening as for foliage effect in the garden. In the variety *aureum* the young leaves unfold. red tinted, turn golden yellow for several weeks, then change to green, finally reverting to yellow again in the autumn. In *rubrum* the leaves of the new shoots on young trees are blood red, while on older trees the unfolding leaves are deep purple red. Striking and unusual effects are created by associating these two varieties together.

The snake-bark maple, *A. davidii*, is a small Chinese tree of open spreading habit. This is one of the group of maples notable for the attractive, white, snake-skin-like striations on the bark of the trunk and branches. The leaves colour a rich red in the autumn when the winged fruits or 'keys', also suffused red, hang thick clustered along the branches. The form usually available is called George Forrest (syn. *horizontalis*), in honour of the great plant collector who introduced it to western gardens in 1922. There are several allied species exhibiting similar snake-bark qualities as well as autumn

colour of leaf. Among these are *A. capillipes*; *A. grosseri*; *A. hersii*; *A. pensylvanicum*, and *A. rufinerve*. All make attractive small or medium-sized garden trees and are of Asiatic origin with the exception of the North American *A. pensylvanicum*.

The choice Chinese species *A. griseum*, the paperbark maple, is generally regarded as one of the most striking and beautiful of all garden trees. The peeling from the trunk and main branches of its mahogany-brown outer bark to reveal orange or cinnamon-coloured underbark is its most outstanding feature. Delightful soft red and orange autumn colouring of leaf, unfailingly produced, is a further attri-bute. An ideal specimen tree for the small garden, it usually assumes a neat vase or wine-glass shape in outline, slowly attain-ing 10 or 12 ft. in about fifteen years. *Acer griseum* grows well on most soils including chalky ones; it may make as much as 45 ft. on rich loamy soils.

A. japonicum is one of the group known as the Japanese maples. It is a slow-growing, small, bushy-headed tree, usu-ally represented in cultivation by the following varieties. *Aureum* is a choice, rather slow-growing but very beautiful form effective throughout the growing season by reason of its handsome soft yellow leaves. For the best effect plant in a sheltered, semi-shaded position preferably facing west in order that the late afternoon sunlight is projected most tellingly through the yellow leaves. Care in siting is important as the leaves will scorch in full sunshine. With leaves up to 6 in. across, *vitifolium* is the largest-leaved Japanese maple and one which contributes a vivid kaleidoscope of colour to the autumn scene. Yellow, orange, scarlet, crimson, purple and green are usually represented particularly on neutral or acid soils. It is a more vigorous small tree than *aureum* and often as wide as it is high.

The box elder, *A. negundo*, a North American maple, is usually seen in cultiva-tion as a medium-sized tree with a wide-spreading head. The bright green young shoots are a notable feature; the pinnate leaves have a variable number of leaflets, bright green with paler undersides. A useful screening tree, the box elder, requires plenty of room if allowed to develop its full spread and is perhaps better represented in small gardens by its several variegated forms which are gener-ally more modest in ultimate growth and more striking in garden effect. *Auratum* is one of the few garden trees retaining its bright golden-yellow leaves throughout the growing season. It is a striking small

Acer davidii George Forrest

tree. *Elegans* (*elegantissimum*) is a form with its leaves broadly margined bright yellow. *Variegatum* (*argenteovariegatum*) is the most commonly planted variety and is most effective with its leaves irregularly bordered with white, some leaflets may be completely white. These three varieties are very worthy garden trees but have a tendency to produce branches where the leaves have reverted to the more vigorous green of *A. negundo*. Such branches should be carefully pruned out as soon as they are noticed; if neglected they will tend to dominate, eventually suppressing the variegated form.

A. nikoense, the Nikko maple, a small to medium-sized, round-headed tree from Japan and central China, is related to *A. griseum*. The large leaves, consisting of 3 to 5-in. long leaflets with grey under-sides, colour magnificently a combination of scarlet, flame and yellow unfailingly each autumn. Suitable for all soils, this is one of the most beautiful, hardy, autumn-colouring trees that we can grow.

In cultivation *A. palmatum*, the Japan-ese maple, is seen as a small round-headed tree, up to 20 ft. high and as much through. The five or seven-lobed bright green leaves assume rich autumn tints of red, orange and yellow. This and the more robust of its many forms will grow in a moist but reasonably well-drained situa-tion on most soils including alkaline or chalky ones. A sheltered semi-shaded site

53

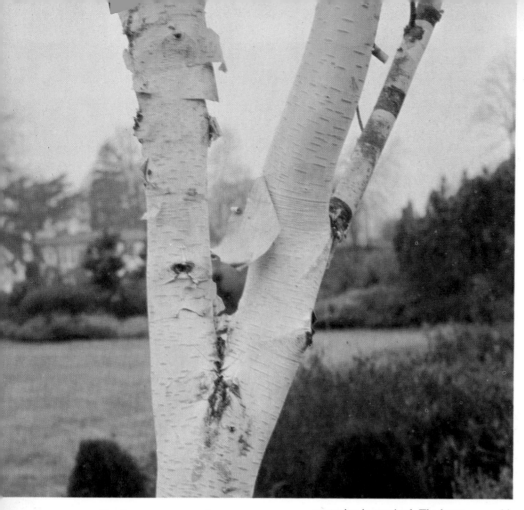

Betula costata

is desirable as these maples will resent exposure to full sunshine and to cold winds. The following are among the most worthwhile of those varieties which will reach the proportions of small trees. *Atropurpureum* is often seen as a small vase-shaped tree up to 10 or 12 ft. high. Good forms have rich crimson leaves consistently throughout the growing season; this is justifiably the most popular Japanese maple. Equally *heptalobum osakazuki* is generally regarded as the finest Japanese maple for autumn colour. The seven-lobed green leaves, larger than in the type species, turn brilliant shades of scarlet and orange. It is a small tree of similar dimensions to *atropurpureum*. Although the soft yellow or orange autumn colour of *senkaki*, the coral bark maple, is not to be despised, this variety is most notable for its coral-red young twigs and branches which are most conspicuous in winter. It makes a small tree of erect habit.

A large, fast-growing, broad-headed, hardy tree, the Norway maple, *A. platanoides*, is now much planted as a landscape tree. Like the sycamore, it transplants readily even at semi-mature size and is often used in gardens where immediate screening is required. The leaves resemble those of the sycamore but are thinner in texture and a brighter green turning clear yellow in the autumn. If need be it may be pruned to keep it within bounds. There are a number of varieties usually slower growing and less large in ultimate growth. Of French origin *columnare* makes a large tree of erect habit. The form Crimson King is much valued for its dark crimson-purple leaves which retain their colour throughout summer. Goldsworth Purple and Faasen's Black are very similar. *Globosum* is perhaps the most suitable form for the small garden as it makes a small mop-headed picturesque tree. The leaves of the compact-headed variety *drummondii* are regularly bordered with white.

Although invaluable in extreme exposure the sycamore, *A. pseudoplatanus*, a large vigorous tree, is best represented in gardens by its slower-growing forms notable for the brilliance of their young leaves in spring. These include *brilliantissimum*, a small slow-growing tree with a neat, compact head. The unfolding leaves in spring are for three or four weeks a delightful tawny pink, changing to pale yellow green and finally mid-green. Another slow-growing variety is Prinz Handjery which makes a small shrubby tree; the young foliage is tinted with yellow on the upper surfaces and with purple beneath. *Nizetii* and Simon-Louis Frères are similar, often with pink tinting in their leaves.

Aesculus

Commonly cultivated species and varieties of the well-known horse chestnut are among the most beautiful of spring and summer-flowering trees and make magnificent large round-headed specimens for a parkland setting. The American buckeyes, less spectacular in flower and variable in their garden value, make small shrubby trees. The following are particularly useful in smaller gardens.

Aesculus carnea briotii is a compact medium-sized variety of the red horse chestnut having deeper coloured, larger flower panicles. *A. pavia atrosanguinea*, the best-coloured form of the red buckeye, is an unusual small round-headed tree producing its deep red flowers in June. All the chestnuts and buckeyes are trouble free and thrive in all well-drained soils.

Amelanchier

Several members of this genus assume the dimensions of small trees and provide us with two seasons of effect – a dense canopy of small white fragrant flowers in the spring, often with the developing young leaves, followed by rich colouring of the foliage in the autumn. The snowy mespiluses are more successful on moist but well-drained lime-free soils. Their nomenclature is confused but the following species are usually available in tree forms. However, avoid specimens grafted on thorn (crataegus).

The true species under the name *Amelanchier canadensis* (*oblongifolia*) forms an erect-growing shrubby tree, native of swampy land in eastern North America. The leaves are oblong in shape and the flowers produced in compact erect racemes. Another North American species is *A. laevis*; here the bronzy-pink young leaves appearing with the fragrant white flowers are an added feature. It is often wrongly grown under the name of *A. canadensis*.

A. lamarckii (*grandiflora*) is the best species for general garden planting; it will form a small specimen of rather spreading habit. A striking tree in flower and autumn colour, it is now naturalized in several areas of Europe including England. *A. lamarckii rubescens* (*grandiflora rubescens*) is a variety with flowers purple pink in bud and tinted pink when open.

Arbutus

Arbutus andrachnoides (syn. *hybrida*) (*andrachnae* × *unedo*) is a small evergreen tree, grown mainly for the glorious cinnamon-red shaggy bark on trunk and branches. Racemes of parchment-coloured, pitcher-shaped flowers appear on the ends of twigs in the late autumn or winter. It is a hybrid between the Grecian and Killarney strawberry trees.

The Killarney strawberry tree, *A. unedo*, is a handsome small tree, gnarled with age; this species produces white or pale pink flowers, together with the hanging strawberry-like red and yellow fruits in the autumn of the year. It is a native of the Mediterranean and south and west Ireland. Its variety *rubra* has deeper pink flowers and a compact habit.

Both the above-mentioned strawberry trees are remarkably successful in chalky or limy soils.

Betula

The birches are a well-loved genus of hardy medium-sized trees, much valued for their elegance of habit and for the striking effects created by the silvery-white or orange-brown bark of trunk and branches. Those species or varieties with light, narrow heads are often planted quite closely in groups to give a multi-stemmed effect. Soft golden autumn colour of leaf is a further feature of many species.

Although ultimately a tall tree, *Betula ermanii*, a handsome species from north eastern Asia, is, with careful siting, truly magnificent in the garden from quite an early age. The trunk has cream or pink-tinted peeling bark while the upright-spreading branches are a glistening orange brown. Species with similar qualities of effectively peeling bark, making fine specimen trees, are *B. costata* with cream-white bark and *B. jacquemontii*, a west Himalayan species with vivid white trunk and branches.

The common silver birch or lady of the woods, *B. pendula*, is one of the most attractive of the European native species but trees raised from seed can be variable in the quality of their silver-white trunks and in the size and spread of head. In small gardens, the species is perhaps best represented by its selected forms though the type tree is excellent for small copses or where multi-stemmed effects are required. *B.p. dalecarlica*, the Swedish birch, is remarkable as much for its slender, graceful, drooping habit and finely cut leaves as for its silvery-white trunk. *B.p. tristis* makes a fine, narrow-headed, white-trunked, tall tree with pendulous

branches and is of more robust constitution than the Swedish birch. *B.p. youngii*, Young's weeping birch, forms a small, mushroom-headed garden tree with branches weeping to the ground.

Carpinus

The hornbeams are handsome, hardy trees of medium to large size suitable for all soils. Their hop-like seed clusters are unusual and attractive. The common hornbeam is *Carpinus betulus*, a British

Acer griseum

and European native tree often with a rounded picturesque head and grey fluted trunk. The foliage, superficially resembling that of the beech, is markedly ribbed and toothed, turning yellow in autumn. The following forms, which are of architectural interest, are particularly useful in gardens. *Columnaris* is a slow-growing, dense-habited, small tree of narrow upright growth. Although quite narrow when young, *fastigiata (pyramidalis)* matures to a medium-sized tree of broadly pyramidal, almost onion-like shape.

Catalpa

Catalpa bignonioides, the most usually planted Indian bean tree, forms a small to medium-sized tree of wide-spreading habit. The large, handsome leaves may grow up to 10 in. long and 8 in. wide while the conspicuous panicles of foxglove-like flowers, white with yellow and purple spots, appear towards late summer. After hot summers, the long cylindrical seedpods are quite effective and remarkable. The catalpa thrives in any well-drained soil but should not be sited in an exposed position. A native of the eastern U.S.A., this is one of the most beautiful and desirable of all flowering trees. It has a striking variety, *aurea*, whose soft golden leaves maintain their colour throughout the summer and autumn. A fine lawn specimen.

Cercis

The redbuds or Judas trees are a small genus of late spring-flowering trees or large shrubs suitable for warm sunny sites on any well-drained soil. *Cercis siliquastrum* is the Judas tree. Although often grown as a shrub, it is best seen as a small picturesque tree; the bright rose-purple, pea-shaped flowers are produced in clusters along the bare branches as the round leaves begin to unfold, bronze tinted in the late spring. In late summer and autumn, the purple-tinted seedpods are a conspicuous feature. There is also a white-flowered variety *alba* and a fine deep purple form, Bodnant. The Judas tree from the eastern Mediterranean is the most satisfactory species in European gardens while the North American redbud, *C. canadensis*, is popular in the U.S.A. and Canada.

Cordyline

Cordyline (Dracaena) australis, the cabbage tree of New Zealand, is a small tree of exotic aspect for mild or maritime areas, slowly forming one or more cylindrical stems crowned by dense heads of arching sword-like leaves up to 3 ft. long. Panicles of small fragrant white flowers are produced early in the summer. There is also a form *atropurpurea* with purple-tinted leaves.

Cornus

Those members of this genus which reach

Above: *Catalpa bignonioides*
Right: *Cercis siliquastrum*

the proportion of small or medium-sized trees are most desirable and ornamental, contributing both striking floral and autumn-colouring effects. The flowers are conspicuous by reason of white or coloured bracts or modified leaves which surround the true flower clusters. The cornels or dogwoods will grow on most soils but several species make poor growth in shallow chalky conditions.

Cornus capitata (Benthamia fragifera) is an evergreen Himalayan species making a small bushy tree often wider than high. Its leaves are up to 5 in. long, grey green and downy making a pleasing background for the mid-summer 'flowers' which comprise four to six large pale yellow bracts surrounding the remaining flower parts. Equally conspicuous in the autumn are the large, strawberry-shaped, crimson fruits. Regrettably this handsome tree is only successful in the mildest coastal districts of south and west England and similar climates.

A fine and architecturally significant Japanese species, *C. contraversa* eventually makes a medium-sized tree with tiers of horizontal branches. These are arrayed at mid-summer with clusters of cream-coloured bracts. On most soils the leaves turn purple in the autumn.

The flowering dogwood, *C. florida*, form a small tree, often with a wide-spreading head conspicuous in late spring when it displays masses of white petal-like bracts. This is also one of the trees responsible for the spectacular fall colour of the eastern U.S.A. where it is native. After a hot summer, the leaves colour well in the British Isles but it is generally less happy here thriving best in east or south-east England in sites free from spring or early autumn frosts. This species is rather intolerant of chalk soils. There are a number of varieties selected on account of the exceptional colour of their flower bracts. The variety *rubra* is rose red; Cherokee Chief is a deeper rose red, an American selection, and White Cloud, another American selected form, has brilliant white bracts freely borne.

C. kousa chinensis is a geographical form of the Japanese *C. kousa* and a most beautiful hardy small flowering tree. It produces its large long-lasting white bracts at mid-summer followed by round red edible fruits. The leaves, also larger than in the type, colour well for a long period in autumn. It is less successful on chalky soils.

The Pacific dogwood, *C. nuttallii*, is the doyen of the cornels, a native of western North America where it attains a height of 50 ft. or more. The large white bracts

open in late spring. Regrettably it tends to be short lived in Great Britain but it is often seen as an upright shrubby small tree spectacular in flower from the ground to its summit. It is not suitable for chalk soils.

Crataegus
The thorns are very useful and ornamental small, hardy trees mostly with wide-spreading and dense twiggy heads; spring flower, mainly white, is followed in the autumn by attractive haws. Equally at home in city street or exposed coastal or moorland garden, and on all soils, they are deserving of wider planting.

Crataegus crus-galli, the cockspur thorn, is a particularly worthwhile species from eastern North America making a flat-topped picturesque tree. It is a copious flowerer, notable for both brilliant red autumn leaf colour and for the crimson haws which often persist until spring. The hybrid *C. lavallei (carrierei)* makes a splendid small garden tree; both glossy green leaves and orange-red fruits persist until the New Year making an attractive and unusual winter feature.

A form of the common hawthorn, *C. monogyna stricta (fastigiata)* with a narrow, erect-growing branch system, is particularly useful in cold windswept sites. *C. oxyacantha* is the European and British native hawthorn or May, and it has given rise to a number of varieties or hybrids some with double and coloured flowers which form excellent small garden trees with compact heads. Paul's Scarlet is a double red; *plena*, double white, and

Cornus nuttallii

rosea flore pleno, a lovely double pink.

C. phaenopyrum, the Washington thorn, is one of the most outstanding of the American thorns; a handsome round-headed tree with shining maple-like leaves which colour well in autumn and masses of scarlet haws often persisting until spring.

C. pinnatifida major from northern China is perhaps the most effective of all thorns in respect of its rich autumn leaf colour and hanging clusters of large glossy deep red berries.

Davidia
Davidia involucrata, the handkerchief or ghost tree, is a most ornamental hardy Chinese tree ultimately of medium size with a broad, spreading habit. The large handsome leaves are reminiscent of those of the lime (tilia). The tree receives its popular names by reason of the two large and conspicuous white bracts which surround each small flower cluster appearing in late spring and early summer. This imposing tree, which is happy on all soils of reasonable depth, is ideal as a lawn specimen particularly in the larger garden. Flowering usually commences about ten years after planting and is well worth waiting for. The variety *vilmoriniana* is of equal garden merit and differs only in minor botanical details.

Eucalyptus
Although widely planted in coastal areas of tropical and sub-tropical countries,

Davidia involucrata

there are a number of species of this large Australasian genus suitable for milder areas of Great Britain and countries with similar climates. The evergreen foliage often differs greatly even within a species – juvenile leaves on young specimens being quite distinct from the adult foliage found on older trees. In mild districts many species will make medium-sized or large trees and are frequently in danger of blowing over if exposed to strong winds. In such circumstances and indeed in small gardens generally, the gum trees are best grown as multi-stemmed bushy plants when their attractive foliage can be enjoyed at eye level. Such bushes also provide quantities of excellent and easily accessible foliage for floral arranging. Although less successful on chalk, most species will grow on a considerable range of soils. Spring planting of small pot-grown plants is to be recommended. Once established and growing vigorously, cut back to about 18 in. to strengthen anchorage. Then select the best newly formed stem to make a tree, or grow as a multi-stemmed bush if desired.

One of the hardiest species is *Eucalyptus dalrympleana* which makes a medium-sized tree with silvery-white patchwork trunk and branches; the adult foliage, 4 to 7 in. long, is scimitar shaped.

E. gunnii, the cider gum, a hardy Tasmanian species, is now much planted in the British Isles. The juvenile leaves are round, stem clasping and bright glaucous blue while adult foliage is sickle shaped and sage green. It is most striking if grown as a bush.

The snow gum, *E. niphophila*, is a remarkably hardy species from Australia's Snowy Mountains. It is a small attractive tree which is very garden worthy with its grey and cream-coloured peeling trunk and branches and long, lance-shaped, blue-grey adult leaves. Young branches and twigs are covered with blue-white bloom and new leaves open mahogany red.

A very hardy species, *E. parvifolia*, makes a medium-sized tree and is successful on chalk soils. The juvenile leaves are usually dark green, ovate-lanceolate and pointed while adult foliage is narrower (linear-lanceolate), blue green, about $2\frac{1}{2}$ in. long.

Eucalyptus niphophila

Eucryphia

The evergreen *Eucryphia nymansensis* Nymansay is a magnificent small or medium-sized tree of upright habit. Maturing specimens are spectacular in late summer or early autumn when increasing quantities of large white flowers with prominent stamens are produced. It is a hybrid between two South American species and very worthy of a sheltered site in most gardens having deep moist lime-free loam.

Fagus

The common beech, *Fagus sylvatica*, is a European species, also indigenous to the British Isles. It is without doubt Britain's most impressive large landscape tree, admired equally for its fresh green young leaves, for its handsome smooth grey trunk and winter-branch tracery and for the rich golden brown of its autumn foliage. It thrives on all well-drained soils and is particularly at home where the subsoil is chalk. There are many forms in cultivation, some of which are restricted enough in ultimate growth for use in small gardens.

F.s. aurea pendula is a remarkable form of tall slender habit, with branches which hang down almost perpendicularly. The foliage is golden yellow. It should be sited in semi-shade. *F.s.* Dawyck (syn. *fastigiata*), the Dawyck beech, becomes a handsome tall tree of conical habit and *F.s. heterophylla*, the fern-leaved beech, is one of the most beautiful and unusual forms making a large tree. The fern-like leaves are variable in shape but usually deeply cut and lobed. There is also a beautiful variant, *rohanii*, with purple leaves.

F.s. purpurea, the purple or copper beech, is a popular large tree but it is often variable in foliage colour if raised from seed. The best variety *riversii*, which nurserymen supply as a grafted young tree, has large, deep purple, lustrous leaves.

F.s. purpurea pendula, the weeping purple beech, makes a magnificent small weeping tree and is perhaps the best form of purple-leaved beech for the small garden.

Fraxinus

The ashes are a large genus of hardy, fast-growing deciduous trees, mainly native of the temperate regions of the northern hemisphere countries. Many of the large-growing species make stately parkland trees, noted for their elegant, large, pinnate leaves, while the flowering ashes form interesting and attractive summer-flowering specimens of more moderate growth. They are generally happy in any fertile soil, and are tolerant equally of town

Eucryphia nymansensis **Nymansay**

conditions, seaside and exposed localities and moist situations.

Fraxinus excelsior, the common ash, is a familiar large and handsome tree for parkland or similar circumstances, with typical long pinnate leaves and distinct black winter buds. Some of its forms are suitable for gardens. *Aurea (jaspidea)*, the golden-barked ash, makes a compact small tree of slow growth, notable for its yellow young shoots and yellowish winter bark. The leaves turn clear yellow in the autumn. *Pendula*, the weeping ash, is a vigorous weeping tree, usually forming a wide-spreading mound of stiffly pendulous branches. It is excellent as a lawn specimen where there is ample room for its development.

F. mariesii is perhaps the most ornamental of the flowering ashes bearing quantities of cream-white flowers at midsummer, followed by unusual fruits which quickly turn purple. It is a small tree with a rounded head, ideal for many gardens.

The manna ash, *F. ornus*, forms a medium-sized, round-headed tree and is the most commonly planted of the flowering ashes. White flowers are abundantly produced in late spring.

F. oxycarpa Raywood is a selected form of an elegant eastern European species, making a fine specimen tree of medium height, but compact and upright habit. The blue-green summer foliage turns purple in the autumn.

A striking and unusual Japanese flowering ash, *F. spaethiana*, forms a small to medium-sized tree, remarkable for its very large leaves and leaflets with distinctive swollen bases to the leaf stalks.

Gleditsia

Gleditsia triacanthos is a handsome large central North American tree, allied to the false acacia (robinia). The beautiful frond-like glossy dark green leaves turn clear yellow in autumn. In warm and sunny climates formidable spines of 3 to 12 in. develop on the trunk and branches, a feature less marked in cooler climates or shaded areas. In autumn, glossy brown pods 1 to 1½ ft. long hang effectively along the branches. The honey locust is happy in all soils and is tolerant of industrial air pollution. In small gardens it is best represented by either of the following forms. *Bujoti (pendula)* makes an elegant small weeping tree. The leaflets are narrower than in the type. Sunburst *(inermis aurea)* is a thornless variety forming a small or medium-sized tree of somewhat spreading habit. Bright yellow young leaves at the ends of the branches appear effectively among the older emerald-green leaves. This is a striking garden tree.

Halesia

The snowdrop trees are beautiful North American flowering trees, suitable for well-drained (lime free) soils in sunny, sheltered gardens. The hardiest species is *Halesia monticola*, the mountain snowdrop tree, from the mountains of the south eastern United States. In gardens it makes an imposing small spreading tree, its branches hung in late spring with multitudes of pure white bell-like flowers. These are followed by unusual four-winged fruits. It is a tree worthy of wider planting; the variety *vestita* has larger flowers often tinted pink.

Juglans

The walnuts are medium-sized to large stately trees traditionally planted in gardens for many centuries, as much for their noble appearance as for their fruit and timber value. They have large and imposing pinnate leaves which are reminiscent of ash. Walnuts are happy in most well-drained soils.

The black walnut, *Juglans nigra*, is a native of east and central U.S.A., forming a large wide-spreading tree with deeply channelled bark and magnificent leaves, 1 to 2 ft. long, which are aromatic when crushed.

The common walnut, *J. regia*, is a slower-growing, less imposing, south eastern European and Asiatic species forming a medium to large-sized round-headed tree. There are a number of varieties of French origin grown only for their nuts and making large bushes or small compact trees.

Koelreuteria

Koelreuteria paniculata is a very handsome Chinese summer-flowering tree, ultimately broad headed and of medium size. Long fern-like leaves emerge pink tinted and colour yellow in the autumn. Large upright panicles of golden-yellow flowers are followed by unusual bronze-tinted bladder-like seed vessels. To flower freely, the golden-rain tree or pride of India requires a sheltered but sunny situation in any well-drained soil. There is also an interesting, though rare, narrow upright form, *fastigiata*, ultimately growing about 25 ft. high and 3 ft. wide which is ideal for small gardens and for confined areas.

Laburnum

These spectacular, early summer-flowering, small, hardy trees have the descriptive common name of golden rain and are much planted in gardens, thriving on any soil. Large crops of unattractive seedpods, containing poisonous seeds, if left on the trees, tend to sap the vigour and decrease the life span of an already rather short-lived tree. *Laburnum anagyroides pendulum* is a dwarf form with long drooping branches while *L. vossii* is the best laburnum for general planting in gardens. The long racemes of bright yellow pea flowers are produced freely.

Ligustrum

The Chinese tree privet, *Ligustrum lucidum*, becomes a fine evergreen small or medium-sized tree of upright-growing habit, forming ultimately a dense rounded head. The large deep green leaves, 3 to 6 in. long, are an excellent foil for the erect panicles of white flowers, 6 to 8 in. high, produced in late summer. *Excelsum superbum* is a striking variant of similar ultimate size with its large leaves effectively variegated with yellow and white.

Liquidambar

Liquidambar styraciflua, the sweet gum, is a handsome hardy large tree from the eastern U.S.A., ultimately forming a narrow pyramidal head. The lustrous maple-like leaves are alternately produced and colour magnificently deep red or crimson in the autumn; corky protrusions on the older branchlets are a winter feature. This tree is conspicuous from an early age but it is not successful on chalky or alkaline soils.

Liriodendron

Liriodendron tulipifera, the tulip tree, a noble large tree from North America, is much valued for its stately appearance and remarkable blunt-ended leaves which

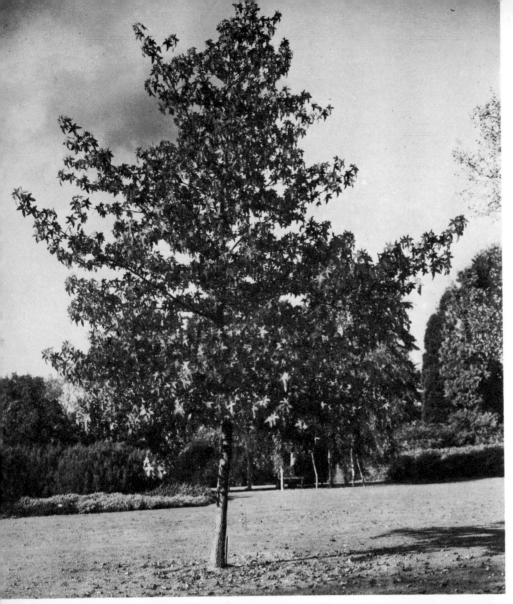

turn golden yellow in autumn, and for the unique tulip-like flowers, yellow green with orange basal markings, appearing on older trees at mid-summer. It is successful in most deep loamy soils.

The variety *aureomarginatum* has leaves conspicuously bordered with yellow and is a striking and unusual variegated tree for the smaller garden while *fastigiatum (pyramidale)* is a narrow upright-growing form, ultimately of medium size.

Magnolia

The large members of this exotic genus are perhaps the most distinguished and magnificent of early-flowering trees that can be grown in gardens. They transplant more successfully from the open ground in the spring and grow well on good, well-drained loams and clays. A number of species are lime tolerant. Regrettably, some of the most magnificent tree species do not flower for many years after planting.

Perhaps the most remarkable and spectacular of the magnolias, *Magnolia campbellii* is a giant tree in its native Himalaya and it reaches considerable proportions in favoured gardens. The immense tulip-shaped flowers, in varying shades of pink, are produced early in the year on maturing trees. The flowers open like water lilies before falling. A number of varieties have now appeared which, unlike the type tree, may flower within ten or fifteen years of planting. In particular these are *mollicomata*, Charles Raffill and Sidbury. All have pink or rose-purple flowers and show signs of greater hardiness than the type. Lime-free soil is necessary.

One of the best small magnolias for general planting is *M. kobus*, producing quantities of white early spring flowers usually within fifteen years of planting. It is a very hardy Japanese species which is happy on all soils and particularly successful on chalk.

The hybrid *M. loebneri (kobus × stellata)* makes a handsome small shrubby tree producing its fragrant white strap-like flowers at a very early age. Like its parents, it succeeds on all soils. There are several varieties now available from this cross, particularly noteworthy are Leonard Messel, lilac pink; Merrill, an American selection with larger fragrant white flowers, and Neil McEacharn, white pink-flushed flowers.

M. salicifolia, an elegant Japanese species, forms a small broadly pyramidal tree with narrow willow-like leaves, usu-

Above left: *Liquidambar styraciflua*
Below left: *Liriodendron tulipifera*

60

ally glaucous on the undersides. Fragrant white flowers are produced in early spring, even on young trees.

Although often grown as a wall specimen in cooler localities, the magnificent *M. grandiflora*, from the southern U.S.A., can perhaps claim to be the finest of flowering evergreens, reaching the proportions of a small to medium-sized tree in southern European and similar favoured localities. The handsome, leathery, glossy, dark green leaves, 6 to 10 in. long, have attractive red-brown felt on the undersides and form a perfect background to the immense cream-coloured, globular, fragrant flowers which are produced continuously in late summer and autumn. The variety Exmouth flowers at an early age. Fortunately, this species is tolerant of all soils of reasonable depth.

Malus

The flowering crabs or rosyblooms are an invaluable group of hardy, small, occasionally medium-sized garden trees providing a variety of shapes and attractive spring bloom in a range of colour from white to deep wine red. Some have purple or red-tinted foliage and many give attractive autumn fruits which are also useful for crab apple jelly. A few provide autumn-tinted leaves. All the following species and varieties thrive on any reasonably fertile soil and make a short list of the best of the numerous varieties available today which combine beauty with vigour and reliability.

Almey is a Canadian-raised small tree, ultimately of rounded habit with reddish young leaves, and large red flowers with white centres, followed by orange-red persistent fruits. *Malus coronaria charlottae (flore pleno)*, a form of an eastern North American species, makes a small tree of spreading habit. The large, semi-double, violet-scented, shell-pink flowers are produced in late spring and early summer. The large leaves colour richly in autumn.

M. floribunda is the Japanese crab. It forms a small free-flowering tree of graceful habit, semi-pendulous or umbrella headed with age. This handsome species is truly spectacular when in bloom in the early spring, its arching branches densely wreathed in apple-blossom pink flowers which are crimson in bud.

Golden Hornet makes a small round-headed tree with erect-growing branches. The white spring flowers are followed by heavy crops of persistent bright yellow fruits. This is a fine fruiting crab. A small tree of somewhat pendulous habit in maturity, John Downie is generally re-garded as the best fruiting crab for both appearance and preserve making. The attractive conical scarlet and orange fruits are reliably produced each autumn.

Katherine is a small round-headed tree of American raising. It has very large semi-double pink flowers which slowly fade to white and these are followed by bright red, yellow-tinted fruits. Profusion *(lemoinei × sieboldii)* is the best of several varieties with red young leaves and wine-red flowers. A small tree of good constitution, its large flowers are profusely borne in clusters of six or seven, and are followed by small ox-blood red fruits.

M. tschonoskii is a Japanese species of medium-sized erect pyramidal habit. It is notable for its silvery-white felted young shoots and in particular for its magnificent display of autumn leaf colour. The large pink-tinted flowers fade to white. Finally there is Van Eseltine which is an ideal small garden tree of distinct narrow upright form. The large semi-double flowers, red in bud, open soft pink and are followed by yellow fruits.

Mespilus

Mespilus germanica, the medlar, is a picturesque small hardy tree of low spreading habit. The large distinctive hairy leaves turn russet brown in autumn. In the spring, five-petalled large white flowers are produced singly and are followed in the autumn by the typical brown edible fruits. Cultivated for centuries, the medlar rivals the black mulberry for architectural effect.

Metrosideros

This is a small genus of Australasian evergreens related to the myrtles. Two or three species make spectacular small or medium-sized flowering trees for gardens in the mildest maritime districts preferably on neutral or acid soils.

Metrosideros excelsa (tomentosa) is a native of North Island, New Zealand, where it is known as the Christmas tree. In summer, this species appears as a solid crimson mass of large bottle-brush flowers. *M. robusta* with thick rounded leaves and scarlet autumn flowers produces a similar effect.

Michelia

Michelia doltsopa is a most desirable small semi-evergreen Himalayan tree related to the magnolias but it is suitable only for lime-free soils in mild or sheltered districts. The handsome leathery leaves, 6 to 7 in. long, are glaucous beneath. White fragrant magnolia-like flowers, opening in the spring, are borne in the axils of the leaves.

Morus

Planted for centuries for their picturesque form and for their edible fruits, the mulberries make small or medium-sized hardy trees on most well-drained soils. *Morus alba* is an economically important Chinese species, long cultivated for its handsome large heart-shaped leaves upon which silk worms are fed. The sweet fruits are white, changing to deep pink. Its variety *pendula* makes an outstanding small weeping tree, suitable as a focal point in the garden.

The black mulberry, *M. nigra*, is a well-known, small, wide-spreading tree renowned for its longevity. The large, heart-shaped, rough-textured leaves are down covered beneath; the deep red fruits are produced in increasing quantities from an early age.

Myrtus

In mild and maritime localities the very beautiful myrtle, *Myrtus apiculata (luma)*, makes a small evergreen tree, covered in the late summer with white myrtle flowers. In addition, the peeling cinnamon brown of trunk and branches is a striking feature. Best sited in a sunny position in any well-drained soil.

Nyssa

There are two species of the tupelo especially worthy of mention. *Nyssa sylvatica* is

Malus Golden Hornet

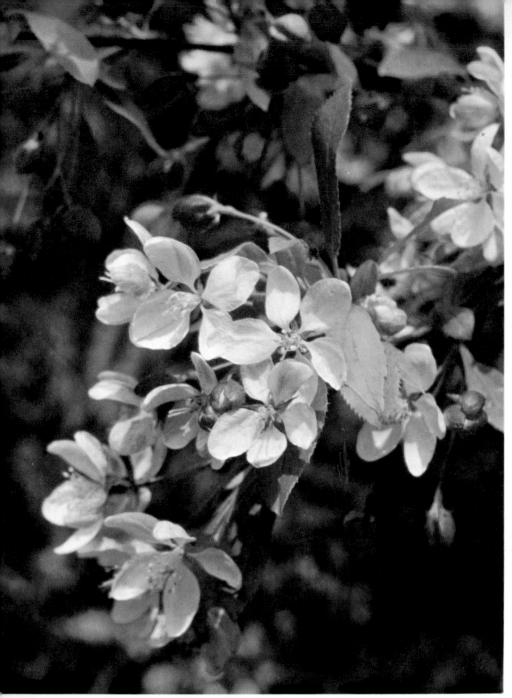

Malus floribunda

a broadly pyramidal medium-sized North American tree for moist lime-free soils. It is one of the most spectacular autumn-colouring trees for the large shining green leaves turn red, orange and yellow. *N. sinensis* is a Chinese species attaining small tree size and of equal merit in the autumn. In addition its young growths appear red throughout the growing season. Both species are excellent by the side of water.

Ostrya

Ostrya carpinifolia, the hop hornbeam, is a medium-sized, round-headed south European tree, usually grown on any fertile soil and worthy of wider planting. In the spring, the long male catkins are

attractive, while later in the year the branches are hung with decorative, hop-like fruits. The double-toothed, hornbeam-like leaves turn yellow in autumn.

Paulownia

This genus contains small to medium-sized Chinese trees grown for their large handsome leaves and unusual foxglove-like flowers, opening in erect panicles in the spring. On pruned trees these often attain 2 ft. or more across. *Paulownia fargesii* makes a medium-sized tree producing at a relatively early age fragrant heliotrope flowers liberally speckled with purple. The best-known species, *P. tomentosa (imperialis)*, forms a smaller round-headed tree with deep heliotrope-coloured flowers.

Platanus

Although a magnificent large broad-headed tree for parkland, I must mention the well-known hybrid *Platanus hispanica (acerifolia)*, the London plane, for its handsome large maple-like leaves and mottled flaking bark. No tree is more tolerant of city conditions and, if necessary, may be restricted by severe pruning. The hanging burr-like fruit clusters are effective for much of the year.

The Oriental plane or chennar, *P. orientalis*, is again a magnificent large long-lived south eastern European tree, much planted in Mediterranean lands as a shade tree. The deeply lobed leaves are particularly attractive when newly opened in the spring, appearing with the hanging fruit clusters.

Populus

This is an extensive genus of fast-growing, medium-sized or large deciduous trees, very useful as specimens or as a tall summer screen where circumstances allow. However, the majority, by reason of their vigour, surface-rooting habits and thirst for moisture, are quite unsuitable for small gardens and for planting near buildings. We will therefore not consider them in detail in this work beyond an honourable mention for *Populus tremula pendula*, the weeping aspen, a very effective small weeping tree particularly conspicuous in early spring when the branches are hung with long purple-grey male catkins and *P. tremuloides pendula*, parasol de St Julien, which makes a charming small pendulous specimen tree of French origin.

Although a large tree *Populus serotina aurea*, the golden poplar, an effective golden-foliage tree, may be restricted by pruning to control the size of the head and to encourage brightly coloured young foliage. The large heart-shaped leaves are bright yellow in the spring and early summer, and again in the autumn.

Prunus

A large family of beautiful flowering trees (and shrubs) of small or medium size, many of which are ideal for the small garden. In addition to spectacular spring or winter flower, many give a second display in their autumn leaf colour. Although some species and hybrids are not long lived, all succeed in any well-drained soil in a sunny position. Under this heading we will consider a selection of the best flowering ornamental species and hybrids of almond *(Prunus dulcis)*, Japanese apricot *(Prunus mume)*, Japanese and other cherries, peach *(P. persica)* and plums *(P. cerasifera)*.

Flowering Almonds These are extensively cultivated and naturalized throughout the Mediterranean lands for their edible almonds and universally grown in gardens as an early spring-flowering small tree. They are generally trees of upright, but often ungainly, habit and like peaches subject to peach leaf curl in country districts. They are good trees for town conditions. There are a number of varieties and in particular: *Prunus dulcis macrocarpa*, with very large pale pink or white flowers and large almonds; *P.d. praecox*, a very early-flowering form with pale pink flowers; *P. amygdalo-persica (dulcis × persica) pollardii*, a hybrid between almond and peach which makes a very beautiful small tree, the deep rich pink flowers are particularly striking when

seen against a dark evergreen background.

Flowering Apricots The Japanese apricot, *P. mume*, forms a charming small garden tree, producing almond-scented pink flowers opening over an extended period in late winter and spring. A sheltered sunny site is desirable. Particularly good forms are: *alboplena*, with semi-double white flowers; *alphandii (flore pleno)*, semi-double, pink, and Beni-shi-don, fragrant flowers which are an unusual shade of rich deep pink.

Japanese and other Flowering Cherries Accolade *(P. sargentii × subhirtella)* is an early April-flowering variety of upright spreading habit, slightly pendulous with age. Semi-double, pale pink flowers are produced in clusters of three.

Amanogawa *(serrulata erecta)* is a well-known variety which forms a slender

Platanus orientalis (yellow) **and** *Acer palmatum* (red)

pillar up to about 15 ft. high by 2 to 3 ft. in width and is ideal for small gardens or restricted places, and for architectural planting. The flowers are fragrant, pale pink opening in mid-May.

A handsome species native of the woods of Europe (including the British Isles) and western Asia, *P. avium*, the gean or wild cherry, forms a medium-sized tree conspicuous in spring with its clusters of large cup-shaped white flowers, and again in autumn, when the leaves colour red. The double gean, *P.a. plena (grandiflora)* is a tree of pyramidal habit and one of the best double white cherries for garden planting.

P. hillieri (incisa × sargentii) is a prolific early-flowering hybrid of rather broad-headed habit. Masses of pale, soft pink, spring flowers are followed in the autumn by fiery-red leaf colour. A selection of narrow upright habit, *P. hillieri* Spire, forming a tree about 25 ft. high and about 8 ft. through at the widest part, is much in demand as a street tree, and is ideal for restricted circumstances in gardens.

Kanzan *(sekiyama)* is a popular, perhaps overplanted variety forming a vigorous medium-sized tree with stiffly ascending branches, assuming a typical funnel-shaped head in maturity. The rather harsh purplish-pink large double flowers are freely produced. For those who prefer a less garish pink, and require a tree of similar ultimate size and habit, Pink Perfection (Shimidsu Sakura × Kanzan) is ideal. Its large double bright pink flowers, often two toned in effect, are produced on long drooping clusters with the bronzy young leaves.

Kiku-shidare Sakura makes an attractive weeping tree with arching branches, ideal as a focal point specimen for the small garden. The deep pink, very double flowers are like miniature chrysanthemum blooms.

Kursar *(kurilensis × sargentii)* is a very desirable early spring-flowering hybrid of upright-spreading habit. The flowers are an unusual shade of deep cerise pink. Autumn leaf colour is rich orange. Okame *(campanulata × incisa)* is very similar in flower and autumn colour. Both varieties were introduced by the renowned authority on ornamental cherries, Captain Collingwood Ingram.

P. padus, bird cherry, is a small or medium-sized hardy tree of wide distribution. The buddleia-like flower spikes are produced in late spring after the Japanese cherries have faded. *P.p. watereri (grandiflora)* is considered the best form, making a tree of broadly pyramidal shape, festooned with exceptionally long racemes of slightly fragrant white flowers.

P. sargentii, Sargent's cherry, is a small to medium-sized, round-headed tree, often considered to be the most desirable of all cherries; it displays its large deep pink flowers in early spring before the foliage opens; in the autumn it is one of the earliest trees to colour in rich tones of orange, scarlet and crimson.

P. serrula (serrula tibetica) is a Chinese species, forming a small round-headed tree, remarkable for the beautiful shining mahogany-coloured bark of its trunk. The white spring flowers are not conspicuous, but nurserymen are now top grafting large-flowered varieties of Japanese cherries,

such as *hillieri*, Shirofugen or Ukon on to 6-ft. stems of this species, in order to make a more garden worthy combination.

Shimidsu Sakura (longipes, Okumi-yako), a variety of considerable distinction and beauty, forms a small mushroom-headed tree, ideal as a lawn specimen in the small garden. The large hanging flower clusters are a delightful shell pink in bud, opening to pure white semi-double blooms, each reminiscent of a ballet dancer's skirt.

Shirofugen forms a small flat-headed tree with wide-spreading branches. Its flowers, pale pink in bud, opening pure white and fading again to purplish pink, are produced with the young coppery-bronze leaves, making a particularly beautiful combination. The flowering period is later and more long lasting than most other Japanese cherries.

Shirotae (Mount Fuji) is an outstanding cherry most distinct in its flat-topped, horizontal-branching habit, the branches extending sometimes to a width of 30 ft. in favourable circumstances. It is best planted in isolation where there is adequate room for its development. The large snow-white single or semi-double flowers festoon the branches in early spring. One of the most effective varieties.

P. subhirtella, spring cherry, is a notable but very variable species, cultivated for centuries in its native Japan, where specimens of great size may be seen. It is usually represented in cultivation today by a number of distinct varieties which are among the finest of all spring-flowering

trees. The variety *rosea (ascendens rosea)*, pink spring cherry, forms a small tree with upright-ascending branches. The flowers are an exquisite shell pink and are enhanced by red-purple calyces. The foliage colours red and yellow in autumn. *P. s. autumnalis*, the autumn cherry, is a popular variety forming a small tree of open wide-spreading habit. The white, pink-tinted flowers are intermittently produced from autumn to spring as weather allows. *Autumnalis rosea* is identical apart from its deep shell-pink flowers. The weeping spring cherry, *P. s. pendula (pendula rosea)*, makes a small weeping tree, ultimately about 10 ft. high and 20 ft. wide, with a dense pattern of thread-like branches weeping to the ground and arrayed in early spring with pale pink flowers. *Pendula rubra* has deeper pink flowers and is equally desirable.

Tai-haku, the great white cherry, forms a small tree of robust upright-spreading habit, remarkable for its very large single pure white blooms, produced most tellingly with the bronzy young leaves. It has the largest flowers of any cherry.

Ukon *(serrulata luteovirens)* makes a strong-growing, wide-spreading tree, of good constitution, distinct in its green or yellow-green flowers. It is very effective when planted in association with Pink Perfection or Kanzan, whose blooms are produced at the same time.

Umineko *(incisa × speciosa)* is a welcome addition to the few varieties of narrow upright habit. It is a tree of vigorous growth with single pure white

Above left: *Prunus* Kanzan
Above: *Prunus serrula*

early spring flowers. The leaves colour well in autumn.

Prunus yedoensis (speciosa × subhirtella rosea), the Tokyo cherry or Yoshino, becomes a vigorous small to medium-sized tree; its arching branches and graceful habit are typical of Japan, where it is widely planted in the Tokyo district. The single blush-white, almond-scented flowers are produced early in the spring. *Perpendens* is a smaller form with branches weeping to the ground.

Flowering Peaches There are a number of varieties of peach, *P. persica*, grown for the beauty of their flowers in spring. Most make small bushy-headed trees, some with pendulous habit. As with the fruiting peaches, it is necessary to maintain these trees in good health by spraying, against peach leaf curl, with lime sulphur or a copper fungicide, twice in early spring as the flower buds swell, and again in early autumn.

The following varieties are particularly recommended: Crimson Cascade, a weeping variety with double carmine-red flowers; Iceberg, semi-double, snow-white flowers, freely produced; Klara Mayer (Clara Meyer), the best pink double-flowered peach; Russell's Red, the best double red-flowered variety.

Flowering Plums *P. cerasifera*, myrobalan or cherry plum, a long cultivated western Asiatic species, is usually represented in ornamental plantings by several purple-leaved varieties or hybrids which make round-headed small trees of dense branching habit.

P. c. pissardii (atropurpurea), the purple-leaved plum, a popular if somewhat over-planted form, makes an attractive combination when associated with laburnum or one of the silver-leaved pears (pyrus). The early spring flowers are single pink in bud opening to white. *P. c. nigra* is an even darker-leaved form in which both stems and leaves are black purple and the flowers single pale pink.

P. blireana (P. cerasifera pissardii × mume alphandii) I consider the most beautiful of this group, both in foliage and flower, the leaves are coppery purple and the large double flowers rose pink.

Pyrus
The pears are a genus of small trees mainly from south eastern Europe. Those with silver or white woolly leaves are most ornamental hardy garden trees, tolerant equally of town conditions and of seaside exposure.

Pyrus nivalis becomes a conspicuous tree in early spring when masses of snow-white flowers appear with the white woolly young leaves. It makes a pleasing contrast when planted with the purple-leaved plum. *P. canescens (nivalis × salicifolia)* provides a similar effect.

P. salicifolia pendula, the weeping willow-leaved pear, is a very effective tree, suitable for most gardens. The branches of this elegant and picturesque small tree usually weep to the ground. The narrow silvery leaves are effective throughout the growing season while the cream-white flowers with red stamens are an added attraction in the spring. A first-class weeping garden tree.

Quercus
Surprisingly there are several hundreds of species of oak widely distributed throughout the temperate and tropical regions of the world. Both evergreen and deciduous, they vary from small dense shrubs to large noble trees of great ornamental and timber value. With a few exceptions, most species succeed in any deep rich soil, whether alkaline or acid. While the majority of quercus species must be looked upon as collectors' pieces, the following selection is very worthy of a place in gardens large enough to contain them.

Quercus cerris, the turkey oak, is notable for its elegance and rapidity of growth, and for its tolerance of chalk soils and seaside exposure. The variegated form, *variegata*, with leaves boldly margined creamy white, makes a striking variegated tree, ultimately of medium or large size.

The scarlet oak, *Q. coccinea*, is a large broad-headed tree from eastern North America, magnificent for six or eight weeks in autumn, when its glossy green leaves turn brilliant red. Its variety *splendens* is a fine form selected for the brilliance and reliability of its autumn colour.

Allied eastern North American species exhibiting similar, though less spectacular, qualities of autumnal leaf colour are *Q. palustris*, pin oak, a more elegant large tree with smaller, five or seven-lobed leaves, and *Q. rubra*, red oak, a vigorous, large, broad-headed species, its leaves are matt green turning russet red in the autumn and are larger than those of either *Q. coccinea* or *Q. palustris*. All three species are not successful on chalky or alkaline soils.

Q. frainetto (conferta), the Hungarian oak, is a stately and handsome species worthy of wider planting. The deeply lobed obovate leaves are exceptionally large. It is successful on all soils.

Q. ilex, the holm oak or evergreen oak, is a Mediterranean species and perhaps the most majestic of all large hardy evergreen trees; its leaves are dark glossy green with grey downy undersides. In early summer the woolly young shoots and yellow catkins are a striking feature. At home in any well-drained fertile soil, the holm oak is excellent in maritime exposures. In small gardens its growth may be restricted by clipping – indeed it makes an excellent evergreen hedge.

Q. phellos is the willow oak, a handsome species for lime-free soils from the eastern United States of America. Usually forming a large round-headed tree, the willow-like leaves colour yellow and orange in autumn. A much renowned large, broad-headed tree, *Q. robur (pedunculata)*, the common or English oak with its rugged bark, is notable for its longevity and for its timber value. Several varieties are particularly appropriate in gardens including *concordia*, golden oak, a small, very slow-growing form with bright golden-yellow leaves throughout spring and summer. This is a rare variety which is difficult to obtain but it is well worth the effort. *Q. r. fastigiata*, the Cypress oak, forms a large tree of dense, narrow, upright habit and *fastigiata purpurea* makes a smaller tree of similar shape, but with young shoots and leaves red purple throughout the spring and summer.

Rhus
The stag's-horn sumach, *Rhus typhina*, is commonly seen in gardens as a small

naturalized in parts of Europe; its white flowers are produced in early or mid-summer. It is best represented in gardens by one of its varieties which are generally small or medium-sized trees of more compact habit. The best of these includes Frisia, a small or medium-sized tree of recent introduction and one of the most striking of foliage trees available today. Its bright golden-yellow leaves maintain their colour from spring to autumn. It is most effective when associated with purple-leaved trees or shrubs. The variety *inermis*, the mop-head acacia, is a small, round-headed tree, formed by a dense mass of spineless branches and deep green pinnate leaves. It is a popular tree for street or public planting, particularly in France.

Salix

The large members of this family are usually seen as graceful waterside trees in gardens or landscape planting. Many are also conspicuous in their coloured winter bark which is more attractive if the trees concerned are pollarded or heavily pruned in spring every other year. In many species, the spring catkins are an additional feature. Most succeed in any deep, moist soil.

One of the most beautiful of large trees for landscape planting is the white willow, *Salix alba*, but the silvery colour of its silky hairy leaves and shoots varies from tree to tree. It is very successful in maritime conditions if planted in moist soil. In small gardens, several of its varieties are good value. *S. a. chermesina (britzensis, chrysostella)*, the red or scarlet willow, is particularly conspicuous in winter when the bark of twigs and young stems appears bright scarlet. Pollard every other year in spring to maintain this feature at its best.

S. a. sericea (argentea), the silver willow, makes a small round-headed tree with consistently shining silvery leaves. It is considerably less vigorous than the type, and ideal for the small garden. The golden willow, *S. a. vitellina*, has brilliant yellow winter shoots which make it the perfect companion for *S. a. chermesina*. It should be similarly pruned every other spring.

S. chrysocoma (alba tristis, alba vitellina pendula, babylonica ramulis aureis) is a handsome, fast-growing, medium-sized weeping tree with a wide-spreading habit, extensively planted for its grace and beauty and particularly for its long golden-yellow weeping branchlets. Although ideal for public planting, it will quickly become too large for small gardens. Regrettably,

shrubby tree with a familiar wide-spreading, antler-like branch system. A native of eastern U.S.A., this small suckering tree is most spectacular in autumn when its large pinnate leaves turn vivid shades of red, orange and yellow. Conical hairy clusters of crimson fruits are attractive particularly after the fall of leaf. There is also an equally worthy variety *laciniata* with more deeply divided leaves.

Robinia

Hardy North American trees which are most ornamental in their elegant habit and attractive pinnate leaves. Pink or white pea-shaped flowers are produced in summer. They thrive on all soils and are particularly valuable in dry, sunny positions, sheltered from wind. If grown in lush or

Prunus **Kiku-shidare Sakura**

exposed circumstances, their brittle branches are liable to break in gales. Many of the smaller forms are successful in town gardens.

Robinia ambigua decaisneana (pseudoacacia decaisneana) becomes a handsome, medium-sized tree; the large racemes of pale pink flowers are very conspicuous. *R. fertilis* Monument is a small tree of narrow upright growth also bearing pale pink flowers.

A graceful and elegant tree for the small garden, *R. hillieri (kelseyi × pseudoacacia)* has lilac-pink flowers which are produced at mid-summer. The common or false acacia, *R. pseudoacacia*, is a large picturesque suckering tree with spiny twigs,

Robinia pseudoacacia Frisia

in country districts, this hybrid is also particularly prone to willow scab or canker (anthracnose) which is difficult to control on large trees. It is, however, worth spraying young trees two or three times during spring and summer with a liquid copper fungicide to reduce the incidence of this disfiguring disease.

The violet willow, *S. daphnoides*, makes a vigorous, upright-growing small tree, conspicuous in winter when its violet-tinted shoots appear over-laid with a white waxy bloom. The bright yellow catkins of male trees (var. *aglaia*) are a striking feature each spring.

The purple osier, *S. purpurea*, is rarely more than a tall shrub of loose open habit with attractive oblong leaves with blue-white undersides. However, its variety *eugenei* forms an upright-growing small tree with unusual grey-pink male catkins; in particular its variety, *pendula*, the purple weeping willow, makes an effective small weeping tree and is particularly suitable for small gardens and for sites where *S. chrysocoma* would be too large.

The purple osier and its varieties are very worthy of garden space, and succeed even in dryish positions if need be.

Sophora

Though widely planted in Japan, *Sophora japonica*, the Japanese pagoda tree, a hardy medium-sized to large round-headed tree, is a native of China. The handsome, long, pinnate leaves consist of up to fifteen leaflets; the creamy-white, pea-shaped flowers are produced in late summer and autumn on maturing trees, and particularly in the hot dry summers of the Mediterranean countries. It is successful in all fertile well-drained soils. The variety *pendula* is a very desirable pictur-esque tree for the small garden, with its stiffly pendulous branches forming a low natural arbour.

Sorbus

A large family of hardy, small or medium-sized trees indispensable in the garden for their flower, attractive foliage, berry and autumn-colouring leaf. In the main, they have an elegant and compact habit of growth. For our purposes the sorbus may be conveniently divided into two groups –

67

the whitebeams (*aria* group) and the mountain ashes or rowans (*aucuparia* group).

All species and varieties will thrive in any fertile soil, but the whitebeams are notably successful on chalk and limestone and the rowans happiest and longest lived on light neutral or acid soils. The following species and varieties are among the best of the many available today.

Sorbus aria, whitebeam, a small to medium-sized round-headed European tree, with oval or obovate dentated leaves, green above and vivid white beneath. The spring flowers, although dull white, are heavily scented. In autumn, bright red fruits are produced in quantity; it is tolerant of wind and maritime exposure and is best represented in small gardens by one of its varieties. *Decaisneana (majestica)* is the largest-leaved whitebeam with elliptical leaves up to 6 in. long and 4 in. wide and with larger fruits than in the type. The best whitebeam is *lutescens*, a variety which is particularly effective in spring and early summer, when its new leaves are downy white on both surfaces.

S. aucuparia, the rowan or mountain ash, is a familiar European species forming a small or medium-sized tree, usually of erect habit. In marked contrast to those of the whitebeam, the leaves are pinnate, 5 to 9 in. long, and composed of up to nineteen leaflets. The flat terminal white flower heads 3 to 5 in. across, which open in late spring, are followed by quantities of scarlet berries. There are a number of equally worthy garden varieties; Sheerwater Seedling, a recent introduction of narrow, upright and compact habit, is ideal as a street tree or for a restricted site in the small garden. The foliage is an attractive blue green and the fruits orange scarlet in large clusters. The variety *xanthocarpa (fructuluteo)* has golden-yellow fruits which are less attractive to birds.

S. commixta (aucuparia group), a Japanese species, also of upright habit, is notable for the brilliant flame or scarlet autumn colouring of its leaves and for the freely produced orange-red fruits.

S. hupehensis (aucuparia group) is a distinct and beautiful Chinese species, forming a compact head of ascending branches. The foliage is of an unusual blue-green hue, acting as a perfect foil for the white or pink-tinted fruits, which are produced in drooping clusters, and persist well into winter. The varieties *obtusa* and *rosea* are equally worthy variants with pink fruits.

Salix chrysocoma

The Swedish whitebeam, *S. intermedia* (*aria* group), is a very hardy small or medium-sized tree useful in exposed or bleak situations. The distinct leaves are lobed towards the base, green above and grey felted beneath. The large orange-red fruits are conspicuous in autumn.

The variety Joseph Rock (*aucuparia* group) is an outstanding introduction from China and an ideal small garden tree of dense narrow habit. The pinnate leaves assume rich autumn tints of red, orange, bronze and purple, making an excellent background for the amber-yellow fruits.

S. pohuashanensis (conradinae) (*aucuparia* group), the Chinese rowan, is a hardy and robust small or medium-sized tree, spectacular in autumn when laden with heavy bunches of large orange-red fruits. A choice Chinese species, *S. sargentiana* (*aucuparia* group) slowly attains about 25 ft. The sticky winter buds are reminiscent of those of the horse chestnut (aesculus). The handsome pinnate leaves, among the largest of the genus, colour magnificently a rich red in the autumn.

A small tree from western China, *S. scalaris* (*aucuparia* group) is distinct in its wide-spreading head, and in its unusual

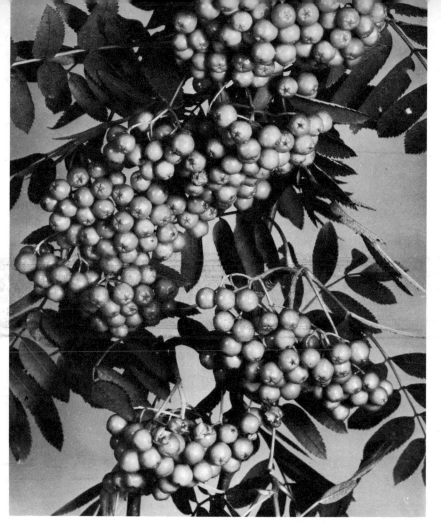

Sorbus aucuparia

dark glossy green fern-like leaves with grey downy undersides. The orange fruits are freely produced and the foliage turns crimson and purple in autumn.

S. vilmorinii is an elegant and delightful small tree from western China. In late summer and autumn the branches are hung with clusters of rosy-red fruits which turn pink and finally fade to white, tinted pink. This is an excellent tree for the smallest garden.

Styrax

Styrax japonica fargesii, the snowbell, is handsome both in leaf and flower. This distinguished, small, broad-headed Chinese tree is worthy of wider planting. The magnolia-like leaves are obovate or broadly elliptic and the white bell-shaped flowers, about $\frac{3}{4}$ in. across, hang all along the branches at mid-summer. Fertile lime-free soil is necessary and although quite hardy, a sheltered west-facing site is desirable, particularly where there is danger of late spring frosts.

Tilia

The limes are stately, medium-sized or large trees with handsome leaves produc-ing great quantities of cream-yellow flow-ers during the summer. They are successful in any fertile soil, and are magnificent in parkland or in public places, but they are in the main too large for the small garden. However, several species are tolerant of pollarding or hard pruning, and are often used for street plantings or in gardens as pleached lime screens.

Pleaching consists of planting standard or half-standard specimens, 8 or 10 ft. apart, and training the side branches to link together to form a curtain-like screen; any shoots growing forward or backwards are pruned flush to the main stem.

In parkland, for municipal planting, or in the larger garden the following readily available species and varieties are particu-larly worthy of consideration.

Tilia americana, the American lime, forms a medium-sized tree with rugged bark on older trees. It is remarkable for its exceptionally large leaves. The variety Redmond is an interesting selection of dense, narrow habit.

T. cordata, the small-leaved lime, is a medium to large-sized European tree of neat rounded habit, bearing compara-tively small heart-shaped leaves. The fra-grant flowers appear somewhat later than those of other species.

A very graceful, medium-sized tree, *T. euchlora (cordata × dasystyla)* has lower branches which are pendulous on older specimens while immature trees have arching branches and bright glossy green leaves. This hybrid is free from aphid (greenfly) attack – a troublesome com-plaint of many limes.

The weeping silver lime, *T. petiolaris (americana pendula)*, forms a most grace-ful and beautiful tall weeping tree, with a rounded head and downward-sweeping branches. The long-stalked leaves are white felted beneath, and in a breeze add considerably to the attraction of this fine tree. The heavily scented flowers produced in late summer are regrettably narcotic to bees.

T. platyphyllos, the broad-leaved lime, becomes a large and rapid-growing tree of rounded habit, now much planted in park-land or public places instead of *T. europaea*, the common lime, which has a densely suckering habit. Its variety *T. p. rubra*, the red-twigged lime, has the additional attraction of red-brown winter shoots, and a more upright habit of growth.

Trachycarpus

Trachycarpus fortunei (Chamaerops excel-sa), the chusan palm, is the only tree palm species reasonably hardy in the warmer counties of the British Isles and in similar favoured or maritime areas in the northern hemisphere. It slowly forms an unusual and picturesque tree, its trunk clothed with dark brown fibrous bases of old leaf stalks, and its head an umbrella of great fan-like leaves. On maturing trees, the conspicuous panicles of yellow flowers are produced among the leaves in summer.

Ulmus

The elms are a genus of fine stately land-scape trees, growing well in any fertile soil, and tolerant of seaside and other exposed positions. There are several picturesque lower-growing forms, some with coloured leaves, which are particu-larly suitable for small gardens. Regret-tably, most species and varieties must be considered to a lesser or greater extent vulnerable to the dreaded Dutch elm disease (a fungus disease spread by elm bark beetles) which in recent years has killed large quantities of the English elm *(Ulmus procera)* and the Dutch elm *(U. hollandica major)* in Europe, the British Isles and elsewhere. However, it is en-couraging to find that varieties of the Dutch and Huntingdon elms resistant to Dutch elm disease are now available from nurserymen. It is hoped that public authorities and owners of private gardens will be encouraged to re-furnish the landscape by planting these resistant varieties, several of which are mentioned below.

U. angustifolia cornubiensis (stricta, carpinifolia cornubiensis), the Cornish elm, is an excellent street tree, ultimately of large size and distinct in its conical head of upright-growing branches. It is a native of Devon and Cornwall in England and of Brittany in France.

U. glabra, the wych or Scotch elm, makes a large tree with a dome-like head of wide-spreading branches. The large coarse-toothed leaves are very rough to the touch. The fruits densely wreathing the branches in spring are particularly attractive. Unlike most other species, the wych elm does not produce sucker growth. There are two weeping forms, both suitable as lawn specimens for gardens. These are *camperdownii*, the Camperdown elm, a small or medium-sized tree with an umbrella-like head of weeping branches

and branchlets, and *pendula (horizontalis)*, the weeping wych elm, which makes a flat-topped head of stiffly pendulous spreading branches. It may also be used to form a natural arbour.

U. hollandica is a natural hybrid of wide-spreading distribution throughout Europe. A form of this hybrid, *major*, is the Dutch elm, a large suckering tree, very vulnerable to Dutch elm disease. However, the following resistant selections have appeared in recent years and should now be readily available from nurserymen. Bea Schwarz, a resistant selection made originally from seedlings collected in northern Europe, and Christine Buisman, a tree of slender upright-branching habit when young, but ultimately a large tree of rounded outline.

U. sarniensis (angustifolia × hollandica), the Jersey or Wheatley elm, is a large tree which develops a dense head of upright branches, narrower than those of the Cornish elm. It is excellent in seaside

exposure. *Dicksonii (wheatleyi aurea)*, the Dickson's golden elm, becomes a compact-headed specimen with golden-yellow leaves. A most effective small tree for the garden.

U. vegeta (carpinifolia × glabra), the Huntingdon or Chichester elm, is a hybrid found in the Midland counties of England. It forms a handsome, vigorous, large tree, with elliptical long pointed leaves of large size. There are two interesting disease-resistant varieties now available. Commelin is a moderately resistant variety of Dutch origin, with smaller leaves than those of the type and a narrower habit of growth, and Groenveld is a slow-growing, small or medium-sized tree of columnar habit. It is said to be very disease resistant and possibly the most appropriate of the new forms for the small garden or for street planting due to its slow rate of growth.

A mixed planting of trees on a large scale

Conifers and Heathers

Adrian Bloom has made a name for himself as a specialist on dwarf and other conifers and the heaths and heathers which associate so superbly with them.

As visitors to Bressingham Gardens, near Diss in Norfolk will be well aware, Mr Bloom has added to the famous collection of herbaceous perennial plants there a heather and conifer garden of the greatest interest and beauty. He sees these as very much plants of the future with their ease of maintenance and year-round visual appeal.

In a very real sense Adrian Bloom is attracting to this group of plants the kind of acclaim which his father, Alan Bloom, has brought to perennials. The collection in his own garden has been built up over the past ten years, during which time he has also been responsible for the commercial production of the huge range of hardy plants raised by the Bressingham establishment. Before that he worked in Europe and the United States of America.

In recent years he has often appeared on television gardening programmes, and he is the author of a book on conifers.

It may seem strange to put together in one section two unrelated families of plants, but I have chosen to do this because I believe the combination of conifers and heathers in the garden makes an unbeatable formula. Given the right treatment initially, a garden should be provided with year round – and I mean in the depths of winter too – colour, contrast and ground cover. If this is the sort of garden which appeals to you, then I hope I can begin to give you some further ideas as to how to achieve it, however small it may be.

Conifers in the Garden

Before rushing out to buy a conifer to fill an odd corner in the garden, assess, if you know, what you require.

The conifers you obtain from any source will in all probability be quite small initially. This you must be prepared for but it is most important to find out the name of the tree and how large it might become because some conifers will grow only 2 ft. in twenty-five years whilst others may reach 70 ft. during the same length of time. It depends upon the species and variety.

So what are the uses of conifers? All but a few are evergreen but such is the tremendous variety that one can choose from almost any form, shape, colour and eventual height. They can serve as a backcloth to a garden, as a windbreak or a hedge, as ground-cover plants or purely as ornamental specimens in their own right.

Cultural Requirements

Few gardens would be complete, in my opinion, without conifers and few are too inhospitable to grow most types successfully.

However, conifers require a reasonable amount of moisture especially in the first year or two after planting when root systems are becoming established. Although not essential, moist peat incorporated with the soil prior to planting will help the plant get away to a good start, whether it be a specimen from the open ground or a container plant. The ideal times for planting conifers are September, October, March and April, but with the advent of the container plant any time of the year will do though in summer constant watering is essential.

Some conifers will tolerate shade but very few will put up with dry shade, with the exception perhaps of the yews. The golden varieties certainly need sun to obtain their best colours and you will find

both green and blue types will appreciate it more if planted in sunny open situations.

Three cultural hints which particularly apply to conifers are: firstly, the importance of planting in soil that is free from perennial weeds; secondly, to allow a perimeter of soil around a specimen which is planted in grass. This should be at least to a width of 6 in. from the base of the plant, and preferably 12 in. I have seen more conifers spoilt this way than by any other.

A hessian screen erected around a newly planted conifer to prevent wind rocking

Thirdly, I have found it always pays when planting a conifer to spray with an anti-dessicant such as S-600. This helps quite considerably in allowing the plant a breathing space to make fresh root without losing moisture through the foliage and thereby preventing much of the burning often seen on conifers in the late spring. The larger the plant the more important it is to spray it – conifers are valuable and worth a little extra effort.

Conifers for Garden Use

The majority of gardens these days could not accommodate the large forest trees and so the following list consists mainly of dwarf, slow-growing and medium-sized conifers. To make this more easily understood, approximate height, and spread where relative, of each plant is given at an age of ten years and at maturity. Of course this can be a guide only as rates of growth for the same plant can vary considerably from one side of the country to the other.

Selected Conifers

Abies

The silver firs consist of mostly large-growing forest trees but some attractive dwarf forms are well worth growing.

Abies balsamea hudsonia is a very hardy,

71

very slow-growing shrub which is useful for the rock garden. It has dark green glossy leaves and is particularly attractive when making bright green fresh shoots in spring. At ten years it will be 8 to 12 in. high and at maturity 2 to 3 ft. high with a spread of 3 to 4 ft.

A. koreana is a somewhat choice plant. Commonly known as the Korean fir, it is slow growing but eventually forms a medium-sized tree. However, it is best known for its bright purple cones which appear quite early in its life. The habit is neat, and the leaves glossy green above, silvery white beneath. Not an easily obtainable plant but well worth searching for! After ten years it will be 5 to 6 ft. high; at maturity 40 to 50 ft.

Araucaria
Araucaria araucana is much better known as the monkey puzzle tree and this species still seems to have a certain popularity. Although one sees some very scruffy specimens in gardens, it can make a very attractive tree – but it needs space. Its long tentacle-like branches have dark glossy green leaves, the points of which are very sharp. It prefers moist soils and will not usually succeed in industrial areas. It is a large tree attaining a height of 4 to 5 ft. after ten years and 70 to 90 ft. at maturity.

Cedrus
The cedars are some of the most useful and beautiful of conifers but once again must be planted with care, as most species grow extremely large in time. All have spirally arranged tufted leaves and, with age, large cones.

The Atlas or blue cedar, *Cedrus atlantica glauca*, is one of our most attractive conifers but it grows too large to be considered ideal for the average suburban garden. At ten years it will be 10 to 15 ft. high; at maturity 100 to 120 ft. Most plants on sale will be grafted and will need a cane or stake to train the leading shoot upwards. Once over 5 to 6 ft. it will find its own way upwards with no further assistance. This variety has striking blue foliage but there is a golden and much slower-growing form *aurea* which is a worthwhile garden plant.

C. deodara, the Himalayan or Deodar cedar, is a graceful and imposing tree but I cannot stress too much that with such large-growing trees – at ten years it will reach 10 to 15 ft. and ultimately 130 to 150 ft. – it is sometimes better to avoid the temptation to try it in a small garden. Its branches, which are clothed in long green needles or leaves, droop at the tips and the leader is typically arched in growth.

Chamaecyparis
This group, commonly known as the false cypresses, consists of a number of species and innumerable varieties of plants and includes some of the most popular garden conifers in the United Kingdom.

However, none of the species is native to the United Kingdom or to Europe, as one might expect, but they mostly originate from North America and Japan.

Many are still referred to as *Cupressus* but this is in fact a separate group (see p. 74).

Most are easy to grow, preferring situations of good drainage but a reasonable amount of moisture.

Chamaecyparis lawsoniana, the Lawson cypress, is perhaps the best-known conifer type planted in Britain, but was itself only introduced from western North America barely a hundred years ago. A great many varieties of this species have since been introduced and are often lumped under the general heading of Lawson's but such is the variety of colours, shapes and sizes in this group that this can be misleading. *C. lawsoniana* itself is often used as a hedging plant these days but seldom as a specimen, having been superseded by some of its varieties for such purposes. Although varying somewhat in habit and rate of growth, most seedlings would grow 10 to 12 ft. in ten years and eventually anything from 75 to 100 ft. at maturity.

C.l. allumii is one of the most widely grown varieties with bluish foliage and a narrow pyramidal habit. Of medium growth, it could be expected to grow 8 to 10 ft. in its first ten years and eventually 30 to 40 ft. In my opinion *C. l. columnaris*

Chamaecyparis pisifera nana

sometimes listed as *columnaris glauca* is a more attractive variety, varying in its denser foliage and as the name suggests a more columnar habit. The blue is if anything more intense. Its rate of growth is a little slower than *allumii* and it would be likely to reach only 30 ft. at maturity.

There is little doubt that *C. l. ellwoodii* is the most popular garden conifer in Great Britain. It has close grey-green foliage and although often classed as a dwarf or rock garden conifer it grows quite vigorously in the first ten years to 6 ft. or so and eventually reaches 20 ft. or more. However, it is an attractive and valuable variety, the habit of which can vary but would normally be described as columnar.

Of fairly recent introduction is Ellwood's Gold, a copy in habit of *ellwoodii* if a bit slower in growth. Less a real gold than the name suggests, it is nonetheless a good garden plant and particularly pleasant in spring when the new yellow-tipped growths appear. *C. l. lanei* is one of the popular medium-growing, golden-yellow varieties and still one of the best. Because there is so little else to see in the winter I feel it is important when choosing conifers to make a selection with this in mind. *Lanei* suits this purpose admirably, being nearly as bright a yellow in winter as in summer. The variety *lutea* is equally useful but lacks the bright winter colour. Both reach about 8 to 10 ft. after ten years and ultimately 30 to 40 ft.

C. l. minima aurea is, as one might suspect, a dwarf form but to my mind one of the most beautiful of all conifers. It has densely packed, bright yellow foliage the year round, ideal for a rock garden or at the front of a heather border. Growing about 1 ft. in ten years and even after twenty or thirty years still likely to be under 6 ft., it could not be described as a plant that gets out of hand! Plants on sale are likely to be small as one might expect.

There is a green and more rounded variety in *minima glauca* which has a similar rate of growth to *minima aurea* and tends to grow on you with age! Pembury Blue has probably the bluest colour of all the medium-growing varieties especially in summer when its foliage attains a brilliant silvery hue. Broadly conical in habit, its leaves are coarser and more open than either *allumii* or *columnaris*. At ten years of age it can be expected to be about 10 ft. and eventually 30 to 40 ft. tall.

C. l. pygmaea argentea is another gem of a plant. A really slow-growing conifer which will even in maturity not exceed 3 ft., reaching perhaps 1 ft. after ten years. Compact and rounded in habit the bottom foliage is sea green but all the exposed growing tips are silvery white the year round. If planted in a sunny position against a contrasting background, a quite startling effect can be created.

C. l. stewartii is one of the oldest of the golden varieties but is still distinct and remains a useful plant for a medium to large garden. It is in fact more golden than yellow, but tends to lose its colour more in winter than either *lanei* or *lutea*. At ten years it will grow to about 10 to 12 ft. and ultimately 30 to 40 ft.

Although there are a great many other golden varieties grown, many are not as proven as the three so far mentioned, although Stardust, a recent introduction from Holland, looks distinct and seems to be an easy grower with good, year-round colour.

It is inevitable that many good varieties cannot be mentioned because of space, but a last and distinctive *C. lawsoniana* form is of a completely different habit. *C. l. tamariscifolia* is a spreading variety eventually forming a large bush much wider than high. It has bright green foliage winter and summer and this comes in overlapping sprays. It is sometimes listed in catalogues under the name of *knowfieldensis*. In ten years it will have attained a height of 3 ft. and a spread of 5 ft., and at maturity possibly 8 to 10 ft. high by 12 to 15 ft. across, so it will eventually need considerable space.

C. nootkatensis originates from western America and is generally much hardier than *C. lawsoniana*, but certainly not so well known. It is perhaps better known as one of the parents to the hybrid *Cupressocyparis leylandii*, although a useful tree in its own right. Reaching 10 to 15 ft. in its first ten years, it will eventually attain forest-tree proportions of 90 to 100 ft. There are one or two useful forms – *glauca*, similar in habit but a more glaucous tinge to the foliage, and an attractive form *lutea* which deserves wider recognition. There is also a weeping form *pendula* which becomes an extremely beautiful plant with age but admittedly does not make much of a show in its first five to ten years. All are medium to large growers and not really suitable except for the larger garden.

C. obtusa originates from Japan and although the species known as the Hinoki cypress is a large-growing tree, it has given us a great many attractive garden forms, only a few of which can be mentioned. Perhaps the most widely known variety is *nana gracilis* which has the typical dark glossy green foliage of the species. It has large, shell-shaped, flattened sprays and although eventually assuming a broadly conical shape it spends some years as a rounded bush. It is often seen as the typical Japanese garden or bonsai plant. Although at ten years reaching about 2 ft., it can at maturity attain 15 to 18 ft., but one could be safe for a number of years planting it on a rock garden.

There are several extremely dwarf forms which even after fifty years may not be more than 2 ft. in height. The true *C. o. nana* is one of these, forming a flat-topped miniature bush. One of my favourite conifers is *C. o. nana lutea* which is again of a very slow growth – at ten years it will be about 1 ft. high but will be unlikely to ever exceed 3 ft. It has wonderful golden foliage the year round with a touch of white in the outer leaves. A choice plant but ideal for a small garden and once again it needs planting in the sun.

C. pisifera is another species originating from Japan and is known as the Sawara cypress. The species is not a good garden plant although there are many varieties of great merit. However, all varieties share the likes of the species in that they like ample moisture at the roots and not too arid an atmosphere or cold winds. They do not normally grow so well in highly alkaline or heavy clay soils as in acid or peaty conditions.

C. pisifera Boulevard was introduced some years ago in the United States but seems far more suited to the English climate and has achieved quite rapid popularity for a relatively recent introduction. Although attractive the year round it is at its best in summer when the foliage turns an intense silvery blue. Its habit is conical, the foliage dense and although classed as a dwarf conifer it will after ten years reach 6 ft. and ultimately perhaps 15 to 20 ft.

A most unusual but nonetheless attractive variety of the Sawara cypress is *filifera aurea*. Of a bright golden-yellow colour both winter and summer *filifera aurea* and its green forms have unusual thread-like foliage. As young plants they can look scruffy but give them a year or two and they will build up into extremely graceful bushes of a broad conical outline. *Filifera aurea* at ten years old will be about 3 to 4 ft. and eventually will reach 15 to 18 ft.

For a real dwarf *C. p. nana* takes some beating. It has tightly congested foliage of mid-green although there are forms which are more than open in habit. The true plant will remain less than 6 in. high in its first ten years and probably never exceed 18 to 24 in. at maturity, but many have a spread of 3 ft. or more by that time. Any signs of a stray shoot trying to grow away should be pruned out immediately.

Lastly to varieties which are popular and useful garden plants but which sometimes get confused with each other – and one can hardly wonder at it when the names are so similar. *C. p. plumosa aurea* and *C. p. plumosa aurea nana* both have soft feathery foliage but *plumosa aurea* grows 4 to 5 ft. in ten years and ultimately over 20 ft. whilst *plumosa aurea nana* as the name suggests would reach about 2 ft. and ultimately only about 6 ft. The latter is also much more golden in winter and in my opinion a much more desirable plant.

Cryptomeria

The genus *Cryptomeria* consists of only one species *C. japonica* which is native to Japan and China, but this has given rise to a multitude of varieties, many of which are excellent for the garden, others just oddities. *C. j. elegans* is one of the better-known varieties of medium growth with soft juvenile foliage. It turns from a summer colour of light browny green to copper bronze in autumn and winter, blending well with the more usual autumn tints of other trees and shrubs. From about 6 ft. in ten years, it will grow to 20 to 25 ft.

C. j. lobbii nana is a slow-growing form making in time a rounded bush with bunches of foliage making separate growths over the plant. Light green in summer, it turns bronze green during the winter. After ten years it will make a bush of about 2 ft. high and as much across and eventually 6 to 8 ft. high and maybe 10 ft. broad.

A dwarf variety ideal for the rock garden is *C. j. vilmoriniana* which makes a very tightly congested bush. Hardly reaching 1 ft. after ten years, it will not be likely to exceed 3 ft. after fifty years. It turns from a bright green in summer to almost a reddish-purple colour in winter depending upon the plant's exposure to the weather.

Cupressus

If the genus *Chamaecyparis* is called the false cypress, this must be termed the true cypress. It is, in fact, a quite distinct genus. Most species are columnar or conical in habit and have thin rounded leaves, one main central stem and a tap root. Usually of vigorous growth they do not transplant easily as older specimens and in fact are most successful when planted small and from containers. Some species and varieties are not reliably hardy in the British Isles.

Cupressus glabra was until recently more commonly known as *C. arizonica*. The variety usually listed as *conica* is most often used as a garden plant and makes an extremely attractive tree of blue grey. It could not be considered for a small garden as it grows in ten years 10 to 12 ft. and eventually may reach 60 ft.

Although the species *C. macrocarpa* is seldom planted these days because it has been to a large extent superseded by the much hardier and more useful hybrid *Cupressocyparis leylandii*, it has given rise to several golden forms ideal for garden use. One of the best must surely be Goldcrest which has bright yellow foliage the year round. This is quite vigorous and grows to 12 to 15 ft. in ten years and ultimately 40 ft. or more. All forms of *C. macrocarpa* seem to do well in seaside areas as far as withstanding salt spray but are not so good at withstanding strong winds.

Cupressocyparis leylandii The Leyland cypress must by now be one of the best-known conifers in England. It is a hybrid between *Cupressus macrocarpa* and *Chamaecyparis nootkatensis* and has been given the rapid growth of the former with some of the hardiness and more attractive habit of the latter. Although of fairly recent commercial introduction it is now widely used for screening and hedging for which purposes it is admirably suited. Because of its rapid growth and ultimate height, if left to its own devices, of nearly 100 ft., it will not stand being kept at a hedge height of under 8 ft. indefinitely. Even after ten years it will probably be in the region of 25 to 30 ft. – prodigious growth indeed and understandingly popular in this age of instant gardening!

The foliage is of a rich green during summer, dulling somewhat in winter. It transplants quite easily but plants under 3 ft. are more likely to become established quicker than larger specimens. As a hedge, plants should be spaced about 3 ft. apart and trimmed once or twice annually. It is not fussy as to soils and one would find it difficult to criticize this as a plant except to warn gardeners of planning before they plant.

Ginkgo

The unusual name *Ginkgo biloba* covers a very unusual conifer known commonly as the maidenhair tree. It is a deciduous conifer which may seem a contradiction in terms but it is not unique in that so much as its direct ancestors go back 150 million years!

Of very slow growth it eventually makes quite a sizeable tree of over 50 ft. It has fan-shaped leaves of pale green which turn to a beautiful golden yellow in autumn before dropping. One might imagine it would be a difficult plant to grow but it is quite amenable as to soils and will even succeed in industrial areas.

Juniperus

The junipers are deservedly gaining in popularity as garden plants and a much wider range is being introduced to the British Isles from other parts of the world to give the gardener an even better choice. Most species are very hardy and grow successfully in even the poorest of soils, whether acid or alkaline. There is such a wide range of colours, shapes and forms in this genus that one would make quite an attractive garden growing only junipers. Unfortunately only a limited selection can be made here.

Juniperus chinensis aurea is an excellent garden variety of the Chinese juniper. Although very slow growing initially, even to the point of finding it difficult to assert a leading shoot, it eventually makes a beautiful golden columnar-shaped specimen. What adds to the attraction is that the plant usually carries both adult and juvenile foliage giving it more variety in shade and texture. Perhaps growing only 3 ft. in ten years, it eventually may get as high as 30 ft.

One of the bluest junipers is *J. c. pyramidalis* which has a broadly conical habit and very prickly foliage. After ten

Above left: *Cupressocyparis leylandii*
Left: *Ginkgo biloba*

74

years it will grow to 5 or 6 ft. and with age broaden and grow as high as 15 to 20 ft. Like many junipers it is better planted in an open position.

J. communis is one of the three conifers native to the British Isles. It has given us several useful garden forms, some upright, some prostrate. *J. c. compressa* is quite a unique variety with its perfectly symmetrical outline, its slowness of growth and its usefulness as a sink or trough garden conifer. It is a must for the rock garden also and looks particularly attractive planted in groups of three or more. Bright green in summer, it turns a bluish-green hue in winter. Perhaps at ten years reaching 12 to 18 in., it will be very rare to see a specimen over 3 to 4 ft.

J. c. depressa aurea is a golden prostrate form of great merit. It needs to be planted in an open position for best effect where its butter-yellow shoots in spring provide a beautiful effect. The foliage turns a bronzy hue in winter with the silver undersides of the leaves more prominent. One should expect a spread of 3 to 4 ft. in ten years and increasing after many more years to 10 to 12 ft.

J. c. hibernica, known as the Irish juniper, is useful where an upright conifer is required. This will eventually reach 18 to 20 ft. One of the best ground-cover junipers is *J. c. repanda* which makes a very vigorous dark green carpet which turns a greeny brown during the winter months. It has a similar rate of growth to *depressa aurea*.

J. horizontalis is commonly known as the creeping juniper and this name describes the habit of the species and its many varieties admirably. The species originates from North America where it and many varieties are grown widely for garden and landscape use.

The most popular form in Europe is *J. h. glauca*, a carpet-forming plant which roots from runners as it spreads across the ground. The foliage is bright steel blue in summer, grey green in winter. To increase the density the runners can be pruned back occasionally. Similar forms occur in *douglasii*, Bar Harbor and *wiltonii*. All will spread quite rapidly covering a diameter of 6 to 8 ft. in ten years and ultimately considerably more. New and distinct varieties are likely to be introduced to Europe from the United States but one which is available and probably the best for ground cover is *J. h. plumosa*, the Andorra juniper. Where varieties so far

Above: *Juniperus communis depressa aurea*
Right: **Many dwarf conifers can be accommodated in a relatively small space**

mentioned grow flat to the ground, this will reach 1½ to 2 ft. in height providing a more effective smother to weeds. The foliage is softer and more feathery, the colour grey green turning a purple hue in winter. All *J. horizontalis* varieties are extremely hardy.

J. media includes some forms which may be listed under *J. chinensis* in books and catalogues. I think it is now generally accepted that they should belong in this grouping but the main thing from a gardener's point of view is that all those mentioned here are excellent garden plants. *J. m. hetzii* is an extremely vigorous semi-prostrate variety. It has grey-green foliage the year through and can be used as a specimen plant, as a low hedge or as a ground-cover plant. To increase density pruning will be necessary but in no way detrimental to the plant. Tolerant of alkaline soils it will grow better in sun than shade. An all-purpose plant but give it room as by the time it is ten years old it will be 5 ft. high and 6 ft across, eventually spreading 12 ft. across by 8 to 10 ft. in height. But also remember the pruning! Old Gold is in my opinion better in a smaller garden than *J. m. pfitzeriana aurea*. It is much more compact in growth with a better, year-round golden colour. It will probably reach 2½ to 3 ft. in ten years and spread 3 to 4 ft. against 3 ft. by 6 ft. for *pfitzeriana aurea* over the same period. Ultimately it may be 6 ft. high and 8 ft. across whilst *pfitzeriana aurea* might be 6 ft. high but 12 ft. or more in diameter. The green *J. m. pfitzeriana* is even more vigorous although like the garden form an excellent ground coverer. It is not for the small garden I suspect but hardy and adaptable succeeding well on chalk. Forms may vary from nearly prostrate to maybe 10 ft. or more in height. The growth rate for *pfitzeriana aurea* applies but perhaps add 30 per cent. on both the ten-year and ultimate figures.

J. sabina, the savin juniper, has given us many useful garden forms, mostly prostrate or semi-prostrate in habit. All have the pungent odour of the species when the foliage is crushed. The variety Blue Danube doesn't really live up to its name as far as the blue is concerned but otherwise it is a very attractive garden plant, especially when used as a ground coverer. It will grow quite rapidly – in ten years about 3 ft. high and a spread of 6 to 8 ft., eventually 4 ft. high and 15 ft. across.

Almost the most popular prostrate variety of juniper is *J. s. tamariscifolia* which makes a beautiful specimen with age, building itself up in layers and covering a wide area. It is particularly attractive

on a large rock garden or a bank where it moulds itself into the contours. The foliage colour is grey blue. After ten years it should grow about 1 ft. high but spreading 3 ft. However, as branches root along the ground, it can spread to 15 ft. or more in time and attain a height of 18 in. to 2 ft.

Of recent introduction to Europe are forms of *J. scopulorum*, the Rocky Mountain juniper, which are very popular in the United States. They are mostly medium growers with conical or pyramidal habits. They would appear to be tolerant of most soil conditions but need to be placed in exposed or sunny situations for best results. Perhaps the best known is Skyrocket, a name which speaks for itself. This makes an extremely narrow column of blue grey, growing 7 to 8 ft. in ten years and ultimately 20 to 25 ft. It is extremely useful as an accent plant as are some of the others such as Blue Heaven of similar growth rate but a more pyramidal habit. The colour of the foliage is an intense silvery blue in summer but dulls somewhat in winter. Springbank has bright silver-grey foliage but much thinner branches. It is somewhat slower in growth than the previous two mentioned.

J. squamata has given us a few good forms and Blue Star, although only of recent introduction, promises to be one of the best for the smaller garden. It is slow growing with dense steel blue foliage and a bushy habit. It is likely in ten years to be 12 to 18 in. in height with a similar spread, and (taking a guess at it) probably at maturity 2 to 3 ft. high by 3 to 4 ft. across. Probably the best-known form of the species is *meyeri* which was introduced from China early this century and is now

grown all over the world. It is also steel blue in colour, making a somewhat irregular bush with nodding leading shoots which are typical of the species. It needs an open position and some trimming may be necessary from time to time – these precautions will help to prevent the browning of the foliage sometimes seen on older specimens.

J. virginiana is native to the eastern United States and Canada and there is known as the pencil cedar as the species generally has a narrowly columnar shape. It and the garden forms it has produced are all very hardy and amenable to most soil conditions. The variety *burkii* is known in the British Isles but not used widely which is a pity. It is a useful plant with a broadly conical habit, the dense foliage blue grey in summer, turning a purplish hue in winter. Growing 8 to 10 ft. high in ten years, it will ultimately reach 20 to 25 ft.

One of the best of all the semi-prostrate junipers is *J. v.* Grey Owl which has thin spreading branches of grey blue and is extremely vigorous in growth. A useful ground-cover plant it will, however, eventually need more space than is available in some gardens. After ten years it will probably reach 12 to 18 in. in height and spread 8 to 10 ft. and after several more years 3 to 4 ft. in height with a spread of 15 to 18 ft.

Larix

The larches, whilst beautiful trees in any context, are generally unsuitable for all but the largest gardens. All species drop

Juniperus media pfitzeriana aurea

76

Above right: *Metasequoia glyptostroboides*
Above: *Picea breweriana*

their leaves in the autumn many keeping in tune with deciduous trees by turning yellow and golden before doing so. Most have the distinctive tufted growth of the new leaves in the spring which is most attractive. Both species normally seen in the British Isles are used as forest trees and of course attain eventual heights of around about 100 ft. These are *Larix decidua*, the European larch, and *L. leptolepis*, the Japanese larch.

Libocedrus

The species most commonly associated with the genus is *Libocedrus decurrens* which is now often listed by botanists under the genus *Calocedrus*. *L. decurrens* or *Calocedrus decurrens* is known as the incense cedar and whilst eventually making a large tree it is quite slow growing and being quite narrow in habit could be used more as a garden plant. It has rich green foliage throughout the year with fan-shaped flattened branches. Growing 8 to 10 ft. in ten years, it will under good conditions eventually grow to 80 to 100 ft. so be careful!

Metasequoia

Metasequoia is, as they say, 'a tree with a story'! There is only one species known and this is *Metasequoia glyptostroboides*, more easily remembered under the common name the dawn redwood. It was dis-

covered in China as recently as 1941 and was before that time thought to be extinct and only to be found in fossilized form. Since that one plant was found it has now been distributed throughout the world and is generally available from many nurseries.

It has an open pyramidal habit with feathery bright green plumed leaves in summer turning bronze in autumn and dropping its leaves before the winter. This is not strictly a good garden plant on account of its size reaching 15 to 18 ft. after ten years and ultimately about 100 ft.; it is nonetheless attractive with a very unusual and interesting history.

Picea

The spruces have given us a multitude of good garden varieties, although many are not generally available except from specialist nurseries. This is primarily because many varieties have to be grafted which is a specialist propagation procedure. Many fine varieties are likely to become widely known when supplies become more readily available, but in the meantime prices are likely to be high and some searching through specialist catalogues will be necessary to track down some of the most desirable forms.

Picea abies is known more commonly as the Norway spruce or even more commonly as the Christmas tree in the British Isles. The species is used only as a forest tree and is not recommended as a garden conifer even though it may look attractive in its early years.

Some confusion exists with the naming of many of the dwarf forms but here follows a selection of some of the most distinctive.

P. a. gregoryana makes a very slow-growing hummock of tight dark green foliage which is prickly to the touch. Most of the *abies* varieties have brownish resinous winter buds which add to their attractiveness. After ten years *gregoryana* will make a cushion-shaped plant about 6 to 8 in. high and will ultimately only reach 18 to 20 in. in height but spreading perhaps 3 to 4 ft.

P. a. nidiformis is a most attractive dwarf spruce for any garden. It has a flat-topped and spreading habit, dark green with typical brown resinous winter buds which open in spring to produce the bright green shoots for the next season's growth. From 12 to 15 in. high by perhaps 2 ft. in width after ten years it will grow eventually as high as 3 to 6 ft. and spread 8 to 9 ft. A variety with a more upright habit is *ohlendorffii*. It has the same dark green foliage as the previous variety and dark orange-brown winter buds.

P. breweriana must be classed as one of the most beautiful of all conifers – but it takes many years in most situations to attain this stature. Broadly conical in habit it has long pendulous branches with dark blue-green foliage. It prefers a situation of some shelter and even slight shade but enjoys plenty of moisture. Although eventually becoming a large tree it will probably only grow 4 to 5 ft. in its first ten years and after a great many more attain possibly 45 to 50 ft.

One of the most popular and widely grown spruces is *P. glauca albertiana conica*. It is very hardy and not difficult to grow, a splendid garden plant, making a perfect cone-shaped specimen. The foliage is dark green except for the period in spring and early summer when its new growth gives it a bright emerald-green colour. This plant should in my opinion be in every garden although one has to admit it does seem to get attacked by its fair share of pests such as red spider mite. However, these can be controlled quite easily by spraying with a systemic insecticide once or twice through the summer months. After ten years it will grow to about 4 ft. and at maturity maybe as much as 10 to 12 ft.

P. omorika, the Serbian spruce, is once again rather too large for all except the largest of gardens, but is one of the most trouble-free conifers and certainly one of the most attractive of spruces. With its narrow pyramidal habit and leaves of dark green, it associates well with silver birch and makes an excellent screening or accent plant with its stately bearing. Reaching 8 to 10 ft. at ten years of age, it will eventually grow to 60 to 75 ft.

P. pungens has given us some of the most exciting silver and blue varieties of any genus – but all named forms need to be propagated by grafting – hence the scarcity of these in general circulation. Selections of seedlings from the species *P. pungens* are often made and these forms will generally be listed as *P. p. glauca* and can of course vary considerably. A selected dwarf form of great merit is *P. p. globosa* which makes a dense bush of silver blue. It is a beautiful foliage form and particularly useful for the small garden, growing in ten years perhaps 2 ft. high and eventually 4 to 5 ft. with a similar spread.

Of the upright and larger-growing forms there is quite a wide selection but any of them could be considered worth having. Perhaps the most widely available is Koster. This has a pyramidal shape but like all the grafted forms it may take a year or two of training the leading shoot in a vertical position before it decides to grow that way on its own account. It is a silver blue the year round but the colour is particularly pronounced in the early summer when new shoots appear. Growing 6 to 8 ft. in ten years, it will eventually reach 20 to 30 ft. Normally these *P. pungens* varieties have no particular fads or fancies but they prefer an open position. Other varieties of merit are *spekii* and *moer-*

heimii and there are many more as yet almost unobtainable in Britain.

Pinus

The pines are some of our most picturesque trees, both in the landscape and in gardens whilst among the many species and varieties in this genus are some to fit every purpose. Once again many of the varieties have to be propagated by grafting and so will not be so readily available as seedling raised plants or those which come from cuttings. They are also likely to be more expensive. Most are easy to grow, many succeeding on very poor dry soils where other conifers would fail. Some species are used for forestry purposes and among these is one of our three British native conifers, *Pinus sylvestris*, the Scots pine. All pines have needle-like foliage and most species grow cones when well established which vary somewhat in size, shape and attractiveness.

P. cembra to my mind should be grown more widely than at present. Its common name is the Swiss stone pine and it makes a broad conical-shaped tree in time, retaining its bottom branches even as a mature specimen. The dark blue-green foliage only changes each spring when distinctive orange-brown shoots appear to herald another season's growth. Slow growing during its first few years, it may only be 6 to 7 ft. at the ten-year stage but eventually reaches 30 to 40 ft.

P. densiflora, the Japanese red pine, is somewhat similar to the Scots pine, *P. sylvestris*, but although it is not often used in the British Isles it has given us a few useful dwarf forms, the most notable of which is *P. d. umbraculifera*. This unwieldy name when translated from latin means umbrella and this is indeed somewhat descriptive of the habit of a mature specimen of this plant. It has long dark green leaves which turn somewhat bronzed in winter. At ten years old it will be 3 to 4 ft. and ultimately perhaps 10 to 12 ft. high with almost a similar spread.

Although again perhaps too rapid growing for all but the largest gardens *P. griffithii*, or *P. wallichiana* as it should be now known, is such a beautiful tree that I feel it should be included in this section. It originated from the Himalayan Mountains and is commonly known as the Bhutan pine. It has long bluish-green needles and a very graceful broadly conical habit. Reaching 15 ft. in ten years, it will grow to well over 100 ft. at maturity.

P. mugo, the mountain pine, grows wild all over the mountains of central Europe, varying considerably in habit and rate of growth and as a garden plant can be

expected to make a medium to large shrub. It is therefore somewhat difficult to give any more explicit indications as to rates of growth. Nonetheless it can make a most attractive garden plant but if a more regulated form is required the variety Gnom is worth looking for. This is of course grafted and can be expected to grow 2 to 3 ft. high and spread about the same in its first ten years, eventually reaching a height and spread of 5 to 6 ft.

P. nigra, the Austrian pine, offers an alternative to the Scots pine for use as a windbreak and screen. It has dark green foliage, a colour held throughout the year, is hardy and adaptable to most soil conditions. It is conical when young but loses its bottom branches with age becoming more mop headed or flat topped. Eventually growing to 60 to 100 ft., it will at ten years reach 6 to 10 ft. so could not really be considered for the small garden. It has produced some useful dwarf forms.

P. parviflora, the Japanese white pine, is an attractive species which is not grown widely in the British Isles at present. It has light bluish-green leaves and cones of greenish blue until they ripen. There is a selected form which is one of the most beautiful slow-growing pines, *P. p. glauca*. It has a narrower and more ascending habit than the species with distinctively blue leaves. Both have similar rates of growth reaching 6 to 8 ft. in ten years and eventually 20 to 30 ft.

a. *Thuja occidentalis* **Rheingold**
b. *Chamaecyparis lawsoniana lanei*
c. *Santolina chamaecyparissus*
d. *Chamaecyparis lawsoniana* **Blue Nantais**
e. *Chamaecyparis lawsoniana lutea*
f. *Juniperus squamata meyeri*
g. *Calluna vulgaris* **Golden Carpet**
h. *Erica cinerea* **Atrosanguinea Smith's Variety**
i. *Abies koreana* **Prostrate Beauty**

P. sylvestris is a familiar sight on the British landscape with its craggy appearance as a mature specimen. The Scots pine varies as do most species in habit and rate of growth but it normally makes a medium to large tree. Conical when young it becomes mop headed or flat topped with age losing its lower branches in the process. The foliage is blue green, the bark reddish when it becomes exposed. At ten years it will grow 10 to 15 ft. and at maturity anything from 45 to 100 ft. It has given us some useful garden forms not least of which is the golden Scots pine, *P. s. aurea*, which is similar to the species in all respects except that the leaves turn a wonderful yellow during the winter months – a real bonus! It will grow 4 to 5 ft. in ten years and eventually maybe 15 to 20 ft.

One of the dwarfest pines is *P. s. beuvronensis* which makes a dense blue-green bush wider than high. Like all plants and particularly dwarf conifers if grown on poor soil or with a restricted root run, it will be much dwarfer than if given extremely fertile conditions. With age it may become more vigorous than my growth estimates suggest, but at any rate it is a first-class garden plant. After ten years it may have made 2 to 3 ft. in height and spread, ultimately 4 to 5 ft. in height and spreading as much as 8 to 10 ft.

Many other dwarf and slow-growing forms of *P. sylvestris* are in existence but not many will be readily available in nurserymen's catalogues at present. On that sad note we leave the pines.

Podocarpus
Podocarpus is a genus which originates from the southern hemisphere and apart from a few species it is not hardy in our climate. The best known and to my mind most useful species is *Podocarpus nivalis* which is a native of New Zealand. It makes a compact bush with very dark green leaves reminiscent of a yew. Hardy and amenable to most soil conditions including those containing lime, it could be more widely known. Plants vary but at ten years it will grow perhaps only 6 to 8 in. and after many years perhaps 1½ to 2 ft. in height and 3 to 4 ft. across.

Pseudotsuga
The genus contains five species, the best known of which is *Pseudotsuga menziesii*, the Douglas fir, a giant tree not at all suitable for gardens. However, this species in turn has produced a few dwarf forms, the best known of which is *fletcheri*. This makes an irregular flat-topped bush with blue-green foliage. It is quite different to

any other dwarf conifer and extremely attractive at all stages of development and in my opinion needs to be better known. At ten years it will make a bush 2 to 2½ ft. in height by 3 ft. across and after many more years perhaps 3 to 6 ft. high by 8 to 10 ft. in width.

Sciadopitys
Sciadopitys, known as the Japanese umbrella pine, is a genus with only one species. *Sciadopitys verticillata* is a most distinctive tree looking rather like a pine which it is not. It has glossy green leaves or needles which are quite thick and rigid rather than grassy to the touch. It is an extremely slow grower for the first few years reaching perhaps 3 to 4 ft. in ten years but gaining strength and vigour with advancing years to eventually end up as a tree of some 30 to 35 ft.

Sequoia
Sequoia has also only one species attached to its name, this being *Sequoia sempervirens*, the Californian redwood, which can in no way be considered a garden plant growing even in the British Isles over 150 ft. However, it has produced one interesting slow-growing or dwarf conifer in *S. s. adpressa*. This, if left to its own devices, would make a straggling bush or small tree of up to 30 ft. Trimmed regularly to a bush of not more than 3 ft. in height it will give a great amount of pleasure as a most beautiful artificial dwarf variety. The tips of the foliage in the summer will turn creamy white so that the bush looks as though it is covered in snow. Worth a bit of trouble, this plant!

Sequoiadendron
Sequoiadendron again is represented by one species *Sequoiadendron giganteum*, more commonly known in the British Isles as a wellingtonia. It is also called the mammoth tree on account of its ultimate size and whilst an attractive and spectacular tree it will eventually grow to 150 ft. or more so cannot be considered for the garden.

Taxodium
Taxodium is one of the few deciduous genera among the cone-bearing family which we call conifers and it originates from the south eastern United States and Mexico. The best-known species is *Taxodium distichum*, the swamp cypress. When grown in water or very close to the water it develops large roots which protrude well above ground. It will succeed in all soils where not too dry. Bright fresh green leaves in spring and summer turn bronze

in autumn before dropping. A beautiful and stately tree it will get large in time. After ten years it will grow to about 15 ft. and eventually will attain 100 ft. or more.

Taxus
The yews are a very variable but useful group of plants which have somewhat dropped from favour in the public eye over the past few years. As commonly seen in the British landscape they are dark and sombre and associated somehow with cemeteries and graveyards – an association which needs dispelling as there is a very wide range of shapes, forms and colours available for garden use.

They are adaptable to most soil conditions, succeeding well on chalk and lime and tolerating quite dry shady conditions but all require good drainage. Some forms make excellent hedges and all withstand clipping well.

Taxus baccata, the common or English yew, is one of Britain's three native conifers and as such is so variable in shape and habit that no clear indication as to rates of growth can be given. There have been a great many varieties produced from this species, one of the most widely used being *fastigiata*, the Irish yew. This makes a narrow column, broadening considerably with age with the typical dark, almost black-green foliage of the species. A far more attractive form for the garden is the golden *fastigiata aurea* which has a similar habit but has deep yellow-green leaves turning a golden hue in winter, particularly when planted in an open sunny position. At ten years it will be 5 to 6 ft. in height and eventually may reach as much as 15 to 18 ft.

A useful ground-cover plant is *T. b. repandens* which is almost prostrate in habit with dark green leaves. It will grow well in shade which gives it particular importance as a landscaping specimen. Of similar habit though a little more prostrate and open is *T. b. repens aurea* which is a golden-variegated variety and particularly attractive when the new season's growth begins each early summer. A newish variety from Holland called Summergold also looks promising. This is semi-prostrate and as the name suggests has foliage of a soft golden colour. Both can be expected to grow 12 in. or so in height and spread 3 to 4 ft. in ten years and eventually 2 to 3 ft. in height and perhaps 10 to 12 ft. across after a great many years. Naturally I am only making a rough guess at this!

Lastly one of the most attractive of the golden-foliaged yews is *T. b. semperaurea* which is slow growing and makes a vase-shaped bush of golden yellow throughout the year. After ten years it will grow to perhaps 3 ft. in height and eventually will reach a height of 8 to 10 ft. with a similar width.

T. cuspidata, the Japanese yew, and its forms are not grown much in Europe but are widely used in the United States because of their superior hardiness to *T. baccata*. It makes a small to medium-sized tree in its native Japan but it is in its selected varieties that it is most useful. *T. c. nana* is the variety most seen in Europe, making a dwarf, irregularly shaped bush which will need pruning to keep it attractive. Not in my opinion a particularly desirable conifer.

T. media is a hybrid between *T. baccata* and *T. cuspidata* and in truly American fashion has been dubbed the Anglo-Japanese yew. This hybrid makes a medium to large-sized spreading shrub and it and its varieties are widely used in the United States. The most commonly seen variety in Europe is *hicksii* which makes a dense columnar bush of dark green and is probably the best form for hedging purposes. Growing 5 to 6 ft. in ten years, it will eventually reach 20 ft. or more with age.

Thuja

This genus has produced a great many good garden varieties and in appearance they are very like some of the false cypresses. There are only three species and all except some forms of *Thuja orientalis* are hardy in the British Isles. Apart from a dislike of badly drained situations all are reliably easy to grow.

T. occidentalis, the white cedar, originates from eastern North America and is the hardiest of the three species. The species itself is not used as a garden plant but it has given us many forms suitable for individual specimens and for hedging purposes. It has aromatic foliage particularly when crushed.

T. o. danica, as the name suggests, originated in Denmark. It is a very attractive dwarf variety forming a dense rounded bush somewhat like a cushion with erectly held flattened foliage sprays. Bright green in summer, it turns slightly bronze in winter. After ten years it can be expected to be about 1 ft. high by the same width and eventually 2 to 3 ft. high by a width of 3 to 4 ft. The variety Holmstrup makes a dense narrowly conical bush of bright green, holding its colour well throughout the year. A first-class reliable plant which was introduced a few years ago in Denmark and worthy of wider recognition, it will grow perhaps 3 to 4 ft.

in ten years and eventually 12 to 15 ft.

A similar form but faster growing and more open in habit is *T. o. lutea nana* which is golden yellow in summer, a colour which is almost intensified in winter – certainly a point to commend it for the garden. It is an extremely easy grower and will withstand exposed situations which cannot be said of some of the golden chamaecyparis varieties. Growing 4 to 5 ft. in ten years, it will probably end up at the 15 to 20-ft. mark.

The best variety for hedging is probably *T. o. pyramidalis* which is also known as *fastigiata*. It has a narrow columnar habit and if used as a hedge would need to be planted at not more than 2-ft. intervals. Tolerant of a wide range of conditions including some shade, this variety also makes an attractive specimen in its own right. It has densely held sprays of bright green foliage in summer, bronzing somewhat in winter. It of course withstands clipping well. At ten years it will grow 6 to 8 ft. and if allowed to grow to maturity probably 20 to 25 ft.

One of the best garden conifers is *T. o. Rheingold*, a slow-growing form which turns from golden yellow in summer to rich coppery gold in winter and in very hard winters almost reddish bronze. Quite often one will obtain plants with very soft feathery foliage which appear different to the more typical flattened sprays, or more often both types of foliage will appear on the same plant. Rheingold is an excellent garden plant and associates well with winter-flowering heathers. Like all golden forms the best colour will be obtained by placing it in a sunny position. After ten years it will reach approximately 4 to 5 ft. and eventually will make a broad-based bush 10 to 12 ft. high and as much across.

T. orientalis is known as the Chinese arbor-vitae or tree of life coming as it does from north and western China. The species makes a small tree mostly of conical habit which is not used much as a garden plant, although it has produced several useful dwarf and slow-growing garden varieties.

One of my favourite dwarf conifers is *T. o. aurea nana* which makes a densely foliaged bush of bright golden yellow in summer, turning yellow green in winter. The flattened foliage sprays are held erectly giving the plant a very neat attractive appearance. It will grow 2 to 2½ ft. in ten years and ultimately 5 to 8 ft. There appears to be more than one form in cultivation.

T. o. conspicua is a pyramidal variety of great attraction, a golden-yellow colour

Taxus baccata fastigiata

through most of the year but particularly bright in summer. It is a medium grower reaching 6 to 8 ft. in ten years and eventually as much as 18 to 25 ft. There is a similar but slower-growing variety in *T. o. elegantissima* which turns a deep bronze in winter.

Lastly a dwarf juvenile-foliaged form of some attraction is *T. o. juniperoides*, a rounded bush turning from a summer colour of greyish green to a striking deep purple in winter. Unfortunately like a few other forms of similar foliage and habit, it is not reliably hardy and tends to open up with age. Reaching 2 ft. in ten years, it is unlikely to exceed 3 ft. at a somewhat young age of maturity!

T. plicata, the western red cedar, as one might guess originates from western North America and is a very important timber tree. It is also an extremely useful tree for hedging although the selected form *atrovirens* is much better. *T. plicata* will grow too large as a garden specimen reaching well over 100 ft. at maturity. The foliage of this species is generally more rounded and glossy than the two so far mentioned and has a very pleasant odour when crushed. The species and all forms used for hedging withstand clipping very well and this is one of the few which will break new shoots from old wood if cut back hard – a definite advantage for this purpose.

T. p. rogersii is an unusual but very useful conifer for the small garden. It has very dense foliage, dark green inside the plant and tips of golden, yellow and bronze, particularly pronounced in winter, the whole effect giving a variegated look. Mostly globular in shape it will sometimes assume a leading shoot which alters its habit to conical. In ten years reaching 18 in. to 2 ft., it may ultimately grow to 5 to 6 ft. with a similar width.

A quite choice form which is not generally known is *T. p.* Stoneham Gold, a slow-growing variety with foliage of a really old-gold colour. The habit is somewhat irregular particularly in the early stages of growth, but the plant develops into a broadly conical bush. The inside of the plant is dark green, accentuating the golden tips of the leaves which turn bright golden bronze in winter. After ten years perhaps reaching 2 to 2½ ft., it will eventually grow to 6 to 7 ft. If a more regular-shaped plant is required then a hard trim will not be resented.

Thujopsis

Thujopsis is a very similar genus to thuja, but is only represented by one species *Thujopsis dolabrata*. This makes a medium-sized tree with a broadly pyramidal habit which has large flattened sprays of glossy green. Growing 6 to 8 ft. in ten years, it will eventually reach 30 to 35 ft. in the British Isles. There is a dwarf spreading form in *nana* of no great attraction.

Tsuga

This genus is usually known more commonly as the hemlock and has produced some very worthwhile garden forms which are not generally known to gardeners in the United Kingdom. This applies particularly to *Tsuga canadensis* and its varieties which are very popular in the United States and likely in time to become so in Europe. The foliage is generally similar to the yews but with much thinner leaves and branches of a more arching habit. They are tolerant of most soil conditions succeeding particularly well in soils that are both moist and well drained.

T. canadensis, the eastern hemlock, originates from the eastern United States and makes a large tree of pyramidal outline not really suitable for any but the largest gardens. It makes a tall graceful tree usually forked near the base, growing 12 to 15 ft. in ten years and ultimately between 75 to 100 ft. This species and its

varieties tolerate alkaline soil and in fact seem to prefer them to very acid conditions. There are several dwarf forms which will probably only be available from specialist nurseries at present.

Bennett makes an attractive flat-topped bush with graceful drooping branchlets. This and a very similar semi-prostrate variety Jeddeloh are distinct in offering new forms and texture to the choice of conifers available to the gardener. Both have the mid to light green foliage typical of the species. Both have similar rates of growth making plants of 12 to 18 in. high by a width of 3 to 4 ft. in ten years and eventually a height of 3 to 4 ft. and a width of up to 10 ft.

Cole is an extremely prostrate form which closely hugs the ground spreading slowly to a diameter of perhaps 2 to 3 ft. in ten years and ultimately up to 10 ft. or so. Probably the most familiar variety in Great Britain is *pendula* which makes a spreading bush, slowly building up in height but always with a very pendulous branching habit. Although slow it will eventually make a large plant as high as 6 to 8 ft. and as broad as 20 ft. although at the ten-year stage perhaps only 18 to 24 in. and 2½ to 3 ft. across. It is particularly effective if placed on a bank or a wall where the branches can cascade down the slope or over the edge as the case may be.

Heaths and Heathers

Few types of plants have risen in popularity to such an extent in recent years as heaths and heathers and it is easy to see why.

They are relatively trouble free, look attractive the year round and provide excellent ground cover. Furthermore they associate well with other plants and to my mind none better than with conifers.

Heathers in the Garden

Heathers is the term usually applied to both *Erica* and *Calluna*, although strictly speaking all ericas should be referred to as heaths and callunas as heathers. It should at the outset be stated that all the callunas and most of the summer-flowering ericas dislike alkaline soils. This problem can be overcome to some extent by the addition of quantities of peat, or, even better, by building a raised peat bed and with the help of a chemical called sequestrene. However, both remedies can be expensive so one should give it some thought before spending vast sums of money!

I hope this will serve as a warning but not a deterrent for there are a great many ericas that will grow well on alkaline soils, notably *Erica carnea* varieties and *E. darleyensis* varieties. These types are in many ways the most useful to the gardener because they give flower throughout the winter and early spring, a time when most gardens are notable for the absence of colour.

Heathers have one definite requirement whether they succeed on acid or alkaline soil and that is to be placed in a sunny position. They will grow in some shade but they will not usually flower well and will tend to become straggly. As with conifers, golden-foliaged forms will turn dull without sun to brighten them.

Planning

We have ascertained what sort of soil we have and that we need a sunny position for best effect. The next stage, if a heather border is to give the most worthwhile result, is to decide on the amount of the space available and which varieties to choose to give as much year-round colour as possible. This doesn't mean only selecting for colour of flower but colour of foliage, and of course the height the varieties will eventually grow to.

According to the space available one will need to decide how many plants of each variety can be used. Never plant less than three of a kind except for tree heaths where one will be ample. It will of course be more effective to use larger quantities than three but this will be entirely governed by the size of border you are able (or willing) to give.

Three plans are given overleaf which will give an indication of what can be done with a small or larger border, together with appropriate conifers for such a situation. Plans A and B are similar but B is for alkaline soils.

Planting

The first step should of course be the preparation of the border which in the case of heathers can be considerable according to the type of soil you have in your garden. Most soils will benefit from the addition of peat but if your conditions are either sandy and well drained or to the other extreme, heavy clay and poorly drained, they may need a considerable amount. But like most plants, good soil preparation is a basic principle for success.

Dig the soil well, cleaning out perennial weeds and mixing in moistened peat. If possible get some slight elevation to your border either in the middle, or rising from where it will be most often viewed. This

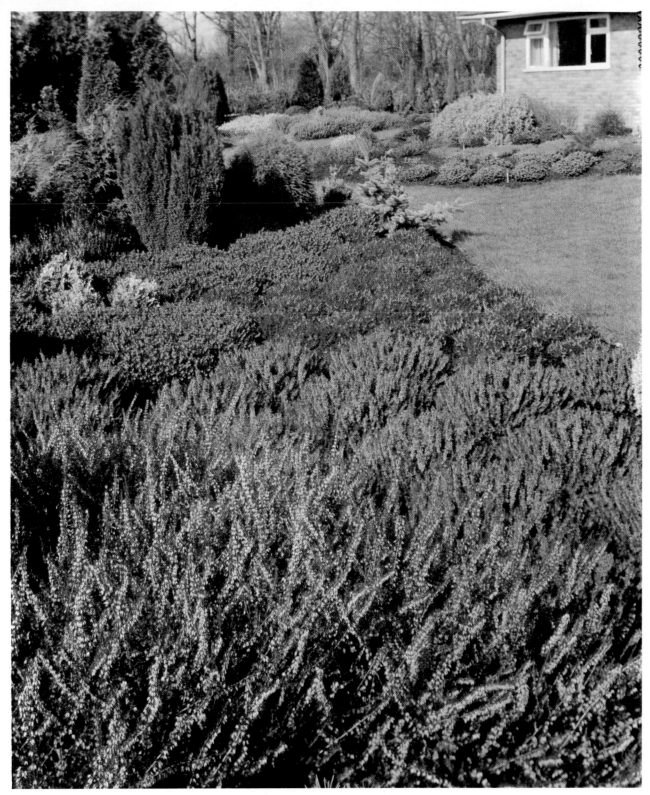

A mixed planting of heathers

always adds interest to a border and will be particularly useful if your soil is badly drained.

Having now ordered and received your plants of good quality and true to name we hope, you can start planting. This can be undertaken at almost any time of the year if the plants are in containers but

spring and autumn if they are from the open ground. Correct spacing of plants is important as some heathers grow much more quickly than others. Generally most varieties can be planted at a density of five to the square yard but for more vigorous types such as *E. carnea* Springwood White and *E. darleyensis* Arthur Johnson three plants to the square yard will be ample. It is a good idea to place

your plants before planting in the positions you wish them to be planted – this ensures you have even spacing and don't end up with a gap at one end of the bed!

Remove the container – it is surprising how many people forget – and with a spade or a trowel dig a hole for the plant – mixing two handfuls of moist peat around the roots of each plant – which should of course also be moist. The plant can be

PLAN A

A heather bed for year-round colour in neutral or acid soil. The heathers are planted 12 to 18 in. apart so that they produce rapid ground cover. Where not otherwise indicated, groups are of five plants each. The bed is 15 ft. long and 9 ft. wide

(a) *Erica carnea* King George
(b) *Calluna vulgaris* Gold Haze
(c) *Erica cinerea* C. D. Eason
(d) *Erica carnea* Springwood White
(e) *Erica carnea* Vivellii
(f) *Erica vagans* Mrs D. F. Maxwell
(g) *Calluna vulgaris* Robert Chapman
(h) *Erica cinerea* Purple Beauty
(i) *Erica mediterranea* W. T. Rackliff (3)
(j) *Calluna vulgaris* H. E. Beale
(k) *Erica darleyensis* Arthur Johnson

Conifers

(l) *Picea albertiana* Conica
(m) *Chamaecyparis pisifera* Boulevard
(n) *Thuja occidentalis* Rheingold

PLAN B

A heather bed for year-round colour in acid, neutral or alkaline soil. The dimensions of the bed are the same as those for Plan A

(a) *Erica carnea* Foxhollow
(b) *Erica carnea* Praecox Rubra
(c) *Erica carnea* Springwood White
(d) *Erica darleyensis* J. H. Brummage
(e) *Erica vagans* Mrs D. F. Maxwell
(f) *Erica carnea* Myretoun Ruby
(g) *Erica mediterranea* W. T. Rackliff (3)
(h) *Erica vagans* Lyonesse
(i) *Erica darleyensis* Arthur Johnson

Conifers

(j) *Thuja occidentalis* Rheingold
(k) *Picea albertiana* Conica
(l) *Juniperus chinensis* Pyramidalis

PLAN C

An island bed for year-round flower and foliage effect on neutral or acid soil. The heathers are planted in groups of ten, unless otherwise indicated. The bed is 20 ft. long and 15 ft. wide. The smaller bed is a mixed planting of dwarf conifers; in this bed the plants should be at least 18 in. apart

(a) *Calluna vulgaris* Gold Haze
(b) *Erica vagans* Mrs D. F. Maxwell
(c) *Erica cinerea* Pink Ice (5)
(d) *Calluna vulgaris* Darkness
(e) *Erica carnea* Springwood White (5)
(f) *Erica carnea* King George (5)
(g) *Calluna vulgaris* Robert Chapman
(h) *Erica darleyensis* Arthur Johnson
(i) *Erica cinerea* Purple Beauty
(j) *Erica darleyensis* Silberschmelze
(k) *Erica carnea* Myretoun Ruby

Conifers

(l) *Chamaecyparis lawsoniana* Elwoodii
(m) *Thuja occidentalis* Rheingold
(n) *Picea glauca albertiana conica*
(o) *Juniperus media* Old Gold
(p) *Cryptomeria japonica lobbii nana*
(q) *Chamaecyparis pisifera* Boulevard

Dwarf Conifer Bed

(a) *Abies balsamea hudsonia*
(b) *Chamaecyparis lawsoniana minima aurea*
(c) *Chamaecyparis obtusa nana*
(d) *Juniperus squamata* Blue Star
(e) *Chamaecyparis obtusa nana lutea*
(f) *Thuja occidentalis danica*
(g) *Juniperus communis compressa*
(h) *Thuja plicata* Stoneham Gold
(i) *Thuja occidentalis* Holmstrup
(j) *Cryptomeria japonica vilmoriniana*
(k) *Chamaecyparis lawsoniana pygmaea argentea*
(l) *Chamaecyparis pisifera nana*
(m) *Thuja plicata rogersii*
(n) *Chamaecyparis pisifera filifera nana*
(o) *Thuja orientalis aurea nana*
(p) *Juniperus horizontalis glauca*
(q) *Chamaecyparis obtusa nana gracilis*

inserted slightly deeper than the level of the soil in the pot so that the foliage of the heather rests on the soil. After planting the bed it is a good idea if you have any peat left, and even if you haven't, to mulch around each plant to a depth of an inch or two. This can of course be extended to the whole bed but it can become expensive. The mulch serves to prevent weeds and drying out of the roots – it also enables the heather to root along the stem, keeping it younger, more healthy and more vigorous.

Having finished the planting you will, I hope, find that your heathers will give you pleasure for many years to come.

Maintenance

All plants need some maintenance at some stage in their life in a garden situation and heathers are no exception. It should be unnecessary to mention that any seedling weeds need to be kept under control – eventually most will be smothered by the spreading heathers. Summer-flowering types will always improve in appearance and flowering if the old flower heads are trimmed each spring, just as the next year's growth begins – this normally being in March. Also all callunas will benefit from a trim at the same time even if they do not normally flower – such as *Calluna* Golden Feather. The more vigorous the growth the more trimming or pruning is required. Winter-flowering heathers will seldom need any pruning as most are fairly compact in habit anyway, but taller varieties such as *E. darleyensis* Arthur Johnson or the tree heaths should be pruned immediately after flowering.

In dry periods it is advisable to water your heathers, and particularly during the first season or two after planting until their root systems are established.

There are only a few species of heathers but such is the choice of varieties among those in cultivation some qualified selection has to be made. Many varieties may only be available from specialists but all of those listed here have been selected because they have been tried under most conditions and for a number of years.

PLAN A

PLAN B

PLAN C

Selected Heathers

Calluna

Calluna vulgaris, the common heather or ling, grows wild throughout many parts of Britain and Europe. It grows in a variety of places, from the Highlands of Scotland to the sandy Breckland of East Anglia but it will not grow where lime is present in the soil. Normally very hardy in the wild, on rich soils it will often grow soft and straggly and therefore more susceptible to winter damage. This is particularly true of some modern varieties and foliage forms. The common heather varies in height from 1 to 3 ft., but some of the named varieties will differ even more. The flowering period is normally from August until November.

Alba Plena This variety has bright green foliage and 1½-ft. spikes of double white flowers in August and September. It is not the most vigorous grower and occasionally one will notice a reversion from double to a single flower.

Beoley Gold One of the best of the yellow-foliaged varieties, it retains its colour throughout the year whilst producing attractive white flowers in August and September. It grows to 1½ ft.

Blazeaway Grown primarily for its startling foliage effect turning from golden orange in summer to a burnt red in winter. It grows 1½ ft. tall and has somewhat unattractive mauve flowers in August and September.

County Wicklow Growing only 9 to 12 in., this is one of the best double pink-flowering heathers. The flowers are very freely produced in August and September.

Darkness Of fairly recent introduction, this is a valuable addition to the range, producing deep crimson flowers on 1-ft. spikes in August and September. It is a vigorous grower but compact – further qualities to commend it to the gardener.

Foxii Nana A really miniature heather growing to a small mound of only 6 in. high with rather sparse purple flowers. Ideal for the rock garden but not so much for a mixed heather border, as it is likely to look a little out of place!

Golden Carpet An apt description for one of the best foliage varieties, this almost prostrate variety is useful for the front of the border. Golden in summer, it becomes a more orange red in winter and is of interest the year round.

Golden Feather Rarely has a flower but in many ways this is an advantage. It has soft feathery golden-yellow foliage turning burnt orange in winter. Not always the easiest to grow or the longest-lived variety in my experience.

Gold Haze Has bright golden foliage the year round and, like Beoley Gold, white flowers. To my mind it neither flowers so well as the latter nor does it retain such a bright yellow foliage colour in winter. August and September flowering and growing to 2 ft., it is still one of the most popular varieties.

H. E. Beale Is probably one of the oldest varieties but still one of the best. It has beautiful double pink flowers which last well through September and October on 2-ft. spikes and is especially effective in a large grouping.

J. H. Hamilton Is also a double pink of a similar vintage to H. E. Beale. However, it flowers earlier in August and September, is deeper in colour and only 9 in. or so in height. These two varieties have really proved themselves garden worthy.

Mair's Variety Grows vigorously to nearly 3 ft. with long spikes of single white flowers in August and September. The bright green foliage is an attractive foil to the flowers which are useful for cutting.

Multicolor Is also known as Prairie Fire and both names are descriptive of this excellent dwarf-growing variety. It changes through the seasons but at most times has yellow, orange and red hues reflected in its foliage. The flowers are purplish during August and September and if anything detract from the pleasing foliage.

Peter Sparkes Is of similar habit and flowering time to H. E. Beale, double but the flowers are a much deeper pink. An excellent variety but there may not be room in most gardens for both.

Robert Chapman To my mind one of the most reliable foliage varieties, giving a range of colour the year round and only marred by its purple flowers in August and September. It is quite vigorous in habit growing to 1½ ft. or so, the foliage colours turning from orange in summer to red in winter, particularly during frosty weather.

Silver Knight Has soft woolly foliage of silver grey and mauve-pink flowers in August and September. A good compact variety growing to only 1 ft.; like Silver Queen extremely attractive used in association with golden-foliaged varieties.

Silver Queen Also has silver-grey foliage which is a good deal tighter in habit,

Good species of heaths and heathers which are readily available

(a) *Calluna vulgaris*
(b) *Erica vagans*
(c) *Erica arborea* Alpina
(d) *Erica cinerea*
(e) *Daboecia cantabrica*
(f) *Erica tetralix*
(g) *Erica carnea*
(h) *Erica darleyensis*

a   b   c   d

e   f   g   h

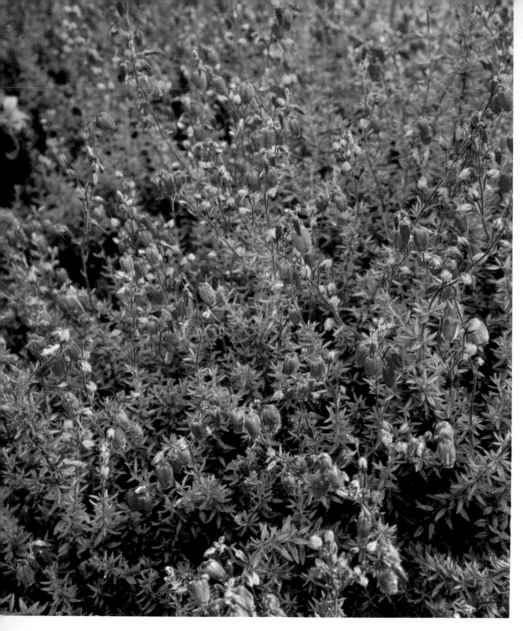

Daboecia cantabrica

although the flowering spikes reach 1½ ft. with purple flowers in August and September.

Sister Anne Grows to a very compact 6 in. with somewhat woolly foliage. It has pink flowers which are produced freely in August and September. Although very attractive in summer it looks somewhat dead and raggy in winter.

Sunset Is a foliage variety of fairly recent introduction. Orange in spring and summer, it turns reddish bronze in winter particularly in an exposed position. The flowers are a rather nondescript pink in August and September, the plant growing about 1 ft. tall.

Daboecia

Daboecia cantabrica is commonly known as the Irish bell heather and as one might expect from a plant originating from western Ireland it likes moist conditions

and is not considered fully hardy in some parts of the British Isles. The species and varieties dislike lime. The flower heads should be trimmed back lightly after flowering, either in late autumn or early spring. Not every garden will be able to grow daboecias successfully but when well grown they offer a delightful contrast to other heathers.

Alba Has large white bells hanging on nearly foot-long spikes from July to October. The whole plant grows to nearly 2 ft.

Donard Pink Is a strong grower to 2 ft. with pale pink flowers from June until September.

Hookstone Purple Another vigorous grower to 2 ft., it has bright purple bells, flowering from June to October.

William Buchanan A cross between *D. cantabrica* and *D. azorica*, the Azores heath, this has a long flowering period from June until October with crimson flowers on compact foot-high bushes.

Erica arborea

As the latin name might suggest this is known as the tree heath and in fact it does grow in its native Mediterranean habitat to about 20 ft. However, the species is not hardy in the British Isles and the variety *alpina* is the one usually offered. This grows only 6 to 8 ft. and will withstand most British winters. It has pale green foliage and white flowers which make a much better show on alkaline than acid soils, covering the period from March until May. It makes a useful addition to the heather range but is more suited to the larger heather garden where it can be allowed to grow unrestricted.

Erica australis

This species originates from Portugal and western Spain and is generally hardy in Great Britain but can be easily damaged by snowfalls and strong winds. It grows from 4 to 6 ft. carrying purple flowers from April until June, extending the flowering season of heathers through what is generally a quiet period for colour. A variety called Riverslea seems to be a definite improvement on the type with larger flowers of fuchsia purple. The species will withstand some lime.

Erica carnea

The winter heath or mountain heath is probably the most versatile and widely used heath in gardens. Originating from the European Alps, it is exceptionally hardy flowering even through a snow and ice cover. It grows successfully on alkaline as well as acid soils, flowering better if planted in an open position although it will grow quite well in shade if not too dry. Most varieties grow less than 1 ft. in height, but vary considerably in vigour and therefore spread. No trimming is required. There is a wide range of varieties in cultivation but unfortunately many are very similar, but all flower within the November to April period. Here are some of the best and most distinct.

Aurea Has golden-yellow foliage which is particularly pronounced in spring and early summer when new growth begins. From February until April it is covered with pale pink flowers. It is a most useful and attractive variety reaching about 9 in. and fairly compact in habit.

Foxhollow Is similar in having golden foliage but it is much more golden and more spreading in habit than *aurea* and with far fewer pink flowers. It seems to turn slightly bronzed in winter in exposed positions. Height similar to *aurea*.

King George Most heather enthusiasts I think would agree that this is probably the best of the *carnea* varieties although first introduced over fifty years ago. It has a compact habit growing to 9 in. or so with masses of rich pink flowers from January until April.

Myretoun Ruby Also goes under the more descriptive name of Winter Jewel but whichever name is used it is an outstanding new variety. The habit is compact to 9 in. high and against the dark green foliage are borne the most beautiful red flowers of any *carnea* variety. Flowering is from February until April.

Pink Spangles Is another recent introduction of great merit. Similar to the better known Springwood Pink in habit and, like it, excellent for ground cover, the large flowers are bi-coloured pale lilac and deep rosy red, lasting from January until March.

Praecox Rubra An early-flowering variety, as the name suggests, it has deep rosy-red flowers on 9-in. bushes from December until March.

Ruby Glow Flowers in March and April and it is an attractive variety with a spreading habit. Rich ruby-red flowers give a colourful display although some seasons it seems a bit shy in flower.

Springwood Pink Like its white-flowered counterpart is one of the most popular varieties and one of the best for ground-cover use. Dark green foliage, spreading rapidly but only to about 6 in. high, is covered with masses of pale pink flowers which darken with age during February and March. Like all varieties, of course, the length of flowering can be dependent upon the season.

Springwood White Must be the most vigorous *carnea* variety and is a real carpeting plant, rooting along the surface of the soil as it spreads. The foliage is a pleasant fresh green, particularly in early summer and reaches to only about 9 in. The flowers last from February until April with the real show coming in March when the foliage is made invisible by the pure white flowers.

Vivellii Really should be classed as a foliage plant, although its carmine flowers from January to March are distinct enough for it to be put in a collection on their own merit. The foliage is dark green in summer changing to bronze green in winter, a startling contrast to golden-foliaged heathers and conifers and against a variety such as Springwood White.

Erica ciliaris

The Dorset heath will not take lime soils at any price and prefers moisture so this immediately restricts its use in a great many gardens. Although in favourable conditions *Erica ciliaris* varieties will give an excellent show of flowers from June until October, they can be most frustrating and difficult to grow for the average gardener, being intolerant of atmospheric pollution and inclined to be tender in hard winters.

Aurea Is the only golden-foliaged variety of the species with pretty pink flowers from July until October. It is somewhat weak in growth reaching 12 in. but most attractive when grown well.

Camla Is useful for ground cover and is hardier than most varieties. It is 12 in. high and has rosy-pink flowers from July to October.

Corfe Castle Has soft salmon-pink flowers from July to October on compact plants 9 to 12 in. in height.

David McClintock Is of recent introduction with bi-coloured flowers which open white and turn to pink with age. Again flowering from June until October, it is taller than some at 15 to 18 in.

Stoborough Grows vigorously to 24 in. and its pearl-white flowers over apple-green foliage from July until October make it one of the best *ciliaris* varieties.

Erica cinerea

Erica cinerea has a number of common names but is probably best known as the Scotch heath or bell heath. It is found growing wild through most of western Europe and throughout the whole of the British Isles. It dislikes lime but withstands drier conditions better than many heaths and is often found on cliffs and growing among rocks in association with *Calluna vulgaris*. It prefers sun and good drainage so these two factors should be borne in mind when planting in the garden. There are a great many varieties in cultivation and, as one might expect with such a free-seeding species, too many of a similar colour. Varieties vary in height from 6 to 24 in., but all benefit from trimming each March or early April just as new growth begins.

Alba Minor Has masses of white flowers from June until October on compact 9-in. bushes. One of the best white varieties.

Atrosanguinea Smith's Variety Flowers profusely from June until September. These are of an intense scarlet colour on 6 to 9-in. spikes.

C. D. Eason Has dark green foliage which contrasts well with the bright red flowers appearing in June and lasting until September. A first-class plant which has proved its reliability over the years.

C. G. Best Like the preceding variety, it is not likely to be popular by name alone! It has long stems with salmon-pink flowers from July until September. The flower heads remain, like most *E. cinerea* varieties, attractive throughout the winter, but should be pruned fairly hard in March from 18 in. to about 6 in. This will improve both habit and flowering.

Foxhollow Mahogany Is of fairly recent introduction and has masses of rich mahogany-coloured flowers from July until September to about 12 in. in height.

Golden Drop Can sometimes be difficult to establish but is well worth the effort as when growing well it is an outstanding foliage variety. The pink flowers are of little consequence but the foliage turns from copper orange in summer to red in winter and grows only 6 in. high. It is particularly effective planted next to *E. carnea* Springwood White.

My Love Has flowers of a bluish-mauve colour from July until September on erect 12-in. spikes. An extremely bright-flowered variety which is somewhat similar to another called Vivienne Patricia.

Pink Ice Is of recent introduction and a first-class plant with a distinct compact habit and beautiful pure pink flowers. The rounded dark green bushes reach only 9 in. and are excellent at the front of a border. The short flower spikes give colour from June until September.

Purple Beauty Grows vigorously and flowers freely and to my mind is one of the best *cinerea* varieties. The foliage is very dark green and is covered with masses of bright purple flowers right from June through until October on plants reaching to 12 in. or so. A variety that should be in every heather garden!

Velvet Night Must be the darkest flowered of all having almost black-purple flowers on 12-in. stems from June until August. The foliage is also very dark, giving a slightly sombre appearance but once again if used as a contrast to golden foliage or white flowers extremely effective.

Many other good, distinct and worthwhile varieties exist in this species, but obviously space does not allow more to be mentioned. The problem, of course, is more often what not to have than which ones to choose!

Erica darleyensis

These hybrid varieties all arose from a chance seedling between *E. mediterranea* (*E. erigena*) and *E. carnea* producing what has been known for years as *E. darleyensis*. As this was first raised at Darley Dale Nurseries in Derbyshire, this is now known as *E. darleyensis* Darley Dale and all other seedlings which arose from it are classed as varieties of *E. darleyensis*.

One way and another the botanists

have kept us all busy, but the plants are the main thing and these are very valuable to the heather garden. Most varieties grow between 2 and 4 ft. All are vigorous, useful for ground cover and all grow successfully on alkaline soils.

Arthur Johnson To my mind this is one of the finest heathers introduced, flowering from December to April. Taller than most varieties at 2 ft. and with long spikes of deep pink blooms, it is vigorous, an easy grower and reliable in flower.

Darley Dale Formerly *E. darleyensis*, it is more compact than Arthur Johnson with much shorter spikes of a pinky-mauve colour which last from November until March. One of the best for ground cover growing between $1\frac{1}{2}$ to 2 ft. in height and quite amenable to a variety of soils and situations.

Furzey Is also listed in some catalogues as Cherry Stevens. The dark green foliage is covered with masses of deep rose-pink flowers from January until April. A good variety of fairly recent introduction.

Jack H. Brummage Has golden-yellow foliage which is more prominent in some gardens than others. It seems to prefer heavier, slightly alkaline soils to give its best in both foliage and flower. The latter are a pleasing shade of pink in February and March on $1\frac{1}{2}$-ft. bushes.

J. W. Porter Flowers from February to April on large rounded bushes of dark green which reach $1\frac{1}{2}$ ft. in height. The flowers are a direct contrast to the foliage, being a strong reddish purple but unfortunately are not always produced as freely as those of some other varieties.

Silberschmelze Probably has been given more names than any other variety, mainly because of the Englishman's lack of knowledge of the German language where this plant was first raised! Molten Silver, *darleyensis alba* Silver Beads and Silver Bells are just a few synonyms for what is really a white Darley Dale and an excellent garden plant. It flowers from December until April on bushes $1\frac{1}{2}$ to 2 ft. high. Also a good ground cover with a vigorous habit, Silberschmelze has single flowers of silvery white with distinct brownish stamens in the centre of each, creating a most pleasing effect.

Erica mediterranea

As might be imagined this species (syn. *Erica erigena*) is known as the Mediterranean heath but what is not known so widely is that it is also native in western Ireland, northern Spain and south western France. Normally in the wild it makes a shrub varying in height from 4 to 8 ft. with small pink flowers from March until

May. It grows well on lime soils but although withstanding some frost and snow is easily damaged by severe winter weather though seldom killed outright. Some varieties are more adaptable to British gardens than others and most will benefit from sheltered positions – at the same time requiring full sun. They are useful in that they extend the flowering period in the heather garden from the *E. carnea* varieties finishing in April almost to the *E. cinerea* varieties which begin in June.

Alba Reaches 3 to 4 ft. with rich green foliage covered with white flowers from March until May.

Brightness Has a compact bushy habit growing slowly to 2 ft. The foliage is dark green, the flower buds turning bronze before opening in March into a purple-red colour and lasting until May. Flowers on this variety do not always appear freely all over the plant which seems to be typical of some others of this species.

Superba Will under most conditions reach 6 ft. or so and has larger rosy-pink flowers more freely produced than the type which have an added bonus in being honey scented during the March to May flowering period.

W. T. Rackliff Grows in compact rounded bushes of rich green to 24 in. and is covered with pure white flowers in March and April. Like most *E. mediterranea* varieties flowering can be spoilt by frost.

Erica tetralix

The cross-leaved heath is distributed in the wild through most of north western Europe where the moist airstreams flow in from the Atlantic. To thrive it must be in lime-free conditions and will undoubtedly succeed better in areas of high rainfall and where its roots can be assured of a constant supply of water. Grey foliage is a predominant feature of the species and most varieties, with flowers held in clusters mostly from June until October. Like *E. ciliaris*, *E. tetralix* cannot be expected to grow well in all gardens.

Alba Mollis Is quite a striking plant with silver-grey foliage and white flowers from June until September. Like most varieties of the species it grows about 6 to 9 in.

Con Underwood Has large crimson flowers on 9-in. bushes from June until October and is one of the best and most reliable varieties.

Hookstone Pink Flowering from June until October and growing to 12 in., it has terracotta flower buds opening to clear pink over grey foliage.

Ken Underwood Has very dark grey-green leaves and an upright habit to 12 in. The

long flower spikes carry cerise flowers from June until August.

Pink Star Is of recent introduction but appears to be different to varieties already in cultivation in having star-like flowers held upright rather than drooping as is the case with most. The contrast of bright pink against the grey foliage is most attractive.

Erica vagans

The Cornish heath in the wild makes a low spreading shrub from 1 to 3 ft. in height. Mostly found in Cornwall, it is also native to parts of western France and the Iberian peninsular. It will grow in acid, neutral or slightly alkaline soils and will occasionally get damaged in severe winters. There are several varieties in cultivation but as white and pink are the two main colours many are very similar.

Although the dead flower heads remain attractive the whole winter, they should be trimmed fairly hard back in the spring when new growth begins to be assured of both compact plants and improved flowering during the next summer.

Cream Is a strong-growing, creamy-white variety growing to 2 ft. and giving a good show in August until October.

Lyonesse Flowers in August and September and is almost the purest white among the many white *vagans* varieties and although introduced nearly fifty years ago has stood the test of time and still remains one of the most popular. It is quite compact in habit, reaching only $1\frac{1}{2}$ ft. with foliage of a fresh light green. When the spiky white flowers fade, they become an attractive golden brown, remaining so through the winter.

Mrs D. F. Maxwell Is often partnered by Lyonesse because both were introduced about the same time and both have become old favourites. This is a very beautiful free-flowering deep rose cerise of compact habit. Like many *vagans* varieties it will have an eventual spread of 4 to 6 ft. if space is given though only reaching $1\frac{1}{2}$ ft. in height. It flowers from August until October on dark green foliage – a must for every collection!

St Keverne Received an Award of Merit from the Royal Horticultural Society as long ago as 1914, but still remains one of the best varieties. Clear salmon-pink flowers are a distinctive feature on $1\frac{1}{2}$-ft. compact yet vigorous bushes.

Valerie Proudley Of recent introduction has golden-yellow and white flowers, an attractive combination even though the plant understandably lacks the vigour of the green types. The gold remains summer and winter on compact 1-ft. plants.

Perennials

Alan Bloom, V.M.H., has had a lifelong association with plants being the son of a pioneer market flower grower in Cambridgeshire. Having gained experience in various nurseries after leaving school, he decided to go in for the production of plants rather than market flowers and began in business on his own account in 1931 at the age of twenty-four years.

In 1934 his business was made wholesale only and by 1939 thirty-six acres of hardy perennials and alpines in nearly two thousand species and varieties were being grown at Oakington, near Cambridge. With stocks down to six acres by the end of the Second World War, a search for a new site ended in the acquisition of Bressingham Hall near Diss in Norfolk with its 220 acres, but it was not until 1950 that restoration of the property and nursery business got under way. With pre-war production of the property exceeded a few years later, at last came the opportunity to indulge fully in a love of plants by converting five acres of meadow into a garden, a garden now internationally famous, which attracts many thousands of visitors on Thursday and Sunday afternoons between spring and autumn.

About five thousand species and varieties of hardy herbaceous plants are grown, making it by far the most important collection of its kind in Europe. They include not only a wealth of uncommon species but several new varieties which have been bred at Bressingham. Many have received awards from The Royal Horticultural Society, and the island bed method of growing perennials as practised at Bressingham and described in Alan Bloom's books, is widely accepted as the most effective and trouble free.

The farm and nursery now extend to 430 acres and although the business is still essentially wholesale there is a retail mail order catalogue of the greatest interest to discerning gardeners.

Mr Bloom was awarded the Victoria Medal of Honour by The Royal Horticultural Society in 1971, in recognition of his great services to horticulture.

Hardy perennials are no longer a neglected subject in the gardening scene. The time is happily past when they were relegated in so many gardens because the rewards they gave were disproportionate to the trouble entailed. The conventional herbaceous border was largely at fault because of its long narrow shape with a backing wall, hedge or fence. The plants it contained suffered from overcrowding, weakly growth and excessive competition for light and air. Quite often such borders were too narrow in relation to the height of the plants they contained. All this accentuated the main disabilities to which perennials are prone if not given a fair chance – difficulty of access to a border and the need for supports.

The factor of adaptability must be reckoned with. The majority of kinds grown and offered by nurseries are adaptable to ordinary garden conditions, but it would be as much a mistake to plant something which is by nature shade or moisture loving into a dry open situation as it would the other way round. It would also be a mistake to plant as neighbours something rank or invasive with what is by nature of slow or lowly growth. The need then is to have some foreknowledge of the habits of what one wishes to grow and to avoid indiscriminate planting.

The principle to apply is that of making a selection of plants best suited to the place in which they are to grow. The range of subjects existing in gardens and nurseries is sufficiently wide for this to be achieved, no matter how small the garden, or unkind the soil, so long as it is not completely hemmed in by tall buildings or overhung by large trees to exclude both light and air.

Overcrowding and overhanging by trees or other taller growth inevitably leads to stem weakness, and plants in close competition for light and air becomes excessively tall and spindly. In the majority of cases where border staking is necessary, it is not the fault of the plants but of the conditions under which they are grown. Light and air are vitally necessary to sturdy growth for all kinds of plants that prefer sunlight, or an open situation as most perennials do.

Bearing in mind the need to make a selection of plants best adapted to the site, the preparation for a bed or border of hardy plants should include drainage if the soil appears excessively wet or sticky in winter or hard baked in summer. Thorough digging will mostly suffice, since the surface may have been panned down by builders' vehicles or machines.

Summer and autumn are of course the best times for deep digging on heavy soil, which will enable winter frosts to break down hard lumps and clots into quite fine tilth for spring planting.

On both light poor soils and heavy clays, humus, in the form of peat, compost or farmyard manure, are recommended. These will improve the texture, as well as the fertility of the soil, and give plants such a good start that nothing but occasional topdressings of fertilizer will be needed for years.

There is no doubt whatever that island beds give the best reward in terms of value for money and effort in maintenance. An island bed can be sited anywhere so long as all-round access is possible, even if it is only a narrow path on one side or end. It is quite feasible to convert a backed border into an island bed so long as there is sufficient width for no matter what the backing consists of, rear access can be provided either by a narrow path of grass or paving used as stepping stones.

If the backing is of a wall, it can be used for climbers and a strip allowed along the foot for bulbs or any of the wide variety of dwarf plants or climbers that like such a spot. The rear part of the bed itself should have, as edging groups, dwarf early-flowering perennials such as bergenias, pulmonarias, epimediums, for even if the border has a sunny aspect, the taller kinds of perennials facing the adjoining groups will provide for summer shading. This strip at the rear will prove a source of delight in spring and if colour has gone by summer, one has at least easy access to the rest of the bed for maintenance work, and there will be far less staking anyway, because the weakening effect of the backing is greatly lessened.

Only one-sided beds which are on a small scale, where heights of plants grown are in keeping with the effective width of the border, are worthy of consideration. If a garden admits of no compromise, or has no site suitable for an island bed, fair enough, but a one-sided border will inevitably be more troublesome to maintain unless a very careful selection of plants is made.

Whatever type of border one decides to plan and plant, its success and potential interest will depend not only on a well-chosen site, well-prepared soil and the right selection of plants, but on its width. The narrower the bed, the more restrictive one should be on the height of subjects grown. Nothing looks more incongruous than to see plants flowering at 4 or 5 ft. high in a bed only 4 or 5 ft. wide. A safe guide in making a selection of plants is to measure the effective or plantable width of the border in feet, and halve it to arrive at the maximum height of plants it should contain. This would restrict a 4-ft. wide border to plants of no more than 2 ft. tall, but a little latitude or discretion could be allowed for the very erect spiky plants – such as kniphofias – to exceed the limit.

This is a rule that can apply to any type of border – island or one-sided – bearing in mind that in the former, the tallest are in the centre parts, and at the rear in the latter.

Grouping is another factor worthy of careful consideration. Where space is very restricted and where there is a preference for variety, then a case could be made for having only one plant of each kind – but grouping of subjects or kinds should on the whole be practised from say three of a kind together for a small bed of about 100 sq. ft. in area, to ten or fifteen plants for the largest beds up to a 1000 sq. ft. or more.

The average spacing to be recommended if good quality nursery-grown plants are used is about five to the square yard. If, for example, groups are of five plants of a kind, this gives a planting distance of about 16 in. from plant to plant within a group. But the space around it, up to the outer plants in adjoining groups, should be more, say 20 in. Spacing required depends of course on the spread or robustness of the subject. It can vary all the way from a single plant occupying a square yard in a few cases, to nine plants of some dwarf slow-growing subjects.

If in the process of making a new bed or border, an error in placing occurs, it will show up during the first flowering season and can easily be rectified then.

Selected Perennials

Acanthus

Acanthus are best placed in isolation in a sunny place rather than in a mixed border. *Acanthus longifolius*, *A. mollis* and *A. spinosus* will in time take up more than their allotted space as a group and then curbing becomes an annual task. Of the three *A. mollis* is the least satisfactory, flowering less freely than the other two. All have long classically jagged leaves, which die back in winter, of deep glossy green and from this welter of foliage arise spikes 3 to 4 ft. high of curiously hooded flowers of lavender lilac tinged with white.

They prefer a well-drained soil, and a group can be very effective, especially as flowering lasts from early July onwards for many weeks.

Achillea

The yarrows or milfoils include a few good and very showy plants, but some of a weedy nature as well. All achilleas have serrated leaves which enhance the plant as a whole, and are flowers useful for cutting. They like a sunny position. *Achillea filipendulina*, with its plate-like heads of deep yellow on erect 4-ft. stems, is worthy of the popularity it holds. It is easy enough to grow in any well-drained soil, and needs the minimum of attention for years at a stretch. Usually offered under the name of Gold Plate, the stems, when cut at their best, can be dried for winter decoration. The variety Coronation Gold is less tall than Gold Plate and with smaller heads of deep yellow flowers. Moonshine is much dwarfer and combines the best qualities of the species *clypeolata* and *taygetea*. It flowers from May to July, at about 18 in., keeps its silvery backcloth for almost the whole year, and often throws a few late heads of glistening canary yellow in autumn.

A. millefolium is the wild milfoil of meadows and hedgerows. Deep pink and almost red varieties, such as Cerise Queen, can make quite a brave show for a season or two before they need curbing or replanting back into position. Another disability is that the 3-ft. heads become top heavy and often need supports. This applies also to the white achilleas, The Pearl and Perry's White. Both have double button-type flowers on loose heads, and grow up to 3 ft. All achilleas should be divided in early autumn or spring.

Anaphalis

The anaphalis are no longer the neglected subjects they once were. This is because some have good ground-cover properties and will adapt themselves to rather harsh conditions. All are silvery grey and all have white or ivory flower heads of a crispy everlasting texture.

There is not much to choose between *Anaphalis margaritacea*, *A. nubigena* and *A. triplinervis* except in height. The first named is about 1½ ft. high in flower and it carries a rather loose crop of branching heads. The other two are 9 to 12 in. high, and all three have the virtue of surface spread unmarred either by unsightly fading or by an aggressive weedy nature in spite of fairly rapid growth.

A. yedoensis dies back in winter to a spreading root system but the new shoots in spring are like silvery-white fingers. These run up to a good 2 ft., making a solid bush of stems topped by papery white heads which are useful for cutting and drying.

Anchusa

Bright though anchusas are, I would not class them as good garden plants from a reliability standpoint, though quite well known under such names as Loddon Royalist, Morning Glory and Opal. The black fleshy roots send up large coarse abrasive leaves and spikes which carry a profusion of small but intensely blue flowers from late May to July on stems up to 4 ft. which mostly need supporting. After July there is a somewhat blank space, and too often it is still largely blank next spring because plants have failed to survive the winter. The wetter or richer the soil, the more this is likely to happen.

Anemone

The anemones or windflowers are too diverse for any general remarks, and only one group will be mentioned covered by the name *hupehensis*, which was long known as *Anemone japonica*. No garden should be without these charming plants which can contribute so much to the late summer display. Though shades of pink and white are the only colours to be seen, it is the way their flowers are borne that makes for so much charm. Individual flowers ranging from 1½ to 3 in. across remind one of the dog rose in shape, with yellow-stamened centres. From a base mass of vine-like leaves rise wiry, branching stems, tipped by nodding flowers and close set buds still to open. After a slow start in spring, most varieties begin flowering in late July or early August and will continue until autumn has set in. Good drainage and a mainly sunny position are the only essentials to cultivation and they are especially good on chalky soil.

The tallest varieties are white. White Giant leads in both size of flower and height at 3½ ft., with Louise Uhink very close. There is little to choose between some of the single pink varieties such as Queen Charlotte, Max Vogel and Kriemhilde, which are about 2½ ft. high. The semi-double Lady Gilmour is much dwarfer, as are the deeper rose-pink Profusion and Bressingham Glow. These are only 20 in. tall, which is the height of the single-flowered September Charm, a clear pink.

Right: A well-contoured herbaceous border with *Monarda didyma*, the bee-balm, in the foreground

Anthemis

Most anthemis flower freely and for a long time, but their chief fault is that of a short life. The varieties of *Anthemis tinctoria* are especially prone. The yellow daisy-type flowers come on somewhat twiggy and not very erect growth 2 to 2½ ft. high from June to late August and, if the woody rootstock fails to produce new basal growth in autumn, there can be no survival.

Grallagh Gold is even trickier than the light yellow Wargrave or Mrs Buxton, but the dwarfer species, *A. sancti-johannis*, is, in my experience, much more reliable. It has the same deep green somewhat parsley-like leaves and the deep yellow flowers are carried quite neatly on 20-in. bushes.

Armeria

The common thrift is *Armeria maritima* and it has produced some variations and hybrids of real garden value. Vindictive is one that can be used as an effective edging for it will make a continuous evergreen row 1 ft. wide within a year or two. The closely mounded deep green foliage is like sheep-grazed grass, and in May and June it is ablaze with 8-in. drumstick heads of bright carmine pink.

The best clones of *A. m. alba* serve a similar purpose, both for edging and grouping. The tallest, largest flowered and brightest is Bees Ruby though the colour is in fact a deep carmine of lustred texture. Plants are mounded, much broader in the leaf than others, and the central root stem just below ground is so bare that division is seldom possible. Cuttings are not easy to strike, but some success comes from basal cuttings taken in early autumn or spring and inserted in a cold frame. Armerias need full sun and a very well-drained soil.

Artemisia

The wormwoods would not have any claims but for their foliage effect and the most brightly silvered, with the most finely cut leaves, are not very reliable in my experience, mostly because they dislike winter wet. *Artemisia argentea*, *A. discolor* and *A. splendens* run a little below ground and lose compactness after a year or two. They are best in a hot dry spot, and so is the semi-shrubby *A. nutans*. This is my preference amongst the silver-filigree species which have effective foliage up to about 12 in. and very ineffective dirty white flowers above that height.

Another section, less silvery and less delicate of leaf, are decidedly more vigorous, so much so that curbing is necessary.

These include *A. ludoviciana*, *A. palmeri*, *A. pontica*, *A.* Silver Queen and *A. villarsii* – useful amongst shrubs or on a dry bank but of little charm in a mixed border of perennials.

The only species I know that is worth growing as a border subject for its flowers is *A. lactiflora*. This of course denotes milky white flowers, but the terminal heads of beady flowers are more of a creamy-ivory shade. These come on stiff-growing stems, reaching 4 ft. at least in the rich or dampish soil this splendid plant prefers and make a very effective, contrasting display in late summer and early autumn. It needs no staking.

Aster

The garden would be rather dull in autumn if no Michaelmas daisies were to be seen. New varieties have been produced over recent years and although decided advances have been made, enhancing the range of height and colour as well as the size of flower, it is purely a matter of personal preference when such a welter of choice exists. There is little point in my making recommendations, except to emphasize the need to keep to varieties which do not need staking, and to replant every three years, using only the outer healthier shoots.

There are many other asters in existence, apart from Michaelmas daisies, which have been somewhat overlooked and which are virtually trouble free. *Aster acris*, for example, is a first-rate plant with myriads of starry, blue, yellow-centred flowers on bushy growth 2½ ft. high in late summer.

A. amellus, of which there is a number of varieties, is long lived in well-drained soil. The varieties grow erectly at heights varying from 1½ to 2½ ft., with greyish leaves and woody stems from a compact rootstock. The best known is the violet-blue King George, but I like the deeper-coloured, very reliable Violet Queen. Pink shades are not the easiest to grow, but Lady Hindlip and Sonia are amongst the best, whilst Nocturne, lavender lilac, and Lac de Geneve, light blue, more or less complete the colour range.

A. frikarti, a hybrid, grows taller at 3 ft. than either of its parents (*A. amellus* and *A. thompsoni*). It has 2-in. wide light lavender-blue flowers with the usual yellow centre on widely branching stems from July onwards for many weeks. *A. thompsoni nana* is a splendid little plant which makes perfectly shaped greyish-leaved bushes up to 18 in. or so, and set with 1-in. lavender-blue flowers from July to October. It is slow growing, and quite reliable

if grown in reasonably well-drained soil.

A. ericoides is worth considering because it is neat and trouble free. The flowers are tiny, smothering the small-leaved and shapely bushes 2½ ft. or so high in autumn. The colour range is limited; Brimstone being a buff-yellow shade, Cinderella, lavender blue, and there is also White Heather. *A. linosyris* is deep yellow, the flowers being carried on a terminal head like a bunch of little puffs. This species is August flowering, and a variant named Goldcrest is a little later and a trifle more graceful. All asters are best divided in spring.

Astilbe

Astilbes grown in good soil with adequate moisture achieve perfection from every point of view as plants of incomparable beauty. Attractive wide-based foliage often mounds up to a shapely pyramid formation through which the plumed spikes appear of every imaginable shade from white through pink, salmon and cerise to fiery red and deep red. Some are erect, others arch and droop, and heights vary from 6 in. to 6 ft. None ever need staking and as plants they are completely hardy and can be left alone for years, trouble free and reliable, though they cannot stand hot, dry conditions. They respond heartily to mulching in spring, which of course conserves moisture, and all can safely be divided when dormant. In general, the tallest-growing astilbes are the strongest and least fussy about moisture, but these do not include the brightest colours.

One of the best of the taller kinds is *Astilbe taquettii superba*, with imposing spikes, straight and strong, of an intense lilac-purple shade, about 4 ft. in height and at its best in July and August. *A. davidii* and the varieties Tamarix, Salland, Venus and Salmon Queen are all quite tall and very robust with colours ranging from the pale pink of Venus to the crimson magenta of *A. davidii*.

Given the right conditions, the more colourful range of dwarfer astilbes will provide a much longer flowering period. These are hybrids, growing from 1½ to 3 ft. tall and flowering between late June and mid-August. Cologne, a deep carmine rose, and Dusseldorf, salmon pink, are about 2 ft. high, as is Rheinland, early, clear pink, and Deutschland, a fine white. For reds of this height, Fire is a very intense shade and Red Sentinel is almost brick red. Glow, at 2½ ft., is stronger and Spinell is another fiery shade. The 2½-ft. Federsee is a rosy-red variety and Bressingham Pink has fine clear pink spikes.

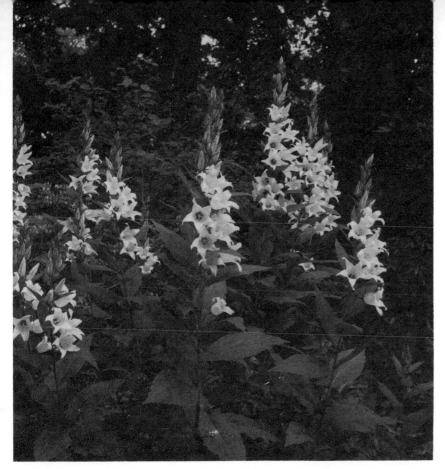

Campanula latifolia alba

Fanal is a deep red dwarf variety, barely 2 ft. high, and another white variety of rare charm with dark green leaves is Irrlicht. *A. simplicifolia* Sprite has very dark foliage as background to the 12-in. spikelets carrying countless ivory-pink flowers like a cascade. This is a sturdy miniature of great charm.

The deeply divided foliage makes a big contribution to the beauty of astilbes and there is infinite variation in the shades of green to be found among them, including some of bronzy and purplish hue.

Bergenia

As space fillers for any but the hottest driest situations bergenias would take some beating. The large shiny leaves are almost evergreen – mostly dying off in late winter in readiness for the spring-flowering period of April and May, when the stubby spikes, from 9 to 24 in. high, open to show a spray of little bell-shaped flowers. The usual colour is pink, rather washy in older species, but deeper, bordering on red, in such modern varieties as the dwarf Abendglut (Evening Glow) and Ballawley, which is the largest of all. Silberlicht is a free-flowering almost white shade. Where flowering is less important, any *cordifolia* form or *schmidtii* are cheaper to buy.

The value of bergenias is their bright foliage from May to March, and their ability to spread fairly quickly but unobtrusively in awkward places, almost regardless of soil, sun or shade and to smother most weeds.

Brunnera

The one species *Brunnera macrophylla* was formerly *Anchusa myosotidiflora*. It differs from most anchusas by being a good reliable perennial, with much less fleshy roots, forming clumps of rounded leaves, which have weed-smothering properties, all summer. In April, the sprays of tiny but brilliant blue forget-me-not flowers extend on low branching stems outward to make a pleasing display until June. In good or moist soil, plants become fairly massive.

A very bright-leaved form, *variegata*, grows rather less robustly. The leaves are up to 6 in. wide and more than half of each is a primrose shade. Flowering is similar to the green type, but for the sake of foliage effect it is best planted where hot sun does not scorch it.

Campanula

The bellflowers comprise a genus where a wide range of adaptability exists, as well as a range of height, from being prostrate to 5 or 6 ft. tall. With such diversity, recommendations will be easier to follow on the basis of height. Beginning with the

dwarfest, the semi-prostrate hybrid *Campanula* Stella can adorn not only a rock garden, a wall top, path edging or the front of a border, but makes a first-rate pot plant for an indoor or outdoor position. Its normal flowering time is June to August, but if cut back, divided when old, and re-vitalized it will flower again in autumn. Cultivation is easy in any reasonable soil, in sun or partial shade.

Almost any of the varieties of *C. carpatica* are valuable for frontal groups. They vary in height from 6 to 12 in., having upward-facing, cup-shaped flowers 1 to 2 in. across, are neat in habit and flower through June to August. Colours vary from white to violet blue and, though easy to raise from seed, one must obtain named varieties to avoid mixed shades.

C. burghaltii is distinctive for its near opaque smoky-blue bells, elongated in shape and dangling from 15 to 18-in. stems. It flowers from June onwards from quite vigorous but not invasive plants. *C.* Van Houttei is similar in habit with equally large bells of a pale blue shade.

C. glomerata has many forms. With all, the flowers grow in clusters, either as a terminal head or hugging the spike. The earliest is Joan Elliott with fine deep violet-blue flowers on 15-in. stems from May to July. Other dwarf forms exist, notably *nana* – both the white and mauve blue in this have flowers along the 12 to 18-in. spikes for many weeks from early June, but the little Purple Pixie does not begin until well into July. The best of the top-clustered group is *superba*, which grows to 3 ft., flowering June and July, with upturned violet flowers.

C. lactiflora is also variable. The deepest-coloured named variety is Prichard's, growing leafily and erectly to 2½ to 3 ft., with open clusters of bell-shaped flowers facing the sun. The pygmy of this long-flowering species is Pouffe, which grows outwards rather than upwards, making a green cushion for the light blue flowers from June to September. The tallest is Loddon Anna, reaching a rather precarious 6 ft., with heads of palest pink. The white *alba* is only a foot or so shorter. All these, however, are reliable plants and will grow quite happily in shade as well as sun.

C. latifolia (syn. *macrantha*) is similarly adaptable and although its flowering season of June to July is briefer, it stands well, with strong spikes to 4 ft. or so carrying obliquely large pointed petalled bells. There is a good white *alba* and Brantwood is deep violet blue, but the near opaque Gloaming is of an entrancing pale sky-blue colour.

93

C. latiloba (formerly *grandis*) makes a surface mat of bright green rosettes and sends up 3-ft. spikes on which saucer-shaped flowers are set for much of its length. The best variety for colour and reliability is Percy Piper, with flowers of a deep china blue 3 in. across. This type may need replanting every two or three years to ensure full flowering, but *C. persici-folia*, of somewhat similar habit, has greater faults. It is prone to rust disease, and to die out sometimes from exhaustion. Stems are apt to topple over and self-sown seedlings to appear in wrong places. This is not to condemn it entirely, and it can be quite showy with large saucers for much of its 2 to 3-ft. stems. Good named varieties are Snowdrift and Telham Beauty, the latter a good blue.

The only double-flowered variety that can be recommended appears to belong to the nettle-leaved campanula species *C. trachelium*. Bernice is of obscure origin but it is reliably perennial, growing up-rightly to 2 ft. from a compact rootstock. The double powder-blue flowers cluster on the stem in June and July.

Catananche

Catananche caerulea, Cupid's dart, is quite a popular subject, with a very long season of papery blue cornflowers on wiry stems. It reaches 2 to 2½ ft. and in well-drained soil will flower for three months from June onwards. Its faults are lack of long-evity and a tendency to loll over so that flowers droop rather than stand up to face the sky, especially in damp weather. It comes from seed sown in May, or root cuttings taken in March.

Centaurea

This is another genus that includes coarse as well as choicer species with heights varying from 2 in. to 6 ft. or more. *Centaurea dealbata*, as a species, is not to be recommended when the much brighter, deep pink-flowered *stenbergii* is an improvement. John Coutts is another improved variety with even larger flowers of a lighter clearer pink shade. Both reach 2½ ft. to flower freely in June to July, with ample greyish foliage. This is a vigorous, easy-growing type even in poor soil.

C. macrocephala has yellow tufty flowers on plants to 5 ft. *C. hypoleuca* is charming with a profusion of clear pink flowers on compact grey-foliaged plants. The stems are wiry, rising to 12 in. above and round the mounded foliage, to make a pleasing display from late May to July. *C. pulchra major*, though sturdy in light well-drained soil, is a choice plant. It has jagged leaves of silvery grey unfurling to

12 in. or so in length, and then come ramrod spikes topped by handsome fluffy heads of a rosy hue in June and July to 3 ft. tall.

Finally *C. ruthenica*, which is distinctive for its shining deep green foliage, gracefully slender 4-ft. stems carrying very pretty canary-yellow, fluffy-headed flowers from June to August. The centaureas are easy but best divided in early spring.

Centranthus

Many a garden would be the poorer without *Centranthus ruber*, keys of Heaven, for it has the capacity for making good the neglectful use of a garden and can be seen naturalized on old walls as well as in old borders. If it seeds about, unwanted seedlings can be treated as weeds, leaving a group where it belongs to be self-replenishing. Flowering is profuse on 2 to 3-ft. stems. The usual deep but rather dull pink heads are not especially attractive, a switch to the brighter red *coccinea* is advised, and if considered too common for a bed in which choicer plants are preferred, usually some odd dry corner exists where it can fill a need for colour.

Chrysanthemum

In the minds of many people, the name registers only as a florist's flower and

Centaurea macrocephala

though strictly the genus includes pyrethrums (p. 106), it also includes marguerites or shasta daisies. The well-known *Chrysanthemum* Esther Read was raised as a novelty when only single white-flowered varieties existed. Single white varieties are still widely grown including the very large-flowered, lacy-petalled Thomas Killin. Everest, large single white, Wirral Supreme, double white along with other doubles including the ineptly named Cobham Gold, as well as Esther and Jennifer Read still appeal. *C. corymbosum* grows stoutly to 3½ ft., carrying hundreds of 1-in. wide white daisies, with greyish foliage, from June to August.

Cirsium

Cirsium rivularis atropurpureum is unmistakably a thistle, but it has no vices and is decidedly handsome. The long not too prickly leaves hug the ground and the spikes topped by reddish-purple thistle blobs reach 4 ft., flowering from June to August, to give a good over-all appearance in any open situation.

Coreopsis

Coreopsis grandiflora is easily raised from seed in such varieties as Sunburst and

Mayfield Giant, but they deteriorate after one season's profligate show of deep yellow flowers, rather laxly carried on thin stems to about 2 ft. The midget Goldfink not only smothers itself in deep yellow, maroon-marked flowers on 8-in. stems from June to September but mostly survives the winter as well. Hardiness is not in doubt, but if odd plants exhaust themselves, those remaining divide easily in spring to make replacements.

The most remarkable and distinctive coreopsis is *verticillata*, for it forms shapely 18-in. bushes with an abundance of narrow foliage, decked with 1-in. yellow-rayed flowers from June to late August. This sterling little plant is fully perennial with a slowly expanding rootstock and has a slightly deeper coloured edition in *grandiflora*.

Crambe
Crambe cordifolia is a decidedly ornamental species of sea kale, but too massive for a small mixed border. The leaf spread of a single fleshy rooted plant can exceed 3 ft., and the much-branched spikes of white flowers even more, as well as reaching 5 ft. in height. The effect of such a profusion of flowers is quite startling during early summer but after that the space it has taken steadily becomes bare until another season.

Crepis
Though a member of the dandelion tribe, *Crepis incana* is a little charmer for a frontal position in full sun and very well-drained soil. The open flowers are mainly 1 in. across and overall a soft pink shade, with silvery-grey mounded foliage that gives instant appeal, even if only about 10 to 12 in. high, and flowers on and on from June to September.

Cynoglossum
These are long-lived, easy-to-grow members of the same family as anchusas. *Cynoglossum grande* is a trifle untidy but it makes a brave show of intensely blue flowers on 1½ to 2-ft. stems in May and June. The sprays tend to become top heavy later on but cutting as flowering fades promotes more basal greenery and probably some more flowers as well. *C. nervosum* is a shorter and neater subject, inclined to be grey leaved on hummocky plants, above which come 10-in. arching sprays of small but bright deep blue flowers from early June to August.

Delphinium
These majestic plants may be considered indispensable, but almost invariably they

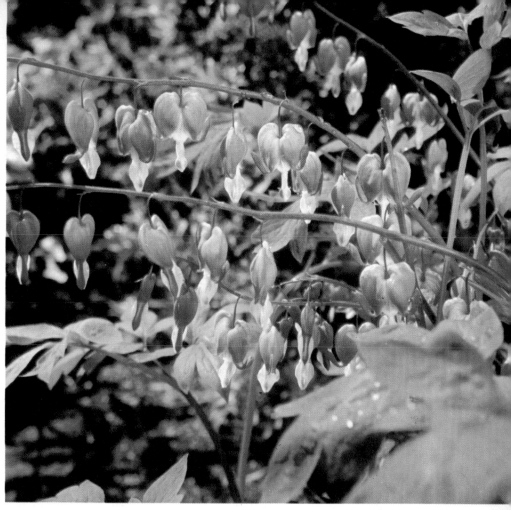

need staking in good time. They also need soil fertility for best results, and in some gardens slugs can be a menace. From seed sown under glass in spring it is possible for some plants to flower in late summer, otherwise sow out of doors to obtain stock to flower freely the following year after transplanting. Named varieties of flowering size are obtainable, but these will not flower true from seed, which mostly produces mixed shades of blue. A few strains come reasonably true especially in the shorter-lived Pacific Hybrids, having names taken from the Arthurian legends.

Belladonna delphiniums are less tall with more open spikes, and in their way are as attractive as the large-flowered varieties, though it is in the latter that double flowers occur.

Dianthus
The name covers both pinks and carnations. The latter are excluded but the former are garden favourites for both perfume and colour. There are a number of named varieties, mostly double, which include white, pink and red shades. These are increased by cuttings or divisions but from seed they throw singles as well as variable colours. All garden pinks are in the 6 to 12-in. height range and much

Dicentra spectabilis

prefer an open position with well-drained soil, flowering from June to August.

Dicentra
The true bleeding heart, *Dicentra spectabilis*, has few faults as a hardy perennial, and it is worthy of a little extra fussing to give of its best. The lush foliage, the arching sprays dangling red and white lockets are a gladdening sight from April to June. The fangy but brittle roots should be planted carefully in well-drained soil, where some sun but not the worst of the winds can reach them. Division is tricky, but the vernal shoots, with a good base, will root in a cold frame.

D. eximia (or *formosa*) is a dwarfer plant which will spread below ground to give a mound of greenery and 12-in. sprays of deep rosy-coloured flowers in early summer. There is a pretty, though less reliable, white form but the brightest and largest flowered is Adrian Bloom. Flowers have twice the size of the type and much more colour as well as a longer flowering period. Bountiful is another improvement, slightly less colourful but no less vigorous. These are quite easy to divide and indeed are best divided and replanted after about three years in newly enriched soil. They will grow in sun or partial shade, and are less susceptible to gale damage than *D. spectabilis*.

Dictamnus
Dictamnus fraxinella, the burning bush, is a deeply rooting plant that likes full sun and perfect drainage where it will live for years to send up bush-forming spikes to 3 ft. carrying a bright array of lilac-pink flowers from June to August. This is not a plant on which to attempt division, and from seed it is rather slow to reach maturity.

Diplarrhena
The stiff, tufty, iris-like leaves of *Diplarrhena moraea* are evergreen and through these in June and July come wiry 18-in. stems and distinctive 1½-in. open three-petalled white flowers, tinged purple at the base. This is a good-natured plant for well-drained soil and not too exposed a position.

Doronicum
The leopard's banes are easy-to-grow subjects making a bright display of yellow in spring. The earliest to thrust up their widely rayed yellow daisies are the dwarfest. *Doronicum* Goldzwerg reaches only 6 in. from late March to May followed quickly by the 15-in. Miss Mason. This is the height of the fully double-flowered Spring Beauty, an outstanding variety. Harpur Crewe is the tallest, with wide-rayed flowers on 3-ft. stems. Doronicums are easy to divide (preferably in early autumn) and respond to such replanting every few years.

Echinacea
Echinacea purpurea (syn. *Rudbeckia purpurea*), the purple cone-flower, has a special appeal with its somewhat drooping petals accentuating the cone from which they radiate, on stems up to 3½ ft. Named varieties as well as variable seedlings are offered but the best-known variety The King is not in my opinion the best garden plant. The colour is deep purple rose on stems apt to need supports. Robert Bloom is a much warmer rosy-red shade, and it should not need staking. The strain from which this was selected, Bressingham Hybrids, has only slight variations in colour. All give their best display from July to September. Echinaceas like good deep soil, well drained but not too dry, and can safely be divided in early spring.

Echinops
Without exception, the deep-rooting globe thistles are reliably hardy and perennial,

but one or two are too massive for small gardens. All have greyish, jagged and slightly prickly leaves and branching stems to carry rounded flower heads of mainly light blue.

Echinops ritro grows erectly to 3 ft., is a deeper blue, and is less troublesome than the taller, more massive kinds. *E. humilis* is amongst the larger ones and includes the 5-ft. variety Taplow Blue and the 4-ft. Blue Cloud. Veitch's Blue is less robust at 3 to 4 ft., and has deeper blue flowers, but these varieties look somewhat shabby after flowering ends by late August, so that one is tempted to cut them hard back to encourage a tuft of new leaves instead. Old plants are easier to divide than to dig up, and roots left in the ground will mostly sprout again.

Epimedium
The barrenworts are valuable for pretty ground-cover foliage which lasts for most of the year and follows the dainty flower sprays in spring. Though adaptable, light shade is what they prefer, and quicker growth spread comes where not too dry. Roots are increased by dividing in autumn. Foliage effect is freshly green in all varieties, but flower colour varies, from yellow in *Epimedium perralderianum*, orange in *E. warleyense*, pink in *E. macranthum* and *E. rubrum*. The white *E. youngianum niveum* is the dwarfest at only 6 in. tall. The stems support the foliage like a canopy, and though a new set of leaves is made every year, it is only during early spring, when flowering time comes, that foliage is absent.

Epimediums have a great potential in the modern way of gardening, which accounts for their steady rise in popularity. But although they are adaptable to some of the less hospitable shady places, they do respond to kindness with an occasional mulch with peat and added fertilizer.

Erigeron
The fleabanes are useful members of the daisy family, giving a good display from May to August, and some are excellent for cutting. They are happy in open positions, in any well-drained soil and are best increased by division in spring. The most reliable include the varieties Darkest of All, which is single flowered, violet blue, 20 in., and Foerster's Liebling, near double, bright pink, of similar height. Lilofee and Adria are lavender blue, 2½ ft., Prosperity, light lavender blue, 20 in., almost double. Amity, lilac pink, 2 ft., Gaiety, single, pink, and Sincerity, mauve blue, single, are long flowering and Dignity is violet blue. The old variety Quakeress,

pale lilac pink is still garden worthy, though not erect growing in a confined space.

Eryngium
By comparison with most flowers the sea hollies are freakish, as all have flowers without visible petals. In some the stems are as brightly coloured as the flower bracts and in others the flowers and leaves are both green. Such species as *Eryngium serra*, *E. bromeliifolium* and *E. pandanifolium* grow from large green rosettes of vicious-looking, saw-edged leaves and send up stiffly branching spikes tipped by green spiny thimbles as flowers.

E. alpinum is very handsome, with rounded green leaves and sturdy 2½-ft. stems crowned with large, whiskery, silver-blue flowers. *E. bourgati* is reliable. This is very silvery with a tinge of blue in the 20-in. stems as well as in the terminal bract. *E. variifolium* has marbled evergreen foliage. This reaches 2 ft. and *E. dichotomum* is also good on somewhat similar lines. *E. planum* is easy, green and leafy except for the blue flowering tips, but these are not so bright as in the widely branching *E. tripartitum* which is the best of this group growing 3 to 3½ ft. Some eryngiums will come from seed, but the usual method of increase is from root cuttings in spring.

Euphorbia
This vast and varied genus includes oddities, weeds and a few good garden plants. All have bracts or clustered flower heads and the characteristic white sap in the leaves and stems. *Euphorbia characias* and *E. wulfenii* are so much alike for garden purposes that they can be described together. They are sub-shrubs, with year-round, blue-grey foliage of a succulent nature, and slowly build up into imposing plants 3 ft. high or more till they startlingly burst into almost a fountain of sulphur-yellow heads of flower in spring. These are scarcely plants for an ordinary border, but they look well with shrubs or on a wall. They prefer privation to richness, and though old plants may die out and severe winters may reduce them to pulp, there are usually sufficient self-sown seedlings around to refurnish the group. These are best transplanted when quite small.

One of the best of all spring-flowering herbaceous plants is *E. polychroma* (syn. *E. epithymoides*). It is very sturdy and hardy and remains compact, producing heads of bright sulphur-yellow bracts in April and early May. These reach 18 in.

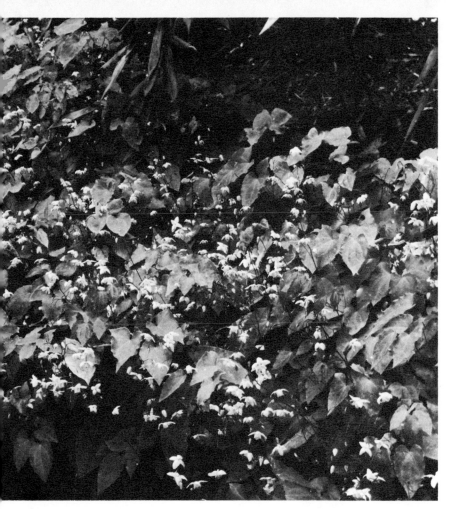

Epimediums used as ground cover

by the time they begin to fade to green, and remain a neat bush of foliage until autumn.

Given an open site *E. griffithii* Fireglow is a very good plant, with slow-spreading shoots from below ground that come through at first like asparagus to show the deep fiery heads in May and June. Afterwards these too fade into the greenery of a stiff shapely bush, 2½ ft. high. *E. niciciana* makes a splendid show of sulphur yellow for many weeks of summer. Wiry stems with narrow leaves terminate in flattened heads to form a bush about 2 ft. high from a compact rootstock. It is best in well-drained soil and full sun.

E. robbiae makes a wealth of deep green leaves and occasional flower heads with effective leaf cover at 10 to 12 in. high. *E. amygdaloides* and *E. macrostegia* are on similar lines – deep green foliage and a reasonably rapid spread, but these are more suitable amongst shrubs than in a perennial border.

Gentiana

The name gentian has become so closely associated with alpines and rock gardens

that many people are surprised when they learn that some species grow to 4 ft. high. In between the true alpine and these tall and not very special herbaceous species, there are a few first-class garden plants, of which one outstanding example is the willow gentian, *Gentiana asclepiadea*. This carries deep blue trumpets on slender stems about 2 ft. high in late summer, but is much better in cool shade than in fully open or dry positions. It dies down in winter to a compact root which dislikes being moved, much less divided. In just the right conditions it will naturalize.

Too little use is made in frontal border groups of the summer-flowering gentians of which *G. septemfida* is best known. Although none exceed 9 to 10 in. in height they make such a wonderful show and are quite happy in ordinary soil, with or without lime. All have bright blue trumpets clustered on somewhat lax, leafy stems, and all much prefer to be left alone once planted.

Geranium

True geraniums, crane's bills, are hardy garden plants, and the majority are of the easiest culture with many adaptable for both sun and shade. *Geranium armen-*

um (a name preferable to *psilostemon*, now said to be correct) will grow up to 3 ft. in a dense bush given ample moisture as against barely 2 ft. where starved and dry. The flowers, over 1 in. across on wide branching stems, are fiercely magenta from June to August, but Bressingham Flair is less intense, with more pink showing in the flowers.

Geranium endressii forms dense mounds of light green, and sprays of light or bright pink make a good show in June and July, about 20 in. high. A. T. Johnson, Rose Clair and Wargrave Pink are all pink with not much variation. *G. grandiflorum* spreads too quickly for what it gives in flowers, but Johnson's Blue is very good indeed. It smothers itself in early summer in wide, blue, saucer-shaped flowers, and reaches a height of 18 in. *G. ibericum platypetalum* is taller at 2 ft. or so, dark of leaf and a rich deep blue in flower.

G. renardii is a little charmer, in spite of its having a rather brief period in flower. The flowers are shallow cups of lightest mauve blue, marked with delicate crimson veins within. These disappear in June under a 10-in. canopy of greyish leaves, downy and stippled and so remaining until autumn.

G. sanguineum spreads, though not to become a nuisance, and has a long succession of magenta-rose flowers in the solid twiggy-stemmed mound it makes, only 12 in. high, and there is a white form, *album*, also a good pink known as *lancastriense splendens* which makes a 12-in. mound and keeps flowering for about ten weeks.

G. sylvaticum Mayflower is among those that flower in May and June with light blue salver-shaped flowers nestling above the very pretty canopied foliage of buttercup shape, on 20-in. stalks. Deeper blue flowers come for several weeks on the densely spreading mounds of the uncommon but easy *G. wlassovianum*. This covers the July to September period and is worth a place where space is not restricted though the root itself is compact. Deep and inhospitable shade will not prevent the 2-ft. *G. phaeum* from flowering in May and June. It has tough roots and abundant foliage which, like so many of the taller kinds, needs to be cut back after flowering so as to encourage new greenery.

Geum

The best-known varieties are the least reliable as perennials, but for reliability *Geum borisii* deserves a high rating with its intense orange single flowers on 12-in. stems above leafy plants in May and June and sometimes later. The shortest lived are the popular double red Mrs Bradshaw and double yellow Lady Stratheden. These flower very freely, but after a couple of years they lose vigour and die in most gardens.

Other hybrids of value, though all will need replanting and dividing every two or three years to retain vigour, are Fire Opal, orange red, and Rubin, deep red, which both grow to about 2 ft. Georgenberg is single yellow, long flowering and hummocky in growth, height 12 in., April to June, whilst Lionel Cox is similar but soft yellow. *G. rossii* is a distinctive species, neat growing with somewhat carroty foliage, and in May and June it sends up 9-in. sprays of bright yellow.

Gillenia

Gillenia trifoliata is a subject for good moist soil, with or without shade, in which grace and charm compensate for lack of brilliance. Erect willowy leaved bushes grow to 3 ft. to give open panicles of small white flowers from June to August. Its roots are tough, long lived and trouble free.

Gypsophila

The tallest but still popular baby's breath is not an ideal border subject because of its floppy habit. The double-flowered Bristol Fairy has little advantage over the single, longer-lived type. Both are charming in their way, with clouds of tiny pure white flowers, but the fangy rooted plants need space, as well as free-drained soil, in which to make their expansive display in late June to September. There is a dwarfer neater double-flowered variety named *Gypsophila compacta plena*. This makes a mound 18 in. high and 2 ft. across and is to be preferred in a mixed bed or border. Two dwarfer double pink varieties exist. One is Pink Star, with small pale pink flowers on mounded growth to 18 in. and the more prostrate Rosy Veil.

Helenium

The sneezeweeds are quite indispensable for providing a rich display of colour, but neglect can cause some disappointment. As plants become old, starvation makes leaves wither to spoil the flowering effect, and this can only be corrected by dividing and replacing every three years or so in enriched soil. Heleniums are very easy to grow, but do best in fully open positions.

The tallest varieties should be avoided and browny reds as Bruno and Moerheim Gem are in the 4-ft. range of heights, for July to September flowering, with Butterpat, a good yellow. Earlier sturdy varieties are Bressingham Gold, Coppelia, Gold Fox and Mahogany, all with orange and browny-flame shades. Golden Youth is a fine clear colour, about 2½ ft., and Wyndley is also quite dwarf, parti-coloured. The dwarfest, under 2 ft., is Crimson Beauty, but the colour is brownish red. Division of heleniums is safe in early autumn or spring.

Heliopsis

These have obvious family connections with heleniums, but they can be left alone for several years and relied upon to flower freely unsupported. All varieties are basically yellow, tinged green in Goldgreenheart, to the rich buttery yellow of Golden Plume. Both are semi-double flowered, and two good single varieties are Ballerina and *Heliopsis patula*. The branching stems produce a long display of 3-in. flowers from June to September, on a somewhat bush-forming habit of growth with ample greenery to about 3 ft.

Helleborus

The true Christmas rose has a never-failing appeal even though it seldom opens in time for Christmas. But January–February flowering is exciting enough to make this a very desirable plant, though it is best placed in shade, not where overhung or very dry, preferring a cool position. Old plants do not move or divide at all well, and young seedling plants do best.

Helleborus niger is followed in time of flowering by a complex range which includes the Lenten rose, *H. orientalis*. This varies in colour from white to deep pink and even plum-purple shades. Flowering shoots appear long before winter is over and in March and April they can prove a real joy, with their up-turned, saucer-shaped, golden-stamened flowers, up to 3 in. across, on 12 to 18-in. stems. The annual change of leaf takes place as flowering fades, with the broadly fingered foliage, freshly green at first, making a 12-in. canopy for eleven months of the year. The *orientalis* hybrids – seldom available to name or colour – are most rewarding. A colony or just a few plants can permanently fill an odd corner of the garden even where it becomes quite dry in summer, so long as it is not sunbaked. Where moist enough, self-sown seedlings will appear, but they can be divided in autumn.

H. corsicus makes quite a show of pale greenish-white flowers on 2-ft. stems in spring. A somewhat more compact and reliable hybrid exists named *H. sternii* and this has the same saw-edged leaves, but of a darker green as well as whiter flowers than *H. corsicus*.

If hellebores in general are not altogether suitable for a summer border, they fit in well amongst shrubs, which can provide the shade they like, and the 2-ft. tall *H. foetidus* can fill a really inhospitable place in dry shade to the extent of becoming naturalized, even though it is not long lived, after a full spring flowering of greenery has taken place.

Heuchera

Heucheras have that rare combination of compact well-foliaged evergreen growth and a show of brightly coloured flowers carried daintily on sprays or spikes for several weeks in early summer. Many have very pretty leaves, shaped much like the geraniums, in varying shades of green, sometimes with darker zonings. The stems are thin and wiry, varying from 15 to 30 in. high, and the number of individual flowers, small and bell shaped on a well-grown plant, run into hundreds. Colours range from white to every shade of pink, through to scarlet and red including coral, salmon and coppery crimson. Heucheras must firstly have good drainage, and are best in sun or only partial shade. They flower better for being enriched, yet they are drought resistant. Crowns become woody with age, and the remedy, often needed every three to four years, is to mulch deeply with soil or compost, or to dig up and replant deeply, using only the most vigorous shoots and discarding older woody growth.

Several named varieties are available, true to colour, but Bressingham Hybrids are a mixed strain giving a wide colour range. They do not come true from seed and division is best after flowering ceases in July. Scintillation, bright pink, tipped coral, 2 ft.; Sparkler, carmine and scarlet, 2 ft.; Splendour, salmon scarlet, 2 ft.; Red Spangles, 20 in.; Pretty Polly, soft pink, 15 in.; Hyperion, strong growing, coral rose, close-packed spike, 2½ ft., and Greenfinch, greenish white, 2½ ft., are recommended varieties.

Heucherella

Heucherella Bridget Bloom is a splendid little plant for fairly good light soil, preferring a little shade, and has been known to flower almost as freely in autumn as its normal period of May and June, with a profusion of light pink sprays 15 in. high. This and *H. tiarelloides* are hybrids between a heuchera and tiarella. The latter gives good ground cover with soft, slightly golden leaves and sends up in April and May a display of 12-in. foamy pink spikes. This is an easily grown plant for any but hot dry positions.

Hosta

The plantain lilies have indeed come into their own of recent years because all are such good garden plants, possessing hardiness, adaptability, reliable growth and good foliage, coupled with pleasing overall appearance. They will grow in shade or sun so long as their roots can find moisture and nutriment. In any but parched or starved conditions they can be left for years to develop into solid clumps. Ideally they are happiest in cool shade, especially those with variegated leaves. All lose their leaves at the onset of winter, and can be divided when dormant.

Hosta crispula has handsome creamy-buff marginal-edged leaves, with lavender-mauve flowers in June to August on 3-ft. stems. This is the period when most hostas flower, but *H. fortunei* and its varieties are earlier than others. The type has large pointed blue-green leaves and 2-ft. stems carrying pale lavender flowers. *H. f. picta* comes through in spring with bright and very attractive variegations which last until flowering at mid-summer before turning green. Honeybells is a green-leaved variety, with 2½-ft. spikes, freely produced, carrying sweetly scented lavender trumpets. *H. lancifolia* is a likeable plant, shapely of growth, with narrow, deep green leaves overlapping and having a fair show of 20-in. spikes in late summer. *H. rectifolia* is a splendid free-flowering plant growing to a stately 4 ft., with lavender-mauve spikes.

The name *H. sieboldiana* is still to some extent in dispute because some consider *H. glauca* to be the correct name. There is a glaucous-leaved type which is less distinctive than the massive *H. sieboldiana elegans*. This also has pale mauve flowers but the spikes reach 3 ft. and the leaves are up to 18 in. across. Then there is what I call *H. s.* (or *glauca*) *coerulea*. This has large but more rounded leaves, and they have a more definite bluish hue, though the flowering is very similar.

Thomas Hogg – a variety raised over a hundred years ago – is virtually identical with *H. albo-marginata*. The glaucous leaves are very large, inclined to be rounded and with a creamy-white edge – the 2-ft. spikes carry mauve flowers. This is not very different from *H. crispula*, and they are certainly alike in preferring a place away from strong sun and wind to look their best.

H. undulata medio variegata has brightly variegated leaves all summer. It is much smaller than most hostas and the deep mauve flowers are on 12 to 18-in. spikes. *H. ventricosa* is easy and reliable. It flowers freely in July–August, with deep lavender trumpets on 3-ft. stems. The leaves are deep green, but in *H. v. variegata* they have streaks of yellow which, with a free-flowering habit, make it one of the most attractive. The new variety Royal Standard is green leaved with perfumed white flowers 2½ ft. tall and is a welcome addition to the range.

Incarvillea

Once the deep fangy roots decide in early May to sprout, growth is rapid and startling. Within two or three weeks, the exotic-looking trumpet flowers of deep reddish pink begin to open. The deeply cut dark green leaves follow, and in the case of *Incarvillea delavayi* the stems reach 2 ft. or more before the last flowers fade in early July. *I. grandiflora* begins flowering almost at ground level and seldom exceeds 12 in. Well-drained soil and sun is much preferred.

Inula

This is another genus of yellow daisy flowers, all of which have rayed petals. *Inula barbata* makes a fairly quick spread of soft leafy mounds on which 1½-in. flowers nestle for many weeks after June, and *I. hookeri* is similar, but about twice as tall at 2½ ft., with larger flowers. The variety named Golden Beauty is neat growing and long flowering. It forms 2-ft. upright bushes, and the yellow flowers keep coming from June to September.

I. ensifolia compacta is a most useful little plant for frontal positions and is long lived and trouble free, and although *I. orientalis* grows only to 20 in. or so, the flowers are 3 to 4 in. across and very finely rayed. All inulas are easily increased by division and need no special treatment.

Iris

The most popular section of iris is the *germanica* or June-flowering varieties. There is a welter of varieties in existence in a fascinating range of colours. Whilst agreeing that they make a glorious display, their period of glory is short. This is the chief fault also of so many kinds of iris, but there are some that help in spreading the flowering season. *Iris pumila*, for example, is at its best in April and May, in shades of yellow, blue and white, and all are under 12 in. in height.

I. foetidissima is the wild Gladwyn iris with deep evergreen foliage, and it will grow in quite deep shade. One seldom notices it flower, but cannot fail to notice the vermilion seedpods in autumn as they burst open. There is an excellent variegated form of this very useful plant, as there is of the old *I. pallida*, the poor man's orchid of cottage gardens.

I. missouriensis is easy and attractive and makes a bright display of light blue flowers on 2-ft. stems, as does *I. beesiana*, and the deep blue *I. setosa* is also good value. All these flower for most of June and July.

Kirengeshoma

Kirengeshoma palmata is a native of Japan and it has waxy-looking flowers like small daylilies of soft yellow for many weeks in later summer, nodding over a mass of light greenery. The leaves are fingered and of nettle type but the whole plant has a distinctive appearance, at once bushy and graceful, reaching 3 ft. high where moist. It likes a humus-rich soil, some light shade and no lack of moisture and though it makes no brilliant display, it is the type of plant one feels glad to have.

Knautia

Knautia macedonica (syn. *Scabiosa rumelica*) cannot be faulted on the score of distinction and long flowering, though it does not usually survive for more than about three seasons. It makes considerable mounded growth from a fairly small rootstock and gives a long display of deep red pincushion flowers from June to September. The habit is lax, and should be left that way for the best effect, because it will at least give ground cover at about 20 in., and the short-stemmed flowers rise just above this.

Kniphofia

All red hot pokers like a sunny open position, and the range is now so wide that the six months from May to October can be covered, whilst heights range from 18 in. to 6 ft. when in flower. The variety Atlanta makes quite massive broad-leaved plants with heavy red and yellow spikes at 3 ft. Bees Sunset, deep orange; Gold Else; Springtime, red and yellow, and *Kniphofia tubergenii*, light yellow, are all in the 3-ft. range from June to August flowering, along with the salmon-flushed-ivory Jenny Bloom, and the ivory-white Maid of Orleans. Bressingham Torch and Bressingham Flame also flower at this time. These last two have the grassy foliage and slender spikes of the dwarf October-flowering *K. galpinii*, but reach about 2½ ft. Two splendid and more reliable variations of *K. galpinii* exist in Bressingham Comet and Bressingham Gleam flowering in September–October, at about 1½ to 2 ft.

Helleborus niger

For taller late flowering (August–October), there are some of majestic stature, such as the brilliant flame Samuel's Sensation and the orange C. M. Prichard. *K. caulescens* is distinctive – half-way to a yucca in habit, with thick stems to the heavy, broad-leaved, glaucous rosettes above ground. The spikes are stumpy, yellow and red, in late summer.

Liatris

This is a showy, distinctive perennial. An unusual feature is that the bright lilac-purple furry flowers begin to open at the top of the 2½ to 3-ft. stems, in contrast to nearly all other spiky plants. The species *Liatris callilepis* is most often listed, but those who order *L. spicata* or *L. pycnostachya* will be sent much the same plant though there is a dwarfer ace in Kobold. Flowering begins in June and lasts several weeks, especially on young plants. Old

Liriope

This name is seldom listed in hardy plant catalogues, but *Liriope muscari*, especially, is a first-rate plant. It forms a hefty tuft of narrow deeply evergreen leaves through which appear, from August till late October, little pokery 15 to 18-in. spikes like grape hyacinths of a bright lilac-mauve shade. With small tubers amid the densely fibrous root system, it is fairly impervious to drought and is hardy, long lived and trouble free.

Lupinus

Ranking as they do amongst the indispensables to be seen in practically every garden, little need be said about them here. With new varieties coming on to the market year by year, the choice must rest with the purchaser, as far as names are concerned. Many people prefer to have the cheaper seedling plants, even if they turn out as a mixture. Lupins prefer neutral or acid to alkaline soils, but do not revert, as some people imagine. Deterioration is due to self-sown seedlings taking the place of those originally planted.

Lychnis

Lychnis chalcedonica is a good perennial, making a compact plant and producing leafy stems capped with a head 2 to 3 ft. tall of small but intense red flowers in the June–August period. *L. coronaria* is silver-grey leaved, and has loose sprays of pink or carmine flowers for a long period. This showy plant is best in a dry place, but will

Below: *Kniphofia* **C. M. Pritchard**

Island beds in the author's garden

plants are best dug up in spring and rejuvenated by division into enriched soil.

Libertia

There are several species in existence, but even the best known *Libertia formosa* is not often seen. Plants make quite a packed mass of narrow evergreen iris-like fans but from a mainly fibrous root, and through this come 2-ft. spikes of open-petalled white flowers in June–July. Hardiness is not a strong feature with libertias, and they thrive best in light soil and need a sunny place. *L. ixioides* is shorter than *L. formosa*. Divide in spring.

Limonium

The most reliable is *Limonium latifolium* and it makes a large plant with a fair spread of shining leaves and wide branching 2 to 3-ft. sprays of tiny blue flowers from July to September. For drying, cut stems before fading begins. Named varieties are offered in Blue Cloud and the deeper blue Violetta. These deep-rooting plants should be in a well-drained, open position.

Linum

The blue *Linum perenne* is not very perennial, seldom living beyond two summers. *L. narbonnense* is much longer lived, so long as the soil is very well drained and where happy it is one of the finest of dwarf border plants. The flowers are richly blue and $\frac{3}{4}$ in. across and are borne on narrow-leaved bushes about 20 in. high, giving a brilliant show for ten weeks or more from June to September. The yellow linums also prefer sun and good drainage.

   L. dolomiticum makes a compact root and sends up erect stems to about 18 in., crowned with a wide cluster of brightest yellow rounded flowers $\frac{3}{4}$ in. across from mid-June to late August. *L. campanulatum* and *L. flavum* are on similar lines but dwarfer.

produce seedlings to make up for being rather short lived. *L. viscaria* in the double form *plena* has flowers on sticky 10-in. stems of a very bright deep pink. Plants are neat growing with deep green narrow leaves, flowering June–July.

Macleaya

These easily grown plants make strong spikes up to 6 ft., with powdered stems and pretty leaves which are brownish beneath and bluish above, and sprays of tiny flowers in late summer. In the true *Macleaya cordata* the flowers are more definite – little ivory-white tubes $\frac{1}{2}$ in. long and as a background plant – by itself or against a dark background – it is very effective.

M. microcarpa has a wider branching spike, but the flowers are of a brownish yellow, to be appreciated as a whole and not for individual florets. The name Coral Plume was given to a slightly more colourful variation. The somewhat fleshy roots tend to wander and shoot up amongst neighbouring subjects unawares, though they are not difficult to check or eradicate. Both types will grow in quite dry soils and do not object to shade.

Meconopsis

Few plants have achieved such an aura as the blue Himalayan poppy and, as *Meconopsis baileyi*, common usage has stood firm against the more recently imposed name of *M. betonicifolia*. Like all meconopsis, this needs light leafy soil and some shade, and spikes attain 3 ft. where suited. It is not long lived, but comes freely from seed. *M. chelidonifolia* is easy and fully perennial. The fingery light green leaves hang from wiry stems up to 2$\frac{1}{2}$ ft. tall and from June to August, 2-in. yellow flowers dangle above.

Monarda

These have both colour and curiosity appeal. All grow from mat-forming plants that may spread rather quickly in rich or moist soil, and make leafy bushes varying in height from 2 to 4 ft. accordingly. The terminal heads are of bract-like flowers, with arching lipped petals in red, pink and purple shades. Named varieties are best. Adam is cerise red; Melissa, bright pink; and there is Croftway Pink, and the old favourite Cambridge Scarlet. Prairie Glow is salmon red, not so tall, and both Prairie Night and *Monarda magnifica* are purple. Monardas respond to the rejuvenating effects of replanting every two or three years, best divided in spring and young plants flower longer, are less tall and are altogether superior.

Moraea

For those who seek worthy but uncommon plants, *Moraea spathacea* is one which is not at all difficult to grow. It forms clumps of iris-like leaves, and above during May and June come 2-ft. stems carrying bright yellow flowers, not closely resembling iris in shape, but quite open petalled. It is long lived and trouble free in well-drained soil.

Morina

Morina longifolia has long spiny leaves in bright green rosettes like a thistle, but they are shiny and hairless. It also has a thistly tap root but the spike of 2 ft. or so develops to show the drooping-lipped pink flowers. In sun and any well-drained soil it will throw flowering stems on and off all summer, even into November.

Nepeta

The popular species of catmint is *Nepeta mussinii* which gives such a long succession of lavender-blue flowers from 12-in. spikes, from grey-leaved clumpy plants. Though adaptable to sun or partial shade, winter losses occur where drainage is poor. Division is best in spring. A larger edition exists in Six Hills Giant which has sprays up to 2 ft. tall over the same June–September period. Blue Beauty differs in having erect spikes of larger violet-blue flowers, 20 in. tall and plants expand by creeping shoots below ground. The plants when crushed have a distinct mint-like fragrance which cats especially like.

Oenothera

The name evening primrose applies to the short-lived *Oenothera biennis*, but there are several fully perennial kinds that make a bright display with their big yellow cup-shaped flowers. *O. cinaeus* comes through in spring with bright parti-coloured leaves – buff, pink, purple red, but these fade to deep green as the loose sprays of rich yellow cups open. Fireworks is a deep yellow similar in habit but with purplish-green leaves, as is Yellow River with green foliage, and the 2-ft. tall Highlight has a neat basal growth of clustered rosettes which when older increase easily from division in early spring.

O. linearis has smaller flowers on 1$\frac{1}{2}$-ft. twiggy branching sprays and *O. glaber* is erect at 15 in. and bright yellow. Both are good plants of somewhat similar growth. The most distinctive oenothera is *O. missouriensis* but it is virtually prostrate in habit. It makes a quite wide spread of greenery which from July to October has saucers 4 in. across of light canary yellow. This needs sun and good drainage.

Omphalodes

One species is worthy of inclusion for although it is of very lowly stature it has real carpeting value in shady places. *Omphalodes cappadocica* has crinkly grey-ish-green foliage of about 6 in. and sprays of tiny but brilliant forget-me-not flowers in April and May. The variety Anthea Bloom is sky blue and very free flowering. They are long lived, trouble-free plants for cool positions.

Origanum

This genus includes some that have aromatic foliage and are of culinary value. The true marjoram is *Origanum vulgare, and the neater-growing O. compactum* makes deep green bushes 10 in. high covered in tiny blue flowers in late summer. The golden-leaved form *O. v. aureum* has no flowers worth mentioning though the aromatic foliage has almost year-round brightness. *O. laevigatum* makes a pretty show of tiny purple-blue flowers on wiry branching stems 15 in. high.

Paeonia

These are amongst the longest lived of all perennials. They should be planted with permanence in mind, space in which to expand, and in an open situation. Peonies like rich deep soil, and respond to mulching after a time. Old plants can be divided, with the careful use of a knife with which to separate the liveliest chunks. This should always take place in the August–October period. Planting depth is important. The new buds should rest 1 in. only below surface.

Varieties of the popular June-flowering period are legion. Some have huge flowers, in shades of pink, red and white, mostly double. Some are more fragrant than others, but most specialist catalogues give details of this point as well as of colour and height. Varieties under the specific name of *Paeonia sinensis* can be had to cover the whole of June – both double and single flowered. Doubles and singles occur, with a more limited colour range, in the earlier *P. officinalis*. *P. lobata* is single flowered, intense orange red in the variety Sunshine, but the earliest is the charming single yellow *P. mlokosewitschii*, which often opens in April. Other worthy single-flowered species are *P. smouthii* and *P. arietina*, deep pink, and the white *P. obovata*.

Papaver

For size of flowers Oriental poppies, *Papaver orientalis*, can easily compete with peonies. For brilliance of colour, they can excel them but they are not so

Papaver Mrs Perry

permanent nor do they have the merit of pleasing foliage to carry on, as do peonies, after flowering. All flower from late May until late June, but not all are capable of standing without support which should be provided as unobtrusively as possible.

The most erect I know is the blood-red Goliath, standing nobly at 3 ft. or more, though the orange-scarlet Marcus Perry is pretty good in this respect. Other varieties include brownish red, various shades of pink, also white. Some of the double flowered are rather floppy. These poppies like a very well-drained soil, not too rich. Their fleshy roots are deeply penetrating. After flowering, growth should be cut back so as to encourage new leaves, without which an unsightly bare patch may occur.

Penstemon

The showiest kinds are the least reliable as hardy perennials. Some are used as bedding plants by taking cuttings in late summer or autumn and keeping them under glass until planting out time in spring, when they quickly fill out into bushy plants to flower from July to October. Flowers are of trumpet shape, coming on spikes up to 2½ ft. tall, with ample base greenery. In milder localities, the deep crimson Garnet and blood-red Firebird will mostly survive for several years, along with the clear pink Endurance. These have smaller flowers, but are colourful and long flowering.

Phlox

These rank very high amongst the brightest and most indispensable of border plants. They are happiest in light rather than heavy or alkaline soil. Phlox are offered in a bewildering range of varieties but the newest introductions do not necessarily supersede older varieties. Recommendations include older varieties which have stood the test of time.

The best dwarf white is still Mia Ruys, and for a taller one there is White Admiral at 3 ft. Mother of Pearl is a vigorous, weather-proof pink suffused white of similar height. Prospero is soft pink and Dodo Hanbury Forbes is somewhat deeper with Windsor, a carmine-rose shade. Endurance, salmon rose; Brigadier and Spitfire, orange salmon, and the intensely bright Prince of Orange should not be missed.

The most reliable deep red is Starfire, with Tenor, an early-flowering blood red while Aida, San Antonio and Vintage Wine are good representatives of the magenta-purple range. The King, Parma Violet and Marlborough are recommended violet purples. In lighter lavender-blue shades Skylight and Hampton Court are good whilst Balmoral has a tinge of lilac.

A much neglected section of phlox is *Phlox maculata*. The pure pink Alpha and the almost white purple-eyed Omega are the only representatives of this distinctive range. Flowers come on column-type trusses, up to 3 ft. tall, from a spreading mat-like rootstock, and make a long standing display from early July onwards.

Physostegia

The so-called obedient plants are good garden subjects, all having tapering spikes and subsidiaries from lower down and they remain in flower for several weeks. *Physostegia speciosa* Rose Bouquet has a profusion of light rosy-lilac flowers on 2-ft. spikes from July to September, but the dwarfer Vivid flowers later, and is often at its best in October. The deep pink flowers make a bright display, but the shooting roots wander so widely that it pays to round them up every spring to replant back where they belong.

The others including the pretty white Summer Snow and the deeper rose-pink Summer Spire belong to *P. virginiana*, and have more slender spikes about 3 ft. high. These flower from July to September, and have a vigorous rootstock consisting of spreading whitish crowns which tend to fall apart when lifting, and in moist or rich soil need curbing after two or three years. They are reliably perennial and need no special treatment.

Platycodon

When the buds of *Platycodon grandiflorum* expand, the petals are joined together to form a hollow globe of about walnut size, changing into saucer-shaped campanula-type flowers. As garden plants the balloon flowers have real merit. They are long lived, having quite fleshy roots, and need only well-drained soil. Heights vary from the 12-in. *P. g. mariesii* in shades of light blue to 2 ft. with the tallest clones of *P. grandiflorum* available in white, blue and

very pale pink. Plants are slightly variable in colour, but old plants will divide. Dormancy extends till April, and newly emerging shoots can be damaged by winter and spring cultivations if the exact site of plants is not marked or seen.

Polemonium

Some of these are short lived and seed about to become a nuisance. More reliable and seldom setting seed, *Polemonium foliosissimum* is not only a good perennial but has a much longer flowering period, sometimes lasting from June until September, growing to 2½ to 3 ft., with heads of lavender-blue, bird's-eye flowers.

Polemoniums are not fussy plants, and when old can be divided to promote rejuvenation. This applies especially to the dwarfer quite vigorous kinds, such as the light blue Sapphire, flowering in May and June at 15 in. and the 10-in. Blue Pearl. Pink Pearl makes a clumpy growth and has slightly bronze-tinged foliage, but the flowers are well short of a true pink. The common name of polemoniums is Jacob's ladder.

Polygonum

Most knotweeds have pokery spikes made up of tiny flowers so closely set together that the spike itself is the colourful part. In the robust *Polygonum amplexicaule*, the spikes are thin, topping a rounded dense bush of pointed leaves, reaching 4 to 5 ft. high and at least 3 ft. in diameter. The dull red form *atrosanguineum* and the lighter, brighter red Firetail can be recommended not only for reliability, but for a three-month flowering season.

P. bistorta superbum is worthwhile. The stems run up to 3 ft. or so, carrying 4-in. stumpy pokers of a clear light pink in May and June. *P. carneum* grows more compactly, with smaller but deeper pink pokers during June and July.

From narrow-leaved tufts come bottle-brush heads for weeks of the startling red-flowered *P. milettii*. *P. macrophyllum* has long wavy deep green leaves and branching stems 18 in. high of clear pink pokers from July onwards. To make a trio of the choicest polygonums, *P. sphaerostachyum* must be included. Low dense bushes intricately branched show their bright rosy-pink pokery heads in late spring and where happy continue to make a bright show all summer. All three are slow growing as plants, all like good moistish soil, and much prefer shade to an exposed position. Some other polygon-

Left: *Campanula glomerata* (foreground) and *Polygonum bistorta* (pale pink)

A traditional herbaceous border

ums are of a weedy nature and should not be used in gardens indiscriminately.

Potentilla

For rich colourings, long flowering and reliability many of the potentillas rank highly. They are mostly dwarf plants, easy to grow in any ordinary soil, and all have a good base of foliage, either green, grey or silvery, of strawberry shape.

Potentilla argyrophylla atrosanguinea has silvery leaves, vigorous growth and sprays of ¾-in., bright red flowers. Flamenco is similar but larger flowered and green leaved, carrying sprays up to 2 ft. Both flower from May to July, but it is from June to September that the more prostrate but equally brilliant Gibson's Scarlet takes over. Firedance is orange salmon, Miss Willmott is pink, and good semi-double flowered varieties are Glory of Nancy, orange and red; William Rollisson, flame orange, and Yellow Queen. All grow about 18 in. Potentillas are easy in open positions and can be divided in autumn or spring.

Prunella

These easy-to-grow plants, with the common name of self heal, are useful for frontal positions, and need only occasional replanting or curbing. Under the name Loveliness can be obtained white, lilac and pink shades. From mat-forming plants come stumpy spikes 9 to 10 in. high in June and July to make a bright if rather brief display. *Prunella webbiana* is a little later with deep green mats and 9-in. spikes of deep pink flowers.

Pulmonaria

These spring-flowering plants, the lungworts, are pretty adaptable, and can be effectively used in places one can more or less forget when summer comes. The brilliant blue little bell-shaped flowers of *Pulmonaria angustifolia azurea* come on 9-in. sprays from March to May and Munstead Blue is a little dwarfer and later to flower. *P. saccharata* is much more coarse, and even the red-flowered Bowles Red takes up space with large rough leaves. Those with prettily white spotted leaves are effective even when flowering is over and Pink Dawn is worthwhile, having flowers pink at first, on 12-in. sprays, which fade to blue, to give at times a two-colour effect without excessive growth.

Pulsatilla

Pulsatilla vulgaris is widely variable in both height and colour though basic features are constant. The Pasque flowers are deeply rooting plants, which in early spring send up goblet-shaped flowers with silvery gossamer surroundings, followed by grey-green ferny leaves which last on through summer. Plants become larger with age but do not spread. Flowering ceases in May and is followed by prettily tufted seed heads. Colours range from pale lavender to purple, and include white and ruby red, with prominent golden stamens, reaching 9 to 12 in. in height.

Pyrethrum

These brightly coloured daisy-type flowers are decorative from late May till July but unless planted with ample light and air space they need supporting even though they are mostly under 3 ft. high. Well-drained soil and sun are essential. Planting in autumn is not advised but apart from March and early April, old plants can be lifted and divided immediately after flowering. Named varieties include single-flowered white, various shades of pink, as well as rich salmon red and crimson. Double-flowered varieties hold a similar colour range.

Rodgersia

These are all moisture lovers with handsome foliage worth protecting from damaging winds. All species are otherwise robust and hardy, forming steadily expanding clumps made up of crowns almost at ground level. An annual mulch does a power of good in providing a show of large chestnut-type leaves 1 to 2 ft. across on stems up to 3 ft. high.

Flowers are mostly creamy white but the best known *Rodgersia pinnata* has pink variations with *superba* quite outstanding. There is a bronzy-leaved, pink-flowered form known as Irish Bronze. Other species not differing greatly from one another are *R. podophylla* and *R. purdomi*, but *R. tabularis* is distinct with its 2½ ft. high, almost flat-topped umbrella leaves 12 in. across. This is not so robust growing, but none could be regarded as difficult given their basic necessities and all can be safely divided or planted in autumn or spring.

Roscoea

These are out of the ordinary plants which grow from brittle tuberous roots having a yellowish sap. They need deep planting since they establish themselves about 6 in. below surface, and do not emerge until well into May. The pointed shiny leaves sheath the stems which then carry a long succession of prominently lipped flowers.

In *Roscoea beesiana* stems come in close profusion, and the flowers are bicolour, purple and buff, 12 in. tall, from June to August. *R. cautleoides* is a little earlier and much looser in habit, with pale yellow flowers dangling a little on arching sprays to 1½ ft. *R. purpurea* has pretty light violet-blue flowers, but the variety *procera* is more colourful, and makes a good show from late June onwards.

Rudbeckia

Except for the short-lived and virtually annual *Rudbeckia hirta* and *R. purpurea* (syn. *Echinacea purpurea*), all the perennial species are yellow, but their variations in form make all but the tallest of value. Varieties of *R. laciniata* include the well-known Autumn Sun (Herbstsonne) which reaches an unsteady 6 or 7 ft. Goldquelle, however, grows unaided to a shapely 3 to 4 ft., with dense dark green foliage, set with fully double chrome-yellow flowers 3 in. across from July to October.

The grey-green leaved *R. deamii* makes a wonderful show from August to October with its black-eyed, deep yellow flowers on 2½-ft. stems. Bright green foliage sets off the amazingly free Goldsturm which often begins in June–July and continues into autumn. No rudbeckias like to be in parched conditions and where reasonably moist and in good soil will flower for much longer. All are easily divided in spring.

Salvia

The best hardy salvias flower from June to August. The variations of *Salvia superba* make erect sage-leaved stems, topped with slender spikes of tiny lipped flowers which attract bees and butterflies. May Night grows to about 20 in., with East Friesland rather more compact and later. Lubeca is 2½ ft. and the original *S. superba* is still the tallest at 3½ to 4 ft.

All are long lived, hardy and easy in any well-drained soil, and can be increased by division or basal cuttings in spring. *S. haematodes* is best from seed. In some gardens it will survive for years, as will the attractive cross between this and *S. superba*, named Indigo. *S. ambigens* grows erectly to 4 ft., and makes steady surface spread. The flowers are deep blue on terminal spikes from July onwards but the

roots need a winter covering of litter in cold districts.

Sanguisorba

The most stately is *Sanguisorba* (or *Poterium*) *sitchensis* which may be a form of the wild burnet, *S. officinalis*. It has 5-ft. stems, ample fingery leaves, and is topped by a profusion of short near-red pokers. This has tough roots, and will grow in almost any soil.

Satureia

Two of the savories are useful for frontal positions where they make a low mound of greenery all summer, and then in August and September are covered with tiny blue flowers. *Satureia cunaefolia* makes deep green little bushes but *S. montana caerulea* gives a wider more permanent spread. Both are very easy to grow.

Scabiosa

The blue *Scabiosa caucasica* is a firm favourite and is splendid for cutting. The range of colour is blue and white, growing about 2½ ft. tall and flowering from June to September. Scabious dislike wet, especially in winter and survive longest in free-draining alkaline soils. The open saucer-shaped flowers on wiry 2 to 3-ft. stems need to be cut or dead-headed to promote the long flowering. They are best planted or divided in spring, but can also be reared from seed.

Clive Greaves is mid-blue in colour, Moonstone is lighter of shade and Moerheim Blue is deeper. The white Miss Willmott or Bressingham White make for a contrast. A species worth noting is *S. graminifolia*. This makes a compact mound of silvery grassy leaves and gives a long succession of rounded pincushion heads on 10-in. stems of light lavender blue from June to September. The variety Pinkushion has soft pink flowers 1 in. across with similar habit. Both are reliable and easy in any sunny position.

Sedum

The taller herbaceous sedums include some that are well-established favourites, especially the so-called ice plant, *Sedum spectabile*, with wide heads densely packed with glistening pink flowers. The named varieties Brilliant, Carmen and Meteor do not differ greatly from one another, all flowering 12 to 18 in. in late summer. Autumn Joy grows sturdily to 2 ft. and the heads up to 12 to 15 in. across open first as light pink in September changing slowly to salmon rose.

S. heterodontum is also easy. From a

Scabiosa caucasica

somewhat fleshy rooted but compact plant, the crowns open in spring to reveal fuzzy heads of a burnt-orange colour, followed up by bluish succulent foliage on the stems. This is only 9 to 12 in. tall as is the yellow-headed *S. rhodiola*, the rose root sedum, with a similar dwarf bushy habit, with no fads as to soil and no rapid spread.

Selinum
For those attracted to the unusual and stately, *Selinum tenuifolium*, the milk parsley, might well appeal. Strong stems run to 4 or 5 ft. with lacy parsley-green leaves horizontally and topped by a wide head of whitish flowers 12 in. or so across. It is a trouble-free plant of considerable charm.

Serratula
Two of these are sufficiently compact and colourful to include, especially as they flower at an off-peak period. *Serratula macrocephala* has deep green deeply divided leaves and 18-in. branching stems carrying heads of light purple tufty flowers from August to October.

S. shawii is fairly similar, but only 12 in. high and more compact as well as being later to flower and deeper in colour. Both are easy to grow in any soil, without giving an excessive spread.

Sidalcea
These spike-forming plants flower gracefully between June and September, in shades of pink to rosy red. They are easy to grow, best in full sun with good drainage, and can be divided in spring. Mrs Alderson, Wm Smith and Rev. Page

Roberts are light satiny pink with slender spikes to 4 ft. but Puck is shorter at 2½ ft. Deeper shades are Rose Queen, Wensleydale and Croftway Red, at 3 to 4 ft. All have small, mallow-type flowers and when finished spikes should be cut back to promote new basal growth which will carry them over winter.

Sisyrinchium
Sisyrinchium striatum is one of the most adaptable of plants. The growth is very much like that of *Iris germanica*, of a flattened fan of sword leaves, but without tubers. The flowers, unlike iris, are open petalled on 2-ft. spikes from June to August. In spite of the small amount of fibrous root made by this plant it will grow in quite inhospitable soils and situations, as well as amongst fussier subjects and tends to naturalize itself from seed. There is a rarely seen and very pretty form with variegated leaves.

Solidago
Some species and named varieties too of golden rod are far too tall and invasive for good gardening, and one would do well to omit any that grow over 4 ft. tall, including the variety Golden Wings. Mimosa will reach 4 ft., but the plants grow compactly and do not seed about, as do some, after the handsome yellow plumes have finished in September.

Those growing less than 4 ft. are worth having, though all have the fault of a rather short flowering season. The range of colour varies from the deep yellow of Golden Mosa, Golden Shower, or Golden Falls to the lighter shades of Lemore and Leslie. All these grow about 2½ to 3 ft. varying somewhat in the shape of the plume and flowering between July and September. Peter Pan is earlier with distinctive lateral branches to the crested plume. Crown of Rays is on similar lines, but very bushy in habit as well as being dwarfer at 2 ft., whilst Cloth of Gold is only 18 in. tall, with a vigorous outward spread.

The neatest-growing dwarfs are the miniatures, Queenie and Golden Thumb. They do not differ much from each other and form bright almost golden-leaved bushes 9 to 12 in. high, flowering from August to October. Although so easy to grow, these better solidagos are best planted or divided for replanting in early spring.

Stachys
The species *Stachys lanata*, with its felted silver leaves to which the donkeys' ears name has stuck, is an easy-growing, mat-

Stokesia laevis **Blue Star**

forming plant seen in most gardens with its thin spikes of small pink flowers in June–July. It has ground-covering properties in quite dry positions, and for those who prefer a complete foliage backcloth, the non-flowering variety Silver Carpet is available.

S. macrantha is a charming, easy-growing plant which produces bushy greenery topped with short spikes of rosy-purple lipped flowers in June–July, 2 to 2½ ft. tall. *S. spicata rosea* has 12-in. spikes of deep pink and in the form *densiflorum* the flowers are closely packed on 15-in. stems. This is a showy plant, as is the sturdier 20-in. *robusta*. All these are long flowering and easy to grow and divide in autumn or spring.

Stokesia
Stokesia laevis has wide open semi-double blue flowers. Where happy, in deep light soil, the 3-in. flowers come in long succession on 18-in. branching stems from early July to September. The leaves are long and leathery, but the plant itself does not spread much, and old plants can be divided in spring. There are slight variations in shade from seed, but the named variety Blue Star has proved to be the most reliable.

Strobilanthes
Strobilanthes atropurpurea is a little known but trouble-free plant which has a stout long-lived rootstock. Twiggy branching stems carry small greyish leaves from a dense bush about 2½ ft. high on which appear small violet-purple lipped flowers from July to September. It makes no great show, but is interesting and distinctive.

Old plants will divide in spring, and are best planted in fairly rich soil.

Stylophorum

Stylophorum diphyllum has rich yellow poppy-like flowers 1½ in. across which nestle amongst a profusion of glaucous-green leaves in spring to make this an attractive subject for semi-shady situations, where not too dry. The somewhat fleshy roots have a fairly vigorous spread though not to become a nuisance for they can easily be curbed. Height 9 in. when in flower with leaves fading in autumn.

Telekia

Telekia speciosa (syn. *Buphthalmum speciosum*) is a hefty, deep-rooting plant making a wide spread of broad leaves and demanding more space than the 3 to 4-ft. spikes of yellow daisy-type flowers deserve. It has a short season in flower, during June–July, and though easy to grow, there are other subjects, such as heliopsis, which will provide a longer better display in a smaller space.

Tellima

This is an unpretentious plant, grown mainly for its soft carpeting foliage rather than its 2-ft. sprays of greenish-buff flowers in May–June. *Tellima grandiflora purpurea* has rounded, mounded leaves of a bronzy-purple tinge, and is to be recommended for its adaptability to shady positions where more colourful subjects will not grow. Plants divide readily and planting is safe in autumn or spring.

Thalictrum

Without exception, meadow rues respond to fertility and all dislike drought. The

Pyrethrums E. M. Robinson (pink) and Kelway's Glorious (magenta)

so-called hardy maidenhair, *Thalictrum minus adiantifolium*, is the easiest to grow, but it is by no means showy, having buff-green flowers on 2½-ft. sprays. The tiny leaves are pretty, and this feature is shared, in varying forms, with all the species. The stately *T. angustifolium* has deep green deeply divided foliage beneath the fuzzy flower heads on strong 6-ft. stems. This flowers from June to August, as does the blue-grey *T. glaucum*, with fluffy heads of light yellow.

The earliest to flower is *T. aquilegifolium*. This is another easy-to-grow species, with bluish-green foliage, which comes into flower by early June. The strong stems are branched and they carry fluffy heads in shades of mauve and purple. There is also a pure white, and all grow to 3 to 4 ft. *T. dipterocarpum* makes a much smaller rootstock than the above, but sends up, where happy, a vast amount of rather lax top growth. This consists of small-leaved, much-branched stems which, if supported, will reach 6 ft. This species has individual flowers of mauve blue with orange stamens, and remains in flower from late June to September. The variety Hewitt's Double is not so tall and is less vigorous, and in greater need of rich moistish soil to give of its charming best.

T. rocquebrunianum is robust, with stems both strong and thick of a purplish glaucous hue. From the tip up to 4 ft. high, and from lateral branches, are borne the ½-in. wide, lilac-coloured flowers with prominent yellow stamens from June to August. It needs rich soil to give of its splendid best. Most species will divide.

Thermopsis

With strong resemblance to its cousin the lupin, thermopsis is a long-lived plant for a sunny position and well-drained soil. The best known *Thermopsis montana* is, in my opinion, far from being the most worthy, for its runs underground and will not keep to its allotted space. The yellow-flowered spikes, on 2-ft. stems, are less imposing than either *T. lanceolata* or *T. mollis*. Both these are light yellow with a compact bushy habit reaching 3 ft. high, with the former flowering in May and June, and the latter in June and July. Old plants do not easily divide and roots are tough.

Tovara

Tovara virginiana makes a shapely bush up to 3 ft. high, on which the flowering spikes are so thin that it makes a rather dull display. The form *variegata* seldom flowers, but it is well worth growing for its foliage alone. The leaf shadings are subdued, but soft and pleasing and given a moist, sheltered position, it will grow to a shapely 2½ ft. retaining its effect till winter comes. Plants are slow growing but long lived and trouble free.

Tradescantia

There is nothing choice about the trinity flowers or spiderworts, but they flower for a long time. Rushy leaves and stems up to 2 ft. carry clustered heads of three-petalled flowers ½ to ¾ in. across in quite bright colours. Named varieties include white, light blue, mid and deep blue as well as purple and magenta, and smaller-flowered doubles exist as well. Flowering begins in June, but by August they may be looking tatty, and are best cut back to freshen

Trillium sessile

them, and to prevent seeding which can be a nuisance. They have the merit of adaptability to varying soils and situations.

Tricyrtis

These are known also as toad lilies and in their way are quite charming given some shade and a not too dry and light humusy soil. They have lily-shaped flowers, often with curious inner markings. All grow from short creeping rhizomes just below the surface and have slender stems on which the pointed leaves are wrapped.

Tricyrtis macropoda is fairly vigorous with buff-white flowers which have purple markings, and soft light green leaves. *T. stolonifera* has shiny deep green leaves and a more rapid surface spread, given cool leafy or peaty soil. The slender but erect stems reach 2 ft. or more and one needs to pause to examine the intricate colour markings of mauve and purple. All the above flower in later summer and remain in flower for several weeks.

Trillium

These, too, are woodland plants for a light humus-rich soil, and a shady position. They have a unique charm but few nurserymen are able to offer them. The best known is *Trillium grandiflorum*, the North American wake robin, which in spring sends up smooth stems topped by a ruff of leaves on which sit pure white, three-petalled flowers 1½ in. across which

are effective from mid-April to mid-May.

Perhaps the most sought after of all double white flowers is the form *plenum*, and no wonder. This rarity has perfection in form and lasts unspoiled for a longer period than the single – reminding one of a small pure white camellia. The single will come from seed, but to increase a stock of the double is a very slow process.

T. chloropetalum is spectacular with its mottled leaves and plum-red flowers in April on 18-in. stems. *T. sessile* is of similar height and not far off the same colour, but the petals stand erectly and the leaves again just below the flowers are quite broad. *T. nervosum* is quite vigorous with a greater increase of crowns than those above. The flowers are pink on 12 to 15-in. stems in April–May. Left alone in the right conditions, these trilliums will form quite large clumps, and produce more flowers as they expand.

Trollius

Though not for hot dry positions, the globe flower can add much to the garden scene in early summer. The vital period when plants need moisture for their tress-like fibrous roots is after flowering has ended, and for the rest of summer. Mulching with peat helps greatly and cuts down the need for watering. The lush green leaves emerge in early April and flower buds top them within two or three weeks. The globe effect appears just before the buds open.

Trollius europaeus superbus is a reliable light yellow, 2 ft. tall, and Canary Bird is paler and larger flowered. Goldquelle has large mid-yellow flowers with Orange Princess and *T.* Fireglobe good representatives of the deeper shades. The dwarfest of the *europaeus* range is the very pale yellow Alabaster. The distinctive *T. ledebouri* should not be missed. The petals open to reveal an upstanding crest of stamens of egg-yolk colour and stems reach 3 ft., flowering in June–July. *T. pumilus* grows only 9 to 12 in. in early summer, with shining yellow flowers.

Veratrum

Though the false hellebores cannot be regarded as colourful they always appeal. Broad-ribbed basal foliage and statuesque pokery spikes up to 6 ft. have black, greenish or off-white flowers for a long time. They also live a long time without attention and though preferring cool deep soil are surprisingly adaptable, once safely established. The best-known species – and about the only one available from nurseries – is *Veratrum nigrum*, which is almost black, 4 to 5 ft. tall and at its best

during June and July. *V. album*, greenish white, and *V. viride*, yellowish green, are also in cultivation.

Verbascum

Although some of the brightest of the mulleins are not fully perennial or long lived, a collection needs such spike-forming plants to break up uniformity. The most reliable have the stoutest rootstock, thick and fleshy or tap rooted and for a good yellow *Verbascum chaixii* (syn. *vernale*) can be recommended. From a base of large pointed dock-like leaves, strong spikes rise to 4 to 5 ft. and the open-petalled flowers on both terminal and secondary spikes give a good show for several weeks from June onwards. A dwarfer yellow species (4 ft.) is *V. thapsiforme* (syn. *densiflorum*).

Gainsborough is 3 ft., lighter yellow with woolly grey foliage, but it is rather allergic to winter wet. The hybrid Golden Bush is distinctive, reliable and long flowering, though individual flowers are small. The habit is bushy with very twiggy laterals and it grows only 2 ft. high. The deep rose Pink Domino grows to 3½ ft.

Verbascums do not need rich soil and in fact prefer sandy or stony soil with perfect drainage to survive the winter. All are increased, true to name or colour, from root cuttings taken in early spring.

Vernonia

The iron weeds have the distinction of being even later to flower than Michaelmas daisies, but only the species *Vernonia crinita* is listed in catalogues, though others exist. From a stout fibrous-rooted clump rise strong erect stems carrying narrow leaves to reach 5 ft. or so by the end of summer and then from mid-October till well into November, the broad head of small purple flowers can be seen. It is not a spectacular plant, but in its way it is quite attractive and has no fads or vices.

Veronica

A genus that provides several good garden subjects, few of which are difficult to grow. The varieties of *Veronica teucrium* are all blue and make a bright display in June–July, ranging in height from the 12-in. Shirley Blue; 15-in. Crater Lake Blue; 18-in. Royal Blue, and 24-in. Blue Fountain, all of mounded or bushy growth topped with short spikes.

V. gentianoides is early flowering, at its best in May. Spikes come from mat-forming, shiny-leaved plants, and heights are 6 to 12 in. in the light blue type. *V. spicata* is also mat forming, but the flower spikes open in June and July. Silver-grey leaves and violet-purple spikes to 15 in. are seen in the form *incana* and though Saraband is much freer to flower, the leaves are less silvery, as is the case with the taller and less tidy Wendy. Pretty pink-flowered varieties are Barcarolle and Minuet, the latter having greyish leaves and lighter pink spikes than the former, both being about 18 in. tall. The variety Snow White completes the colour range.

V. exaltata is late flowering with tall leafy spikes of light blue to 4 ft. It is quite attractive, though sometimes needs supports. This does not apply to *V. virginica* which also grows strongly to 4 ft. but both the blue flowered and the pale pink *rosea* are soon over, and by far the most attractive is *alba*. This reaches an imposing 5 ft., with whorled leaves at intervals along the stem, which branches to carry white-flowered spikes from August to September.

Zygadenus

One or two species of this little known genus are now coming in for attention. They have a demure charm, with a spray of green-tinged white flowers on 12 to 18-in. stems from a slowly increasing rootstock. The leaves are deep green, pointed and leathery, and flowering continues from June to September. *Zygadenus elegans* and the slightly larger *Z. nutallii* both need fairly moist soil and prefer some shade.

A mature island bed planting

Annuals and Biennials

Francis Perry, M.B.E., V.M.H., F.L.S., writer, journalist, lecturer and broadcaster, has achieved fame as a horticulturist and as the first woman member of The Royal Horticultural Society's council since the Society was founded in 1804. This singular honour was accorded her in 1968.

Her influence on gardening has been immense through her work in the field of education – she was the first principal of Norwood Hall College of Agricultural Education and Horticultural Organizer for the County of Middlesex for many years – her fourteen books on many aspects of gardening, her many writings which include a weekly article in *The Observer* newspaper, of which she is gardening correspondent, and her many appearances on radio and television.

Mrs Perry was trained at Swanley Horticultural College in Kent, and early on came under the influence of that great gardener and near neighbour, the late E. A. Bowles. With his guidance and that of her father-in-law, the late Amos Perry, a plantsman of great distinction, she had unique opportunities of which she made the most.

She has travelled in all five continents, often lecturing and always looking for plants. A widow, her only son, Roger, was for six years the Director of the Charles Darwin Research Station in the Galapagos Islands and he, too, is an author of repute.

In 1972 The Royal Horticultural Society awarded Mrs Perry the coveted Victoria Medal of Honour, and, eight years prior to that, a Veitch Gold Medal. She was awarded the M.B.E. in 1962.

Her most recent honour has been the Sarah Francis Chapman Medal from the Garden Club of America, for literary achivement.

Annuals are plants which complete their life cycle from small dormant seeds through germination, development, flowering and harvesting all within the space of a year. Although their life span is thus short, measured against herbaceous perennials, shrubs and trees, they make up for this with a prodigality of blossom unsurpassed by any other group of plants.

Their gay, long-blooming qualities render them invaluable wherever quick colour is desired. They are particularly useful for new gardens the first season, hiding the bare soil beneath a carpet of flowers. In later years or in established gardens the potentialities are even greater; their uses extending to window boxes, hanging baskets and containers of all description as well as beds and borders.

Biennials are plants which take two years to complete their life cycle. Seed sown one season develops a rosette of leaves that year and flowers and fruits the next. Usually the seed of such plants is sown outside – in shallow drills in late spring. Later the seedlings are pricked out in nursery beds prior to being bedded out in the autumn. While many biennials are mainly used for bedding purposes (for example wallflowers and forget-me-nots) others fit into the annual or mixed border if used during their second season. Canterbury bells and sweet williams are frequently used in this way.

Again, a number of perennials often make better plants or are less subject to disease when treated as annuals or biennials. Antirrhinums, for instance, are almost invariably treated as annuals and polyanthus, hollyhocks and double daisies as biennials.

Another advantage of using annuals and biennials is economic. They are easy to grow and seed is cheaper to purchase than plants. The hardy annuals may be sown where they are to flower and some of them start to bloom within two months of sowing. Half-hardy annuals have to be raised under glass and planted outside when all risk of frost is past. Their use thus presupposes the possession of a frost-free – or heated – frame or greenhouse.

Preparing the Ground

Although annuals have worldwide distribution, many of those which have become most popular with gardeners appear to be native to central and South America and South Africa. Their brilliant colourings seem in some way to be linked with the sunshine of their native lands. Background knowledge of indigenous conditions often provides clues as to treatment and generally speaking monocarpic

plants do best in good soil and open sunny situations. With few exceptions flower beds solely devoted to annuals, window boxes, or groups of annuals in mixed borders should be sited in open positions and away from trees or hedges which can draw up the stems.

For best results the ground should be prepared in autumn; cleared of weeds and deeply dug. Organic material should be incorporated through the top 12 in. to provide a reservoir of food and hold moisture in summer, but this must be well rotted. Farmyard manure, garden compost, leafmould and moist peat are all suitable. When this rots down to friable humus any type of soil, regardless of its original nature, will benefit in tilth and texture.

Because of their adaptability there is a common misconception that annuals do best in poor soil. This is not so. They will grow in a fashion on poor land, but there is no comparison between the resultant plants and those raised under more favourable conditions.

If biennials are to be good, it is equally important that they too be grown in good soil. Stocks and Canterbury bells particularly require fertile land. Others, such as foxgloves, honesty and meconopsis, need moist soil but prefer light shade in summer.

Once the border is adequately prepared hardy annuals will be sown in the positions where they are to flower and half-hardy kinds planted out from pots or boxes when weather conditions allow.

As with herbaceous border plantings, bold groups of the same plant create the biggest impact, so quantities of the same variety must be grown in order to make a show. Unlike permanent bedding, however, it is not essential that each group of plants should be the same shade. Very fine patchwork effects can be obtained by using mixed coloured eschscholzias – for instance – in one block, variously hued linarias in another – and so on.

Sowing Hardy Annuals Out of Doors

Ideal sowing conditions obtain when the soil is moist and the ground has been raked to a fine tilth beforehand. The smaller the seed – and annual seed is often very tiny – the more important this becomes. If soil particles are in contact with one another, the film of moisture surrounding each is readily available to the first, all-important plant roots. Large particles and loose shifting soil make for air pockets and if seedlings fall into these they soon dry up and perish. Tread the ground beforehand therefore if it has been

Before sowing, the areas to be occupied by different annuals are marked on the surface of the soil

The seed is sown thinly and then lightly raked in

Brushwood provides the most natural support for annuals if used sparingly

recently dug and then rake it down to a fine, smooth, even tilth.

Unless the plants are intended for cutting purposes avoid sowing annuals in straight lines. A good idea is to mark out individual areas beforehand, making these informal but running into each other like a jigsaw puzzle. Sometimes it is enough to draw lines with a hoe for this purpose or sand can be used to make a bolder outline. If each section is labelled with the name of the intended occupant it is easier to work methodically, sowing as one goes and also reserving spaces for the half-hardy annuals which cannot be planted out until later in the season.

Seed can either be scattered broadcast within the prescribed areas and then lightly raked in, or a pointed stick can be used to trace narrow drills. Sow thinly and later fill in the drills with the head of a rake – held in an upright position so that the teeth cannot dig into the ground and the seeds are only just covered. Water if necessary.

When the plants germinate weed between the rows and then thin the seedlings to 1 in. apart. If they are to develop to full size and maturity a second and more drastic thinning will be necessary. This final spacing will be determined by the type of plant and its spread and ultimate height, but as a rough guide, plants growing 12 in. in height under good conditions should be thinned to about 6 in. apart; those of 18 in. to 9 in. and any 2 ft. or thereabouts left 1 ft. away from neighbours. Most annuals are self-supporting, but weak-stemmed varieties or plants in windy positions can be made secure with the aid of twiggy peasticks.

Keep the hoe going to eradicate weed seedlings and loosen the soil until the plants have grown sufficiently to render this unnecessary. Late germinating weeds will then be smothered at birth and any

survivors can just be pulled out by hand.

The sowing of hardy annuals takes place out of doors in late spring (April to May in Britain). Typical of plants which can be treated in this manner are Shirley poppies, Virginian and night-scented stocks and nasturtiums. For details see under individual headings.

Autumn Sowing

On well-drained soil and in favoured situations, hardy annuals are frequently sown out of doors the autumn prior to flowering. If all goes well – and it is a calculated risk, for winters are always unpredictable – they make stronger plants and bloom earlier than those raised in spring.

The beginning of September is the best time to sow in Britain; a little earlier in cooler climates and slightly later in warmer areas. The prospects of success are improved if cloches are placed over the seedlings in severe weather.

Although all annuals are not suitable for autumn sowing the following may be tried with reasonable success: calendulas, larkspurs, sweet peas, nigella, eschscholzias, cornflowers, annual scabious, godetias, clarkias and linarias.

Sowing Under Glass

Half-hardy annuals are prone to frost damage, so to give them a good start they are first raised under glass, then potted separately or spaced out in boxes, and finally put outside in their flowering positions when the weather improves. In Britain it is usually safe to do this at the end of May or early in June – a week or two later in northern Europe or the north eastern states of northern America.

Growing temperatures will naturally vary according to the type of plant, but the hardier kinds for outdoor planting will do quite well in a frame or greenhouse

from which frost can be excluded. Tender annuals will need temperatures of approximately 15 to 18°C. (60 to 65°F.) later.

In all cases the soil should be light and friable. Equal parts of coarse sand (or perlite), good sifted loam and peat moss or sphagnum moss provide the foundation of most home-mixed composts. Alternatively one can buy packaged composts, which have the advantage of added nutrients. John Innes Seed Compost is commonly used in Britain or General Purpose Soil in the United States.

The containers, whether pans, pots or boxes, must be scrupulously clean and crocked if there is only one drainage hole, with a little peaty material above the crocks to prevent blockage. They should then be filled with damp compost. Firm lightly and leave a smooth finish.

Now sow the seed thinly and cover it with silver sand or finely sieved compost. Label the pots and stand them in a shallow bath of water so that the liquid is just below the rims. Leave them there until the soil surface looks damp. This method

Sowing half-hardy annuals in a seed pan
(a) Silver sand or finely sieved compost
(b) The seeds
(c) Compost
(d) Peaty material
(e) Crocks
(f) The initial watering is carried out by immersing the seed pan in water

does not dislodge the seed as much as top watering with a can.

Remove the containers to a frame or greenhouse and cover them with glass and a sheet of newspaper. The glass must be turned daily to prevent too much condensation and both coverings removed when germination takes place.

When large enough to handle prick out seedlings 2 to 3 in. apart in boxes or pot them separately and grow on.

Biennials

Biennials are sown outside in shallow drills in spring or early summer (normally between April and June) for flowering the following season. Some, like meconopsis and primula, should be sown directly after harvesting as the seed deteriorates with keeping. The procedure is similar to that of hardy annuals except that the plants are raised in sheltered nursery beds (which can be shaded if necessary) and have a fine sowing tilth. They are then thinned to 6 to 9 in. apart in the rows and lifted and planted in their flowering positions in early autumn or the following spring.

Selected Annuals and Biennials

ANNUALS AND BIENNIALS FOR WINDOW BOXES AND OTHER CONTAINERS

Annuals are ideal for containers of all kinds, but particularly window boxes, jardinières, strawberry jars, patio pots and tubs. Many remain in flower for weeks – even months – their gay colours brightening sombre spots and masking dull features.

Where window boxes are used they must always be securely fastened and ideally should be 1 in. wider than the sill and have wedges pushed under the front edges so that they tip slightly backwards. Drainage holes are not essential if plenty of drainage material (crocks covered with rough peat) is placed in the bottom and they are carefully watered. Loose liners are the ideal for as each crop of flowers becomes shabby these can be lifted out and changed in minutes by previously prepared replacements.

Window boxes can also be fastened to brackets secured to boundary walls, which affords interest and provides more space and colour in very small gardens. Arrange these at different levels for a more artistic effect.

Hanging baskets have many uses. They can be hung from rafters in sun lounges, pergola arches and over doorways or the flat-backed kinds may be fixed to house walls. These again must be very secure and lined with moss or green plastic sheeting (with a few holes pierced round the sides about 1 in. up from the base to avoid waterlogging after storms) to conserve moisture in dry weather.

Tubs full of annuals, urns and pots can be stood about in various situations or a strawberry pot used to mask an obvious and inconveniently sited manhole cover. Stand terracotta strawberry pots in large saucers and fill these with water daily. This is the best method of watering. The polyester and glassfibre types should not be filled too full as these have no drainage holes and being non-porous have to be watered from the top. Feed all container plants occasionally – foliar sprays are ideal in summer – and change the soil annually.

F_1 hybrid varieties (first cross seed) are preferable in some instances but not invariably, as the larger flowers produced can suffer in storms and windy situations.

Alyssum

Alyssum maritimum, now more correctly *Lobularia maritima*, is the familiar sweet alyssum so popular for edging window boxes, borders and beds or for growing in pavement crevices. Strictly a perennial, it is invariably grown as a hardy annual and flowers continuously from June until October. Growing 6 to 9 in. high, it has tufts of small pointed leaves and racemes of white, honey-scented little flowers. Varieties with pink and violet flowers are available. Seed can be sown where the plants are to flower in spring or raised earlier under glass and after hardening off planted outside towards the end of May. Germination takes about five days.

Bellis

Bellis perennis is the English daisy, a perennial which has produced a number of fine double varieties. These come true from seed when treated as annuals or biennials. The flowers are large and showy on 5 to 6-in. stems, the colours white, pink or red and the simple oval leaves ground hugging. Seed is sown in June, when they are treated as biennials, in a nursery plot outside and, after thinning and growing on, the young plants are set in their flowering positions in early autumn. They can also be raised under glass, by sowing seed in June or July and transferring the seedlings – by stages – to 4-in. pots. Daisies like rich, moist soil and flower out of doors from May to July. They can be

If liners are used in window boxes, planting is made easier and more rapid

A strawberry pot

used in beds as well as containers, or as carpets in light shade beneath trees, or grown as cut flowers.

Dahlia

Dwarf bedding dahlias are often treated as annuals and make useful container plants with a flowering season extending from June until frosts cut them in early autumn. Seed production does away with the chore of overwintering the tubers and the results are reasonably predictable and true to type. Treat them as half-hardy annuals and pinch out the growing tips when the plants are 3 to 4 in. high to induce a bushy habit. The seedlings should be separately potted and when weather conditions allow may be turned out and planted. They need full sun and rich soil, with plenty of water, and the occasional feed in the growing season. The most suitable races for container work are such kinds as the double Dwarf Early Bird Mixture or Unwin's Dwarf Mixture; both in bright colours and about 12 in. tall. If singles are sought any of the Coltness types, such as Sparkle Mixed, are ideal although they are taller (15 to 18 in.).

Lathyrus

Lathyrus odoratus is the sweet pea, a much-loved flower with a delightful colour range and exquisite scent. Whilst most sweet peas are more suitable for the cut flower bed or mixed border, there are dwarf strains well adapted for use in window boxes and other containers. They include the American Knee-Hi which grows around 2 ft. and needs no staking. Each flower stem carries five to seven blooms, the colours are as varied as their taller counterparts. The Little Sweetheart varieties are still more compact, being a mere 8 in. high in various colours. For cultivation details see p. 116.

Limnanthes

Limnanthes douglasii is the meadow foam or fried egg plant, a delightful little Californian, whose white, yellow-centred, saucer-shaped flowers seem irresistible to bees. Seed should be sown where the plants are to flower in autumn or spring. Germination takes about three weeks, when the young plants should be thinned to 3 or 4 in. This is a beautiful little plant for early summer flowering, when it dies down and can be replaced if required. In the garden enough self-set seedlings come up each spring to maintain the stock. The height is 9 to 12 in.

Matricaria

Chrysanthemum parthenium is more likely to be found in seed catalogues under *Matricaria eximia* than its proper name, for which reason it is included here. The type, a British perennial with small white daisy flowers and aromatic deeply cut foliage, is not worth growing, but the double-flowered varieties with branching stems and many ball-like heads are really arresting and stand well in containers. Typical sorts are Silver Ball, Golden Ball, and Lemon Ball, all 9 to 12 in. high with ¾-in. blooms, and there is a golden-foliaged form *aureum*, which makes an attractive background for blue flowers.

Matthiola

Stocks make good container plants if they can be sited away from strong winds which can snap the stems unless these are individually staked. They appreciate deep, rich, moist soil and given this thrive in full sun or partial shade. There are three main groups, all derived from *Matthiola incana*; the Brompton or Queen stocks which are treated as biennials, seed being sown outside in June or July and then put out in their flowering positions the following September (or April in exposed areas); ten week stocks, which are grown as half-hardy annuals and planted out in May from spring-sown seed under glass, and intermediate or East Lothian stocks, which can be grown as biennials or alternatively as annuals for autumn flowering.

In all cases the colour range is varied, from white and apricot to rose, lilac, carmine, mauve, purple and light blue. Since those with double flowers are the showiest always purchase seed from a reliable grower stocking good strains and check the seedlings before growing these on or pricking out. It is the light green foliaged seedlings with long leaves which produce double flowers – the dark green, short-foliaged ones are most likely to be single. Although seed deteriorates with keeping, the most persistent of life and able to survive are also doubles. Incidentally the germination of stocks takes about ten days.

In addition to their usefulness in containers, stocks merit a place amongst mixed bedding as well as for cut flowers or pot work indoors. Their rich scent, silvery foliage and long spikes of flowers commend them to most gardeners, so plant them in positions where these can be enjoyed, such as close to the house or near sitting out areas in the garden.

Petunia

Petunias are among the most desirable container plants for they are cheap and easy to raise and flower all summer. They have showy, trumpet-shaped flowers and entire, rough, rather stocky stems and leaves. If the stems become leggy, the flowering shoots can be cut back to young growths farther back along the stems. These soon take over and throw up fresh flowers. This operation can be repeated several times in a season if one feeds the plants in between times. The F_1 hybrids and doubles are more showy when grown as pot plants or in protected situations, but wind can damage the brittle stems, so that the smaller singles are often more useful in window boxes and hanging baskets.

A strawberry pot filled with pink, mauve and blue petunias makes a magnificent 'all round' feature for summer and the leaves and flowers completely hide the pot in a few weeks.

Petunias should be treated as half-hardy annuals, the seed germinating in about fourteen days and, like stocks, the smaller seedlings are the ones which produce double or most brightly coloured flowers. A light rich soil suits them best, with plenty of water during the growing season. They are highly susceptible to frost and do not take kindly to drought.

For winter bloomers, seed can be sown in a cold frame in June or July, the seedlings potted on and stopped when about 4 in. high to induce bushiness and brought under glass, temperature 55 to 60°F. (13 to 16°C.), in September or October.

Salvia

Salvia splendens is the scarlet sage, a beautiful Brazilian with spikes of fiery red, sage-like flowers and equally vivid bracts on branching 2 to 3-ft. stems and smooth, oval, pointed leaves. For window boxes Dwarf Gem (9 in.) or Fireball (12 to 15 in.) are ideal. There are also white and dull purple varieties, but these are less arresting than the scarlets.

Although perennial the plants should be treated as half-hardy annuals. The seed germinates in eight days and seedlings should have the tops pinched out when 3 to 4 in. high. They require light but rich soil with plenty of moisture and full sun.

Tropaeolum

Dwarf nasturtiums (*Tropaeolum majus*) make good container plants for sun or light shade as they bloom continuously all summer with variously coloured, helmet-shaped flowers and round silvery leaves. Seedsmen recognize and offer various races, particularly the varieties *nanum*, Tom Thumb and the lovely climbing Gleam Hybrids. These have double flowers of orange, primrose, scarlet, pink or salmon, some with dark foliage and another called Alaska has cream-splashed variegated leaves.

The climbing Gleam Hybrids can also be trained up trellises behind window boxes or in tubs to disguise dustbins and similar ugly features. Blackfly may attack the plants, but soon succumb to derris spray.

Nasturtium seed germinates in about ten days and can either be sown where it is to flower or grown under glass and put outside when there is no more risk of frost. The flowers are faintly scented and the crushed foliage has a pungent smell. Both flowers and leaves can be eaten in salads and the seeds used as a substitute for capers. See also p. 118.

Other plants to try in containers and dealt with on other pages are the trailing lobelia, silver-edged centaureas, wallflowers, polyanthus and forget-me-nots and poppies, ageratum, calendulas and calceolarias.

FRAGRANT ANNUALS AND BIENNIALS

Fragrance in flowers gives a bonus to beauty and most people would give extra points to a plant so favoured. A fair proportion should be grown in every garden and since the summer sorts (particularly) seem to smell most sweetly toward the evening, plant these close to the house and enjoy their fragrance at this quiet part of the day or by a garden seat where they may be appreciated at leisure.

Asperula

Asperula orientalis is a pretty little woodruff with 12-in. high slender stems carrying whorls of needle-like leaves and terminal heads of small, sky-blue, tubular flowers. It should be sown in early spring where it is to flower, selecting shady places in moist soil or damp pockets near water. It flowers about twelve weeks later.

Centaurea

Centaurea moschata is the sweet sultan, a popular and sweetly fragrant plant much esteemed for cutting purposes. It has thistle-like heads of white, yellow, rose, red or purple on 2-ft. stems and toothed leaves. Seed can be sown outside in spring and the seedlings thinned to 9 in. apart, or in frames in September for flowering under glass in late winter. Germination takes place in about sixteen days.

Top: *Petunia grandiflora* **Lavender Lady**
Right: *Nasturtium* **Golden Gleam**

Cheiranthus

The sweet scent and showy flowers of wallflowers (*Cheiranthus cheiri*) gives them great appeal for spring bedding and cutting purposes. They are hardy, remain in character for weeks and, apart from mixed strains, seed can be bought to colour to conform with different bedding schemes. Although perennial they are treated as biennials; the seed being sown soon after harvesting. It germinates in about twelve days and then the seedlings should be pricked out in rows 6 in. apart. In order to produce a fibrous root system and make them easier to transplant the tips of the tap roots should be broken at this stage. In early autumn they should be lifted again and planted in their flowering positions, in full sun and 1 ft. apart. The usual height is around 18 in., but dwarf types like Tom Thumb only grow to half that height. The colour range includes reddish brown, blood red, crimson, salmon, ruby, rose, yellow and creamy white.

Dianthus

Dianthus are noted for fragrance and amongst those normally raised from seed are the popular sweet williams (*Dianthus barbatus*). Although perennial these are treated as biennial since they deteriorate after the first flowering, and self-set seedlings usually maintain the stock in future years. After germination the plants produce basal clumps of long narrow leaves and the following spring 18-in. leafy stems terminating in large flat heads of wide open flowers. Reds predominate but other colour combinations of shades occur, also varieties with double flowers. The species has been crossed with *D. allwoodii* (itself a cross between an old English garden pink and the border carnation) to produce the fragrant Sweet Wivelsfield pinks. These are also treated as biennials.

Exacum

Exacum affine is a delightful member of the gentian family with extraordinarily sweet-smelling flowers. These are small and mauve and the leaves smooth and oval in shape. The plant is bushy and low growing (9 to 12 in.) but flowers for months and is especially fine for pot work in the home or conservatory. Treat as half hardy; germination takes about fourteen days.

Heliotropium

Heliotropium arborescens (heliotrope) is a half-hardy perennial from Peru with branching stems carrying dark green oblong leaves and clusters of richly scented violet-purple flowers. This fragrance is most marked towards evening. Heliotrope is often known as cherry pie and white, pink and rose-flowered forms can occur. The plants are popular for bedding and as pot subjects; particularly good forms being propagated from cuttings. Normally, however, they are grown from seed, as half-hardy annuals, since they flower freely the first year. They appreciate a rich, well-drained soil and full sun.

The seed germinates in about fourteen days and seedlings should be separately potted but not planted outside until there is no more risk of frost. To produce bushy plants pinch out the tops when they are 4 to 5 in. high. For standards (which are best treated as biennial) leave the main stem and rub out all side shoots. Once the required height is reached remove the tip and let the side shoots develop.

Humea

Humea elegans is a striking plant for growing under glass or in a light window, although its powerful incense smell may not appeal to everyone. It has large, oval, sharply pointed leaves and loose pendant sprays of small crimson or reddish-brown flowers. Treat as biennial, sowing the seed in mid-summer.

Lathyrus

The sweet pea (*Lathyrus odoratus*) is a universal favourite, particularly for cutting. Almost every shade of colour is represented in the sweet-smelling flowers. To do well, however, the plants require rich well-prepared soil in an open sunny position. The ground should be deeply dug (approximately 2 ft.) the previous autumn, or holes can be taken out to the same depth, and a good layer of well-rotted manure placed in the bottom before returning the soil.

The seed can be sown in late January or February (two or three seeds to a 3-in. pot) in a cool greenhouse or frame and planted outside as the weather improves in early spring (March or April). The plants must be supported with peasticks or trained up netting or strings. They need plenty of water and feeding in summer. Keep the flowers picked to prevent seed formation (which checks further blooming) and remove tendrils and surplus foliage. For early flowering seed is sown in autumn or winter in a cold frame and exhibition flowers are grown on plants restricted to a single stem. See also p. 114.

Others with scented flowers include *Limnanthes douglasii*, *Alyssum maritimum*, hesperis, violas, antirrhinums and *Tropaeolum majus*.

CLIMBING ANNUALS

Climbing plants are useful to cover walls and sheds, mask old tree stumps and clamber over patio fences and loggias. Some can even be grown with perennial climbers like roses, so that they can take over and give colour when the roses have finished blooming. Most of those grown as annuals are only half hardy so have to be raised under glass and grown on in pots before it is safe to put them outside in early summer.

With the aid of climbers small gardens can be enclosed with 'curtains' of flowers and leaves and a shady sitting out area is easily contrived by growing them up a light framework erected around three sides of a garden seat.

Cobaea

Cobaea scandens is the cup and saucer plant, a vigorous Mexican which can reach a height of 20 ft. or more in a season. It needs a sheltered position and full sun. The large 3-in. flowers are greenish or creamy white at first, but the inner bell-like corolla becomes violet or purple with age. All the flowers are set off by green, saucer-like bracts.

Cucurbita

These non-edible members of the cucumber family are amusing to grow up trellises or fences, or the heavier-fruited types can be allowed to scramble over the ground. Treat as for marrows and give them full sun and deep rich soil. The fruits vary considerably – in size, shape and colour – and some are smooth skinned and others heavily warted.

Eccremocarpus

Eccremocarpus scaber, the Chilean glory flower, is best treated as a half-hardy annual, except where it is grown under glass or can be adequately protected in winter. Growing about 15 ft. high, it has slender spikes of tubular orange flowers and pinnate leaves with tendrils. It requires a sheltered sunny situation and makes an attractive drape for a south wall.

Humulus

Humulus scandens (*japonicus*), one of the hops, provides quick cover for unsightly fences and similar features during the summer months and soon forms a dense screen. The seed germinates in about ten days and can either be raised under glass for planting out later or sown outside in April. Either the cream-variegated leaf form called *variegatus* or the golden-foliaged *lutescens* are the most ornamental.

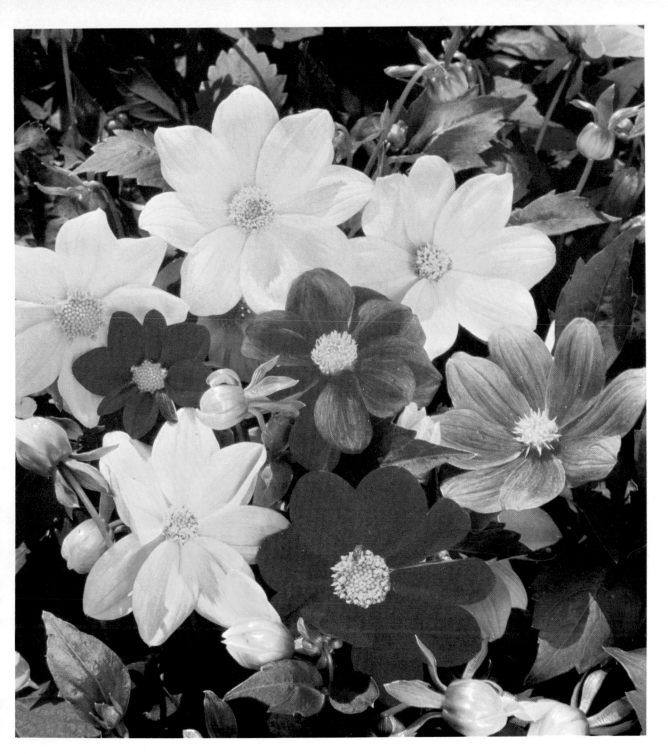

Ipomoea

These delightful ornamental climbers have large trumpet flowers in exquisite shades. The blues are particularly fine. *Ipomoea violacea* (*I. tricolor*; *I. rubrocoerulea*) is one of the loveliest, the deep blue, white-throated flowers 5 in. in diameter. *I. purpurea* (*Convolvulus major*) is the morning glory, a beautiful half-hardy annual with violet flowers which become purple with age, but there are also white, dark and sky blue, and crimson forms. Plant ipomoeas outside in June, choosing a warm sunny sheltered situation.

Maurandya

Maurandya (now more correctly *Asarina*) *barclaiana*, a vigorous, free-flowering climber from Mexico, has violet-purple, foxglove-like flowers about 3 in. long and smooth sharply pointed leaves. There are also white and rose-flowered forms. Treat as half-hardy annuals and grow in a warm sunny position.

Quamoclit

These half-hardy annuals can be grown outside in favourable localities if planted out when all risk of cold is past. Alter-

Dahlia **Disco Mixed**

natively, they make beautiful climbers for a sun lounge or conservatory. *Quamoclit lobata* (*Mina lobata*), from Mexico, grows to 6 or 8 ft. and has three-lobed leaves and showy bunches of scarlet and yellow flowers. *Q. pennata*, the cypress vine, is more delicate, with finely dissected leaves on 8 to 10-ft. twining stems and scarlet, star-like flowers.

Thunbergia

Thunbergia alata, the black-eyed Susan,

can be put out in summer in some localities but generally speaking is best grown under glass in pots and trained over hoops or sticks or up wire fixed to rafter beams. It flowers continuously all summer with vivid orange flowers which have almost black centres in *aurantiaca* or are white with dark centres in *alba*. Seed sown in February or March germinates in about fifteen days and needs growing on in a temperature of 55 to 65°F. (13 to 18°C.). The plants like moist, rich but well-drained soil and sun and should be fed occasionally if grown in pots.

Tropaeolum

Nasturtiums (*Tropaeolum majus* and varieties) are well-known plants, with vivid flowers and round glaucous leaves, which thrive in most soils. Both climbing and bush varieties are available, the former ideal for semi-shade in moist soil. They can be grown up trellises or pergolas and flower all through the summer.

A wide range of garden forms are now available, in many shades, from primrose, yellow and orange to rose, cherry red and scarlet. Seed should be sown where plants are to flower in April and covered with ¾ in. of soil. This takes ten days to germinate and later should be thinned to the recommended distances and allowed to run up supports. See also p. 114.

T. peregrinum (*T. canariense*) is the canary creeper, a South American climber up to 8 ft., with small, five-fingered leaves and fringed golden-yellow flowers. It does well in a shady situation.

ANNUALS AND BIENNIALS FOR DRYING

A number of monocarpic plants have flowers or attractive seedpods which can be dried for winter decoration. If these are picked just before they reach their peak they will be absolutely perfect for this purpose. Dry them in small bunches in an airy situation, protected from rain or strong sun – which might bleach the colours. Those with top-heavy flowers – like helichrysums – are usually mounted on wire 'stems'. The smaller kinds can be made into pictures, tablemats, paperweights and other trifles.

Eryngium

Most species of eryngium (sea hollies) are perennials but *Eryngium giganteum* is a true biennial and also one of the loveliest. Growing 3 to 4 ft. high with branching silvery stems, it has toothed, arrow-shaped leaves and large silvery-blue flower heads backed by silver-veined, glaucous calyces. Once suited it colonizes freely and comes up every year.

Gomphrena

Gomphrenas or globe amaranths can be used as border edgings, pot plants, for bedding or the showy clover-like heads can be dried for winter decoration. They grow about 18 in. tall and have globular heads of white, yellow, red or violet flowers. Treat as half-hardy annuals (the seed germinates in twelve days) and plant out 12 in. apart. *Gomphrena globosa* is the best (and most variable) species.

Gypsophila

Gypsophila elegans or chalk plant is a popular market flower with slender 12 to 18-in. silvery stems, small lance-shaped leaves and masses of little white (occasionally pink or rose) simple flowers. These can be used fresh or dried for winter use. In gardens, the plants look pretty trailing down over steps or rocks. Treat as hardy annuals. See also p. 120.

Helichrysum

Helichrysum bracteatum is the everlasting flower or immortelle, a hardy annual from Australia with lance-shaped leaves and large, papery-scaled flowers up to 2 in. across. These can be white, yellow, orange, purple, rose or red on 2½-ft. stems. They are half-hardy annuals, suitable for most soils if the situation is sunny.

Helipterum

These are pretty Australian composites, frequently catalogued under rhodanthe or acroclinium. *Helipterum* (*Rhodanthe*) *manglesii* makes a bushy 12 to 15-in. plant with many nodding, pink and white, papery-petalled flowers, something like daisies. Treat as half-hardy or hardy annuals – the latter giving later flowers. The very similar *H.* (*Acroclinium*) *roseum* can be sown outside in April and has white, pink or deep rose flowers with either gold or brown centres.

Limonium

Limonium sinuatum is one of the sea lavenders and is often listed as statice. It is a biennial best treated as a half-hardy annual; the seedlings come through in eight days and the plants should be set out 12 in. apart when there is no more risk of frost. They have branching, flattened, rough, 1 to 2-ft. stems with spikes of blue, mauve, lavender, rose, salmon-pink or white flowers. These dry beautifully and are always very popular. The candlewick statice, *L. suworowii*, has long drooping spikes packed with small rose flowers and lance-shaped basal leaves. It makes a good pot plant.

Lunaria

Lunaria annua, a biennial in spite of its name, is the honesty, a good plant for odd corners, even in semi-shaded situations. Seed sown outside in April or May blooms the following spring, the flowers varying from white to deep purple or sometimes bicoloured. There is also a splendid variegated-leaved form called *variegatum* which comes true from seed. In autumn the seedpods should be rubbed between the fingers and thumb to remove the seeds and outer coverings, thus leaving the pearly, moon-like inner portions which are delightful for winter decoration.

Molucella

Molucella laevis or bells of Ireland is grown for its calyces (the flowers are insignificant). These are borne on 30 to 36-in. spikes and are pale green and shell shaped with delicate white traceries. They dry to a biscuit shade. The plant is a half-hardy annual which does well in light soil.

Nicandra

Nicandra physaloides, the shoo-fly plant (it is supposed to repel insects), is a vigorous half-hardy annual from Peru with 3 to 4-ft. branching stems, smooth oval leaves and bell-shaped blue and white flowers. These give place to swollen seedpods something like those of the cape gooseberry (physalis). It needs moist soil.

Nigella

Nigella damascena or love-in-the-mist is attractive both in flower and fruit. The latter are used in dried arrangements. The flowers are 1½ in. across, saucer shaped and usually blue – Miss Jekyll is a particularly rich shade – but there are white and pale forms, also doubles. The seedpods are pale green, barred with brown and surrounded (as are the flowers) with the spiky haloes of the leafy involucres. Sow the seed in moist soil where the plants are to flower in early spring, or autumn in mild locations and thin to 9 in. apart.

Papaver

Poppy heads are always in demand for Christmas decorations; kinds like *Papaver somniferum* (opium poppy) being the most popular. Treat these as hardy annuals. See also p. 126.

Zea

The varieties of maize (*Zea mays*), known as Indian or squaw corn, with multi-coloured seeds of mahogany, gold, slate

Nigella **Persian Jewels Mixed**

blue, red and brown (all in the same pod) are delightful when dried for winter decoration. Treat as half-hardy annuals.

SHADE
ANNUALS AND BIENNIALS

Most annuals produce finer results when grown in an open position, but some are adaptable to shade and others actually prefer it. Given moist soil – for few plants thrive in dry shade – they become indispensable for brightening dull corners, growing in north-facing beds or window boxes or establishing beneath the overhanging branches of trees.

Aquilegia
Although strictly perennial the Long Spurred Hybrids derived from *Aquilegia caerulea* are usually treated as hardy annuals. To this end seed is sown in frames in September or under glass in spring and then planted out. These hybrids come in a wide range of colours and

combinations of shades and all have long protruding spurs behind the flowers. The height varies between 18 and 30 in. They do well in dappled shade and are excellent for borders, also for cutting.

Collinsia
Collinsia heterophylla (*bicolor*) seed can be sown outside in moist soil and light shade in autumn or spring (according to climatic conditions). This germinates in fourteen days and later the plants need thinning out to about 6 in. apart. The large and showy, purple and white-lobed flowers are carried in clusters on 2-ft. stems.

Cynoglossum
Cynoglossum amabile or hound's tongue is a rough-textured biennial from eastern Asia with sprays of turquoise-blue forget-me-not-like flowers on 1 to 2-ft. stems. The leaves are hairy and oblong. Treat as biennial or sow seed under glass in early spring.

Digitalis
The stately spikes of foxgloves (*Digitalis purpurea*) are equally beautiful in the

formal border – with blue delphiniums, tall campanulas, English irises (*I. xiphioides*) and the cerise *Geranium psilostemon* – as in the wild garden amongst ferns and hostas.

Seed should be sown in drills in May or June and the young plants transferred to their flowering positions when large enough to handle. Incidentally, they will move in full flower – useful to fill up gaps. *D. purpurea* is purple or white, spotted with brown inside the tubular flowers, but there are also primrose, apricot and various pink forms, with or without spots, also types in which the flowers are borne horizontally, all round the stems. The usual height is 5 to 6 ft. but a dwarf race called Foxy is only 30 in. tall and flowers in five months from sowing.

Hesperis
Hesperis matronalis is the dame's violet or sweet rocket; a sweetly scented plant something like honesty (*Lunaria annua*) with white, pale mauve or deep purple, four-petalled flowers on 2 to 3-ft. spikes. It is a hardy biennial of branching habit; the perfume strongest towards evening.

Impatiens
The brilliant forms of *Impatiens holstii*, *I. sultanii*, *I. petersiana* (although correctly now grouped under the collective name of *I. wallerana*) are generally still catalogued under their old names. In recent years there have been many colour additions – scarlet, rose, crimson, white, orange and bicolours – also dwarf races which have proved excellent for planting outside. These grow between 5 and 8 in. high and should be treated as half-hardy annuals. Damp soil is essential (peat in the soil helps) in either sun or shade.

Meconopsis
The annual and monocarpic species of meconopsis make beautiful additions to shady borders. All require cool, moist conditions. Seed should be sown soon after gathering in a shady frame and the young plants potted but not put outside until early autumn. The beautiful Himalayan blue poppy, *Meconopsis betonicifolia* (*M. baileyi*), with large, satiny, sky-blue flowers, can be treated in this way, also *M. regia* which has flat rosettes of leaves covered with bronze-gold hairs and spikes of bright yellow flowers. The two look delightful grown together in light woodland conditions. Both are 3 ft or so.

Mimulus
Mimulus are really bog plants, so if they are to thrive they must have moist soil,

preferably away from hot sun. Most garden sorts, derived from *Mimulus luteus* and *M. cupreus*, are treated as half-hardy annuals. Heights vary between 6 and 9 in. and the snapdragon-like flowers come in bright pinks, scarlets, yellows and oranges, often blotched with other shades. Red Emperor Mixed is a particularly good strain.

Nemophila

Nemophila menziesii or baby blue eyes is a delightful Californian annual with deeply cut leaves and masses of large, saucer-shaped blue and white flowers on 6 to 8-in. stems. It is excellent for massing under a light canopy of tree foliage, but will also grow in rock pockets or shady borders. Sow the seed outside in early spring for summer flowering or in autumn in protected spots for spring blooming.

Viola

Pansies are short-lived perennials derived from *Viola tricolor*, usually treated as biennials. Their puckish flower faces, in every conceivable colour, are delightful for edging purposes, as a groundwork for other plants or in beds by themselves. Since they like cool moist conditions they do well in light shade, although the winter-flowering races need more open conditions. Sow seed in summer for the following season's flowering. Violas are very similar except that the plants are tufted and the flowers smaller and frequently self-coloured. Good named sorts have to be propagated from cuttings.

Other annuals which will grow in partial shade are nicotianas, lunaria, *Begonia semperflorens* and *Tropaeolum majus*.

ANNUALS FOR ROCK GARDENS AND SMALL CONTAINERS

Although purists may prefer to exclude ordinary annuals from rock gardens, their introduction certainly extends its season and provides colour into autumn. Since many of these recommended sorts are half-hardy annuals, they will not go outside anyway until late May or June, when the spring flush of rock flowers is waning.

Adonis

Adonis aestivalis or pheasant's eye is a small hardy annual with finely cut leaves and bright crimson flowers like small anemones. It grows 12 to 18 in. tall and needs grouping to make an effect. A deep, rich, loamy soil suits it best.

Ageratum

Dwarf ageratums (*Ageratum houstonianum*) are low-growing (6 in.) hardy annuals with fluffy heads of mauve flowers like candy floss. They flower all summer and make good border edgings.

Brachycome

Brachycome iberidifolia is the swan river daisy, a slender-stemmed, half-hardy annual of 15 to 18 in. with many sweet-scented daisy flowers, 1½ in. across. The colours vary from white, pink and rose to lilac. It is best grown in drifts in moist soil with sun.

Cotula

Cotula barbata is the pincushion plant, a compact half-hardy annual of 4 to 6 in. with deeply cut leaves spangled with golden flowers like daisies without the outer florets. It forms dense carpets of foliage, even in poor soil.

Dorotheanthus and Portulaca

Dorotheanthus bellidiformis (often sold as *Mesembryanthemum criniflorum*) makes dwarf mats of succulent linear foliage studded with vivid daisy flowers of cerise, crimson, buff, red, orange or apricot each more than 1 in. across. On a bright sunny day (the flowers close in dull weather) the effect is brilliant. Treat as a half-hardy annual or sow outside in May for late flowers. Portulaca requires similar treatment and both do well in poor soil.

Portulaca grandiflora is the best species

Above: *Ageratum houstonianum*
Right: Annuals provide colourful summer bedding

with round, succulent stems of 6 to 8 in. carrying cup-shaped flowers of white, deep rose, rose and white, crimson or clear yellow. There are also double varieties and the main flowering season is July and August.

Felicia

Felicia bergeriana is the kingfisher daisy, a dwarf half-hardy annual of 4 to 5 in. with small but brilliant metallic-blue daisies which close in dull weather. Suitable for warm, sunny spots.

Gilia

Gilia hybrida (*Leptosiphon* hybrids) can be grown between flagstones or in small pockets. It does not mind poor soil and only grows about 6 in. tall. It is a hardy annual with finely cut leaves and clusters of white, yellow, rose-pink, purple or violet flowers. All have yellow centres.

Gypsophila

Gypsophila repens is a dainty hardy annual having cobwebby stems and tiny leaves. It is smothered in summer with dense sprays of dainty little white flowers. These look very pretty trailing over rocks or stone steps. There are also pink and red forms. The usual height is 12 to 18 in. Sow seed out of doors in autumn, or in cold districts in spring. See also p. 118.

Iberis

Iberis umbellata is the best of the annual candytufts with racemes of white, four-petalled, sweetly scented flowers in character all through the summer. Lilac and crimson forms are available and the normal height is around 12 to 15 in. Treat as hardy annuals and grow in light, well-drained soil in open situations.

Ionopsidium

Ionopsidium acaule, the violet cress, can be sown directly on the rockery where it is to grow. In later seasons self-set seedlings usually maintain the stock. The violet-blue (sometimes white) flowers bloom from June to September on 2 to 3-in. tufts of rounded leaves and stems. Hardy annual.

Layia

Layia elegans or tidytips has yellow, 2-in. daisies with prominent white petal tips. These occur on 12-in. stems and persist for weeks. Well-drained soil and sunshine suit this hardy annual.

Linaria

Linaria maroccana is a charming hardy annual with slender 10 to 18-in. stems packed with small, snapdragon-like flowers. Normally these are violet with white blotches but white, mauve, crimson and yellow forms occur. The plants need full sun and well-drained soil and should be grouped for maximum effect. They also make good pot plants.

Lobelia

Among the smaller annuals no plant is more adaptable than *Lobelia erinus*, a charming, compact, half-hardy annual with smooth serrated leaves and pale blue, white-throated flowers. These bloom continuously all summer and may be grown in hanging baskets, pots and borders as well as in the rock garden. Selected forms, which come true from seed, include the deep blue, white-eyed Bluestone; white Snowball; deep carmine-red and white-eyed Rosamund, and Mrs Clibran which is brilliant blue with white eyes. The usual height is 6 in. but there are also pendulous lobelias with lax, 18-in. trailing stems, much used in hanging baskets. *L. tenuior* is a good blue for pot work.

Nemesia

Nemesia strumosa is grown as a half-hardy annual. Ideal for bedding in sunny annual borders, the plants also do well in rich, slightly acid soil in rock gardens. The stems grow 9 to 12 in. tall with bunches of bright flowers in scarlet, orange, crimson,

carmine, pink, purple, cream, white or yellow. The race known as Suttonii is particularly fine.

Nierembergia

Nierembergia caerulea (*N. hippomanica*) is a perennial usually treated as a half-hardy annual, although plants are occasionally lifted in autumn and overwintered under glass. It blooms all summer, the 6 to 9-in. stems spangled with cup-shaped flowers of lavender with yellow throats. It needs sun and shelter in moist but well-drained soil.

Phlox

Phlox drummondii does best in deep moist soil and should be treated as a half-hardy annual. The lightly scented flowers come in clusters and persist all summer in vivid shades of scarlet, violet, pink, white and yellow. There are large-flowered hybrids around 12 in. and dwarfs of 6 in. A warm sunny position is preferred.

Sedum

Sedum caeruleum is a lovely little annual with masses of pale blue starry flowers and needle-fine leaves on 2 to 3-in. stems. Sow the seed in rock pockets out of doors in April.

Silene

Silene coeli-rosa, also known and sold under the names *Lychnis coeli-rosa* and *Viscaria oculata*, is a vivid, easy-to-grow

Nemesia strumosa

annual which should be sown where it is to flower in March or April. Sometimes called rose of Heaven, it has slender, 18-in. stems with narrow leaves and many rosy-red, white-centred flowers about 1 in. across.

ANNUALS AND BIENNIALS FOR CUTTING

Many annuals make excellent cut flowers and indeed constant picking – by preventing seeding – prolongs the life and vigour of some, such as sweet peas. For the rest, in order not to denude borders of bloom, it may be advisable to grow these in reserved beds away from general view. Make the beds long and narrow (not more than 3 ft. wide), so that picking can take place in all weathers without treading all over the soil.

Agrostemma

Agrostemma githago is the corn cockle, a beautiful hardy annual with large, five-petalled magenta flowers (pale lilac in the variety Milas), 2 to 3 in. across on 2 to 3-ft. stems. The long narrow leaves are greyish. The plant is also useful for pot culture or in borders.

Amaranthus

Amaranthus are esteemed for their foliage as well as their striking inflorescences.

Amaranthus caudatus or love-lies-bleeding takes its name from the long drooping spikes of flowers which may be blood red, white or green. When these are stripped of their leaves they make interesting cut flowers. The plants grow 2 to 5 ft. according to conditions, although rich soil tends to make them top heavy and coarse. *A. hybridus* (often listed in catalogues as *A. hypochondriacus*) is known as prince's feather on account of the colourful greenish-red leaves and spikes of blood-red flowers. The 18-in. *A. tricolor* or Joseph's coat is the best for foliage, however, this being strikingly patterned in scarlet, yellow and bronze green. All the family need sun and should be treated as half-hardy annuals.

Callistephus

Callistephus chinensis is the China aster, a favourite for cutting but also useful in borders. There is a wide range of types, all of which should be grown in an open sunny position in good soil and treated as half-hardy annuals. Pompon Mixed has button-like daisies in shades of purple, blue, mauve, red, pink and white – also some bicolours, all 18 in. high; Dwarf Queen is a race of small (9 in.) double bedding kinds; Totem Pole has large shaggy flowers 6 to 7 in. across, 2 ft.; the Single Flowered are naturally all singles, on 2½-ft. stems, and Californian Giant produces huge shaggy blooms on 2 to 3-ft. stems in various colours. A virus disease (spotted wilt) sometimes attacks and kills aster plants. Buying seed from reliable sources and not too much warmth in the early stages of growth are the best preventatives.

Centaurea

Centaurea cyanus is the cornflower, a pretty little blue-flowered annual with small thistle-like heads of flowers on branching, 2½-ft. stems. There are also pinks and whites and dwarf forms. This is essentially a flower for cutting since dead blooms remain on the stems, which spoils them for border work. Sow the seed in autumn on light soil and in spring thin the plants to 12 or 18 in. apart.

Chrysanthemum

Annual chrysanthemums make ideal cut flowers and come in self-colours of white, cream and yellow and also with contrasting bands around the petals or different centres. They are derived from such species as *Chrysanthemum coronarium*, *C. carinatum* and *C. segetum*. The usual height is between 1 and 2 ft. and the plants should be treated as hardy annuals.

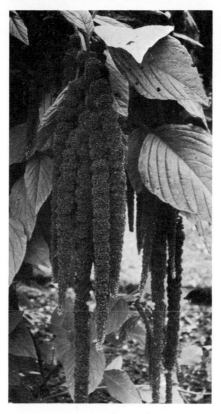

Germination takes place in eight days. Grow them in an open sunny position and good but well-drained soil. *C. frutescens*, the white marguerite, a popular long flowering bedding plant should be treated as half hardy. It has branching 2-ft. stems with deeply cut leaves and many golden-centred, white flowers. There is also a yellow called Comtesse de Chambord and a pink, Mary Wootton.

Clarkia

Clarkia elegans (more correctly *C. unguiculata*) is a branching hardy annual from California which will grow 1 to 3 ft. tall, according to when the seed is sown and the richness of the soil. The flowers are carried on long spikes and can be single or double in shades of pink, scarlet and purple – also white. The buds open up well in water.

Cleome

Cleome spinosa is the spider plant, an unusual half-hardy annual with strong, rather sticky, 3 to 5-ft. stems, spiny, palmate leaves (which smell unpleasant when bruised) and pink, rose, white or mauve flowers with 4 to 5-in. protruding anthers. There is also a yellow form called Golden Sparkler.

Coreopsis

Coreopsis are North American annuals and perennials with daisy flowers mostly in yellow, gold and bronze shades. *Coreop-*

Above: *Clarkia elegans*
Above left: *Amaranthus caudatus*

sis basalis (*C. drummondii*) and *C. tinctoria* are hardy annuals, the former 1½ to 2 ft. tall with large yellow flowers; the latter embracing races and varieties varying in height from 9 in. to 2 or 3 ft. The dwarfs make good border edging or pot plants; the taller kinds are excellent for cutting. The variety *atrosanguinea* has dark red single flowers and there are also singles and doubles in various shades and mixtures of colours.

Cosmos

Cosmos bipinnatus is at its best in late summer and autumn. It is an elegant plant with pale green feathery leaves, tall branching (2 to 3 ft.) stems and long-stemmed white, pink, rose or crimson daisies. There are also semi-doubles which come true from seed. All make excellent cut flowers. Treat as hardy annuals or half-hardy annuals (for stronger plants and earlier flowers). The soil should be on the poor side and the aspect sunny.

Delphinium

The ever-popular larkspurs are derived from two species of delphiniums (*Delphinium ajacis* and *D. consolida*). They are reliable hardy annuals with dainty spikes of pink, mauve, blue or white flowers which blend pleasantly, dry for winter decoration and grace any border. Heights vary from 2½ to 5 ft., and apart from singles there are various doubles and a race of dwarfs at 18 in. Although not fastidious they do best from autumn sowings in open sunny situations and well-drained soil. The seed germinates in about nineteen days and they flower from June over a period of eight to ten weeks. Spring sowing produces later blooms.

Gaillardia

Gaillardia aristata, although perennial, is usually grown as a biennial or half-hardy annual. It has showy daisy flowers up to 5 in. across of bright yellow with zonings of other shades. There are also wine, copper, reds and tangerines in selected races like the Monarch strain. The height ranges up to 3 ft. and the soil should be well drained and the aspect sunny.

Godetia

Godetias are valuable for summer bedding or pot work under glass, as well as cutting. For outdoor cultivation seed should be sown in a warm sunny position about March – or October, in gentle heat, for indoor work. *Godetia grandiflora* grows about 12 in. high with clusters of large flowers which, in the hybrids, range from white and various shades of pink to deep crimson. There are also doubles known as Azalea Flowered. *G. amoena* is taller and slenderer (2 to 2½ ft.) and has a similar colour range. The two species have been crossed to produce the very popular tall doubles.

Rudbeckia

Rudbeckia hirta is a splendid plant up to 3 ft. in height with branching, hairy stems and large daisy heads of flowers 3 to 4 in. across. These are golden yellow with dark centres. The Hirta Hybrida race come in various autumnal shades of orange, bronze, scarlet and yellow.

Salpiglossis

Salpiglossis sinuata is a beautiful half-hardy annual from Chile with dainty 2 to 3-ft. branching stems and many trumpet-shaped flowers of crimson, scarlet, violet, yellow, ivory to buff, usually patterned with gold. Grow in a sheltered sunny position in rich moist soil.

Scabiosa

Scabiosa atropurpurea or sweet scabious make delightful cut flowers with their long, stiff, 3-ft. stems and round pin-cushion heads of white, pink, scarlet,

Left: A well-balanced planting of annuals
Right: Annuals in pot and patio

mauve, blue or maroon. There are also doubles and dwarf strains. They can be treated as biennials or hardy annuals and also make striking border plants.

Zinnia
Zinnias (*Zinnia elegans*) need a rich moist soil and plenty of sun. Without these they invariably disappoint. They also resent transplanting so should be pricked out (from April sowings under glass) into small pots and from these to the garden in early June. Alternatively, seed can be sown outside in May. There are large-flowered strains of 2 to 3 ft. in distinct colours like orange, pink, scarlet and purple. Giant Dahlia and Chrysanthemum Flowered are examples and among the smaller types come Pumila Pompon, doubles, 1½ ft.; Peter Pan and Thumbelina, both 6 in. Envy is a curious chartreuse-green zinnia.

Other good cutting annuals include various grasses such as *Briza maxima* (quaking grass), *Pennisetum longistylum*, and *Lagurus ovatus* (hare's tail), annual lupins, nasturtiums, centaurea, dianthus, polyanthus, violas, calendulas, dahlias, lathyrus and stocks.

LONG FLOWERING PLANTS
These plants remain in bloom for long periods so are particularly useful for container work and bedding; some also make good cut flowers.

Antirrhinum
Because rust disease is widespread and ruins their foliage, snapdragons (*Antirrhinum majus*) are usually grown as hardy or half-hardy annuals. Their varying heights, honey fragrance and showy flowers make them popular for summer bedding, window boxes and as cut flowers. Colours range from white and yellow through shades of pink to scarlet, blood red and near lavender. The F_1 hybrids are particularly good for cutting or forcing under glass. Heights vary from 3 ft. in the Grandiflorum Giant Sentinels range; 4 ft. in Maximum; Nanum Grandiflorum is 15 in. and Nanum Compactum 6 to 8 in. There are also double varieties and Penstemon-flowered types with flat-fronted tubular flowers.

Begonia
Begonia semperflorens are dependable, long-flowering bedding plants which can also be used in window boxes and other containers or rock garden pockets. They are neat and compact, on average 6 to 15 in. high, with green or bronze foliage

and masses of small, pink, red or white flowers. Treat as half-hardy annuals. Suitable for sun or shade.

Calendula
Calendula officinalis is the pot marigold, a splendid plant for bedding and cutting. The round daisy heads come in various shades of yellow and orange, the doubles being most popular. Pot marigolds thrive in sun and most soils and can be raised from autumn or spring sowings out of doors.

Eschscholzia
Californian poppies (*Eschscholzia californica*) are hardy annuals with deeply cut, glaucous foliage, fleshy tap roots and large yellow, orange, cream, pink and red single or double flowers on 12 to 15-in stems. Sow out of doors in spring or autumn in full sun.

Myosotis
Forget-me-nots (*Myosotis alpestris*) are best treated as biennials. These well-known, blue-flowered favourites are ideal for spring bedding, particularly between bulbs. The pink and white forms are less popular. They grow 4 to 12 in. tall in sun or light shade. After flowering shake the old plants over a spare corner of ground, and enough seedlings will come up for the following season's use.

Papaver
Annual poppies should be grouped in borders, otherwise they make little impact. They are easy to grow in any open situation and reasonable soil and may be sown outside in autumn or spring. Shirley poppies are derived from the scarlet, black-based corn poppy, *Papaver rhoeas*, and have larger and white-based flowers in a delightful range of pink and rose shades, also white. Double varieties are also available. *P. nudicaule*, the Iceland poppy, should be treated as a half-hardy annual. The long (12 to 18 in.) stems carry large flowers of glowing orange, yellow, white, pink or rose. *P. somniferum*, the opium poppy, has glaucous leaves and stems and very large single or double, white, salmon or scarlet flowers. Sow these out of doors in spring. See also p. 118.

Primula
Polyanthus, derived in the main from *Primula veris* and *P. vulgaris* crosses, are frequently raised from seed as biennials. They make excellent spring bedding plants with white, yellow, orange, pink, rose, red, blue, purple or violet flowers and

after blooming can be lifted and divided and removed to a cool, moist, shady spot for the summer. In autumn they can be replanted in rich soil and a sunny situation. They grow 1 ft. in height.

Tagetes
Although not natives of Africa or France, nor yet true marigolds, *Tagetes erecta*, the African marigold, and *T. patula*, the French marigold, are reliable half-hardy annuals which bloom right through the summer. The Africans are tall and vigorous with round and heavy, yellow or orange flowers up to 6 in. across on branching stems and unpleasant smelling, cut-edged leaves. There are also dwarf and Carnation and Chrysanthemum-flowered types. Heights vary from 6 in. to 3 ft.; the Burpee Climax strain being particularly fine (2½ to 3 ft.).

French marigolds are smaller and daintier with masses of single or double lemon, gold, orange or mahogany-red flowers, often striped or striated with other shades. The average height is 6 to 12 in. Both kinds like sun but will also flower well in wet seasons.

Verbena
Verbenas (usually listed as *Verbena hybrida*) have flat heads of flowers in pink, red, mauve, blue and purple, also white. They make bushy plants 12 to 15 in. high with simple serrated leaves and there are also dwarf forms. Grow as half-hardy annuals in full sun – although strictly speaking they are perennial and were once propagated from cuttings.

Other long season annuals include ageratum, alyssum, chrysanthemums, impatiens, matthiola and tropaeolums.

OTHER GOOD ANNUALS AND BIENNIALS

Althaea
Because of rust disease the perennial hollyhocks (*Althaea rosea*) and the fig-leaved *A. ficifolia* are usually treated as hardy biennials. Their tall (6 to 9 ft.), stately spikes of single or double rosette flowers are ideal for backs of borders or as accent plants in key positions. They should be planted in full sun in heavy but rich and well-drained soil; staking the spikes if necessary. Colours range from pink, rose and maroon to white, apricot and yellow.

Arctotis
Arctotis or African daisies are vigorous plants with hairy, silvery-grey stems and

Gazania splendens

foliage and 3 to 4-in. flowers of cream, yellow, orange, red, crimson or purple – frequently zoned with other shades – on 1½-ft. stems. To encourage a bushy habit pinch out the tops when the seedlings are 5 to 6 in. tall. Because of their mixed background African daisies are usually catalogued as *Arctotis hybrida*. Treat them as half-hardy annuals and grow them in an open sunny position.

Argemone
Argemone mexicana is the prickly poppy and it likes a hot sunny situation. It grows about 2 ft. with glaucous, prickly foliage and bright yellow, poppy-like flowers about 3 in. across.

Atriplex
Atriplex hortensis cupreata is a wine-red-foliaged spinach, a useful foliage plant for borders and cutting. It grows up to 4 ft. and should be treated as a hardy annual.

Calceolaria
Calceolaria chelidonioides is a South American annual with long succulent leaves and honey-scented, lemon-yellow, pouched flowers on 12 to 18-in. stems. The shrubby *C. integrifolia* (*C. rugosa*) can also be grown from seed; Golden Bunch being a particularly fine flowering, 8-in. variety. Treat as half-hardy annuals and place in a warm, sunny situation.

Campanula
Canterbury bells (*Campanula medium*) are delightful biennials for mixed borders, especially in rich soil with plenty of sun. In windy situations they may need staking. The bell-shaped flowers come with or without 'saucers' in white, pink, blue and mauve and there are dwarf races such as the 18-in. Musical Bells. *C. pyramidalis*, the chimney bellflower, is also grown as a biennial, but with protection in winter. The beautiful blue or white flowers are saucer shaped on 4-ft. (to 8 ft. under glass) spires.

Centaurea
Centaurea cineraria (*C. candidissima*) is grown for its fine silvery leaves which set off bright annuals and have many garden uses. It likes sun and well-drained soil, growing about 15 in. high. *C. gymnocarpa* is similar but with wider leaves and taller at 2 ft. Both plants are perennials but can be killed in cold winters so treat as half-hardy annuals.

Cladanthus
Cladanthus arabicus has deeply cut leaves and bright yellow daisy flowers on 12 to 15-in. stems. It appreciates sun and should be grown as a hardy annual.

Convolvulus
Convolvulus tricolor is a delightful hardy annual for full sun, growing 12 to 15 in. tall with brilliant blue, funnel-shaped flowers with white or pale yellow throats. There are also kinds with white, rose and dark blue flowers.

Echium
Echium lycopsis (*E. plantagineum*) or viper's bugloss is a hardy annual with spikes of bright blue flowers and rough leaves and stems. It grows 9 to 12 in. tall and there are white, pink, purple and mauve-flowered forms.

Gazania
Gazanias are best treated as half-hardy annuals although named or selected varieties can be perpetuated from cuttings. They must be grown in full sun since the flowers fail to open in dull weather or shade. The long, narrow, ground-hugging leaves have a silver reverse and the brilliant daisy flowers come in cream, orange and pink, often with striking zonings such as green on pink and orange on silver.

Helianthus
Helianthus annuus is the common sunflower, a hardy annual with huge plate-like golden flower heads up to 1 ft. in diameter on 4 to 10-ft. stems. Seedsmen also sell dwarf sunflowers on 3 to 4-ft. stems, with orange, yellow, cream and chestnut-brown flowers.

Lavatera
Lavatera trimestris rosea, one of the best of the taller hardy annuals, has large open, satiny-pink flowers like mallows on its branching stems. These are in character all summer and require full sun and good soil. Height 24 to 30 in. One of the best strains is called Loveliness and there is also a white form.

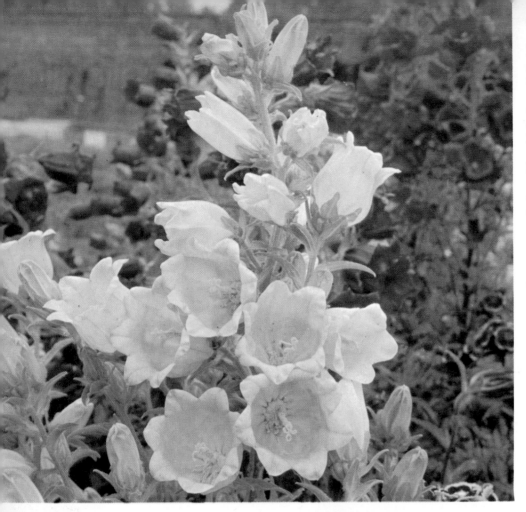

Linum

Linum grandiflorum rubrum is a red-flowered flax, very showy, with slender 12-in. stems carrying many saucer-shaped, deep red blooms. It likes sun and only shows to advantage in bright weather. Hardy annual.

Mentzelia

Mentzelia lindleyi (*Bartonia aurea*), an easy hardy annual, has large, golden, chalice-shaped flowers full of stamens on 18-in. stems. It is also known as blazing star, likes sun and is sweetly scented.

Oenothera

Oenotheras may be annual, biennial or short-term perennials; many are night bloomers. The common evening prim-rose (*Oenothera biennis*) sows itself about after initial establishment, the 2 to 4-ft. stems carrying many 2-in., lemon-yellow, sweetly scented flowers. Another night-scented biennial is the shorter (12 in.) *O. trichocalyx* with white flowers. *O. acaulis*, although perennial, should be treated as a half-hardy annual and is worth the trouble as the 4-in. flowers on trailing stems are very beautiful. They open white and develop to deep rose.

Silene

Silenes are showy plants for the border or rock garden with small white, pink or purple-pink flowers. The annual *Silene pendula*, growing 6 to 8 in., makes compact plants covered with bloom in spring from autumn sowings. In cold soils, however, they may need winter protection. There are double forms as well as singles. *S. armeria* grows taller – 1 to 2 ft. – and has sticky stems.

Tithonia

The Mexican sunflower (*Tithonia rotundifolia*) is a rapid grower, up to 9 ft. and 6 to 10 ft. across. Its broad branching habit supports many large, single, orange, zinnia-like flowers from July onwards. Treat as a half-hardy annual and plant in sun.

Verbascum

Verbascums (mulleins) carry their flowers on long straight spikes. They like sun and well-drained soil. Although perennial, some can be grown as hardy annuals. *Verbascum olympicum* is yellow and 5 to 6 ft.; *V. phoeniceum*, red, purple, pink, white or mauve and 2 to 3 ft. tall.

Above left: *Campanula media*
Left: *Helianthus annuus*

Flowering Bulbs

Percy Thrower, V.M.H., N.D.H., has become a household name to millions of gardeners – and non-gardeners – through his weekly B.B.C. television programme, "Gardeners' World", his books and other writings and his many public lectures.

After leaving school he worked for four years with his father, the head gardener at Horwood House in Buckinghamshire. Then, at the age of eighteen, he became a journeyman gardener in the Royal Gardens at Windsor Castle. He spent nearly five years there, working first in the fruit house and then in the plant houses.

A career in public parks followed. Two years at Leeds and nine at Derby preceeded his appointment as Parks Superintendent at Shrewsbury, a post he held for twenty-eight years until he retired in the spring of 1974. Shrewsbury is, of course, noted for its fine civic gardens and its annual flower show.

Percy Thrower began his broadcasting career over twenty-six years ago and since those days has made hundreds of sound broadcasts and television appearances. He escorts many gardening tours abroad and is also joint owner of a leading rose nursery and general garden centre business in Shropshire.

His services to horticulture were recognized by The Royal Horticultural Society in 1974 when he was awarded the Victoria Medal of Honour.

The bulbous plants provide us with some of the loveliest of the garden flowers. Few other plants give such brilliance and profusion of colour for so little effort on the part of the grower. Many connect the word bulb with the spring-flowering kinds and especially the daffodils which hold such a special place in our affections but there are bulbous plants to give colour throughout the year even in the depths of winter and it is a pity that, with the exception of the gladioli, the lilies and the dahlias, the summer and autumn-flowering kinds are so often neglected.

A bulb is an underground storage organ and the term bulbous plants is a general one which embraces other similar structures known as tubers and corms, and sometimes plants with rhizomes are included in this classification. Although there are botanical differences between these structures, these are largely unimportant from the gardener's point of view as their cultivation is very similar. They are all, with few exceptions, easy to grow and maintain and therefore can be relied upon by the busy gardener.

The function of a bulbous structure is twofold. It allows the plant to survive adverse weather conditions which may range from severe winter cold to drought and it stores food so that the plant grows rapidly when placed under suitable conditions. During the growing and flowering period of the bulbous plant, food is manufactured by the leaves. This is passed back down to the storage organ and the next year's leaves and flowers are formed. After flowering the leaves and roots of the present year's growth gradually die back to leave the swollen storage organ ready to produce the next year's growth.

Bulbous plants can be found to fit into any setting in the garden. There are kinds which look good in formal bedding schemes, others for mixed beds and borders while many look delightful when naturalized in grass. Some, too, adapt well to growing in window boxes, tubs and other ornamental containers on paved areas and patios.

Formal Beds

The bulbous plants which are most suited for formal plantings are mainly spring-flowering subjects. They include the Early Single, Early Double, Cottage, Broken and Darwin tulips, hyacinths, some of the narcissi, snowdrops, crocuses, muscari, chionodoxas and scillas. Many of these look effective when planted on their own or they can be combined with other spring-bedding plants such as wallflowers, pansies, violas, polyanthus, forget-me-nots, arabis and *Alyssum saxatile* in very many attractive combinations. For summer there are the tuberous-rooted begonias and dahlias. It is important when planning and planting formal beds to buy bulbs which are guaranteed to grow to a uniform height and colour and to flower at the same time.

Ensure that the drainage is adequate, then dig the bed over to the depth of a spade. The soil texture can be greatly improved by forking in a dressing of horticultural peat at the rate recommended by the supplier. The peat should be well soaked with water before it is worked into the soil. A dressing of bonemeal or hoof and horn, applied while wearing gardening gloves at the rate of 4 oz. to the sq. yd. and forked in with the peat, will prove very beneficial. Never place fresh manure in direct contact with bulbs but it can be most profitably incorporated below planting level.

Planting depths and distances and the times of planting too are dealt with in the list of plants which follows. It is best to plant the bedding plants first, if these are being used, and then to put in the bulbs using a trowel. After their display is over spring-bedding plants are removed to make way for the summer flowers. However, the bulbous plants must be allowed to complete their life cycle naturally. They should, therefore, be moved to a reserve bed in a secluded part of the garden where they can be lined out in shallow trenches and the soil well firmed around them. In dry weather, water the soil. By about late June the foliage should have withered and the bulbs can be lifted with care making sure that they are not damaged by the spade or fork. Dry in a cool airy shed or

Cleaning narcissus bulbs and removing the dried foliage before storing them in trays

129

room and before storing in boxes, under similar conditions, remove old roots and other extraneous material and throw away any bulbs which appear diseased.

Mixed Beds and Borders

There are houses and gardens which, because of their style and layout, are most suited to a formal treatment of plants. Informal garden plants are, however, becoming increasingly popular and these allow for mixed beds and borders which are planted with a whole range of subjects – small trees, shrubs, herbaceous perennials, bulbs and even annuals and biennials. This type of planting is especially economic where space is limited and with skilful planning it will give the garden year-round interest.

Soil preparation is similar to that described for formal beds though with a mixed border it is seldom necessary to prepare and plant the whole area at once. Plant with a trowel at the times and distances recommended in the following list. Gladioli and lilies are among the bulbs which should be bedded on sand as they will rot in moist soils.

Some subjects may need staking. Firmly secure one bamboo cane to each plant in the ground and tie the flower stem to this loosely with a soft material. The plant should be allowed some freedom of movement in the wind or it will look unnatural so take the tying material round the stake, knot it and then take it loosely round the stem, knotting it again.

Many of the summer-flowering bulbous plants are not reliably hardy. Some, like the dahlia, will have to be lifted and stored each winter, but the soil where others are growing can be covered with straw, bracken or a similar material as a protection against frost. It is better, if possible, to leave bulbs undisturbed for several years. Every third or fourth year they can then be lifted and sorted through and at

this time offsets can be removed. Some protection can also be given to the less hardy kinds if they are planted in beds against warm south or south west-facing walls.

Naturalized Bulbs

Naturalized bulbs, as the term implies, are those grown under as near natural conditions as possible. They can look very attractive indeed in an informal garden setting and once planted they demand very little attention from the grower. In fact this is the least troublesome way of all to grow bulbous plants. They can be planted around trees and shrubs, down banks, in small woodland areas or in drifts on the lawn. How about daffodils around forsythia to produce a brilliant splash of yellow in the spring; blue muscari round a flowering cherry; anemones down a bank; bluebells in a woodland setting, and crocuses on the lawn? The combinations are endless and all are equally lovely.

There is only one important point to remember when planting bulbs in a lawn and that is that the grass cannot be cut until the leaves of the bulbs have died down naturally for the plants must be

(a) A bulb planter
(b) A core of soil removed
(c) The bulb is inserted and the core replaced

allowed to complete their life cycle in order to build up food resources for the next year's growth. The grass when eventually cut may be an unattractive brown colour but watering and feeding with a lawn fertilizer will soon bring it round.

Naturalized bulbs should be planted in drifts, not in rows or rigid clumps. The best way of achieving a good effect is to scatter handfuls of bulbs and plant them where they fall. The easiest way of planting naturalized bulbs is with a special tool known as a bulb planter. This cuts out a core of turf and soil when it is pressed into the ground and removes it intact when it is given a twist and lift. The bulb can then be placed in the hole and the core of soil and turf replaced and firmed with the feet. Small quantities of bulbs can be planted with a trowel. Where only a small area is involved the turf can be lifted, the soil improved with a dressing of bonemeal at the rate of 2 oz. to the sq. yd., the bulbs planted and the turf replaced.

Bulbs in Containers

Patios are now very popular features in many gardens and they will be enhanced by tubs and other ornamental containers filled with bulbous and other subjects. This method of cultivation is especially suited to those slightly tender subjects – agapanthus, amaryllis, crinums, nerines and others – for the containers can be put in to the conservatory, greenhouse or a frostproof shed for the winter.

A most important point when growing bulbs in containers is to ensure that the drainage is good and there should be adequate holes to allow the surplus water to escape. These will either be at the bottoms of the sides of the container

In moist soils, lily bulbs can be planted on sand to avoid rotting

Staking

when the container may stand on the ground or they will be in the bottom of the container itself. In this case the container must be raised a little from the ground to allow the water to escape easily. Cover these holes with crocks and then a thick layer of roughage before the compost is added. If the provision of holes is impossible then a thick layer of drainage material must be laid in the bottom of the container before the compost is added.

I would recommend John Innes Potting Compost No. 2 as the growing medium. If you do use ordinary garden soil, this must have a good texture and it is a good idea to add peat to it and a dressing of bonemeal. Plant at the same time and depth as stated in the plant lists. Watch the compost carefully during the growing season and water when it appears dry. Taller plants may require some unobtrusive staking.

A method of growing daffodils which I have found particularly rewarding is that of planting double layers of daffodil bulbs in tubs at least 12 in. deep. Place a layer of crocks over the drainage holes and cover this with roughage. Add a layer of compost and set the first layer of bulbs in position. Cover the bulbs with compost so that the tips are just showing and then position the second layer of bulbs between the tips of the first layer. Work in the compost among these bulbs and make this firm.

Selected Bulbs

Acidanthera
The lovely *Acidanthera bicolor murielae* comes from Ethiopia and grows 3 ft. high. On each stem, during September and October, are borne five to six fragrant white flowers each marked with a maroon blotch at the centre. Of special interest to the flower arranger is that these flowers will last a long time if picked in bud.

The corms should be planted in April and May 3 in. deep and 6 in. apart in light, well-drained soil and in a sunny position which is sheltered from the wind. An ideal place is against a warm south or south west-facing wall where it should be possible to leave the corms in the ground over winter if they are protected by a covering of straw or bracken.

Acidantheras can be increased by offsets or by seed sown under glass in the spring.

Agapanthus
Agapanthus orientalis (syn. *A. umbellatus*) is the African lily or lily of the Nile. It has large strap-shaped leaves and handsome

funnel-shaped summer flowers which in the species are blue but there is also a fine white form and one of a rich double blue. All grow 2 to 3 ft. tall.

The creeping rootstock should be planted in March so that the crown is just below the surface in a sandy soil and a warm, sunny position. As it is inclined to be half hardy, it makes an excellent subject for flowering in pots which can be taken into the greenhouse or conservatory during the winter months. A single rhizome will give a good display in a 9 or 10-in. pot. A hardier strain, the Headbourne Hybrids, has now been developed, however, with colours ranging from pale to deep violet blue. These can be left in situ during the winter with straw or bracken protection.

African lilies can be increased by offsets, division or seed though from seed they may take five to six years to flower.

Allium
This is the family to which the onion belongs but it has many lovely ornamental relations which only give the characteristic onion smell if their leaves are bruised. Heights range from a few inches to several feet and the colour range is from pure white through yellow and pink to deep purple. All produce ball-shaped flower heads freely from May to July, some being solid and others tasselled. They should be planted in a sunny, open position in the autumn and covered with two to three times their own depth of soil. The smaller-growing species can be planted 2 to 3 in. apart, the larger ones 8 to 9 in. apart. Increase by division of the bulb clusters in autumn or by seed sown in spring in a cool greenhouse or frame.

Allium aflatunense has the descriptive common name of the powder puff. It has dense rounded heads of lilac-purple flowers on 2 to 3-ft. stems. The butterflies' haven, *A. albopilosum*, has heads of lilac starry flowers which can be as much as 10 to 12 in. across on 2-ft. stems. The globular heads of the 2-ft. *A. caeruleum* are cornflower blue.

A. moly is sometimes known as the golden garlic. It has bluish-green leaves and umbels of yellow flowers on 10 to 12-in. stems. Sweetly scented white flowers are the glory of the 15-in. *A. neapolitanum*. And the last which I have room for here is *A. ostrowskianum*, at 6 in. ideal for the rock garden, which it graces with its carmine-pink flowers.

Alstroemeria
The Peruvian lilies are elegant, tuberous-rooted perennials and they make excellent

cut flowers. The umbels of richly coloured, funnel-shaped flowers are in evidence from June onwards on 1 to 4-ft. leafy stems. They should be planted in April in a well-drained sheltered position and established plants will benefit from an annual mulch of well-decayed manure in the spring. This will also afford some protection from frosts.

I would strongly recommend the hybrids of *Alstroemeria ligtu* which can be had in beautiful shades of pink, orange, yellow and carmine. There is also *A. aurantiaca lutea* which has yellow flowers spotted carmine; *A. pelegrina* which is clear pink, and *A. haemantha* which is blood red.

Amaryllis
If you plant the belladonna lily, *Amaryllis belladonna*, under a south wall you will be richly rewarded during the late summer and early autumn with fragrant, rosy-red, trumpet flowers of which up to ten can be carried on the top of each 18-in. stem. An August planting of bulbs 4 in. deep and 12 in. apart will flower within a few weeks. The dull green, strap-shaped leaves are produced after the flowers in the spring. Leave undisturbed but cover in severe winters with bracken or straw. Increase by offsets or by seed sown in heat in spring. This, however, is a very slow process as it can take seven years before flowers appear.

Anemone
Some of the members of this charming genus will have been written about elsewhere in this book but here we are concerned with the lovely tuberous-rooted species.

As its common name implies, the wood anemone, *Anemone nemorosa*, is ideal for naturalizing and as ground cover beneath taller subjects in the mixed border which will give it some shade. The spring flowers of the species are white with pink tips on 6-in. stems and there are several good varieties in the white to lavender-blue colour range. Plant 2 in. deep in a leafy or peaty soil in September or October.

A. coronaria is the poppy anemone and two excellent strains – the St Brigid and the de Caen – have been bred from it. These have flowers of many colours and are, of course, well known as commercial cut flowers. The stems are up to 1 ft. high. Plant the tubers 2 to 3 in. deep and 6 in. apart in November for spring flowering, in April or May for July flowering, and in June for September flowering.

There are numerous varieties of *A. blanda* with flowers from white to blue. They prefer a sunny and sheltered site

Anemone coronaria St Brigid

Bulbocodium

Bulbocodium vernum is especially suited to the rock garden for the crocus-like purple blooms appear on short stems during March and April. Plant in September 3 in. deep and 4 to 6 in. apart in a warm, sheltered place and well-drained soil. It can be left undisturbed for many years.

Calochortus

The butterfly tulips or mariposa lilies are not easy to grow and consequently they are not as widely known as their beauty suggests that they should be. However, the gardener with a warm, well-drained soil would do well to try them for they are like very delicately formed tulips on slender 6 to 24-in. stems, the height depending on the species grown.

Plant in October or November in a warm, sunny position and a light, sandy soil to which leafmould or peat has been added for moisture retention during the summer. If protected with straw or bracken during the winter, or in severe weather with frame lights or cloches, they can be left undisturbed for several years.

Calochortus venustus is perhaps the most readily available with white, cream or yellow flowers with a blotch of dark red on each petal. It flowers in June and July and is 2 ft. tall. *C. splendens* has lilac flowers on 1-ft. stems in May and June.

Camassia

I like to see the amenable *Camassia esculenta* flowering in the summer border. It has spikes of star-shaped flowers which in variety have a colour range from white to deep blue. This species which grows to 2 ft. and flowers in June and July can also be naturalized in light woodland. There is also *C. cusickii* which is 3 ft. and *C. scilloides* (syn. *C. fraseri*) which is half that height. Both have pale blue flowers.

Plant camassias in the autumn 4 to 5 in. deep and the same distance apart in sun or light shade and leave undisturbed for a number of years. Increase by seed or by division when the bulbs are lifted which some gardeners advocate should be every four years to keep the bulbs in a healthy condition.

Chionodoxa

The glory of the snow is native to the mountainous regions of Asia Minor and it is a delightful subject for the rock garden or window box. It should be planted in autumn 3 in. deep and 1 in. apart to flower from early March onwards. There are several good species. *Chionodoxa luciliae* is blue with a white centre; *C. sardensis* is a striking deep

with good well-drained soil. *A. fulgens* has gay scarlet flowers in May and *A. apennina* is a charming plant for naturalizing in grass. It flowers in March.

All are increased by seed or dividing the tubers.

Babiana

The beautiful forms of *Babiana stricta* can be grown out of doors in favoured areas given a light sandy soil and a well-drained sunny border. They will, however, need the winter protection of a covering of straw or bracken if the bulbs are not lifted and stored. The flowers appear in May and June and among the lovely colours available are blue, cream, rose pink and crimson. Plant 4 in. deep and 2 in. apart in March or April and increase from seed or offsets.

Begonia

The tuberous-rooted begonias make splendid summer-bedding plants in their vivid colour range of red and pink through orange and yellow to white. The tubers should be started into growth in February, March or April in a greenhouse with a minimum temperature of 13°C. (55°F.). Plant them in boxes of moist peat or a moist peat and sand mixture and when

growth begins pot into 5-in. pots filled with John Innes Potting Compost No. 2. Harden off before planting out. Lift and store the tubers in October. Increase from seed sown in January or February in a temperature of 18°C. (65°F.) or more.

Brodiaea

The genus now includes those flowers originally listed under milla and triteleia. As if to emphasize the surprising number of bulbous subjects which do flower during the summer and autumn months, these are in full bloom during June and July. They are ideal for the front of the border or rock garden and should be planted in a well-drained soil and a sunny position for the best display.

Californian fire cracker is the very vivid common name of *Brodiaea coccinea* (syn. *B. ida-maia*) which has lovely green-tipped, crimson flowers on 15-in. stems. The 12-in. *B. congesta* has lilac-blue flowers but the best of all is the free-flowering, fragrant *B. uniflora (Milla uniflora)* with pale lavender long-lasting flowers which have a thin violet stripe running down the centre of each petal. It grows to 6 in. with lots of grassy foliage.

Colchicum autumnale

blue, and *C. gigantea* has large clear blue flowers with white centres although its variety *alba* is all white. They grow 6 to 7 in. tall and need plenty of sun and good drainage. Propagation is by offsets or seeds.

Colchicum

There is a point of confusion to be cleared up here. Colchicums are often called autumn crocuses but this is misleading as they are totally unrelated to the true crocus species which flower in autumn. They are much better called by one of their other two common names which are meadow saffron and naked ladies. The name naked ladies arose because there is no foliage to be seen during the flowering season. The broad, lush leaves only appear after flowering is over in the spring.

Colchicums will grow in sun or semi-shade and like most bulbous plants prefer a light, well-drained soil. They should be planted 3 in. deep and 6 in. apart in July

and August and can be increased by division of the clumps at this time or by seeds sown in a cold frame in late summer.

The crocus-like blooms are to be found in white and every shade of pink, mauve and purple and are 6 to 8 in. high. Care must be taken in placing them in a planting scheme, however, as the spring foliage, often 15 to 18 in. high, can smother neighbouring plants. They are perhaps better naturalized though even here caution must be practised as the foliage is poisonous and they must not therefore be planted where there are grazing animals.

Colchicum speciosum comes into flower in September but *C. autumnale* and its varieties flower a little earlier. There is also now a wide range of colchicum hybrids which flower from September to November and these are listed in catalogues under named varieties.

Commelina

The blue spiderwort is easy to grow in a warm sunny position. The best species is *Commelina tuberosa* which has lovely

gentian-blue flowers on 15-in. stems in the summer and long lance-shaped leaves. It should be planted in the spring.

Convallaria

The lily-of-the-valley is not a true bulbous plant but it is usually included as such in any comprehensive list such as this. It likes a soil to which peat, leafmould or old manure has been added and a shady position. The crowns should be planted 3 to 4 in. apart and they can be left undisturbed for many years for they only need lifting when they have become overcrowded. An annual topdressing of compost or decayed manure applied when the foliage has died down will ensure the continued production of large flowers in May. Remember when picking the flowers to leave as many leaves as possible to manufacture the food which will be stored for next year.

Crinum

The beautiful South African crinums are superb plants for those sunny, sheltered sites which are backed by a south-facing wall. They like a rich, loamy, sandy soil containing leafmould or peat or they can be grown in tubs and other ornamental containers. Plant in March so that the tips of the bulbs are just below the surface of the soil and if grown in the border protect in winter with straw or bracken. Propagation is by seed sown in spring in a warm greenhouse or by offsets.

Crinums have ornamental, evergreen, strap-shaped leaves and umbels of handsome funnel-shaped flowers on sturdy stems from July to September. From the large bulbs of *Crinum macowanii* develop 2-ft. stems crowned by fragrant white and purple flowers. The flowers of *C. moorei* are pink and those of *C. powellii*, the most widely grown species, are white veined red with white stamens.

Crocosmia

Crocosmia masonorum is a plant which teeters on the edge of hardiness and it, too, needs a warm, sunny border to be a success in our gardens with a light, sandy soil. The flowers, borne in arching sprays on 2½-ft. stems, are an eye-catching orange-red shade and appear in August and September. The corms should be planted 6 in. deep in spring and lifted and stored at the end of the season if there is any danger of them being damaged by frost. In warmer gardens it may be sufficient to protect with bracken or straw for the winter. Increase by offsets or by seed.

The name *Crocosmia crocosmiiflora* now covers the garden varieties of the montbretia and recently some very reliable hybrids have been introduced. Again they need a well-drained soil, a sunny position and winter protection. I would recommend planting them against a light-coloured wall to show off their bright yellow, orange or crimson flowers. Plant the corms 3 in. deep in March or April and 6 in. apart. Increase by division in March and April.

Crocus

A succession of crocus species and varieties can be planted in the garden to give a wealth of beautiful jewel colours from September to April with few breaks. They are perhaps at their best when naturalized in grass but they also look delightful when planted in borders, in the rock garden or as an edging to paths and borders. They prefer a well-drained soil and to be left undisturbed for several years.

The winter and spring-flowering kinds should be planted in September and October and the autumn-flowering ones in July. The planting depth of them all is

3 in. with 2 to 3 in. between them and propagation is by offsets or seeds.

The list of good species and varieties is almost endless and reference to any good bulb catalogue will provide a plethora to choose from. Here is just a selection starting in the spring with *Crocus imperati*, scented violet flowers; *C. sieberi*, lavender blue; the varieties of *C. biflorus*, with blue or purple feathering on a white or cream ground; *C. ancyrensis*, orange yellow, and varieties of *C. chrysanthus*. The year continues with the cloth of gold crocus, *C. susianus*, and *C. tomasinianus*, silver lavender.

Then there are the large-flowered Dutch crocuses which are so widely planted in parks and gardens. For a really bright display these can be planted in a mixture of named varieties.

For autumn flowering there is *C. zonatus* with large but dainty pinkish-mauve flowers with a gold base and orange-gold anthers. *C. speciosus* has bright blue flowers with violet veinings and orange stigmas and there is a pure white variety *albus* with red stigmas. *C. pulchellus* has sky-blue flowers with white anthers.

Curtonus

Curtonus paniculatus was originally known as *Antholyza paniculata*. It flowers in late summer with handsome orange-red, tubular flowers on branched, arching stems to 4 ft. It likes a light, well-drained soil and sunny position preferably against a warm wall. Give a winter protection of straw or bracken. March or April is the time to plant the corms 4 in. deep and 6 to 8 in. apart. Increase by offsets or by seeds sown in a cool greenhouse.

Cyclamen

The gardener with a cool, shady corner to fill can do no better than plant some of these delightful little flowers. They should be planted during August and September in a peaty soil 1½ in. deep and 3 in. apart. They can then be left undisturbed for many years. Propagation is by seed sown in spring in a cool greenhouse or frame or by division of the old clumps in August or September.

Species can be found to flower from August to the following May and among my favourites is *Cyclamen coum* with dainty carmine blooms in February and March. *C. neapolitanum*, with rosy-pink flowers in August and September, *C. europaeum*, with carmine flowers in autumn, and *C. repandum*, with crimson flowers in spring, are species with beautifully marbled foliage. These make an

extremely attractive ground cover which is with us for most of the year.

Dahlia

Here we are concerned with the growing of dahlias from tubers. These tubers are not fully hardy and so must be lifted carefully and stored each winter in a dry, airy, frostproof place. In late April and early May they should be planted out in a good, well-drained soil and sunny position. Insert stakes before planting and use a trowel or spade, depending on the size of the tubers, to make the hole. The tubers should be firmly covered with 3 to 4 in. of soil. Taller-growing varieties should be planted at least 3 ft. apart and the smaller bedding dahlias 18 in. apart.

As the shoots start to develop thin these to leave about three strong shoots to each plant. When these reach about 8 to 9 in. in height, it is a good idea to pinch out the main growing points. This will encourage the side shoots to grow and will result in a bushy plant with a larger number of flowers. Only the larger-flowered kinds and those grown for exhibition need disbudding to leave one bud at the apex of the shoot.

Dahlias need plenty of water and to conserve soil moisture the area around the plants can be mulched with a layer of peat, leafmould, garden compost or well-rotted manure. Feed regularly with a general fertilizer scraping away the mulch if you have applied one. As the taller-growing varieties develop they will require tying loosely to the stakes.

As the season reaches its climax, it may be necessary to thin out some of the surplus young shoots higher up the plant, otherwise it becomes a mass of foliage with poor quality flowers. This is done by snapping off all the side shoots for about 1½ to 2 ft. from the tip of each stem.

After flowering and before any severe frosty weather cut down the plants to within 9 to 12 in. of the ground and label each with the name of its variety. Lift the tubers and store.

Dahlias are divided into groups according to the shape and formation of their flowers. Grow the small and medium-flowered varieties for garden display reserving the large-flowered types for exhibition work. Dahlias are splendid mixed border subjects, they look striking when grown in a bed on their own and the dwarf varieties are among my favourite bedding plants. The Cactus and Semicactus dahlias have spiky flowers and the flatter-petalled types are called Decoratives. Dahlias with globular flowers less than 2 in. in diameter are called Pompons and above this size are called Ball dahlias. The dwarf dahlias, up to 2 ft. in height, are the bedding dahlias. A good catalogue will offer you a wide choice of dahlias in a wide and beautiful colour range.

Dierama
Like so many other fine bulbous plants *Dierama pulcherrimum* comes from South Africa and as its native habitat suggests it needs a sunny, sheltered position and a well-drained but moist soil. The corms should be planted 3 to 4 in. deep and 3 in. apart in the autumn for flowering in July and August. The bell-like flowers of white or purple hang from long, arched stems and the leaves are grass like. Protect in winter and increase by seed sown in spring in a cool greenhouse or frame, or by division of the clusters of corms in March.

Eranthis
The winter aconites are very useful plants for they thrive in moist, shady conditions where little else will grow. They should be planted 2 in. deep and 2 in. apart in September or October and left undisturbed for as long as possible. They will provide excellent ground cover.

The most widely grown species is *Eranthis hyemalis* which flowers from January to March with a carpet of butter-cup yellow against attractive, much divided leaves. *E. tubergeniana* has handsome deep yellow scented flowers, measuring 2 in. across, and its variety Guinea Gold which is somewhat later flowering has deep yellow fragrant flowers and bronzy foliage.

Increase by division of the tubers in September or October.

Eremurus
These are the foxtail lilies, tall, noble plants for the back of the border. They have strap-like leaves and long tail-like flower spikes which will need protection from the wind. Give them a deeply worked rich soil and plant the crowns from October to December. They may need some winter protection but can be left for three or four years before lifting and dividing.

The golden-yellow flowers of *Eremurus bungei* appear in July and are 5 to 6 ft. high. *E. himalaicus* is taller at 8 ft., flowering in May and June with white flowers which have orange anthers. The 10-ft. *E. robustus elwesianus* produces spikes of large delicate pink flowers in June.

Erythronium
The violets revel in a semi-shady place and moist but well-drained soil. Various forms of the dog's tooth violet, *Erythronium*

Crocus tomasinianus

dens-canis, are available in white, purple, pink and mauve and in heights from 6 to 9 in. The nodding flowers appear in March and April. Slightly later flowering is the handsome *E. revolutum* with delightfully mottled leaves. This species has rose-pink flowers and there is a white variety, White Beauty, with brown markings at the base of the petals. *E. tuolumnense* is another fine species, with golden-yellow flowers and pale green leaves.

Plant in August or September, 2 to 3 in. deep and the same distance apart, in a soil which contains plenty of humus material. Increase by offsets removed in early autumn.

Fritillaria
It is strange that the two most commonly grown members of this genus should be so very different from one another though they share the same month of flowering, April.

Fritillaria meleagris is the snake's head fritillary and it grows about 1 ft. high. The beautiful markings on the bell-shaped flowers are among the most unusual to be found for they are chequered in various shades of purple. There are fine named varieties available like the white Aphrodite, the purple Charon, and Saturnus, a pretty pinkish-purple shade. The snake's head fritillary is a native of Britain and may be found growing wild in some districts. It likes a moist but well-drained soil and looks well in borders or naturalized in grass. The bulbs should be planted in September, 4 in. deep and 6 in. apart, and left undisturbed for as long as possible. Increase by offsets taken at the time of replanting.

Fritillaria imperialis, the crown imperial, is an impressive plant with a close-packed tuft of leaves encircling the tops of the 3 to 4-ft. stems above the nodding yellow, red or orange-red, bell-shaped flowers. It prefers a fairly rich soil which is on the heavy side and is best suited to a partly shaded border or a woodland setting. Plant as for *meleagris*, 6 in. deep and 12 in. apart.

Galanthus

Galanthus nivalis is the very popular common snowdrop which, at 6 in. tall, flowers in January and February. It has two outstanding varieties in S. Arnott, which has beautifully formed flowers, and *atkinsii*. Other species – *byzantinus*, *elwesii* and *plicatus*, all 9 to 12 in. tall – extend the flowering season. Each has the well-known white flowers with green markings.

Grow in beds or borders, rock gardens, banks or in grass, in sun or light shade, and plant the bulbs 3 in. deep and 3 in. apart. Increase by offsets or by dividing clumps of bulbs after flowering in spring when this becomes necessary.

Galtonia

The white-flowered *Galtonia candicans* is an attractive plant with its spikes of bell-shaped, sweet-scented flowers on 4-ft. stems. It makes the best display when planted in groups in a mixed sunny border when it will bring a welcome touch of white to the August and September scene. It can be left undisturbed for several years.

Plant the bulbs 6 in. deep and 1 ft. apart on fairly rich soil at any time between autumn and March when conditions are suitable. Increase by offsets at the time of planting.

Gladiolus

These are lovely flowers which are available in many beautiful colours. The types grown are the large-flowered Grandiflorus, the Butterfly, Miniature and Primulinus. As new varieties are introduced each year I would advise you to consult the

Above left: *Fritillaria meleagris* Aphrodite
Left: *Erythronium dens-canis*

catalogues of gladiolus specialists for a list of varieties. The Grandiflorus varieties flower from July to September and grow to 4 ft. tall. The Butterfly gladioli flower at the same time and reach a similar height but the flowers are smaller and they have handsome throat markings and blotches. Miniature gladioli are, of course, shorter at 2 to 2½ ft. tall and the flowers often have crinkled edges to their petals whereas the Primulinus type are 2 to 4 ft. tall with more or less hooded flowers set more widely in a slender spike.

The mixed or cut-flower border is the place for gladioli and they like a site which receives plenty of sunshine and yet is sheltered from strong winds, and well-drained and well-prepared soil.

Prepare the soil as far in advance of the planting date as possible and plant in succession from March to May to extend the flowering time. The corms should be inserted 4 in. deep and 5 to 6 in. apart. A little sand or old ashes placed above and below the corms will keep them from rotting. They appreciate a feed in June with a good compound fertilizer and the taller varieties will need staking.

Gladioli are, unfortunately, only half hardy and so after they have flowered and the foliage has died down the corms should be carefully lifted and stored in a dry frostproof place until the following spring. Increase by seed or from the cormlets which form round the base of the corm each season.

Hyacinthus

Hyacinths are excellent for spring bedding, although their cost is becoming increasingly prohibitive, and also for planting in ornamental containers and wherever they are grown they will delight with their beautiful fragrance. They like a well-drained rich soil in an open, sunny position and it pays to feed them with bonemeal after planting 3 to 4 in. deep and 8 in. apart in September, October or November, placing a little sand around the bulbs.

The faded flowers should be removed before the seedpods form. The leaves are then allowed to wither naturally when the bulbs are lifted, dried and stored in a dry, airy place until the following autumn. They can be left in the ground from season to season but are not usually grown in borders which allow this treatment.

Varieties in a wide colour range can be found in any good catalogue and if their price stops you from buying many bulbs

Above left: *Galanthus nivalis*
Left: *Gladiolus* Norma (Butterfly)

why not try planting them with other spring-bedding plants like aubrietas, forget-me-nots and pansies.

Iris

The bulbous irises include many superb garden plants and apart from the well-known English, Dutch and Spanish varieties, there are also some very attractive dwarf species. *Iris reticulata* is especially welcome in the mixed border or rock garden because it flowers in January and February. The scented flowers are deep purple each with a prominent yellow blotch on 9-in. stems. There are a number of excellent forms including Cantab, blue and yellow; Royal Blue, bluish purple and yellow, and Harmony rich blue and yellow. *Iris danfordiae* resembles *reticulata* in shape but it is yellow and flowers on 3-in. stems in February. *Iris histrioides* also flowers at the same time and is a rich blue shade with white and gold markings. The form named *major* is particularly fine.

All like a gritty well-drained soil and a warm, sunny position sheltered from strong winds. Plant 3 to 4 in. deep and the same distance apart in August and September and the bulbs can then be left for several years before they will need to be lifted and divided.

There are many varieties available of the Dutch, Spanish and English irises in a good colour range from blue and mauve to yellow and white. All grow from 1½ to 2 ft. tall and make popular cut flowers. The Dutch are the first to come into flower in May, followed by the Spanish and then the English in late June and July. Plant them 3 in. deep and 6 in. apart in September or October in any reasonable, well-drained soil to which a dressing of bonemeal has been added. English irises will do better in a moister soil than either the Dutch or Spanish types.

Ixia

The African corn lilies will grace a warm, sunny border during May and June with their pretty, star-shaped flowers borne in long graceful racemes. They come in a wide range of colours often with a contrasting centre – orange, red, violet and white – either as named varieties or in mixture and grow 1 to 1½ ft. tall.

Plant the corms in September or October 4 in. deep and 2 in. apart in a well-drained, warm and sandy soil. The emerging shoots may need protection with straw or bracken in a cold spring. It is important that the corms are well ripened after flowering and it may be necessary to lift them annually after the narrow, grassy leaves have died down.

Ixiolirion

A warm, sheltered position under a south-facing wall, with a light sandy soil, is also the best place for the May-flowering ixiolirions. The attractive, rather trumpet-like flowers in shades of blue, purple and white are set off against narrow greyish-green leaves. They grow 1 to 1½ ft. high and make very good cut flowers. *Ixiolirion montanum* is the species and several varieties of it are freely available and are listed in catalogues.

Plant the bulbs in October 4 in. deep and 4 in. apart and treat as for ixias. Increase by offsets.

Leucojum

These are the snowflakes, charming flowers which resemble outsize snowdrops. *Leucojum aestivum* is the summer snowflake. It grows to 1½ ft. tall and has white, green-tipped flowers in April and May. The spring snowflake, *L. vernum*, is smaller, some 6 in. high and in favoured districts it may start to flower at the end of January, carrying on through February and March. It is especially good for naturalizing in grass. Both species like to grow in shade and should be left undisturbed for periods of up to five years or so. Plant the bulbs 3 in. deep and 4 in. apart in September or October in a moist but well-drained soil.

The autumn-flowering species needs a warm position in full sun. The white, pink-tinged flowers are carried on 6 to 8-in. stems in September. Plant 3 in. deep and 3 in. apart in April. All three species can be propagated by offsets.

Leucojum aestivum

Lilium

There are two important points to remember when making a selection of lilies to grow in the garden. Some are lime haters and some are stem rooting i.e. they form roots on the lower part of the stem as well as basally from the bulb. This means that they have to be planted deeper – 8 to 9 in. as opposed to 5 or 6 in. for the others. To add confusion, however, there are exceptions to this rule notably *Lilium candidum* and *L. giganteum* (*Cardiocrinum giganteum*), both non stem rooters, which are covered with only ½ in. of soil.

Lilies like a well-prepared, well-drained soil and a cool root run. They should therefore be planted with rather open-habited, low-growing shrubs and herbaceous plants in a mixed border as these will shade the lilies' roots. Plant during October and November and bed on sand as the bulbs have a tendency to rot. Once planted leave lilies undisturbed for as long as possible and mulch each spring with peat or leafmould. When deterioration is noticeable divide the clumps of bulbs and replant in autumn. Stake as necessary.

Lilies can be propagated vegetatively from an original single bulb, by means of scales, division or bulbils, or from seed.

Here is a brief description of some of the best garden lilies in alphabetical order starting with the golden-rayed lily of Japan, *Lilium auratum*. It has many highly scented white flowers with crimson spots, each petal marked with a golden ray in August and September. It is stem rooting and grows 5 to 7 ft. tall. *L. candidum* is the Madonna lily with pure white, fragrant flowers on 6-ft. stems in July. Unlike many lilies, this one actually likes a limy soil. *L. davidii*, the handsome Chinese lily, has red Turk's-cap flowers covered with black spots. It has two fine varieties, Maxwell, a bright orange-red colour and about a foot taller than the type at 6 ft., and *willmottiae*, a very impressive deep orange. These are stem rooting and lime tolerant.

For flowering in August and September, as well as in sun or shade, the lime-tolerant stem-rooting *L. henryi* is excellent with orange-yellow flowers marked with dark spots on 6 to 7-ft. stems. *L. speciosum* (*lancifolium*) thrives in sun or partial shade and flowers in August or September on 3 to 5-ft. stems. It is stem rooting and the variety *roseum* is white, spotted pink; *rubrum* is white spotted red, and *album* is pure white. *L. longiflorum* has lovely, trumpet-shaped, waxy, white flowers on 3-ft. stems in June and July.

L. martagon album is the white variety of the Turk's-cap lily. It does not mind

Above: *Lilium martagon*
Above right: *Lilium auratum*

limy soil and will grow 3 to 5 ft. high, flowering in June and July. *L. pardalinum*, the panther lily, has orange and crimson Turk's-cap flowers, heavily marked with crimson-brown spots. These are borne in July on 5 to 6-ft. stems. They like a damp soil and do not object to lime. *L. regale* has handsome trumpet flowers which are suffused with pinkish purple and maroon shades on the outside and white within, flushed yellow in the throat. It grows to 6 ft. tall, is stem rooting and lime tolerant. *L. tigrinum splendens* is a particularly fine variety of the tiger lily with rich salmon-orange flowers in August. It is a stem rooter which does not like alkaline soils and it will grow 4 to 6 ft. high.

Apart from the species there are many excellent hybrid strains including the Mid-century Hybrids which grow 2½ to 4 ft. tall in a lime-free soil and flower in June and July with an excellent colour range. The African Queen strain of trumpet lilies has large flowers of apricot yellow suffused with reddish bronze. They are 5 ft. tall and flower in late June and July.

The Golden Clarion strain has trumpet flowers in varying shades of yellow, gold and orange, often marked with deep red. They flower in July on 3½ to 4-ft. stems.

The strain of trumpet lilies called Golden Splendour includes only golden-coloured lilies. The Bellingham Hybrids have Turk's-cap flowers on 7-ft. stems. They are usually orange in colour marked with dark spots.

Muscari

The grape hyacinths are delightful subjects for borders, growing around trees or shrubs on rock gardens, and naturalizing in grass. The best-known species is *Muscari armeniacum*, especially the variety Heavenly Blue with spikes of rich blue flowers. Another good variety is Cantab with paler, Cambridge-blue flowers. All are around 8 in. tall. Two varieties of *M. botryoides* look charming when grown together. These are the dark blue *caeruleum* and the white *album*. Both flower in April at 6 in. tall.

Slightly earlier there is the rather unusual *M. tubergenianum* which has flowers in two shades of blue on each spike – pale blue at the top, dark blue lower down. The violet-coloured flowers of the plume or feather hyacinth, *M. comosum monstrosum (comosum plumosum)*, are looser than those of the other muscari and they give a feathery appearance. It looks very effective on a sunny ledge in the rock garden or on the top of a dry wall.

Plant muscari in ordinary soil and a

sunny position 3 in. deep and 4 in. apart in September and October. Most varieties increase rapidly and will naturalize themselves.

Narcissus

The daffodils and narcissi must be the most popular of the flowering bulbs and this large genus offers such a bewildering choice that it has been classified by international agreement into eleven divisions based on the formation and colour of the flowers. I will attempt to give a brief description of each of these sections but because of lack of space will not recommend any varieties. These are constantly changing and it would be better to consult a good catalogue. In catalogues you may find reference to: a mother bulb, one with as many as four growths which will each produce flowering shoots, a double nose bulb, one with at least two 'noses' which will give a minimum of two flowers; a single nose bulb, one which will produce one or two flowers.

Division I is devoted to the Trumpet daffodils – those in which the cup is longer than, or as long as, the backing perianth segments (petals).

Division II, the Large-cupped varieties, has four sections. There is one flower to each stem with the cup more than one-third but less than equal to the length of the perianth segments.

139

Left: *Narcissus* **Bermuda**
Above: *Iris reticulata* **Joyce**

Division III, the Small-cupped narcissi, includes varieties with cups not more than one-third the length of the perianth segment, and here again one flower is carried on each stem. There are four sections in this division.

Division IV, the Double daffodils, is perhaps not universally popular for there are quite a few gardeners with a distinct bias against double flowers.

Division V, the Triandrus daffodils, is where we find the angel's tears daffodil, *Narcissus triandrus albus*, which has small, nodding flowers with very reflexed perianth segments. The resemblance to *N. triandrus* can be clearly seen in all members of this division.

Division VI, for Cyclamineus daffodils,

includes the garden varieties and hybrids from *N. cyclamineus*.

Division VII, the Jonquilla daffodils or jonquils, have small to medium-sized flowers often carried in clusters and sweetly scented.

Division VIII, the Tazetta daffodils, includes the Poetaz hybrids which have several good-sized flowers on each stem and are especially useful for cutting. They are the result of crossing *N. poeticus*, the poet's narcissus, with *N. tazetta*, which has clusters of small, sweetly scented flowers.

Division IX comprises garden varieties and hybrids of *N. poeticus* and is known as Poeticus.

Division X includes those species that occur in the wild.

Division XI is reserved for all those which do not fit in anywhere else.

For naturalizing in grass, daffodils have no equal and they are also splendid for growing informally in mixed borders and for planting in martial rows in formal beds. The dwarf varieties and species are excellent for the rock garden. They are tolerant of widely differing soil conditions but prefer one which is rich and well drained. Well-rotted farmyard manure can be incorporated in the bottom spit of soil, well below the level of the bulbs and a dressing of hoof and horn or bonemeal at the rate of 4 oz. to the sq. yd. should be worked into the topsoil. A sunny, open position is ideal but one in semi-shade would give a good show.

Plant as early in the season as possible. August is best but if planting has to be delayed, up to the end of November is all right but the results can be disappointing. Where permanent plantings are made it is best to leave the bulbs alone until it is obvious that overcrowding is affecting quality. They can then be divided in the autumn when offsets can be removed.

For the larger daffodils, 4 to 6 in. is the recommended planting depth, those plantings made in heavier soils being set rather less deeply than others in light soils. The dwarf daffodils or narcissi are planted 2 to 3 in. deep and these need a rather grittier rooting medium with sharper drainage than their more robust relatives.

Nerine

Given a sunny, sheltered and well-drained border, *Nerine bowdenii* will raise distinctive heads of pink flowers on 1½-ft. stems in September and October. It should be protected from November to April with bracken or straw and topdressed in August with leafmould or manure.

Plant between August and November, setting the bulbs 3 in. deep and 4 in. apart. Increase by offsets between July and September.

Ornithogalum

Ornithogalum umbellatum, the star of Bethlehem, whose star-shaped flowers are white inside and white marked with green on the outside, is a useful plant for a mixed border, for the rock garden or for naturalizing in grass or among shrubs. It grows 10 to 12 in. high and flowers in May. Lift and divide the clumps every three years or so as this is a plant which increases rapidly.

For May and June flowering there is *O. nutans* which is taller at 1½ ft. and greener in its colouring. *O. thyrsoides* is the chincherinchee. It has long, thickish foliage and the dense heads of starry white flowers are excellent and long lasting when cut. It should be given a warm, well-drained position and winter protection of bracken, straw or similar material.

Plant all 3 to 4 in. deep and 6 in. apart between August and November.

Oxalis

The following members of this genus have tuberous rootstocks and as such qualify for mention here. Give them all a well-drained soil in a sunny position.

At 3 in. tall *Oxalis adenophylla* is a plant for the rock garden which it will grace in May and June with pink starry flowers against crinkled foliage. *O. deppei* is a copper-red colour and it can become very invasive. It should be regularly divided every autumn. *O. enneaphylla* has much divided, fan-shaped leaves and white flowers. *O. floribunda (rosea)* has bright pink flowers.

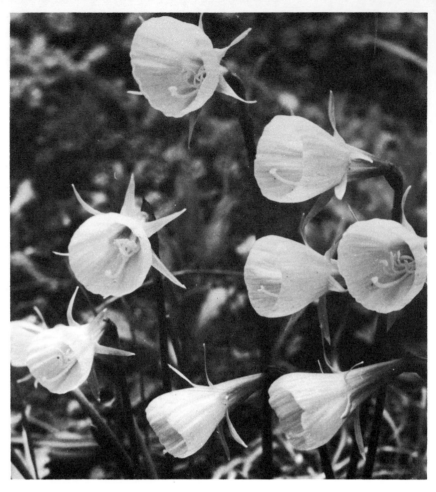

Puschkinia

Puschkinia scilloides, the striped squill, is a distinctive dwarf plant (6 in.) for providing colour in the early spring. The white, blue-striped flowers, as the specific name indicates, resemble those of a scilla (bluebell), to which it is closely related. Plant in a rock garden or sunny border in September or October 3 in. deep and 3 to 4 in. apart. Increase by offsets from old bulbs in late autumn or by seeds raised in a cold frame and sown in August or September.

Ranunculus

The tuberous-rooted ranunculuses are popular as cut flowers and they are also worthy border subjects during May and June. Plant the tubers in October or November, late February or March with the claws facing downwards. The planting depth should be 2 to 3 in. with 4 to 6 in. between the plants. Increase by seeds raised in a cold frame or cool greenhouse. They like sunny, sheltered conditions.

The Double Turban ranunculus are obtainable in separate colours including scarlet, orange and yellow as well as mixed shades. There are also the Giant French varieties and the double Persian mixed strain.

Salvia

Salvia patens is a tuberous-rooted perennial with large blue sage-like flowers on 2-ft. stems from July to September. The tubers can be planted 4 to 5 in. deep and 15 in. apart in mid-April and they can be started into growth in a large flower pot under glass in early April and hardened off for planting out at the end of May.

The tubers should be lifted about the middle of October, dried and stored as for dahlias, for although the roots are hardy frost may kill the young shoots as they emerge in the spring.

Schizostylis

The Kaffir lily is a handsome bulbous subject for the autumn border provided it is given warm, sunny conditions and a good loamy soil. Protection with straw or bracken is necessary in the winter. Plant between October and March and lift and divide the bulbous rhizomes every third year in March or April.

The species *Schizostylis coccinea* has crimson flowers on 1 to 1½-ft. spikes. It has several good varieties of which I would recommend the September–October flowering Mrs Hegarty or the November-flowering Viscountess Byng. Both have pink flowers.

Scilla

This is the genus to which the bluebell belongs and the first species to bloom in the year is the February-flowering Siberian squill, *Scilla sibirica*. The intensely blue blooms are borne in profusion on 4 to 6-in. stems. Larger than the type is the variety *atrocaerulea*, or Spring Beauty, which also has flowers of a rich blue colouring. This is followed by *S. tubergeniana* with flowers of pale blue and white. It is very effective when grown in groups in borders on the rock garden or in grass in sunny positions.

A species for a warm, sunny position is *S. peruviana* with ball-shaped heads of flowers on 9-in. stems in May and June.

The Spanish bluebell is now *Endymion hispanicus* but it used to be *Scilla campanulata (hispanica)*. It looks good naturalized in light shade, among shrubs or under trees, and there are fine named varieties like the pale blue Myosotis, the tall Imperator, with pure white flower spikes, and Queen of the Pinks, a rosy-pink variety. The English bluebell, now *E. non-scriptus*, is very well known. It has both white and pink forms, all being excellent for naturalizing.

Plant in ordinary soil at any time between August and November, 2 to 4 in. deep and 4 in. apart. *S. peruviana* should be planted 6 in. deep and 6 in. apart. Increase by offsets in autumn.

Sparaxis

These brilliantly coloured subjects live up to their common name of the harlequin flowers for the spring blooms come in colours like red, purple, black, white and yellow. The flowers are often up to 2 in. across on stems 6 to 9 in. high. The narrow foliage is also very attractive.

They need a warm, sunny position and a fairly dry soil, and protection from bracken or other material is necessary in very cold weather. Plant the corms in autumn, 4 in. deep and 2 in. apart. Increase by offsets.

Sternbergia

Sternbergia lutea is a charming little plant for autumn colour. The golden-yellow crocus-like flowers will look attractive in a border, in a rock garden, or when naturalized in grass. It grows to about 6 in. in height and has strap-shaped leaves.

The bulbs should be planted 4 to 6 in. deep and 6 in. apart in July in a sunny, well-drained position. Protect in winter with straw or bracken. Propagation is by the new bulbs produced every year.

*Above left: **Narcissus bulbocodium***
*Above: **Ornithogalum thyrsoides***

Tigridia

The unusual and exotic flowers of the tiger flower, *Tigridia pavonia*, are evocative of the country from which they come, Mexico. The orange-red, three-petalled flowers are spotted at the base with deeper colouring. There are also forms with pinkish, mauve, yellow and white colouring. Unfortunately each flower has only a brief day of glory in late summer and early autumn but each 2-ft. stem produces several flowers to open in succession. This plant needs a sunny border and a moist but well-drained soil.

Plant the corms 3 in. deep and 6 in. apart in April and lift to store in October. Increase by offsets removed in April.

Trillium

The wake robin or American wood lily, *Trillium grandiflorum*, is a tuberous perennial. It is valuable because of its liking for rather damp, shady places and is an excellent plant for woodland conditions. Give it a peaty soil, topdress annually with decayed leaves and leave undisturbed for as long as possible, dividing when necessary in March. The white flowers,

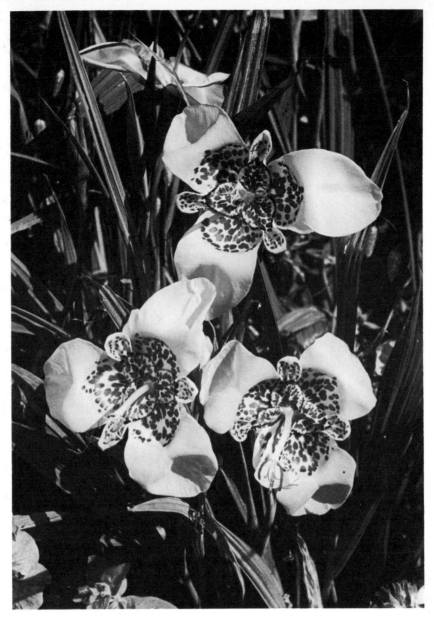

some 3 in. across, are carried on 1½-ft. stems above whorls of practically stemless broad leaves in May. There is a pink variety, *roseum*.

Tulipa

Tulips run a close second to the daffodils for the title of most popular flowering bulb with their bright, dazzling range of colours and diversity of shape and form. They are happy growing in any reasonable garden soil provided it is well prepared and will thrive in sunshine and semi-shade. Tulips can be grown in a variety of situations but possibly look their best when interplanted with subjects which flower at the same time such as aubrietas, forget-me-nots, violas and wallflowers. Many combinations are possible, all of which give a lovely, long-flowering effect. They should all be planted about 4 in. deep and 6 in. apart in October and November and

Tigridia pavonia

can be propagated by offsets or seeds. Those used for bedding purposes should be lifted and replanted in a reserve bed until the foliage has withered when they can be lifted again and stored in a cool, airy room until replanting time comes round. In fact the bulbs of the garden varieties benefit from an annual lifting whereas those of the species can be left undisturbed for several years.

I shall start this brief summary with the species tulips which are becoming increasingly popular. Many of them can be grown on the rock garden or as edgings to other plantings. A warm position with good drainage is needed for *Tulipa clusiana*, the lady tulip, but this elegant species is a joy in April when its red, white and purple flowers are in the full flush of their beauty. *T. eichleri* starts to flower at the

end of March on 15-in. stems. The scarlet blooms have petals marked with black, yellow-margined blotch.

T. kaufmanniana is the water lily tulip, a species which has given us a wonderful range of March-April flowering hybrids, all 6 to 8 in. tall and suitable for rock gardens or borders.

The small flowers of *T. orphanidea* are an attractive, unusual orange shade and those of *T. praestans* Fusilier a spectacular orange scarlet on 9-in. stems. *T. tarda* flowers in late April–early May and has yellow flowers with yellowish-green and white markings on 6-in. stems.

The garden varieties are so numerous that they have been classified into groups as follows. Early Singles which flower in mid-April and are about 1 ft. tall; Early Doubles which are of a similar height and flower at the end of April. Darwin tulips flower in May on 2-ft. or longer stems and have well-shaped flowers in lovely colours: Cottage tulips share the same height and flowering period but the flowers are of a less regimental shape. The elegant lily-flowered tulips have waisted flowers. Rebrandts resemble Darwins in all respects but colour having stripes and blotched flowers. Old English tulips are very regular and refined in form whereas Parrot tulips have flowers with curiously twisted and slashed petals, blotched with green. Then there are the Mendel and Triumph tulips, the late Doubles and the Fosteriana hybrids. The Greigii hybrids are especially notable for their lovely colouration and the handsome markings on the leaves. They are April flowering at 9 to 12 in. The Multi-flowered tulips have several flowers on each stem. The Viridiflora or green tulips flower in May on 9 to 24-in. stems and they have distinctive green markings on the petals. In the Fringed tulips, as the name implies, the edges of the petals are fringed or serrated. Broken varieties have lovely markings on the petals which are unusually attractive.

Zephyranthes

Zephyranthes candida is the zephyr flower of the west wind from America. The handsome star-like flowers appear on 6 to 12-in. stems well above the grass-like foliage in September. It is another subject for a warm sunny border, preferably against a south wall and a light, sandy, well-drained soil. The bulbs should be planted between August and November 4 in. deep and 4 in. apart and given winter protection. It can be increased by offsets during the same period.

Right: *Tulipa* **Dillenburg in spring bedding**

Rock Plants

Royton E. Heath, F.L.S., F.R.I.H. (N.Z.), an amateur gardener who is an acknowledged authority on rock and alpine plants, has been growing these fascinating members of the plant community for over forty years. His books on the subject have been widely acclaimed.

He has studied alpines in their natural habitats on many European mountains, and has arranged displays of plants from his extensive collection at many horticultural shows. His garden is indeed full of good plants, some of extreme rarity.

For his exhibits of rock garden shrubs and other dwarf plants he has won several hundred prizes and awards, including the Lindley Medal of The Royal Horticultural Society for an exhibit of outstanding educational value.

Mr Heath is well known as a judge of alpine plants at provincial and national shows, and he has lectured all over Britain. He has also broadcast on the B.B.C. and appeared on television.

In 1958 Mr Heath was elected a Fellow of the Linnean Society and he is also a Fellow of The Royal New Zealand Institute of Horticulture.

Right: Section through a rock garden on a clay slope.
(a) Original slope with irregularities removed and surface made firm.
(b) Stone or brick rubble to assist drainage.
(c) Infilling compost of equal parts loam, peat and sand.
(d) Rockwork.
(e) Reversed turves or brushwood to prevent clogging or silting.
(f) Drainage pit or trench, three-quarters filled with coarse rubble

Since Reginald Farrer's classic work, *The English Rock Garden*, was first published, there has been a steady but sure interest in the growing of rock plants in the United Kingdom and today two specialized societies of this form of gardening have a combined membership in excess of ten thousand.

With the ever-increasing cost of land, the number of large gardens are fast becoming a minority and the remainder are to be measured in square yards rather than acres. Naturally with restricted garden space, the need for plants of a small stature, which will not readily outgrow their allotted space, is only too apparent and rock plants are well suited for this purpose.

There are a number of methods by which a site can be adapted to grow a worthwhile collection and these will be briefly dealt with here. It is normally quoted in books dealing with rock plants that the site must be open, away from all buildings, trees, shrubs and other growing plants. This idealistic advice would be easy to follow if all the necessary open space was available, but rarely is this so today. By all means choose an open site if possible, but to my knowledge many thousands of rock plants are thriving in alien situations, such as the heart of our industrial areas and even here the rarer plants are grown to perfection. There is only one type of site where this is not possible and that is one adjacent to surface-rooting trees or those producing surface suckers, such as elms, limes, poplars and silver birch. In these circumstances reliance will have to be placed on troughs and other containers raised above the level of the ground and as far as possible from all trees.

If the available space is not large enough to incorporate a rock garden, although even a small one is better than none, it should be possible to build up border edges, or small walls, if the site is a sloping one, to grow a large number of plants. These can be planted with arabis, alyssum, aubrieta, phlox, campanulas and helianthemum varieties which will, if intermixed, provide a carpet of colour from late March until July. An underplanting of dwarf bulbs will also enhance the display. They will add both colour and balance when used in conjunction with other garden features and where necessary provide a natural division between different parts of the garden.

Soils

The ideal soil for rock plants is a light open medium loam with faultless drainage. A lime-free soil is preferable, for lime can be added if required, whereas lime-hating plants will only grow in specially prepared pockets of lime-free soil. Even then they rarely succeed for long. A rich loamy soil can be lightened by the addition of coarse sand or gravel well worked into the top 6 in. The amount to be used will depend on the texture of the loam, the heavier the loam the larger the quantity of sand.

A different approach will be needed if the soil is clay. No attempt should be made to lighten this medium, an almost impossible task, nor should pockets be dug and light mixtures used for filling in as in wet weather these will become just a series of pools, resulting in death traps for the plants. If there is a natural slope, it can be utilized and if possible a pit can be dug at the base and filled with rough drainage material topped with upturned turves or other roughage to prevent soil blocking the drainage. The rock garden is then built up above the ground level using a light well-drained compost. The minimum depth should be 9 in., the height according

Left: Section through a rock garden on a flat clay site.
(a) Structure cut away to show drainage system.
(b) Low retaining wall placed over drainage trench covering.
(c) Reversed turves, brushwood bundles, or flat slabs over drainage trench to prevent clogging and silting.
(d) Drainage trench 3 ft. deep and 2 ft. wide, filled with coarse rubble.
(e) Drainage channels 9 in. wide and 9 in. deep formed to slope down to drainage trench at rear. Channels filled in with rubble for three-quarters of their depth and topped with brushwood.
(f) Channels approximately 4 ft. apart

Left: Concrete-lined pool incorporated in a rock garden.
(a) Allow top of concrete to finish slightly below level of water in places to provide a site for moisture-loving plants.
(b) Concrete sides, 4 in. thick.
(c) Concrete base, 6 in. thick.
(d) Well-rammed hardcore.
(e) Level flange formed at top of concrete to provide bed for paving stones which should project about $1\frac{1}{2}$ in. over water

Below: Polythene-lined pool incorporated in a rock garden.
(a) Rockwork to overhang edge of pool by about $1\frac{1}{2}$ in.
(b) Polythene sheet to overlap flattened edge not less than 9 in. all round.
(c) Stones to hold sheeting in position.
(d) Bed of soft sand or sifted soil to prevent damage to polythene.
(e) Depth can be varied by contouring the soil.
(f) Paving slabs to overhang edge of pool by about $1\frac{1}{2}$ in.

to the type of rock garden under construction. The line drawing gives comprehensive details of building on a flat surface over clay. At the base, adjacent to the drainage pit, leafmould or peat should be added in quantity to the compost, providing an ideal spot for growing the dwarf moisture-loving primulas and other kindred plants.

Instead of the drainage pit, a pool can be built and the line drawings show plans of such pools, one constructed from concrete, the other from polythene which can be obtained either already formed to lay in situ or in sheet form to suit one's own taste.

Whatever type of soil is used, great care must be taken to ensure that this is free of all perennial weeds; a most important point because failure may result in many hours of tedious weeding after planting has been completed, or even having to dismantle and rebuild the rock garden.

Nothing is worse than finding bindweed appearing in the middle of a treasured cushion plant.

Right: Single and multiple rock outcrops.
(a) Natural stratification maintained along outcrop.
(b) Exposed part of outcrop.
(c) General slope

Right: Rock garden constructed from broken paving slabs.
(a) Tilted or dipping strata.
(b) Soil infilling.
(c) Cement.
(d) Paving abutting on to 3-in. layer of hardcore.
(e) Upper layers of slabs should have a more pronounced backward tilt.
(f) Slabs laid in courses with soil between. Gaps left at intervals for crevice and trailing plants.
(g) Lowest course of slabs given a slight backward tilt and cemented to edge of paving.
(h) Crazy paving surround

Rocks

It is difficult to give precise instructions on building a rock garden, much depends on the available space and type of rock employed. The actual placing of the rocks must be left to the gardener's own choice and provided a few simple rules are adhered to a satisfactory result can be achieved. First, the rocks should have two exposed positions, one facing the sun, the other in shade or half shade to suit all types of plants. Second, if the rock has a natural strata, it should be almost parallel to the surface. Lastly, one or two simple outcrops are much better than a pile of stone placed higgledy-piggledy. The line drawings give a general idea of what is required.

There are a number of different types of stone available but for the rock garden they generally fall into three groups. Limestone is the easiest to use for it has a natural stratification which makes correct placing easy. The great disadvantage is

cost for unless you live near to a source of supply it is very expensive. Sandstone is normally less so and it is often possible to find a local source. It also blends in more naturally with the surroundings but a word of warning. If sandstone is used, make sure that it is not composed of soft material as this has a tendency to disintegrate after hard frosts. Tufa has several advantages; it is light to handle, extremely porous and it is easy to drill holes in which to plant cushion and saxitile plants. The disadvantages are cost and only a few sources of supply. A substitute, which can be used if cost has to be considered, is old cement blocks normally obtainable quite cheaply locally. No doubt for a year or so they would look raw, but a covering of plants and the resultant weathering would soon overcome this.

An ideal medium for constructing a rock garden is artificial broken paving slabs which are obtainable cheaply from local council yards. These are used to

simulate a natural outcrop shown in the line drawing. Real walling stone is preferable, of course, but the difference in price is considerable.

When laying rock or other material a firm steady base is essential. Bury as little as possible, consistent with firmness, so that the roots of the plants have no difficulty in finding a cool moist root run. A dusting of BHC powder at the base of each rock will discourage most pests.

Rock Borders and Retaining Walls

The retaining wall is a taller extension of the rock border and a study of the line drawings, which give all the relevant details for their construction, should make this easy. The soil required in these is the same as for the rock garden and the notes on drainage apply also.

Troughs

If the overall garden area is small and as often happens limited to a strip of com-

Diagram 1

Diagram 1
Rock border using a single line of walling stone.
(a) Single line edging.
(b) Bedding stones.
(c) Paving laid on bed of sand over rammed hardcore.
(d) Grass surround or lawn edge as an alternative to paving

Diagram 2
Rock border using a double line of walling stone.
(a) Double line edging.
(b) Slight backward tilt.
(c) Paving or grass.
(d) Bedding stones

Diagram 2

Diagram 3
Dry stone walling.
(a) 'Headers' or 'thro' stones' at intervals in all courses.
(b) Note broken line of joints.
(c) Backward tilt or 'batter', approximately 10 degrees.
(d) Soil-filled gaps for planting up; insert plants as wall is being built.
(e) Headers placed at vertical intervals of four courses

Diagram 3

munal grass and small patios, this method of growing rock plants is ideal. A large number can be successfully grown providing colour throughout the year, especially if some of the really dwarf conifers and berried shrubs are used as dot plants or a scenic backcloth. One of the great advantages of this type of gardening is that an ever-changing colourful landscape in miniature can be built or individual troughs used for collections of plants of specific genera or varieties. For example saxifrages, sempervivums, sedums, miniature willows, crocuses, tulips, narcissi, and iris species are all better suited when grouped individually. Dwarf bulbous plants can be carpeted with prostrate plants such as antennarias, some asperulas, *Campanula arvatica, Gypsophila repens fratensis, Linum salsoloides nanum*, paronychia etc.

The natural stone trough is now a rarity and often difficult to find but there are a number of suitable stone substitutes on the market, the only restriction to their use is that they should not be less than 6 in. deep. The line drawing is self-explanatory with all necessary details. One important point to remember is that the plants must not be allowed to suffer

149

Above: Sink or trough garden.
(a) Stone.
(b) Compost (see below).
(c) Layer of leaf or peat roughage.
(d) Layer of broken crock.
(e) Surface layer of stone chips.
(f) Drainage hole

Composts suitable for trough gardens:
(a) **Equal parts of loam, leafmould and sand. This is a suitable mixture for plants which require a light, open, porous soil with good drainage. A good mixture for troughs in a sheltered position in half shade. All bulbs and conifers do well in this medium.**
(b) **Equal parts of loam, leafmould, peat and sand.**
Retentive of water but well drained. Suitable for plants which like full sun and also for woodland plants grown in half shade.
(c) **Three parts Cornish silversand and one part flaked leafmould.**
For all difficult and rare high alpines, including most of the cushion type. The trough containing this mixture is best sited in half shade

from drought in dry spells. The troughs should be raised off the ground to a height to suit the grower.

Planting

The vast majority of rock plants are pot grown so they can be planted at all times of the year with the exception of frosty weather. Small specimens should be chosen, these are seldom pot bound and acclimatize easier. They should not be allowed to dry out after planting especially during the summer months. The top 1 in. round the collar of the plants should be left bare and when all planting is completed a top dressing of chippings is placed over the whole of the rock garden, troughs, walls or rock borders, including the necks of the plants.

Propagation

The various ways in which the plants can be propagated are mentioned in the A–Z list. John Innes Seed Compost is a suitable medium for raising plants from seed. One without chalk should be used for the lime haters. After germination the plants should be potted on once they have formed their first true leaves.

Cuttings are best rooted in an equal mixture of peat and coarse sand either in a propagating frame or placed round the side of a pot and a plastic bag tied over the rim of the pot. They normally root in a matter of two weeks or so.

When dividing plants make sure that each piece has roots attached.

Pests and Diseases

These can be kept to a minimum by spraying with a systemic insecticide and fungicide when growth commences in early spring, repeating approximately every eight weeks during the growing season. Slugs can be kept in check by spreading slug pellets where they are likely to congregate. Ants and woodlice are discouraged by using a dusting powder containing BHC.

Selected Rock Plants

Acantholimon

This is a small genus, liking neutral or acid soil, which provides interest in winter with the persistent cup-like bracts. One of the easiest to grow is the Armenian *Acantholimon glumaceum* with loose cushions in rosette formation. This species has deep green needle-shaped, spine-tipped foliage and the rosy-pink flowers appear in

June on 6-in. stems. You can expect the prickly thrift to have a spread of 9 in. in maturity. It is increased by cuttings in August.

Achillea

The milfoils or yarrows are mostly grown for their finely cut aromatic foliage. *Achillea ageratifolia* has a tufted habit and is only 2 in. high with deeply toothed, narrow, intensely downy, white leaves and white daisy flowers. It comes from Greece. *A. lewisii,* a garden hybrid, makes a mat of grey-green cut foliage and has light yellow flowers on 6-in. stems. Both have a long flowering season from June to July and can be increased by cuttings in July.

Aethionema

This genus contains a number of easy rock plants known by the common name of the Persian candytufts. They are well represented by *Aethionema armenum,* which has narrow blue-grey leaves and neat heads of pink, veined flowers on 6-in. stems from May to August; and Warley Rose, an improved garden form, with larger, deeper pink-coloured flowers. Both are 4 to 6 in. high with a spread of 12 in. and are suitable for a dry wall as well as the rock garden. Cut back after flowering and propagate by cuttings in June.

Allium

There are a number of ornamental onions which make an attractive display in the rock garden in August. They are all about 9 in. high. *Allium cyaneum* is a Chinese species with grass-like leaves and semi-pendant blue flowers. *A. cyathophorum farreri* (syn. *A. farreri*), with pendant, bell-shaped, reddish-purple flowers, is from Kansu. *A. narcissiflorum* is a native of south eastern Europe and it bears semi-pendant bright rose flowers. Seed is an easy method of increase in March.

Alyssum

The madworts are evergreen plants from 3 to 9 in. high with a spread of 24 in. They are ideal for a wall and together with arabis and aubrieta will provide a riot of early spring colour. They should be cut back after flowering and can be propagated by cuttings in July.

Alyssum alpestre is a sub-shrub from the European Alps with grey oblong hairy leaves and pale yellow flowers in clusters. *A. saxatile,* with its descriptive common name of gold dust, is a sub-shrub with silver-grey leaves. The clustered flowers are golden yellow and named varieties include *citrinum,* lemon yellow; *compactum,* smaller, bright yellow; *plenum,* double yellow, and *variegatum*, yellow and grey-green leaves.

Andromeda

These are evergreen plants for a shady lime-free rock garden and the edge of a pool. *Andromeda glaucophylla* is a dwarf shrub only 6 in. high and 12 in. wide with narrow grey-green leaves and pale pink urn-shaped flowers in May.

A. polifolia, the bog rosemary, is a native of the northern hemisphere and has deep green leaves with pale pink flowers on 6-in. stems in May. Its varieties *compacta* and *minima* from Japan are both smaller with foliage variations. Cuttings are a ready means of increase in May.

Androsace

The rock jasmines are true alpine plants with a world-wide distribution. Their flowering period is April to May and they are from 2 to 4 in. high and 4 to 15 in. wide. All require faultless drainage and can be increased by seed in March or cuttings in June.

Androsace carnea, native to Europe, makes rosettes of narrow, evergreen foliage and the flowers are bright rose with a yellow eye. Good varieties are *brigantiaca*, white; *halleri*, deep pink, from Switzerland, and *laggeri*, smaller rosettes with bright pink flowers from the Pyrenees.

A. sarmentosa is a native of the Himalayas and it forms rosettes of silver-grey hairy foliage. The large pale pink flowers are borne in clusters. The varieties Brilliant, deep rose red, and *chumbyi* with compact clusters of deep pink flowers from the Chumbi Valley are recommended.

Anemone

There are a number of the charming, free-flowering windflowers suitable for the rock garden. *Anemone baldensis* is a herbaceous perennial with deeply cut leaves and starry white flowers, tinged blue on the reverse. Native of Europe, it blooms on 3-in. stems in May and June. It requires a moist spot. Divide in July.

Anemone blanda is a bulbous plant with incurving segments of deeply cut green foliage and, during March and April, blue to purple-blue flowers on 4-in. stems. The variety *atrocaerulea* is deep blue and *rosea* is bright pink.

A. obtusiloba patula, the blue buttercup, comes from the Himalayas. It has rosettes of hairy three-lobed green leaves. The blue flowers are cup shaped and they appear in May and June at the end of prostrate shoots. Propagation is by seed in March.

Antennaria

The blue flowers are cup shaped and they for choice bulbs as well as being attractive plants. At home in the northern hemisphere, *Antennaria dioica* forms 2-in. high mats of evergreen, grey-green leaves and in May and June clusters of pink flowers backed with green, pink-tipped bracts. The variety *minima* is less than 1 in. high and Nyewood has the attractive combination of silver leaves and crimson flowers. Division in August is an easy means of increase.

Anthyllis

There is one species and two forms of the kidney vetch which are very attractive. The European *Anthyllis montana* makes mats of silvery downy leaves 3 in. high and 12in. wide with rose, clover-like flowers over a long period from June to September. *Alba*, white, and *rubra*, deep rose red, are the good varieties. Increase by cuttings in May.

Aquilegia

The columbine is a widely distributed genus of herbaceous perennials containing some delightful miniatures. *Aquilegia bertolonii* is about 4 in. high and forms tufts of grey-green leaves with violet-blue spurred flowers in May. It comes from Italy. *A. canadensis*, from north west Africa, has tufts of green cut leaves and in May red flowers with yellow petals on 8-in. stems.

A. flabellata nana is native to Japan and looks well planted in a trough. It has grey-blue cut leaves on 4-in. stems. and large blue and cream flowers in May. Propagation is by means of seed which should be sown in July.

Arabis

This is a family containing some gems which are all ideal for planting on a sunny wall together with aubrieta for an early spring display. The following species and varieties of the rock cress are to be recommended.

Arabis alpina is a close compact plant with oval leaves and white flowers. It comes from Europe and is about 6in. high and 15 in. wide.

A. caucasica (*albida*) makes a mat about 18 in. wide with leaves in grey rosettes and fragrant white flowers clustered on 9-in. stems. It, too, is a native of Europe. Its variety *billardieri* is rose and *flore pleno* has double white flowers.

A. ferdinandi-coburgi variegata is a form with well-marked bright green foliage which has a marginal band of cream. The flowers are white on 6-in.

stems. They are all evergreen and should be cut back after flowering. Increase by cuttings taken in July.

Armeria

The sea pinks or thrifts are all similar but the one listed here is possibly the best. *Armeria caespitosa* Bevan's Variety forms dense 2-in. evergreen cushions of bright green soft spiny leaves about 6 in. across. The flowers are rounded heads of deep cerise red on short stems in May and June. Increase by cuttings in June.

Artemisia

This is a family of aromatic silver-grey foliage plants useful as foils to other plants. Both the species mentioned are evergreen. *Artemisia glacialis* is a close sub-shrub about 2 in. high and 6 in. wide with narrow silver-downed leaves. The June flowers are yellow. It comes from central Europe and is a good subject for trough culture.

A. schmidtiana nana is Japanese in origin and makes a plant of 2 in. high and 9 in. wide with narrow deeply cut silver-grey leaves. The pendant, yellow flowers appear in September. Both can be propagated by cuttings in July.

Asperula

The woodruffs make good dwarf evergreen plants for the rock garden or trough and are easily increased by cuttings taken in July. *Asperula lilaciflora caespitosa* is a native of south east Europe and it makes a mat of bright green heath-like foliage only 2 in. high with prostrate stems of lilac-pink flowers in June.

The Greek species *suberosa* forms a 4-in. mat of down-covered grey leaves up to 8 in. wide. The long tubular pink flowers which first appear in May continue over a long period.

Aster

The starworts are dainty wildlings, providing colour during late spring. The species *Aster alpinus*, from Europe, has typical large daisy flowers of lilac purple with a golden eye on 4 to 6-in. stems during May and June. It is a variable species, however, with many colour forms which include *albus*, white; *roseus*, pink; *ruber*, deep red and *speciosus*, bright purple. Division in September is a ready means of increase.

Aubrieta

Along with arabis and alyssum, this is one of the widest grown rock plants providing colour in early spring. The forms of *Aubrieta deltoidea*, the wall cress, are 3 in.

151

Aquilegia flabellata nana

high and 24 to 36 in. wide making good plants for a dry wall. The species makes a compact carpet of grey-green hairy leaves and four-petalled mauve flowers in April and May. Good varieties include Barker's Double, double, red; Blue King, blue; Bonfire, red; Bressingham Pink, double, pink; Church Knowle, deep lavender; Dr Mules, purple; Fire King, red; Greencourt Purple, double, purple; Joan Allen, double, crimson; Magician, crimson purple; Russell's Crimson, red; *variegata argentea*, pale mauve, leaves margined silver, and Wanda, double, red.

All should be cut back after flowering and propagation is by cuttings in June or division in September.

Berberis

The barberries are represented here by two forms of *Berberis stenophylla* which are ideal evergreen rock garden shrubs both about 12 in. high and 24 in. across with flowers in May followed by berries in September. *Corallina compacta* has spine-tipped bright green foliage, coral buds, yellow flowers and purple white-bloomed fruit. It is as attractive as it sounds.

Gracilis nana is equally lovely with yellow-flecked holly leaves which are a brilliant orange when young. The flowers are orange yellow and the berries purple. Propagate both by cuttings taken in July.

Calceolaria

The slipperworts are charming, herbaceous plants for a cool moist spot near a pool. They can be increased by division in April. *Calceolaria acutifolia* hails from Patagonia and from a pair of hairy green leaves are borne the pouch-like, golden-yellow flowers, dotted red on the reverse, on 6-in. stems during June to August.

C. tenella, from Chile, is a prostrate plant with minute light green leaves and, during June to August, up to three flowers on thread-like 1-in. stems. These are golden yellow with crimson spots on the tips.

Campanula

The bell flowers are a large family of mid-season plants and they extend the flowering period in the rock garden until late August.

Campanula arvatica, from Spain, forms a mat of minute bright green foliage. Its dainty flowers are like violet-blue stars and they appear on 1-in. stems in June and July. It is excellent for planting in a trough garden.

C. carpatica is a Carpathian species with a large number of garden forms. All open bell-shaped flowers over grey-green foliage and are about 6 to 12 in. high with a spread of 15 in. They flower from June to August and include *alba*, white; *coelestina*, china blue; Isabel, violet, and *turbinata*, purple blue.

The Italian *C. garganica* forms rosettes

of kidney-shaped leaves and its white-eyed blue flowers are to be found in June on 6-in. stems. It is a good wall plant with a spread of up to 15 in. across.

C. portenschlagiana (*muralis*) is a species from Dalmatia suitable for walls. It bears tufted rosettes of kidney-shaped green foliage. The star-shaped light violet-blue flowers are around from June to August on 3-in. stems.

All can be increased by cuttings in June or division in April.

Cerastium

The well-known snow in summer should be avoided like the plague in small rock gardens but *Cerastium alpinum lanatum*, the mouse-ear chickweed from the European Alps, is a small plant with silky oval leaves and shiny white flowers on 2-in. stems during May and June. It is a suitable subject for a trough as its ultimate spread is only 9 in. Propagation is by division in July.

Chamaecytisus

There is only one dwarf broom suitable for the rock garden and that is *Chamaecytisus pygmaeus* from Turkey. It is about 4 in. high and 12 in. wide with prostrate stems and much cut narrow leaves. The bright yellow pea-shaped flowers are to be seen in June and it makes a good plant for a wall. Cuttings can be taken in June.

Chamaespartium

Chamaespartium delphinensis from the Pyrenees is a must for even the smallest rock garden or trough. It is only 3 in. high with zig-zagged branches and winged adpressed grey-green leaves. In June it is covered in a mass of golden-yellow, pea-shaped flowers. It prefers a lime-free soil and can be increased by cuttings in June.

Crocus

There are a large number of crocus species suitable for the rock garden or trough and the following will give a display over a long period. All are from 3 to 4 in. high and can be increased by seed or division.

Among those that flower in autumn (August to October) are *Crocus byzantinus*, flowers bluish purple, eastern Europe; *C. kotschyanus*, large, rose lilac, throat yellow, Asia Minor; *C. speciosus*, lavender blue, veined, Asia Minor, Persia, and varieties Artabir, lavender blue with deeper feathering, and Oxonian, bluish purple.

Those that flower in winter (November to February) include *C. chrysanthus*, flowers deep yellow, brownish-purple veining, Greece, Asia Minor, and varieties

Blue Bird, purplish blue, E. A. Bowles, rounded yellow goblets with bronze feathering, Moonlight, light sulphur yellow; *C. imperati*, bluish-mauve flowers, veined deep purple, southern Italy; *C. laevigatus*, feathered blue-mauve flowers, Greece.

The show continues from February to April with the spring-flowering types. *C. balansae* has goblets of bright orange with mahogany feathering, western Asia Minor; *C. candidus*, variable from white through cream to orange, Asia Minor; *C. fleischeri*, a snowy white species with orange-scarlet stigmata, Asia Minor; *C. susianus*, brilliant orange flowers with dark brown markings, Crimea.

Cytisus

There are some good prostrate species of the common broom for trailing over rocks and walls. *Cytisus ardoinii*, a native of France, is about 6 in. high with bright green leaves in threes and pea-shaped, golden-yellow flowers in May. *C. procumbens* which comes from the same district is smaller at 3 in. high but it has a spread of 24 in. The small oblong grey-green leaves provide a good foil to the bright yellow flowers of May and June. Both are increased by cuttings in June.

Daphne

The garland flowers are interesting dwarf shrubs with normally intensely fragrant flowers. Propagation of both the following species is by cuttings taken in June. *Daphne cneorum*, from Europe, is about 9 in. high with a spread of 24 in. It has narrow oblong leaves and clusters of rich deep pink fragrant flowers in May and June. *D. collina* is a native of Italy and Asia Minor. It grows up to 12 in. high and 18 in. wide and has oblong leaves and terminal heads of fragrant reddish-purple flowers in May.

Dianthus

The pinks are one of the backbones of the rock garden with many attractive flowering plants. *Dianthus deltoides*, the maiden pink, is from 4 to 6 in. high and 15 in. wide. It forms grey-green narrow foliage and deep pink flowers with a darker stripe in June and July. A native of Europe, it has produced a number of good colour forms. These include *albus*, white with a crimson zone; Bowles' Variety, crimson-red flowers; *glaucus*, grey leaves and rose flowers, and the aptly named Huntsman which is scarlet pink.

D. gratianopolitanus (*caesius*) is the British cheddar pink. It is about 6 in. high and 12 in. wide with blue-grey foliage and deeply fringed rose-pink, fragrant flowers in June and July. Good varieties include Baker's Variety, rose red; *flore pleno*, double, rose pink and Icombe, smaller, rose pink. Both the foregoing species and forms are ideal wall plants.

D. pavonius (*neglectus*) from south west Europe is only 3 in. high with smooth

Crocus candidus sub-flavus

tufts of narrow green foliage. The large fringed flowers are bright rose with a green central zone and they are out in June and July. It is a good plant for a trough in a lime-free soil.

There are many named hybrids in most nurserymen's catalogues including Grenadier, double scarlet maroon; Pike's Pink with a crimson central zone, and La Bourbrille, a good cushion pink. All can be increased by cuttings in June.

Douglasia

Douglasia laevigata, from North America, is a good high alpine plant suitable for trough culture. It has tufted cushions of grey-green foliage in rosettes and rose-pink flowers with yellow eyes on 2-in. stems in June. Propagate by cuttings in June.

Draba

This genus contains a number of high alpine cushion plants commonly known as the whitlow grasses and the following two from the Caucasus mountains are ideal plants for the trough. *Draba bryoides imbricata* makes a cushion of grey-green rosettes only 2 in. high and 6 in. wide with golden-yellow flowers in April and May. Flowering at the same time, *D. rigida* has a compact mat of minute green rosettes and large golden-yellow flowers on 3-in. stems. Increase by seed in March.

153

Dryas

The mountain aven, *Dryas octopetala*, is a fine British native dwarf shrub for walls while the *minor* form is suitable for troughs. They are trailing plants from 1 in. high and 6 in. wide to 4 in. high and 24 in. wide with oak-like green foliage. The white flowers are saucer shaped with golden stamens. Cuttings can be taken in June.

Erica

The dwarf forms of *Erica carnea* (*herbacea*) are early peat-loving heaths for the rock garden. They come from Europe and range in height from 9 to 12 in. with a spread of 18 in. They flower from December to March and all can be increased by cuttings in June. The species is flesh coloured and the following varieties are to be recommended: *alba*, white tinged green; Ann Sparkes, yellow-bronze, reddish-tipped foliage, carmine-red flowers; *atrorubra*, carmine red; James Backhouse, pale pink; Loughrigg, pale purple; *praecox rubra*, deep red, and Springwood White, white.

Erigeron

The fleabanes are charming dwarf compact plants with daisy-like flowers and they are small enough for a trough garden. *Erigeron simplex* from North America makes a tufted plant with ash-grey hairy foliage. The lavender flowers have golden centres and appear on 4-in. stems over a long period from May. Increase by seed sown in March.

Erinus

Once introduced, *Erinus alpinus*, a European species, will seed itself in cracks and crevices, either in sun or shade. It forms small compact rosettes of glossy green foliage and has sprays of lilac-purple flowers on 3-in. stems in May and June. Of the three good varieties *albus* is pure white; *carmineus* is carmine, and Dr Hanele is deep carmine.

Euryops

A small genus of shrubs, the one noted here being an extremely decorative evergreen from South Africa. *Euryops acraeus* is an erect-stemmed plant about 9 in. high and 15 in. wide with silver-grey foliage. The large golden-yellow flowers are prominent in June. Cuttings in July are a ready means of increase.

Gaultheria

This is a genus of evergreen lime-hating shrubs of which the following are useful with charming flowers and brightly coloured fruits. They grow from 3 to 9 in. high and can be propagated by cuttings in June. *Gaultheria adenothrix*, from Japan, is an excellent small shrub for a half shady position in a peaty medium. It has thick oval glossy green leaves and white-flushed-pink, urn-shaped flowers in June which are followed by red fruits in October.

The species *procumbens* makes a tufted shrub spreading to 30 in. with oval glossy green leaves, pinkish-white flowers in May and scarlet fruits in October. It comes from North America.

G. trichophylla, from west China, grows 3 in. tall with oval deep green foliage and bell-shaped, pinkish-white flowers in May and rounded lapis-lazuli fruit in September.

Gentiana

Space only allows me to mention a few of this large race of gentians with a wide global distribution and the ones noted here should present little difficulty with regards to cultivation. *Gentiana acaulis*, a native of Europe, is about 3 in. high with large tubular deep blue trumpets over tufts of bright green foliage in early spring. Although easy to grow, it can be temperamental in flowering.

G. farreri, from west China, is 4 in. high and bears radiating laterals with narrow green foliage. The August flowers are Cambridge-blue trumpets striped violet. It requires a lime-free leafy medium. *G. septemfida* is an easy species from south west Asia, about 9 in. high, with straggling leafy stems and terminal clusters of bright blue trumpets in July and August.

G. sino-ornata grows up to 6 in. high with prostrate stems and narrow bright green foliage. The flowers are deep royal blue from September to December. A native of west China, it needs an acid soil composed mainly of leafmould. *G. verna*, the spring gentian from Europe and Asia, is about 2 in. high with tufts of green leaves and erect flowers of deep azure blue in April and May. Seed sown in March is the best method of increase, division in March for *sino-ornata*.

Geranium

The crane's bills are good easy plants for the rock garden. They grow to 6 in. high with a spread of 10 in. They can be propagated by seed in March or division in April. *Geranium argenteum*, from the Alps, has large pink flowers with deeper veinings during June to August over much cut silver leaves. Ballerina is a hybrid with lobed ash-grey leaves and large flowers of blue purple with reddish veinings and a basal blotch of red purple from June to September. *G. sanguineum* is a native of Europe including Britain with lobed green leaves and magenta-crimson flowers from May to October. The variety *lancastriense* is smaller with rose-pink flowers which have purple veinings.

Geum

Geum borisii is a natural hybrid from Bulgaria with roundish lobed, rough-textured, bright green leaves and large orange-scarlet flowers from May to September. It is about 9 to 12 in. high. Divide in March.

Gypsophila

The gauze flowers are good plants to use as ground cover over bulbs in the rock garden. They can be propagated by division in April or seed in March. *Gypsophila cerastioides* is a native of the Himalayas and it makes a mat of tufted green leaves and has clusters of white red-veined flowers on 3-in. stems in May and June.

G. repens fratensis has narrow grey-green leaves and clusters of pink flowers on 9-in. stems in June and July. It comes from south east Europe.

Hebe

This is a wholly Australasian genus and there are a large number of dwarf evergreen shrubs for the rock garden but space forbids the mention of more than just a few.

Hebe buchananii is a compact much branched shrub from 3 to 6 in. high with thick oval dull green leaves and spikes of white flowers in June and July. The variety *nana* is smaller in all its parts and is suitable for troughs. Carl Teschner is a garden hybrid with procumbent purple stems, oval glossy leaves and 6-in. spikes of violet flowers in June.

H. pinguifolia pagei is a garden form, up to 12 in. high and 24 in. wide, with oval leaves and clusters of white flowers with purple anthers in June. All propagate from cuttings taken in July.

Helianthemum

The following forms of the sun rose, *Helianthemum nummularium*, are all about 6 in. high and have a spread of 24 in. They make good plants for walls after the spring-flowering plants have finished. They should be cut back hard after flowering and increased by cuttings in July. The species is a native of Europe and it has trailing stems with oval leaves and clusters of yellow flowers. Good varieties include Amy Baring, bright orange; Apricot, apricot with a deeper eye; Ben Heckla,

Above: *Gentiana sino-ornata*
Above right: *Helianthemum* **The Bride**
Below right: *Dryas octopetala*

brick red; Ben Lawers, deep crimson; *coccineum*, double, deep red; Golden Queen, golden yellow; Jock Scott, light rose; Rose of Leeswood, double, light pink, and The Bride, grey leaves, white flowers.

Hyacinthus

Hyacinthus azureus is a charming dwarf hyacinth from Asia Minor with azure-blue flowers in a tight cluster on 3-in. stems in April. The variety *albus* is white. Propagate by seed in March or division in June.

Hypericum

There are a number of St John's worts suitable for the rock garden and all are extremely free flowering. *Hypericum empetrifolium* is an evergreen shrublet from Greece with slender stems and narrow, grey-green leaves. The pale yellow flowers are borne on 6-in. stems during July and August.

H. nummularium is a European species which grows about 6 in. high with coppery-red young stems and rounded leaves. Like *empetrifolium*, it is summer flowering with golden-yellow flowers on 6-in. stems. *H. reptans*, a sub-shrub from the Himalayas with oval green leaves, is only 3 in. high but it spreads to 18 in. The summer flowers are red in bud but they open to golden yellow. Propagation of all is by cuttings in June or by division in spring.

Iberis

Iberis sempervirens Little Gem is characteristic of the candytufts with dwarf erect 4-in. stems and crowded oblong dark green leaves. The white flowers in large tight heads appear during May and June. Increase by cuttings in June.

Ilex

Ilex crenata Golden Gem is a miniature holly forming a low rounded bush with yellow-green leaves which turn deeper in the winter. After many years it will attain a height of only 12 in. and is therefore a good subject for trough culture. Propagation is by cuttings in June.

Iris

Of the bulbous irises, both *Iris reticulata* and its forms are suitable for the rock garden. *I. reticulata* has deep violet-purple flowers on 9-in. stems during February and its varieties include Cantab, Cambridge Blue; Royal Blue, deep blue, and Hercules, purplish red.

I. pumila, from Asia Minor, resembles a miniature flag iris with purple bearded flowers on 6 to 9-in. stems during April. Amber Queen is amber yellow; *azurea*, pale blue; *cyanea*, dwarf, purple; *gracilis*, lavender pink, and The Bride, white. Divide in June.

Leontopodium

Leontopodium alpinum is the eidelweiss with all its romantic associations. It has lance-shaped, grey-green leaves and the flowers are clustered and enveloped by a circle of thick strap-like woolly bracts. It grows to 8 in. tall and flowers in June and July. Sow seed in March.

Lewisia

The plants in this completely American genus are commonly known as the bitter roots. They are especially attractive when planted on walls. *Lewisia cotyledon* is distinguished by having large rosettes of thick strap-like pale green evergreen leaves with brown markings. The large flowers are salmon, veined pink and they are to be seen in June and July on 9-in. stems. The variety *finchii* is pale pink with deeper veinings; *howellii* is deep rose veined salmon pink, and Weald Rose is cherry pink with deeper veins.

L. nevadensis is a herbaceous plant with narrow fleshy green leaves in rosettes. It has large white flowers on 2-in. stems during May and is suitable for trough culture. Increase by seed in March.

Linaria

The alpine toadflax, *Linaria alpina*, is a close tufted plant only 2 in. high with whorls of grey-green leaves. The summer flowers of the species are violet with an orange lip but the variety *alba* is all white, and *rosea* is pink with a golden-yellow lip. Sow seed in March or divide in June.

Lithospermum

The garden forms of *Lithospermum diffusum* are colourful late flowering plants for the lime-free rock garden. They grow about 6 in. high and 20 in. wide and should be cut back after flowering. Grace Ward has mats of hairy green foliage and gentian-blue flowers, and Heavenly Blue is a deep rich blue with a reddish tinge. Both these excellent varieties will flower from June to October. Cuttings can be struck in June.

Mimulus

The musks or monkey flowers prefer a cool moist root run and are good waterside plants for the rock pool. *Mimulus cupreus* is too rampant for most gardens but its forms are less invasive. Of these Bee's Dazzler is deep red; Dainty, creamy yellow; Red Emperor, crimson scarlet, and Whitecroft's Scarlet, deep scarlet. All are 6 to 9 in. high and they flower from June to August.

M. primuloides, from west America, forms a carpet of rosettes of bright green leaves only 1 in. high and the flowers which come from June to August are yellow with red-brown spots. Divide in April.

Morisia

Morisia monantha (*hypogaea*), the Mediterranean cress from Corsica, forms small rosettes of cut, deep green foliage only

1 in. high. The flowers are stemless and golden yellow and come during May and June. Seed can be sown in March.

Narcissus

The dwarf species of the daffodil are ideal plants for both rock garden and troughs. *Narcissus asturiensis* (*minimus*) is a miniature daffodil from Spain. It is only 3 in. high with golden-yellow flowers in February and March. *N. bulbocodium* has the descriptive common name of the hoop petticoat daffodil. It is a native of the South of France and Spain and has a narrow funnel trumpet and small petals on 6-in. stems in March and April. The type is bright yellow and of the varieties *citrinus* is lemon yellow; *conspicuus*, deep yellow, tinged green on the reverse, and *nivalis*, orange yellow. Sow seed in March or divide in August.

Omphalodes

Omphalodes luciliae is an evergreen subshrub from Asia Minor. It has tufts of

Lewisia cotyledon **hybrid**

light grey oval leaves and grows about 6 in. high. The flowers, which are pink in bud, open to china blue during May to September. *O. verna*, the blue-eyed mary, is a herbaceous perennial with tufts of light green leaves up to 6 in. high. During the spring, it bears bright blue flowers which have a white eye. A native of southern Europe, it prefers shade. June is the month for taking cuttings.

Oxalis

Avoid *Oxalis corniculata* and *O. repens* for once these wood sorrels have been introduced they are impossible to eradicate. However, the following two species are both suitable for trough culture. *O. enneaphylla*, from the Falkland Islands, has fan-shaped, silver-grey, red-brown edged leaves. The flowers are white with a pale yellow-green throat on 1 to 3-in. stems from May to August. The variety *minuta* is smaller with yellow-eyed pink flowers, and *rosea* has pink-flushed flowers.

The Chilean *O. lobata* has lobed green leaves and golden-yellow flowers on 3-in. stems in early autumn. Divide in June.

Papaver

A good poppy for the rock garden comes from the Pyrenees. It is *Papaver rhaeticum* which has divided light green leaves and bright orange flowers on 6-in. stems in early summer. This poppy will seed itself in most gardens.

Paronychia

Paronychia argentea makes a mat of silver-grey evergreen leaves only 2 in. high. Its minute July flowers have conspicuous white bracts. It provides an excellent ground cover for bulbs especially in troughs. The plants can be divided in March.

Penstemon

The beard tongues are all native to America and they are ideal evergreen sub-shrubs for the rock garden. All can be increased by cuttings in June. *Penstemon menziesii microphyllus* is a dwarf shrub, only 3 in. high, with oval toothed green leaves and light purple, tubular flowers in June and July. *P. pinifolius* is a lax shrublet with needle-shaped leaves, about 6 in. high. The clustered flowers, during the summer months, are tubular in shape and mandarin red in colour.

P. rupicola will be found in most catalogues under the name *P. roezlii*. It is a prostrate plant, 4 in. high, with grey-green leaves and large tubular crimson flowers in June.

Pernettya

Pernettya tasmanica is an evergreen sub-shrub with green oval leaves. As its name implies it hails from Tasmania and grows about 2 in. high. It has white, urn-shaped flowers in May followed by red fruits in September. It requires a lime-free leafy soil in some shade. Take cuttings in June.

Phlox

This genus from America provides a good follow on to the flowering season after the spring flowers are over. They make good wall plants and should be cut back after flowering. *Phlox douglasii* is a prostrate plant with narrow green leaves. It is about 2 in. high with an expected spread of 15 in. and the clustered, bright pink flowers appear in May and June.

Above right: A trough in a town garden
Right: A rock outcrop and pool

Good varieties include *alba*, white; Boothman's Variety, mauve, deeper at the base; Eva, bright pink, deeper at the base, and Violet Queen, violet. All prefer some shade in hot gardens.

The moss phlox, *P. subulata*, has narrow light to deep green foliage and grows from 4 to 6 in. high and up to 18 in. wide. The flowers of the species are lavender to purple with a darker central zone in late spring and early summer. In the varieties *alba* is white; *aldboroughensis*, deep red; *atropurpurea*, deep red; Brightness, bright pink; *camlaensis*, large, salmon; *lilacina*, light blue; Temiscaming, glowing magenta crimson, and Vivid, salmon pink with a crimson eye. Take cuttings in June.

Pieris

Pieris japonica variegata is a slow-growing erect shrub about 15 in. high and 18 in. wide with oblong yellow-green margined white evergreen foliage. The white urn-shaped flowers are abundant in April. It requires a lime-free shady spot and can be propagated by cuttings in June.

Polygala

Polygala chamaebuxus is a dwarf shrub with dull green foliage, about 6 in. high and 12 in. wide from Europe. This milkwort has pea-like fragrant flowers which have a white keel and bright yellow mouth in May. Take cuttings in June.

Potentilla

Among the cinquefoils which can be recommended for the rock garden is *Potentilla curviseta* from the Himalayas. It is a mat-forming plant, 2 in. high, with palmate bright green leaves and golden-yellow flowers from June to September. *P. tonguei* is a hybrid with much cut palmate green leaves and orange-yellow summer flowers which become crimson at the base. It is 6 in. high and 9 in. wide and can be divided in April.

Primula

In such a vast family, it is difficult to choose only a few primulas but the following are representative. *Primula denticulata* from the Himalayas has round heads of deep lilac flowers before the leaves in March. It, and the following varieties, grows to about 9 in. tall. *Alba* is white; Prichard's Variety is deep ruby red, and *rosea* is rosy lavender.

P. juliana is the collective name given to the hybrids of *P. juliae*. All are evergreen and about 6 in. tall, flowering from March to May. *Alba* is white; Betty Green, crimson; Blue Horizon, sky blue; *crispii*, wine red; Dorothy, sulphur yellow;

Gloria, crimson, golden eye; Jewel, crimson purple; Sunset Glow, tangerine red, and Wanda, claret coloured.

P. marginata originates from the Maritime Alps. It has silvery-margined, much cut, leafy, evergreen rosettes and lavender fragrant flowers on 6-in. stems during May and June. Good forms include *alba*, yellow-green, silver-margined leaves, white flowers; *caerulea*, light blue; Drake's Form, deep lavender; Linda Pope, lavender blue; Prichard's Variety, bright lavender blue, and *rubra*, ruby red.

The hybrids known by the collective name of *P. pubescens* have rosettes of toothed foliage. The flowers cover a colour range of pink to violet and crimson with a white eye and are borne on 6-in. stems in May and June. *Alba* is white; Christine, old rose; Faldonside, deep crimson; Jane, pale blue; Moonlight, pale yellow; Cardinal, rich velvety red, and The General, brick red.

P. rosea is a species from the Himalayas. It is a good plant for a cool moist spot with rosettes of oval crinkled leaves. The flowers are dark rich rose with a yellow eye on 6-in. stems during March and April. Most can be increased by cuttings in July or division in August.

Ptilotrichum

Ptilotrichum spinosum, from Spain, makes an erect rounded 6-in. shrub with silver-grey leaves. The adult wood is very spiny. The crowded flowers of the species are white, those of the variety *roseum* are pink. Both appear in June and July and seed can be collected and sown in August.

Pulsatilla

Pulsatilla vernalis has the descriptive common name of the lady of the snows. It has much cut, bronzy-green foliage, about 4 in. high. The flowers which unfold in April and May from furry bronze-violet buds are glistening white backed with violet and gold and crowned by a high central boss of yellow stamens.

P. vulgaris is the pasque flower with much cut green leaves. The shaggy haired buds open to reveal rich purple flowers with golden-yellow stamens in April and May. It will grow to 6 to 12 in. as do *alba*, white; *rosea*, rose pink, and *rubra*, deep red purple. Increase by seed sown in July.

Ramonda

The rosette mullein, *Ramonda myconi*, hails from the Pyrenees. It is about 4 in. high with rosettes of rough red-haired oval green foliage. The large rounded flowers are lavender blue with a yellow eye in May and June. Of the varieties the

inevitable *alba* is white, *rosea*, deep pink. September is the month for sowing seed.

Ranunculus

This family contains the buttercups and *Ranunculus alpestris,* a native of Europe, has rosettes of grey-green, three-lobed leaves. The large flowers are white with golden stamens and are borne on 4-in. stems in May and June. It likes a moist soil and is a good trough plant. Propagate by seed in March.

Raoulia

Raoulia hookeri (*australis*), from New Zealand, is only ½ in. in height. It has minute, silver-grey foliage and stemless yellow flowers during the summer. It will look most attractive when planted in a trough. Divide in July.

Rhodohypoxis

A South African species, *Rhodohypoxis baurii*, produces tufts of silky haired channelled green leaves and rose-red flowers in May on 3-in. stems. Recommended varieties include Eva, deep red; The Major, deep pink; Margaret Rose, bright pink, and Ruth, large, white. Divide after flowering.

Salix

The miniature willows are ideal deciduous shrubs for the rock garden in a moist spot. *Salix boydii* is an erect tree-like shrub with a bole which will reach up to 18 in. in time. The grey-white leaves provide an effective background for the silky light yellow May catkins. It is a native of Scotland.

S. reticulata is a dwarf shrublet of only 2 in. high from Europe. It has deep green veined leaves and oval yellow catkins in April. Cuttings can be taken in June.

Saponaria

Saponaria Bressingham Hybrid is a soapwort with reddish stems, narrow green leaves and deep pink flowers with a red calyx in May and June. It is about 2 in. high and can be increased by cuttings after flowering.

S. ocymoides, a species from the Alps and Jura mountains, forms a trailing carpet of bright green oval leaves and bright pink flowers with red-purple calyces in May. It has a white variety *alba*.

Saxifraga

From such a mighty family it is difficult to choose a few for inclusion here. To conserve space, therefore, I have placed the rockfoils in sections according to their cultural requirements. All can be in-

creased by cuttings, best taken in June.
Mossy Section These require a cool, semi-shady position and they make loose carpets of light to deep green rosettes from 18 to 24 in. across. The flowers appear in May and June on 4 to 6-in. stems. Cambria Jewel, rich pink; Darlington Double, double, deep pink; Dubarry, crimson; Flowers of Sulphur, pale yellow; James Bremner, white; Peter Pan, crimson; *rosacea* (*decipiens*) *grandiflora*, large, rose.
Encrusted Section A position in full sun suits these best and they make small to large rosettes of silver, lime-encrusted leaves. They flower in late spring and early summer. *Saxifraga aizoon* is white speckled red from Lombardy and its variety *lutea* is lemon yellow and *rosea* is pink. *S. cochlearis* is white from the Alps; *cotyledon* has huge rosettes and large spires of white flowers; *longifolia* Tumbling Waters has a spire of white flowers 2 ft. in length while *valdensis* is minute with white flowers on red stems.
Kabschia-Engleria Section These make spiny cushions or rosettes of silver-grey to green leaves, 3 to 8 in. wide and require shelter from hot sunshine in summer. They flower in spring on 1 to 3-in. stems. *S. apiculata*, pale yellow; *burseriana* Gloria, white, red stems; *b. sulphurea*, pale yellow; Christine, cherry red; Cranborne, rose; *elizabethae*, yellow; *grisebachii* Wisley Variety, the best Engleria, silver rosettes, crimson woolly spikes; *haagii*, golden yellow; *jenkinsae*, deep

pink; *prosenii*, reddish orange; Riverslea, purple rose; *stribrnyi*, pink, in woolly purple calyces.

Sedum

The following is a short list of the many stonecrops which make fleshy stems and leaves of varying colour and form. They range in height from 1 to 4 in. and flower from May to July. All propagate easily by division in June.

Sedum album Coral Carpet has reddish-purple leaves and pink star flowers; *anglicum minus*, grey-green tipped red leaves and rose-coloured flowers; *caulicola*, rounded, fleshy, green margined, red leaves, deep purple flowers, from Japan; *dasyphyllum*, fleshy oval pinkish-grey leaves, white flowers; *ewersii*, oval glaucous-blue leaves with red margins and pink flowers, from the Himalayas; *lydium*, green turning scarlet leaves, white flowers; *spathulifolium* Cappa Blanca, greyish-white leaves and yellow flowers, from South Oregon, and *spurium atropurpureum*, deep reddish-brown leaves and pink flowers.

Sempervivum

This is a large family and the houseleek owes its popularity to the different colours and forms of the rosettes varying in height from 3 to 6 in. and flowering in June and July. The flowers are mostly indifferent. Increase is by division in May.

Sempervivum arachnoideum, from Eur-

Above left: *Pulsatilla vulgaris coccinea*
Above: *Rhodohypoxis baurii*

ope, has green rosettes covered with spider-web hairs. Its variety, *stansfieldii*, has rosettes which turn red. *S. arenarium* has green tipped red rosettes and yellow flowers. It comes from the eastern Alps. *S. ciliosum*, from Bulgaria, has grey-green, hair-covered rosettes and yellow flowers. In the species *giuseppii* the green rosettes are tipped brown and they are hairy in the centre. The flowers are rosy red and it comes from northern Spain.

Deep reddish-brown rosettes which turn red in winter and red flowers are the attributes of *S. marmoreum* from Bulgaria. *S. reginae-amaliae* has green rosettes tinged purple and red flowers. It comes from Greece.

Silene

The catchfly or campion, *Silene acaulis*, makes a cushion of small narrow leaves only 2 in. high and 6 in. wide. The flowers are pink with a reddish-purple calyx in May and June. It is a native of Europe whereas its variety *exscapa* comes from the Pyrenees and it is lighter green with similar flowers. Divide in March.

Thymus

The thymes are well represented by the many forms of *Thymus serpyllum*. The majority are intensely aromatic and are useful plants for planting in paving or in a dry wall. The species is a native of Europe and makes a rambling plant with narrow leaves from 1 to 3 in. high and up to 24 in. wide. It has semi-hemispheres of purple flowers throughout the summer months. Its varieties include *albus*, white; Anne Hall, clear pink; *aureus*, golden-green leaves in winter, deep lilac flowers; *citriodorus*, lemon-scented leaves, lilac flowers; *c. argenteus*, leaves green and white; *carmineus*, carmine; *coccineus*, crimson, and Silver Queen, variegated leaves of silver and green. Take cuttings in June.

Trollius

Trollius pumilus, the globe flower, is a native of the Himalayas. It has five-lobed green leaves, up to 6 in. high, and many petalled bright yellow flowers in June. It is a good plant for a cool moist spot and it is easily increased by seed sown in March.

Tulipa

The small tulip species are ideal for mass planting in troughs or other containers where they can be left undisturbed. They range from 4 to 8 in. high and flower from April to June. The bulbs can be lifted and divided in August or seed can be sown in March. I would recommend the following species: *aucheriana*, pale rose, bronze basal blotch, Persia; *batalinii*, creamy yellow, greenish-yellow blotch, Turkestan; *biflora*, outer crimson and green, inner white, yellow base, Caucasus; *clusiana*, white, cherry-red bands, basal red blotch, Persia; *eichleri*, bright scarlet, black blotch, outside striped silver grey, Asia Minor; *kaufmanniana*, light creamy yellow flushed rose, central Asia. There are many forms of this tulip, all are good.

The list continues with *linifolia*, bright scarlet, black blotch, central Asia; *pulchella*, crimson, black blotch, Asia Minor; *tarda*, bright yellow, white tipped, Turkestan, and *violacea*, violet blue, bluish-green blotch, Persia.

Veronica

Veronica gentianoides is a compact tufted speedwell from the Caucasus with oval green leaves and spires of pale blue flowers on 6 to 12-in. stems in May and June. Its varieties include *variegata*, leaves variegated and *nana*, a reduced form.

V. spicata nana makes a compact plant only 6 in. high with green rounded leaves and violet-blue flowers in June and July. Propagation is by division in April.

Above left: A limestone rock garden
Left: A well-established collection of rock plants

Pool and Waterside Plants

Francis Perry, M.B.E., V.M.H., F.L.S.,
writer, journalist, lecturer and broadcaster,
has achieved fame as a horticulturist and as the
first woman member of The Royal
Horticultural Society's council since the
Society was founded in 1804. This singular
honour was accorded her in 1968.

Her influence on gardening has been
immense through her work in the field of
education – she was the first principal of
Norwood Hall College of Agricultural
Education and Horticultural Organizer for the
County of Middlesex for many years – her
fourteen books on many aspects of gardening,
her many writings which include a weekly
article in *The Observer* newspaper, of which
she is gardening correspondent, and her many
appearances on radio and television.

Mrs Perry was trained at Swanley
Horticultural College in Kent, and early on
came under the influence of that great gardener
and near neighbour, the late E. A. Bowles.
With his guidance and that of her father-in-law,
the late Amos Perry, a plantsman of great
distinction, she had unique opportunities of
which she made the most.

She has travelled in all five continents, often
lecturing and always looking for plants. A
widow, her only son, Roger, was for six years
the Director of the Charles Darwin Research
Station in the Galapagos Islands and he, too, is
an author of repute.

In 1972 The Royal Horticultural Society
awarded Mrs Perry the coveted Victoria
Medal of Honour, and, eight years prior to
that, a Veitch Gold Medal. She was awarded
the M.B.E. in 1962.

Her most recent honour has been the Sarah
Francis Chapman Medal from the Garden
Club of America, for literary achivement.

In countries with hot climates, water and
shade are the most desirable appurten-
ances of comfortable living. For this
reason homes are frequently built with
their walls surrounding an inner court
yard where fountains play, brightly coloured flowers are grouped and caged
birds sing in the trees. This concept provides the basis for the modern patio.

In cooler climates, however, water
features take on a different image. They
then become an extension of gardening
and are designed to keep fish and grow
aquatic plants under formal or natural
conditions. The fascination of the medium
– its changing nature, the music of a
gurgling stream or splashing fountain and
its magnetism for birds – is another
attraction.

Water is never the same two days
together. As the weather changes so do
its moods – its reflective powers and the
the pattern of its surface.

Siting and Design

Garden pools should be built in an open
position, possibly sheltered on the north
or east by buildings, a hedge or a belt of
shrubs, but never overshadowed by tall
trees. Shade represses flowering, particularly with water lilies, and falling leaves
build up the organic content and become
the chief cause of water discolouration
and infestations of algae.

The shape, size and nature of the pool
will depend on the immediate surrounds.
A formal pool must be of uniform outline,
for example, round, square or rectangular,
and situated in an open position amongst
symmetrical lawns, flower beds or patios.
Its edges can be raised or sunken as long
as they are generously bordered by a
broad coping or flat paving stones. Fountains are permissible and low plantings,
but the symmetry should never be marred

by irregular groups of emergent marginal
aquatics.

Informal pools demand more natural
treatment. They team well with rock
gardens, when waterfalls and stream
effects can be incorporated, or with bog
gardens in a wild or woodland setting.
These pools should always be sunken,
their edges merging into the surrounding
lawns, flower beds or rock garden and
their shape irregular – as in nature.

The Materials

Garden pools can be made of various
materials and in fact any watertight container – even an old bath or water tank –
can become a potential water garden.

Concrete entails the most initial labour
but is strong and durable when properly
made and can be constructed to any shape,
depth or size. A formal pool with raised
curbs must be fashioned of concrete. Use
only good materials for its construction,
otherwise it may leak (ready mixed concrete lightens the labour) and look upon
6 in. as a minimum thickness for sides and
bottom. Reinforcement may be necessary
for large pools and all of them require
maturing (to get rid of free lime) before
plants and fish are introduced. Autumn-
constructed pools which have been kept
full of water all winter, then emptied, are
usually safe for planting by the following
spring. Alternatively the interior can be
painted over with a protective sealing
compound.

Prefabricated glassfibre pools, made in
various shapes and sizes, are available
from garden centres and shops. These are
light to handle and quick to install. A hole
is excavated slightly larger than the unit,
the pool set in place and tested for levels
and soil packed round to make it firm.

A prefabricated pool and cascade (inset)

Planting can take place immediately. Some of these pools can be linked to pre-cast cascade and stream sections for waterfall effects. An electrically powered pump of the submersible or centrifugal (surface) type will work these – or fountains – using the same water over and over again.

The easiest and most modern method of pool making is to excavate a hole and line it with a waterproof butyl liner. This is a flexible sheet of strong, heavy duty, synthetic rubber material which can withstand extremes of temperature and is resistant to pests and fungi infection, also sunlight and ultraviolet rays. It is harmless to plants and fish and can be used for any size of pool since it is possible to join the material (also repair accidental cuts) with a special self-adhesive tape.

Dig the pool to the size and depth, or series of depths, required and if the subsoil is stony spread 1 in. of damp sand or ashes all over the interior. This helps to protect the fabric. Next stretch the material over the hole and weight its edges with rocks or bricks. Run in the water, pleating and tucking the liner into shape as filling goes on. When it is full cut off any surplus fabric, except for about 6 in. all round the edges, and tuck this spare out of sight beneath turves, stone slabs, soil or plants.

Planting

The best time to plant deep water or marginal aquatics is in spring, between April and June, although the submerged kinds and floaters can go into the water at any season. Bog plants move successfully in spring or early autumn.

Water lilies should either be planted in special pockets, made during the construction of the pool, or in aquatic baskets. The latter are made of plastic with openwork sides. Water lily roots are sensitive to confinement and always thrive

best where they can feel the influence of water, so that concrete pockets should have a few holes punched through their sides for the same reason.

After planting, about which more details are given in the section on water lilies on p. 163, lower the baskets into the water but prop them on bricks so that they are only just submerged. The lilies must now recover from the move but when new leaves appear they can be gradually lowered until – six or eight weeks later – the baskets are standing on the floor of the pool. Other deep water aquatics such as nuphars and aponogetons can be treated similarly.

Emergent marginals need very little water above their crowns; their chief desiderata being soil which is always very wet. Some have to have their roots confined to keep them in check. Plant these in solid pockets or suitable containers where they are to grow.

Submerged aquatics have few if any roots so tend to float if they are simply thrown into the water. Anchor them by gently pressing a thin strip of lead around two or three stems and then throw them in. Floaters are simply placed on the pool surface and bog plants inserted – like land plants – with a trowel or handfork.

Pool Depths

Garden pools should be deep enough not to freeze solid in winter, yet sufficiently shallow for the water to warm up quickly in spring. The last is essential for early flowers and in practice means 18 to 24 in. of water above the floor level. Since fish feel the effects of heat they benefit from the greater depth in hot weather, although fountains and waterfalls also help cool water.

The marginal aquatics only require 3 to 4 in. of soil and the same depth of water, so a shallow trough surround (with its

inner edge 1 in. lower than the outer) is sometimes built on to the deeper part during construction. When the pool is full of water this flows over to the outer contours and the trough does not show.

In the case of informal rock pools it is also expedient to build pockets for bog plants where they can be flooded over in dry weather. Alternatively, for large bog gardens, the soil can be taken out to a depth of 12 in. and the area lined with 500 gauge polythene sheeting. Holes should be punched in the sides of this, 6 in. up from the base, so that although it holds a certain amount of liquid it never becomes completely waterlogged. A 3-in. layer of stones or brick rubble is then laid for drainage and the soil returned.

Cultivation

Water plants rarely need feeding, except for water lilies which have been three or more years in their baskets. These can be helped by giving them nutrient pills. Mix equal quantities of wet clay and bonemeal (wear gloves when handling the latter) and mould into tennis ball-sized 'pills'. Push one or two down to the roots of each lily. After a further two years the baskets should be lifted and the lily roots washed, divided and replanted in fresh compost.

Remove old flowers and dead leaves regularly, also seedheads from aquatics likely to become too prolific.

Winter Problems

Falling leaves from nearby trees should not be allowed to accumulate in ornamental pools. Dredge them out with a rake or else make a light framework of 1-in. batons and plastic mesh netting. Lay this over the pool during leaf fall and most of them will be caught.

All pools should be kept full of water in winter and the shallow types protected against a complete freeze up. The instal-

A typical submersible pump for use with garden pools and waterfalls

Waterlilies are planted in baskets of compost topped with gravel to stop the soil floating out when the plant is submerged

A pocket for marginal aquatic plants constructed by laying polythene around part of the perimeter of the pool and allowing water to flow into it. Holes are perforated 6 in. above the base to allow some drainage

lation of a pool heater will keep a small area free of ice and so safeguard fish and plants. Another idea is to float a block of wood or a large ball on the surface and when ice forms take it out by pouring boiling water on top. Now bale out 1 in. of water and cover the hole with plastic sheeting or hessian. The ice will then act like a greenhouse and protect the plants and fish underneath. Naturally, as soon as a thaw occurs, the pool must be topped up again with more water.

Selected Pool and Waterside Plants

There are five main groups among the plants of the water garden: deep water aquatics; floaters; marginal aquatics; submerged oxygenators, and bog plants – all with different functions and requirements.

DEEP WATER AQUATICS

These have floating leaves and flowers and thick tuberous rootstocks anchored in mud at the base of the pool. The nymphaeas (water lilies) are the most important of these, with about seventy species and varieties hardy in this country and suitable for pools of various depths. When making a selection it is important to bear the last in mind and to pick varieties from the right group.

All hardy water lilies need a stiff compost; fibre-free loam enriched with one sixth part well-decayed cow manure or a half pint measure of bonemeal to each bucketful of soil. The compost should be used in a moister condition than is usual for pot plants, otherwise it will not bind and the roots may float upwards. Covering the soil after planting with 1 in. of washed shingle prevents fish from rooting in the mud and making the water cloudy.

There are two main groups of hardy water lilies; one with rhizomatous roots and the other with upright-growing tubers. The last, which includes the British native *Nymphaea alba*, should be planted perpendicularly, with its black and white feeding roots well spread. It should be noted that any thick white roots present are old anchorage roots and useless to the new plant. These should be removed.

Rhizomatous lilies like the North American *N. tuberosa* and *N. odorata* should be planted horizontally – like bearded irises, which they somewhat resemble. Most members of this group have fragrant flowers.

The following water lilies will grow in water 20 to 30 in. deep (less if there is room) and in time should each cover a surface area of approximately 5 to 6 sq. ft.

In this group the variety *gladstoniana* is superb, with large cup-shaped flowers of glistening white, the centres filled with rich golden stamens. The dark green leaves are tough, with a polished texture. Other good whites are Gonnêre, a semi-double, the squat blooms wrapped around with olive-green sepals and *N. tuberosa richardsonii* of globular habit. The only fully double water lily Gloire de Temple Sur Lot is suitable for 18 to 20 in., but is not as free flowering as many others. The creamy-white petals of the flowers curve like those of an incurved chrysanthemum.

Among the pinks *colossea* is flesh coloured; *tuberosa rosea*, soft pink; Marguerite Laplace, deep rose, and Mrs Richmond, deep pink. *Marliacea carnea* and *marliacea rosea* – soft and deeper pink respectively – were given his own patronymic by the great French breeder Latour Marliac – a sure indication of their worth.

There are several good reds in this group, particularly the prolific Escarboucle, a wine-red sort with flowers up to dinner-plate size and, excepting for Wm Falconer, the deepest in colour. *Gloriosa* is a fine red for the shallower depths in this section, also the adaptable and free-flowering James Brydon which produces masses of squat carmine-red blooms throughout the whole of the summer. Colonel Welch is the most robust yellow, but less fine than those recommended in the next section.

The medium growers are suitable for 12 to 18 in. of water and cover a surface area of approximately 4 sq. ft. in time. They are thus ideal for small pools and gardens.

Among the whites are Albatross, a very shapely sort; *caroliniana nivea*, sweetly scented and very prolific, and Hermine, whose stellate flowers stand clear of the water.

Fire Crest is a fragrant pink sort with red-tipped stamens which look as if they have been touched by flame, but *laydekeri lilacea*, rosy lilac, and *laydekeri purpurata*, rosy crimson, are two of the most reliable with only medium-sized blooms but prolifically produced.

Livingstone is bright red flecked with white; Masaniello, deep rose, and Paul Hariot changes colour with age – the new blooms being apricot yellow which gradually deepens to orange red. Two good yellows in this section are *marliacea chromatella*, of a soft primrose shade with chocolate-blotched leaves, and Sunrise,

which is semi-double with deep golden flowers.

There are also several miniatures for rock garden pools. These may need protection or lifting in winter and they can also be grown in small containers on a sunny windowsill indoors. *N. tetragona (pygmaea alba)* is white with green leaves, and *pygmaea helvola*, soft yellow with chocolate-blotched foliage.

OTHER DEEP WATER AQUATICS

Nuphars or pond lilies are strong-growing aquatics allied to but inferior to nymphaeas. Their only advantages over the latter lie in an ability to grow in shade, deep or running water – situations which are anathema to the true water lilies. If used at all in ornamental pools, the roots must be confined and only the weaker sorts like *Nuphar pumila (N. minima)*, with pale yellow flowers; *N. japonica rubrotinctum*, cup-shaped orange flowers with red-tipped stamens, or *N. japonica variegatum*, which has cream-splashed foliage, should be grown. Plant them the same way as nymphaeas.

Nymphoides peltata (Limnanthemum nymphoides), the water fringe, has poppy-like, three-petalled flowers of golden yellow and crinkly edged, almost round, chocolate-blotched, floating leaves. It grows in long strands across the water surface, shading the depths beneath and so discouraging algae, but is easily pulled out if it becomes too rampant.

Aponogeton distachyus, the water hawthorn, takes its name from the vanilla-like scent of the black and white, forked flowers. These float, as do the long narrow leaves. It will grow in depths of 12 to 20 in.

FLOATERS

This group takes its nourishment from dissolved salts in the water, and while some remain in character all the year round, others form winter buds or turons which sink to the bottom of the pool in autumn and reappear in spring. Floating plants shade water and so inhibit algae. They also provide nurseries for young fish and shelter for countless tiny creatures which later feed the fry. Some, however, can become a nuisance and the lemnas (duckweeds) should never be introduced to outdoor pools or, in warm climates, salvinas or water hyacinths (eichhornias).

Among the hardiest are the frogbits *(Hydrocharis morsus-ranae)* with small, white, three-petalled flowers and tiny round leaves and the water soldier *(Stratiotes aloides)* which stays just under the surface and has prickly rosettes of leaves, something like pineapple tops. Male and female flowers – both white and three petalled – are on separate plants.

Azolla caroliniana, the fairy floating moss, is closely related to the ferns and has mossy green fronds which turn red in autumn and then disappear for the winter. The lovely pale mauve flowers of the water hyacinth *(Eichhornia crassipes)* have gold and deeper blue 'peacock' markings on their upper petals. The swollen leaf stalks support the plants which can be carried by wind right across the pool, but the first touch of frost kills them, so they are only suitable for indoor pools or summer effect out of doors.

MARGINAL AQUATICS

These plants have emergent flowers and foliage, with their roots always in shallow water. For best effect they should be grouped in threes, or more, of the same variety and, since many increase vegetatively and can become rampant, the soil should not be rich. Plain loam suits them admirably. Also, to prevent indiscriminate seeding, the spent flower heads should be removed regularly.

Among the best of the flowering marginals are the kingcups or marsh marigolds *(Caltha palustris)*. These are among the first to appear in early spring, the rich golden, buttercup-like flowers borne in great profusion on 9 to 12-in. stems. The heart-shaped leaves are smooth and glossy and completely hidden at flowering time, especially in the double form *plena*. The variety *alba* is white and there are also semi-double kinds and white species. *C. polypetala* is taller (up to 3 ft.) and comes later. It has branching stems, with many single blooms.

The British native *Iris pseudacorus*, or yellow flag, is particularly fine in its variegated form, for the gold and green suffusions on the young foliage are as colourful as flowers. Unfortunately this vivid colouring does not persist but disappears by mid-summer, but then the rich golden flowers appear and provide some compensation. *I. laevigata* thrives in 2 to 4 in. of water and has flat grassy leaves and rich blue flowers in July. There are numerous varieties including a white, *alba*; pink, Rose Queen; variegated-

Above right: *Nymphaea marliacea chromatella*
Right: *Lysichitum americanum*

164

leaved, *variegata*, and two fine blue and whites called *colchesteri* and Benekiron. The approximate height of all these irises is around 2 to 2½ ft.

Another good flowering aquatic is the North American pickerel weed, *Pontederia cordata*. This flowers for weeks from mid-summer onwards, the spikes of soft blue florets set at the ends of 2-ft. leafy stems. The foliage is long, heart shaped and glossy. This plant is very compact and rarely becomes a nuisance.

The flowering rush *(Butomus umbellatus)* has umbels of pink flowers on 2 to 3-ft. stems and long narrow leaves which are bronze purple when young. Several aroids are also useful for shallow water, the most spectacular being *Lysichitum americanum*, which has large (up to 12 in.) bright yellow arums before the leaves in early spring. The foliage which follows, however, is rather massive, so this is a plant which requires plenty of room. It is readily propagated from seed. A white-flowered species, *L. camtschatcense*, is smaller in habit, so more useful in some situations. *Orontium aquaticum*, the golden club, resembles an arum without the outer spathe. It is an adaptable plant, producing floating glaucous leaves and flowers in deep water, or large upright foliage in shallow.

Other flowering aquatics include *Saururus chinensis*, the lizard's tail, a Japanese species around 1 ft. in height, with oval leaves and white-bracted flowers which have long tail-like centres, and also various arrowheads of which the double *Sagittaria sagittifolia leucopetala (S. japonica) flore pleno* is by far the best. This has white flowers in spikes, something like stocks, and arrow-shaped leaves. *Mimulus ringens* is a slender, 1 to 2-ft., mauve-flowered musk and *Calla palustris* (bog arum) is of creeping habit with round rhizomes like thick pencils supporting small glossy, heart-shaped leaves and white arum flowers. Another scrambler is *Menyanthes trifoliata* (bog bean) with trefoiled leaves – like giant clovers – and spikes of small, fringed, pink and white blooms.

Marginal aquatics with variegated foliage are invaluable when there are but few flowers in character. In addition to various irises there is the 2-ft. *Acorus calamus variegatus* or sweet flag which looks something like a bearded iris but with brown spikes of flowers looking like bull's horns protruding from the tops of the stems. If the leaves of this plant are bruised, they have a pleasant aromatic smell.

Glyceria aquatica variegata is the manna

grass, with cream and green leaf patternings, also rosy pink when they are young. It grows around 2 ft. There are also two variegated rushes; *Scirpus tabernaemontani zebrinus*, the porcupine quill rush, with fat round rushy stems, 2 to 3 ft. tall, alternately barred in green and white, and the 5-ft. *S. albescens*, which is striped longitudinally. *Juncus effusus spiralis* grows like a corkscrew, with each green stem spirally twisted.

SUBMERGED AQUATICS

Although largely unseen these are some of the most important plants of the water garden. Their presence, in healthy growing condition, is usually the criteria of a well-balanced pool and their functions are many.

For one thing they are essential as oxygenators. Although plants, as well as animals, absorb a little oxygen during respiration, they alone in the living world can make food from a by-product of this operation. When living creatures breathe they take in oxygen and exhale carbon dioxide, but, certain parts of plants, given fuel for energy, take in carbon dioxide and build this, with water, into simple sugars. This is the basis of all plant foods. However, this chemical change produces a spare product – oxygen – and so this is released back to the air, or water.

The green chlorophyll in leaves is the essential agent which performs this operation and the motivating energy is supplied by sunlight. Fish, snails and other water creatures need oxygen and plants require carbon dioxide and so the aim is to create a balanced pool, so that each utilizes the others' waste products. Additionally, chemical salts in the water build up the food structure, so where there is plenty of

Top left: *Sagittaria sagittifolia*
Top right: *Caltha palustris plena*
Above: *Glyceria aquatica variegata*

underwater vegetation unicellular plants like algae are starved of light and nourishment. Where submerged oxygenators are growing well the water is usually crystal clear and there is little or no algae.

Other functions of these plants include providing depositories for fish eggs and nurseries for the young fry. The latter hide in the tangled masses and so escape from their cannabalistic parents. They also consume a little of the vegetation, as well as the small water creatures which find a haven amongst the foliage. There is also the aesthetic beauty of underwater plants to consider, for looking down on waving stems and leaves is much more pleasant than the appearance of bare soil or concrete. Some species also come to the surface to flower – an extra bonus!

When selecting oxygenators it is important to choose sorts which really are efficient in this respect and some are undoubtedly better than others. Among the most outstanding are the elodeas, particularly *Elodea callitrichoides* and *E. canadensis* (syn. *Anacharis canadensis*), the Canadian pondweed. Both have small, deep green, narrow leaves on branching stems. *Elodea crispa* (more correctly *Lagarosiphon major*) resembles a giant elodea with curly leaves and it too is a splendid oxygenator.

The starworts take their name from the fact that the floating leaves of the spring starwort, *Callitriche palustris* (*C. verna*), form starry masses at the water surface. They are pale green in colour and help to provide shade early in the season. The autumn starwort, *C. hermaphroditica* (*C. autumnalis*), with finer leaves, is more active in the fall and remains submerged.

Crassula (*Tillaea*) *recurva* is a succulent plant with needle-fine leaves and minute white flowers; all the milfoils (*Myriophyllum* sp.) are good; also certain of the pondweeds or potamogetons, particularly *Potamogeton crispus*, the curled pondweed, and *P. densus* or frog's lettuce. These are small plants with leafy, rather brittle stems. Caution should be exercised with certain other potamogetons and particularly with *P. natans*. This will rapidly take over a small pool and can become an obnoxious weed. For deep water both the hornwort (*Ceratophyllum demersum*) and the stonewort (*Chara hispida*) are useful; they have brittle stems with whorls of bristly needle-like leaves.

Among the prettiest of the flowering oxygenators is *Hottonia palustris*, the water violet. This has finely cut, fan-shaped foliage and, in spring, 6-in. spikes of pale lilac, primrose-like flowers above the water. Later the plant forms winter buds and disappears until the following spring.

Ranunculus aquatilis, the water crowfoot, is another spring bloomer; its white, buttercup-like flowers starring the surface of lakes and ponds in March and April. It forms long trails and has two kinds of leaves; the submerged sorts, fan shaped and finely cut; the floating kinds, smooth and resembling small buttercup leaves. This species will also grow in running water.

Utricularia vulgaris is the bladderwort and is a plant which does best in small shallow pools. The 4 to 6-in. emergent spikes of antirrhinum-like flowers are rich yellow and in character in late summer. Utricularias have small bladder-type contraptions on the submerged stems which trap tiny insects for food.

BOG PLANTS
These are plants which link pools, streams and other water features with the rest of the garden. They are moisture lovers which like to feel the influence of water without being in it all the time; so that the soil in which they grow must be always damp but never (except for occasional short periods) be waterlogged.

Since aerobic bacteria work where there are normal air conditions and because of the presence of oxygen in well-drained topsoil, bog plants can be given a richer diet than aquatics. For this reason plenty of humus should be dug into the soil initially or used as mulches in later years. Well-rotted garden compost, farmyard manure, peat or leafmould are all suitable – the aim being to produce a rich friable soil which allows for the easy penetration of plant roots.

Bog plants can be established in spring or autumn and for maximum effect should be grouped in blocks of the same sort of plant. Their numbers include trees and shrubs as well as ferns, grasses, bulbs and herbaceous plants.

HERBACEOUS BOG PLANTS
This is by far the most useful group and includes many which are frequently grown in other situations, such as the herbaceous border or wild garden. Being moisture lovers, however, they give a much better account of themselves when the soil is permanently damp.

The aconitums are good summer bloomers with mostly blue, but sometimes white, cream or bicoloured, helmet-shaped flowers on strong leafy stems. The roots are poisonous but since few people are likely to dig and eat them their cultivation should not be ignored on this account. Among the best are *Aconitum napellus*, the common monkshood, violet blue, and such forms as Bressingham Spire, deep violet and up to 3 ft. and Newry Blue, 3½ ft. The rich blue *A. carmichaelii* (*A. fischeri*) grows to 2½ ft. and the autumn-flowering *A. wilsonii* (by some authorities considered a variety of the preceding) grows to 6 ft. with large violet-blue flowers. *A. vulparia* (*A. lycoctonum*) is a climber reaching to 6 or 7 ft. in moist soil. It has pale yellow flowers.

The actaeas grow well in damp ground and offer both flowers and berries as cultural inducements. *Actaea alba*, the white baneberry, has racemes of white flowers on 12 to 18-in. stems, also deeply cut leaves and white fruits. The red baneberry, *A. rubra*, is similar except for scarlet berries and the cohosh, *A. spicata*, has purplish-black fruits.

Ajugas are adaptable and make good ground-cover plants in most situations – sun or shade, dry or damp – but nowhere do they give a better account of themselves than in soil which is constantly moist. The rich blue, nettle-shaped flowers come in short spikes and the leaves are smooth and entire. *Ajuga reptans*, the common bugle of British woodlands, has a number of forms with variegated foliage, such as *variegata*, grey green and cream; Rainbow, bronze, buff, red and green, and *atropurpurea*, dark purple. There is also a white-flowered form.

The lady's mantle, *Alchemilla mollis*, makes a delightful edging subject for a bog garden, particularly if it is planted where the frothy greenish flowers can be reflected in the water. The silvery cape-shaped leaves are also attractive, but since the plant tends to seed itself about rather too exuberantly, it is wise to remove the old flower heads as these pass from bloom.

Several anemones favour the rich moist soil of a bog garden, particularly *Anemone lesseri*, a garden hybrid of great charm with rounded, shining leaves and cup-shaped, rosy-purple flowers about 2 in. across in early summer. It grows 18 to 24 in. tall and can be propagated by root cuttings taken in early spring.

Aruncus dioicus (*A. sylvester*) is a noble plant for key situations, with massive plumes of hay-scented, creamy-white flowers on sturdy 5 to 6-ft. stems in early summer. The large, deeply divided leaves accentuate their effect. Moist soil and light shade prolongs the flowering season.

Few bog plants are more rewarding than the astilbes, especially when they are associated with waterside irises, primulas and daylilies (hemerocallis). Both the pinnate leaves and plumes of variously coloured, feathery flowers are attractive and, given moist soil at all times, the plants persist for years.

For garden purposes any of the *Astilbe arendsii* forms are the most reliable. These grow between 2 and 3 ft. tall, with pink, red, lilac, crimson and white flowers. Representative varieties are Deutschland, white; Hyacinth, pink; Cattleya, pink with a touch of mauve; Fanal, deep garnet red; Federsee, bright red, and Amethyst, lilac purple.

Among the species *A. davidii* is outstanding for a really damp spot. The stems grow up to 6 ft. with the top 2 ft. packed

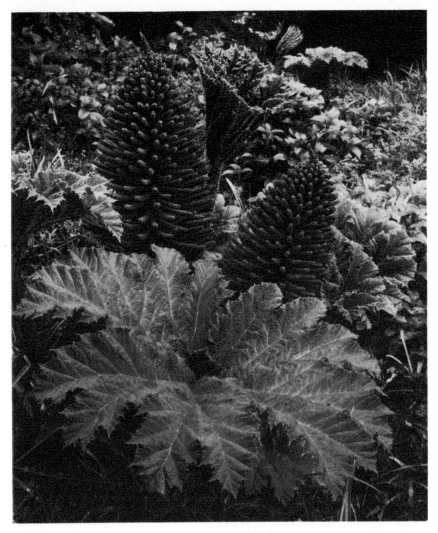

Gunnera manicata

with crimson-magenta flower plumes. The long-stemmed leaves are deeply cut and coarsely toothed. *A. chinensis* is a dwarf for a front row position. Usually less than 1 ft. in height, it has fern-like leaves and deep purple-pink flowers. Astilbes are at their best in mid-summer and can be increased by division of the roots in spring.

Astrantias raised in ordinary borders never attain the quality of bog-grown plants. They need abundant moisture during the summer-flowering season and most borders fail them in this respect. Of erect growth, with lobed leaves and aromatic roots, they have quaint flower heads like tiny Victorian posies, set off by chaff-like bracts. Propagation is by seed or root division in spring or summer. *Astrantia maxima* is pink flowered and up to 2 ft. tall but *A. carniolica rubra* with dull red flowers is the deepest in colour. This likes a little shade and another, *A. major* with rose and green flowers, is the most vigorous and can attain a height of up to 3 ft.

Even lilies will grow in a bog garden; the best for this purpose is undoubtedly *Lilium canadense* which grows up to 5 ft. under ideal conditions, or 2 to 3 ft. when less well situated. Plant the bulbs in autumn 6 to 10 in. deep in moist peaty soil. They dislike lime so chalky ground is unsuitable. The pendant, yellow, bell-shaped flowers are spotted with maroon and purple, with up to twenty blooms on each stem. *L. canadense* can be raised from seed but normally takes three to four years to flower.

L. superbum, the swamp lily of the eastern states of America, is another for damp situations. In very wet soil plant each bulb on a mound so that its roots go down to the water and the bulbs remain free of standing water. The roots should be in semi-shade and the flower stems running up to the sun and light. *L. pardalinum*, the panther or leopard lily, takes its name from the crimson-brown spots which speckle the reddish-orange, turk's cap flowers. These are 3 to 4 in. across, but variable both in size and colour. The stems can attain a height of 8 ft. and like all lilies they should be grouped for maximum effect. Treat as for

L. superbum and divide the clumps every three or four years.

Camassias also belong to the lily family and make useful subjects for damp meadows and similar situations. They flower in early summer, with loose spikes of light to deep blue, funnel-shaped flowers, but white and cream forms are not uncommon. *Camassia leichtlinii* is the best species, but very variable; *plena* is a double sulphur-yellow variety.

The little milkmaids or 'faint sweet cuckoo flowers' of Tennyson (*Cardamine pratensis*) can be allowed to seed and naturalize in damp meadows or the wilder parts of the bog garden. Growing 6 to 9 in. high, they have cress-like leaves (once used for salads) and spikes of simple, pale mauve flowers. *Plena*, a form with double flowers, is more showy but has to be propagated by division.

The snake's heads are *Chelone glabra*, white flowered, and *C. obliqua*, reddish purple, and they flower in late summer with terminal heads of small foxglove-like blooms on 2-ft. stems. These need deep moist soil at all times.

Cimicifugas bloom in late summer and are often seen in herbaceous borders. But they are even more effective in bog gardens, either in sun or partial shade, with their graceful, feathery plumes of fragrant flowers on 5 to 7-ft. stems and smooth, doubly compound leaves. *Cimicifuga racemosa* is one of the best, especially in the varieties Elstead White and White Pearl but *C. dahurica* and *C. cordifolia* follow later in the season and are useful on that account.

Eupatoriums are coarse perennials with large, flat, terminal clusters of white or dull purple flowers and nettle-like or slender pointed leaves in whorls. They are useful for late summer colour especially in the rougher parts of the garden. *Eupatorium cannabinum*, the hemp agrimony, grows to 4 ft. and is dull purple which becomes more effective in its double form; *E. purpureum*, Joe Pye weed, is 3 to 4 ft. with 6 to 9-in., purplish-pink flower heads and *E. rugosum* (*E. ageratoides*), white flowered and 2 to 4 ft. tall, has nettle-like leaves.

Filipendula ulmaria is the meadow sweet, one of the most beautiful of British plants, frequently found alongside streams or in wet ditches. It is perennial with deeply cut leaves and spiraea-like plumes of small flowers. Under damp conditions it grows 2 to 3 ft. tall, or shorter where there is less moisture. The double form *flore plena* is the most effective or any of the foliage variants with golden leaves or cream and green variegations.

Others for the bog garden are *F. camtschatica*, a species from Manchuria with 6 ft. or more of leafy stem terminating in loose panicles of white flowers; *F. purpurea* (*Spiraea palmata* of gardens) with palmate foliage and flat heads of carmine or deep rose florets and *F. rubra* (*Spiraea lobata*) which has clusters of fragant, pink flowers on 2 to 3-ft stems.

Massive-leaved plants are only suitable for large bog gardens, but given the space, nothing looks more impressive than a clump of *Gunnera manicata*. This noble plant produces giant, rhubarb-like leaves 5 to 6ft. across and as much in length (even larger under good conditions) on thick, spiny, 10 to 15-ft. stems. The green-brown flowers come in 3-ft. spikes and look like huge bottle brushes. Since the slightest touch of frost damages the leaves, protection is advisable in cool climates.

Others with large leaves are the ornamental rhubarbs. *Rheum palmatum* is a good waterside plant with creamy-white flowers on 5 to 6-ft. leafy stems and five-lobed leaves. There are also forms with red leaves and crimson flowers.

Primula Inverewe (orange) and Rodgersia aesculifolia (cream)

Among the most beautiful waterside perennials are the bog primulas, especially the candelabra types, which carry the flowers in whorls round their stems. These must have moisture, ideal conditions being provided by a soil which is rich, cool and constantly moist without being water-logged. For most telling effects they should be colonized in bold groups, possibly associated with blue poppies. If allowed to seed naturally, all sorts of interesting forms appear and in a wide colour range. Alternatively, collected seed, gathered as soon as ripe, can be sown in pans or boxes of peaty soil. Keep them cool and in a shady place to germinate, then prick out the young seedlings in boxes or pot them separately. They can then be planted in their flowering positions in spring or autumn.

Primula rosea is the earliest to bloom, often at the end of winter, the flowers brilliant deep pink on 6 to 9-in. stems. Among the candelabra sorts are *P. japonica*, with pink, white or crimson flowers,

often 'eyed' in different colours and up to 2 ft. in height, and *P. pulverulenta*, with mealy stems and rich crimson flowers in the type but variable in such strains as Bartley, when rose-pink, salmon, buff and apricot shades are common. The usual height is between 2½ and 3 ft. *P. beesiana*, violet purple and 2 ft.; *P. bulleyana*, orange, 2 ft., and *P. burmanica*, crimson purple, are others of this type. There are also a number of yellows of which *P. florindae* is one of the best. It is like a giant cowslip, with long, heart-shaped leaves and 3-ft. spikes of pendant flowers. *P.*

Mimulus, irises and primulas are included in this attractive waterside planting

sikkimensis forms rosettes of long and narrow leaves with slender, 2-ft. stems terminating in nodding, pale yellow flowers.

Moisture-loving irises are essential for the bog garden. Closely related to the aquatic *Iris laevigata* (see p. 164) is *I. kaempferi*, the clematis-flowered iris of Japan. This has large flat flowers, either in self blue, white, pink or red, but more often suffused, striated, centre eyed or banded in other shades. They are very striking with their unusual colouration and flat ribbon-like leaves. The species dislikes lime and needs to have the roots moist in summer but drier in winter. Named sorts (often with unpronounceable Japanese names) are available but mixed seedlings are usually very good and much more economical to buy. *I. kaempferi* can be distinguished from *I. laevigata* by the leaves; there is a prominent midrib down the centre of those of *I. kaempferi*, but none on *I. laevigata*. The usual height is around 2 ft.

I. sibirica, also with grassy foliage, has several dainty flowers poised on each 2 to 4-ft. stem. These make excellent cut blooms and are often grown in mixed or herbaceous borders. The flowers are mostly blue, but variable from pale sky blue to deep violet and mauve. There are also white varieties. Although the species and its forms will grow in dry borders and in sun or light shade, they give a better account of themselves in moist soil.

I. delavayi, a native of the Yunnan marshes of China, grows 3 to 4 ft. under favourable moist conditions. The flowers are deep violet with some white spotting and *I. versicolor*, with claret-purple flowers on 2-ft stems, is another for moist soil.

Hemerocallis (daylilies) are indispensable plants for the garden since they seem to thrive in almost any soil, climate or situation; indeed they have even been grown in shallow water. I have seen daylilies in the arctic and others on the equator which gives some idea of their adaptability. Once established the clumps can be left undisturbed for years, the arching foliage attractive even when the flowers are not in character. The large, funnel-shaped, often fragrant blooms only live a day, but since modern hybrids produce countless buds the flowering season extends over several weeks. Besides such species as the tawny-orange *Hemerocallis fulva* and its double form Kwanso and *H. citrina*, pale lemon, there are countless varieties available, many of which are diploids. These come in a wide range of shades from palest lemon to canary yellow, tangerine, pinks (like Pink Domino and Pink Prelude) and crimsons (like Stafford and War Eagle).

Good late summer perennials are the lythrums and ligularias. The purple loosestrifes (*Lythrum salicaria* and varieties) have spikes of bright rosy-red or pink flowers on branching 2 to 3-ft. stems. They should be massed for maximum effect and sited where the setting sun can shine on and through their petals, then they glow like fire. The best varieties are

Brightness, rosy pink; Beacon, rosy red, and Robert, clear pink.

Ligularias belong to the daisy family and are linked – and frequently confused – with senecios. Nearly all the waterside types have large handsome leaves, tall branching stems and showy daisy flowers. They require plenty of water during the growing season and should be given plenty of sun.

Ligularia dentata (Senecio clivorum) has large kidney-shaped smooth leaves about 18 in. across and lots of rich orange flowers on sturdy stems which may go up to 5 ft. when established. It is inclined to be coarse, however, and should not be planted near weaker plants which it can smother, although it makes an excellent subject to grow near a stand pipe, as it masks the latter in summer. Varieties of the species are more popular for planting in water gardens, particularly Greynog Gold, which is more compact and around 3 ft. high with bronze-centred gold flowers; Othello, rich orange, and Desdemona, also orange but with purplish foliage.

L. hodgsonii has purplish overtones on the kidney-shaped serrated leaves and through these come clusters of rich orange flowers on 2-ft. stems. *L. japonica* is the giant ragwort, a plant needing plenty of water when it will run up to 5 ft.; its orange-yellow flowers on branching stems.

The most arresting member of the group, however, is *L. przewalskii (Senecio przewalskii)*, a very distinct plant with stately, wand-like, almost black stems. These grow 5 to 6 ft. high and are tightly packed along their upper lengths with bright yellow, raggle-taggle rosettes of flowers. The dark-stemmed, dark-veined, deeply jagged leaves are also handsome and as long as the roots are damp the plant thrives in sun or partial shade. All the ligularias can be divided in spring.

Lysimachia clethroides is a relative of the primrose and a Japanese species of 2 or 3 ft. with long, pendant, buddleia-like sprays of small white blossoms and broadly lanceolate leaves. It is suitable for sun or semi-shade. The great yellow loosestrife, *L. vulgaris*, is a British species, inclined to spread so best confined to wild garden settings. It has whorls of bright yellow flowers around the stems and tapering leaves. The Romans believed that the flowers put under the yokes of oxen kept them from quarrelling, hence the popular name.

L. punctata, also British and very similar but less rampant, grows around 1½ to 2 ft. The golden-flowered, golden-leaved form of creeping jenny (*L. nummularia*) is often useful at the edge of a

pool since it makes a compact ground cover and will even grow down to the water. It is suitable for sun or partial shade.

Mimulus hybrids are best treated as annuals, sowing the seed in spring under glass and then planting them out in moist soil and semi-shade. The large speckled and marbled flowers grow 6 to 9 in. in height and come in a wide range of colour combinations, but chiefly red, yellow and orange. *Lobelia fulgens*, the cardinal flower, with wine-red leaves and scarlet flowers is a dependable summer bloomer if the roots are moist. It grows 2 to 3 ft. tall and is best renewed frequently from cuttings and protected in winter.

Trollius and ranunculus are other moisture lovers, the former with round, globe-like flowers of yellow or orange. *Trollius europaeus* varieties grow 2 to 2½ ft. tall and associate well with irises and primulas. *Ranunculus acris flore pleno* is a double yellow buttercup and *R. aconitifolius flore pleno*, the fair maids of France, has double white flowers. Both grow around 1½ ft.

Rodgersias have handsome leaves and sprays of spiraea-like flowers. *Rodgersia aesculifolia* has horse chestnut-like foliage and white flowers; *R. pinnata*, also with deeply divided leaves, is rosy red and *R. tabularis (Astilboides tabularis)* has yellowish-white blooms and round umbrella-like leaves.

Finally arum lilies *(Zantedeschia aethiopica)* are often successful in bog gardens, particularly the form known as Crowborough. The roots should receive plenty of water in summer but be kept on the dry side in winter; best effected by covering them with dry leaves and a polythene cover or laying pieces of glass propped on bricks over the crowns.

Zantedeschia aethiopica

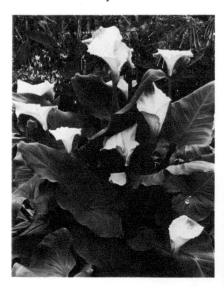

Plant Lists and Index

Shrubs and Climbers

Climbers

Actinidia (all) 10
Campsis (all) 12
Clematis (all those listed) 14
Hedera (all except *H. helix arborescens*) 19
Hydrangea petiolaris 20
Jasminum (all those listed) 20
Lonicera japonica (and varieties) 23
L. periclymenum (and varieties) 23–4
Parthenocissus (all) 24
Passiflora 25
Pileostegia 27
Polygonum baldschuanicum 27
Schizophragma (all) 29
Solanum (all those listed) 29
Wisteria (all) 32

For hot, dry places

Campsis (all) 12
Carpenteria 12–13
Caryopteris 13
Ceanothus (all) 13
Choisya 13
Cistus (all) 13–14
Colutea (all those listed) 15
Cotinus 16
Cytisus (all) 16
Genista (all) 18
Hibiscus syriacus 20
Lavatera olbia 21
Olearia gunniana 24
O. scilloniensis 24
Passiflora 25–6
Perovskia 26
Phlomis (all) 26
Rosmarinus (all) 28
Santolina (all) 29
Senecio greyii 29
S. laxifolius 29
Solanum (all those listed) 29–30
Spartium 30
Tamarix (all) 30
Yucca (all) 32

For shade

Aucuba 10
Azalea (all) 10–11
Buxus 12
Camellia 12
Danae 16
Elaeagnus (all those listed) 16–17
Euonymus fortunei (and varieties) 17
Fatsia 18
Hedera (all) 19
Hydrangea macrophylla 20
H. petiolaris 20
Hypericum calycinum 20
Leycesteria formosa 21
Ligustrum (all those listed) 21–2
Lonicera nitida 22
Mahonia aquifolium 24
Pileostegia 27
Prunus laurocerasus 27–8
P. lusitanica (and varieties) 27–8
Rhododendron (all) 28
Rubus spectabilis 29
R. ulmifolius bellidiflorus 29

Sarcococca (all) 29
Schizophragma (all) 29
Skimmia (all) 29
Viburnum davidii 32

For damp places

Cornus alba sibirica 15
C. stolonifera flaviramea 15
Neillia longiracemosa 24
Sambucus (all) 29
Sorbaria (all) 30
Spiraea billardieri triumphans 30
S. vanhouttei 30
S. veitchii 30
Symphoricarpos (all those listed) 30
Viburnum opulus (and varieties) 30–1

Suitable for chalk

Aucuba 10
Berberis (all) 11
Buddleia alternifolia 11–12
B. davidii 11–12
Ceanothus (all) 13
Cistus (all) 13–14
Clematis (all those listed) 14
Colutea (all) 15
Cornus mas 15–16
Cotoneaster (all) 16
Deutzia (all) 16
Euonymus (all) 17
Genista cinerea 18
Hebe (all) 19
Hypericum (all) 20
Jasminum (all) 20
Lavandula (all) 21
Lonicera (all) 22–4
Mahonia aquifolium 24
Olearia (all) 24
Paeonia delavayi 24
P. lutea 24
Philadelphus (all) 26
Prunus (all) 27–8
Pyracantha (all) 28
Sambucus (all) 29
Schizophragma (all) 29
Senecio greyii 29
S. laxifolius 29
Spartium 30
Symphoricarpos (all) 30
Syringa (all) 30
Vitis (all) 32
Weigela (all) 32
Yucca (all) 32

Requiring acid soil (intolerant of chalk)

Azalea (all) 10
Camellia (all) 12
Enkianthus (all) 17
Kalmia (all) 20
Magnolia (all those listed) 24
Pernettya 26
Pieris (all) 26–7
Rhododendron (all) 28

For seaside gardens

Escallonia (all) 17
Euonymus japonicus (and varieties) 17
Fuchsia (all) 18

Hebe andersonii variegata 19
H. brachysiphon 19
H. hulkeana 19
H. Midsummer Beauty 19
H. salicifolia 19
H. speciosa hybrids 19
Hydrangea macrophylla 20
Lavatera olbia 21
Olearia macrodonta 24
Senecio rotundifolius 29
Tamarix (all) 30
Yucca (all) 32

With coloured or variegated foliage

Actinidia kolomikta 10
Berberis thunbergii atropurpurea 11
Buxus sempervirens (varieties) 12
Cornus alba elegantissima 15
C. a. spaethii 15
Cotinus coggygria (and varieties) 16
Daphne odora marginata 16
Elaeagnus pungens maculata 16–17
Euonymus fortunei (and varieties) 17
E. japonicus (and varieties) 17
Fuchsia magellanica variegata 18
Hebe andersonii variegata 19
Hedera canariensis variegata 20
H. colchica dentata variegata 20
H. helix marginata elegantissima 19
Ligustrum ovalifolium argenteum 21
L. o. aureum 21
Lonicera japonica aureo-reticulata 23
L. nitida Baggessen's Gold 22
Osmanthus ilicifolius aureomarginatus 24
O. i. variegatus 24
Parthenocissus henryana 25
Prunus cistena 28
Sambucus nigra aurea 29
Vitis vinifera purpurea 32

With autumn colour

Azalea (deciduous) 10–11
Berberis Buccaneer 11
B. jamesiana 11
Callicarpa 12
Cotoneaster franchettii sternianum 16
C. horizontalis 16
Enkianthus campanulatus 17
Euonymus alatus 17
E. europaeus 17
E. latifolius 17
E. yedoensis 17
Hamamelis mollis (and variety *pallida*) 18
Hypericum inodorum Elstead 20
Parthenocissus (all) 24–5
Vitis coignetiae 32
V. vinifera Brandt 32

Grown for berries or fruits

Berberis Buccaneer 11
B. jamesiana 11

Callicarpa 12
Cotoneaster (all) 16
Daphne mezereum 16
Euonymus europaeus 17
E. latifolius 17
E. yedoensis 17
Hypericum inodorum Elstead 20
Leycesteria 21
Pernettya 26
Pyracantha (all) 28
Skimmia japonica foremannii (and other female varieties) 29
S. reevesiana 29
Symphoricarpos (all) 30
Viburnum betulifolium 32
V. opulus compactum 31
V. o. fructuluteo 30
Vitis 32

Winter flowering

Chimonanthus 13
Garrya 18
Hamamelis mollis (and variety *pallida*) 18
Jasminum nudiflorum 20
Lonicera fragrantissimum 22
L. standishii 22
Mahonia Charity 24
M. japonica 24
Viburnum bodnantense 31
V. fragrans 31
V. tinus 32

Roses

Crimson

LARGE-FLOWERED BUSH HYBRID TEA
Alec's Red (light) 35
Ena Harkness (medium) 36
Ernest H. Morse (medium) 36
Eroica (deep) 36
John Waterer (deep) 36
Josephine Bruce (deep) 36
National Trust (medium) 36
Red Devil (light) 36
Red Planet (deep) 36–7

CLUSTER-FLOWERED BUSH (FLORIBUNDA)
Dr Barnardo (medium) 38
Lilli Marlene (medium) 38
Marlena (medium) 38
Rob Roy (deep) 39
Stephen Langdon (medium) 39

MODERN SHRUBS
Fountain (deep) 40
Heidelberg (deep) 41
Herbstfeuer (light) 41

MINIATURES
Little Buckaroo (medium) 42
Perla de Alcanada (light) 42

MODERN CLIMBERS
Altissimo (medium) 43
Crimson Shower (medium) 43
Ena Harkness, Climbing (medium) 43
Etoile de Hollande, Climbing (deep) 43
Sympathie (deep) 44

OLD GARDEN ROSES
Capitaine John Ingram (deep) 44
Charles de Mills (purplish) 44
Nuits de Young (deep) 45
Tuscany Superb (purplish) 46

WILD ROSE
Moyesii Geranium (light) 48

MOST FRAGRANT
Alec's Red 35
Eroica 36
Etoile de Hollande, Climbing 43

SHORTEST GROWTH
Little Buckaroo 42
Marlena 38
Perla de Alcanada 42

LARGEST BLOOMS
Alec's Red 35
John Waterer 36
Red Devil 36

BEAUTIFUL SEEDPODS
Herbstfeuer 41
Moyesii Geranium 48

BRIGHTEST COLOURS
Altissimo 43
National Trust 36
Rob Roy 39
Stephen Langdon 39

Scarlet

LARGE-FLOWERED BUSH (HYBRID TEA)
Alexander (light) 35
Baccara (medium) 35
Fragrant Cloud (deep) 36
Pharaoh (medium) 36
Super Star (light) 37

CLUSTER-FLOWERED BUSH (FLORIBUNDA)
Anne Cocker (light) 37
City of Belfast (medium) 37
Evelyn Fison (deep) 38
Irish Mist (light) 38
Lively Lady (medium) 38
Megiddo (medium) 38
Meteor (light) 38
Orangeade (medium) 39
Orange Sensation (medium) 39
Orange Silk (medium) 39
Sarabande (deep) 39
Topsi (medium) 40

MODERN SHRUBS
Bonn (medium) 40
Dorothy Wheatcroft (deep) 40
Fred Loads (light) 40

MODERN CLIMBERS
Danse des Sylphes (deep) 43
Danse du Feu (deep) 43
Parkdirektor Riggers (deep) 44
Paul's Scarlet Climber (medium) 44

MOST FRAGRANT
Fragrant Cloud 36

SHORTEST GROWTH
Meteor 38
Topsi 40

LARGEST BLOOMS
Fragrant Cloud 36
Pharaoh 36
Super Star 37

BRIGHTEST COLOURS
Alexander 35
Anne Cocker 37
City of Belfast 37
Fred Loads 40
Megiddo 38

Roses *continued*

Orange Sensation 39
Topsi 40

Pink

LARGE-FLOWERED BUSH
(HYBRID TEA)
Blessings (medium) 36
Bonsoir (light) 36
Lady Seton (medium) 36
Meinatac (medium) 36
Mullard Jubilee (deep) 36
Pink Favourite (medium) 36
Prima Ballerina (medium) 36
Wendy Cussons (deep) 37

CLUSTER-FLOWERED BUSH
(FLORIBUNDA)
Arakan (light) 37
Busy Lizzie (light) 37
Dearest (medium) 38
Kerryman (deep) 38
Paddy McGredy (deep) 39
Pink Elizabeth Arden (medium)
39
Pink Parfait (light) 39
Queen Elizabeth (medium) 39
Vera Dalton (medium) 40

MODERN SHRUBS
Ballerina (light) 40
Cornelia (medium) 40
Felicia (light) 40
Fritz Nobis (deep) 40
Marguerite Hilling (medium) 41
Penelope (light) 41
Pink Grootendorst (medium) 41
The Fairy (medium) 41
Yesterday (medium) 41

MINIATURES
Humpty Dumpty (medium) 42
Sweet Fairy (medium) 42

MODERN CLIMBERS
Bantry Bay (medium) 43
Morning Jewel (deep) 44
New Dawn (light) 44
Pink Perpetue (deep) 44
Rosy Mantle (light) 44

OLD GARDEN ROSES
Cécile Brunner (light) 44
Cécile Brunner, Climbing (light)
44
Celestial (medium) 44
Common Moss (medium) 44
Crested Moss (medium) 45
De Meaux (medium) 45
La Reine Victoria (medium) 45
Maiden's Blush (light) 45
Old Blush (medium) 45
Petite de Hollande (medium) 45
Pompon de Paris, Climbing
(medium) 45
Souvenir de la Malmaison (light)
45
Spong (medium) 45
Zéphirine Drouhin (deep) 46

WILD ROSES
Californica (medium) 46
Complicata (medium) 47
Farreri Persetosa (medium) 47
Frau Dagmar Hartopp (light)
47–8
Mirifica (medium) 48
Multibracteata (medium) 48
Paulii Rosea (medium) 48
Rubrifolia (light) 48

MOST FRAGRANT
Lady Seton 36
La Reine Victoria 45
Prima Ballerina 36
Wendy Cussons 37
Yesterday 41
Zéphirine Drouhin 46

SHORTEST GROWTH
Arakan 37
Cécile Brunner 44
Humpty Dumpty 42
Mirifica 48
Paddy McGredy 39
Sweet Fairy 42
The Fairy 41

LARGEST BLOOMS
Bonsoir 36
Mullard Jubilee 36
Pink Favourite 36
Wendy Cussons 37

BEAUTIFUL SEEDPODS
Frau Dagmar Hartopp 47–8
Rubrifolia 48

BRIGHTEST COLOURS
Fritz Nobis 40
Kerryman 38
Meinatac 36
Morning Jewel 44
Pink Elizabeth Arden 39
Pompon de Paris, Climbing 45
Prima Ballerina 36
Yesterday 41

Salmon

LARGE-FLOWERED BUSH
(HYBRID TEA)
Evensong (towards rose) 36
Harlow (towards red) 36
Mischief (towards pink) 36
Sweet Promise (towards pink) 37
Truly Yours (towards orange) 37

CLUSTER-FLOWERED BUSH
(FLORIBUNDA)
Charles Dickens (towards
orange) 37
City of Leeds (towards pink)
37–8
Elizabeth of Glamis (towards
orange) 38
Margo Koster (towards red) 38
Michelle (towards pink) 38
Scented Air (towards red) 39
Tony Jacklin (towards red) 39–40

MINIATURES
Coralin (towards red) 41
New Penny (towards red) 42

MODERN CLIMBERS
Compassion (towards orange) 43

MOST FRAGRANT
Compassion 43
Truly Yours 37

SHORTEST GROWTH
Coralin 41
Margo Koster 38
New Penny 42

LARGEST BLOOMS
Evensong 36
Harlow 36
Mischief 36

BRIGHTEST COLOURS
Charles Dickens 37

Harlow 36
Mischief 36
New Penny 42

Bicoloured

The bicolour roses have different
colours on inner and outer sides
of the petals.

LARGE-FLOWERED BUSH
(HYBRID TEA)
Chicago Peace (pink, yellow) 36
Colour Wonder (orange red,
yellow) 36
Curiosity (red, yellow) 36
Kronenbourg (purple red,
yellow) 36
Piccadilly (scarlet, yellow) 36
Rose Gaujard (carmine, white)
37
Stella (carmine, blush) 37

CLUSTER-FLOWERED BUSH
(FLORIBUNDA)
Molly McGredy (red, white) 38

WILD ROSE
Austrian Copper (scarlet, yellow)
46

LARGEST BLOOMS
Chicago Peace 36
Kronenbourg 36
Stella 37

BRIGHTEST COLOURS
Austrian Copper 46
Colour Wonder 36
Piccadilly 36

VARIEGATED FOLIAGE
Curiosity 36

Blended

The blended roses have colours
mixed or shaded on one or both
sides of the petals.

LARGE-FLOWERED BUSH
(HYBRID TEA)
Adolf Horstmann (yellow and
red) 35
Honey Favourite (buff and red)
36
Just Joey (salmon and orange) 36
Perfecta (cream and pink) 36
Typhoon (orange and salmon) 37

CLUSTER-FLOWERED BUSH
(FLORIBUNDA)
Apricot Nectar (buff and yellow)
37
Masquerade (yellow and red) 38
Picasso (red and blush) 39
Redgold (yellow and red) 39

MODERN SHRUBS
Frühlingsmorgen (pink and
cream) 40–1
Joseph's Coat (yellow and red) 41

MINIATURES
Baby Masquerade (yellow and
pink) 41
Little Flirt (orange pink and
yellow) 42

MODERN CLIMBERS
Albertine (light rose and salmon)
42–3
Handel (cream and rose red) 44

Phyllis Bide (yellow and pink) 44

OLD GARDEN ROSES
Camaieux (pink and white) 44
Commandant Beaurepaire (pink
and red) 44
Gallica Versicolor (blush and
red) 45
Lady Penzance (fawn pink and
yellow) 45
Mme Pierre Oger (cream and
pink) 45
Président de Sèze (red and white)
45

WILD ROSE
Mutabilis (buff and red) 48

MOST FRAGRANT
Frühlingsmorgen 40–1
Typhoon 37

SHORTEST GROWTH
Baby Masquerade 41
Little Flirt 42

LARGEST BLOOMS
Perfecta 36

BRIGHTEST COLOURS
Joseph's Coat 41
Just Joey 36
Masquerade 38
Redgold 39
Typhoon 37

SCENTED LEAVES
Lady Penzance 45
Lord Penzance 45

COMPLETE COLOUR CHANGE
Masquerade 38
Mutabilis 48

STRIPED OR WELL MARKED
Camaieux 44
Commandant Beaurepaire 44
Gallica Versicolor 45
Handel 44
Picasso 39
Président de Sèze 45

Orange

LARGE-FLOWERED BUSH
(HYBRID TEA)
Beaute (yellow orange) 36
Troika (red orange) 37
Whisky Mac (amber yellow) 37

CLUSTER-FLOWERED BUSH
(FLORIBUNDA)
Bonfire Night (red orange) 37
Living Fire (red orange) 38
Manx Queen (orange yellow-red)
38
Pineapple Poll (yellow orange,
red) 39
Princess Michiko (red orange) 39
Southampton (orange yellow,
apricot) 39

MODERN CLIMBERS
Maigold (yellow orange) 44
Schoolgirl (pink orange) 44

MOST FRAGRANT
Maigold 44
Pineapple Poll 39

SHORTEST GROWTH
Pineapple Poll 39

LARGEST BLOOMS
Beaute 36
Whisky Mac 37

BRIGHTEST COLOURS
Bonfire Night 37
Living Fire 38
Maigold 44
Princess Michiko 39
Southampton 39
Whisky Mac 37

Yellow

Many yellow roses show at ti
red marks on the outer petals

LARGE-FLOWERED BUSH
(HYBRID TEA)
Diorama (deep) 36
Grandpa Dickson (light) 36
King's Ransom (deep) 36
Peace (light, with pink) 36
Peer Gynt (deep, with red) 36
Sutter's Gold (medium, with
pink) 37
Yellow Pages (deep) 37

CLUSTER-FLOWERED BUSH
(FLORIBUNDA)
Allgold (deep) 37
Arthur Bell (medium) 37
Gardeners' Sunday (deep) 38
Kim (medium, with red) 38
Moonmaiden (cream) 38–9

MODERN SHRUBS
Buff Beauty (cream) 40
Chinatown (deep) 40
Frühlingsgold (cream) 40
Golden Wings (cream) 41

MINIATURE
Rosina (medium) 42

MODERN CLIMBERS
Casino (medium) 43
Golden Showers (deep) 44
Mermaid (cream) 44

WILD ROSES
Banksian Yellow (light) 46
Canary Bird (medium) 47
Cantabrigiensis (cream) 47
Golden Chersonese (deep) 48
Hardii (light, red eye) 48

MOST FRAGRANT
Arthur Bell 37
Frühlingsgold 40
Golden Chersonese 48
Sutter's Gold 37

SHORTEST GROWTH
Kim 38
Rosina 42

LARGEST BLOOMS
Grandpa Dickson 36
Peace 36
Peer Gynt 36

BRIGHTEST COLOURS
Allgold 37
Chinatown 40
Gardeners' Sunday 38
Golden Chersonese 48
Golden Showers 44
King's Ransom 36
Peer Gynt 36
Yellow Pages 37

Damp or waterside positions

Astilbe 92–3
Brunnera 93
Gillenia 98
Hosta 99
Iris (some) 99
Oenothera 102
Polygonum (some) 105
Rodgersia 106
Tovara 109

Fairly dry shade

Anaphalis 90
Bergenia 93
Geranium (some) 97
Helleborus (some) 98
Pulmonaria 105–6
Tellima 108

For shade

(not very dry from tree roots)
Astilbe 92–3
Epimedium 96
Gillenia 98
Helleborus 98
Heucherella 98
Hosta 99
Kirengeshoma 99–100
Meconopsis 102
Omphalodes 102
Polygonum (some) 105
Pulmonaria 105–6
Rodgersia 106
Stylophorum 108
Tricyrtis 109
Trillium 109
Veratrum 110

Useful for cutting or drying

Achillea 90
Anaphalis 90
Anthemis 92
Aster 92
Campanula 93–4
Catananche 94
Chrysanthemum 94
Doronicum 96
Echinops 96
Erigeron 96
Eryngium 96
Helenium 98
Heuchera 98
Kniphofia 100
Liatris 100–1
Libertia 101
Limonium 101
Macleaya 102
Paeonia 102
Phlox 103
Physostegia 103
Pyrethrum 106
Rudbeckia 106
Sanguisorba 106
Scabiosa 106
Sidalcea 107
Solidago 107
Tellima 108
Thalictrum 108–9
Thermopsis 109
Zygadenus 110

Perennials which can usually be left undisturbed for several years

Acanthus 90
Anaphalis 90
Anemone 90
Bergenia 93
Brunnera 93

Campanula (tall kinds) 93–4
Centaurea (tall kinds) 94
Cirsium 94
Crambe 95
Cynoglossum 95
Dianthus 95
Dicentra 95–6
Dictamnus 96
Diplarrhena 96
Echinacea 96
Echinops 96
Epimedium 96
Eryngium 96
Euphorbia 96–7
Gentiana 97
Geranium 97
Gillenia 98
Gypsophila 98
Heliopsis 98
Helleborus 98
Hosta 99
Incarvillea 99
Iris 99
Kirengeshoma 99–100
Kniphofia 100
Libertia 101
Limonium 101
Liriope 101
Moraea 102
Morina 102
Omphalodes 102
Origanum 102
Paeonia 102
Papaver 102–3
Phlox 103
Platycodon 103–5
Polygonum (some) 105
Potentilla 105
Pulmonaria 105–6
Pulsatilla 105
Rodgersia 106
Roscoea 106
Salvia 106
Sanguisorba 106
Satureia 106
Sedum 106–7
Selinum 107
Serratula 107
Stokesia 107
Strobilanthes 107–8
Telekia 108
Thalictrum 108–9
Thermopsis 109
Tovara 109
Tradescantia 109
Tricyrtis 109
Trillium 109
Veratrum 110
Verbascum 110
Vernonia 110
Zygadenus 110

Perennials which are best curbed or divided and replanted every two, three or four years or are relatively short lived

Achillea 90
Anchusa 90
Anthemis 92
Aster 92
Catananche 94
Centaurea (dwarf kinds) 94
Centranthus 94
Chrysanthemum 94
Coreopsis 94–5
Delphinium 95
Doronicum 96
Erigeron 96
Geranium (some) 97
Geum 97–8
Helenium 98
Heuchera 98

Heucherella 98
Inula 99
Knautia 100
Liatris 100–1
Linum 101
Lupinus 101
Lychnis 101–2
Macleaya 102
Meconopsis 102
Monarda 102
Nepeta 102
Oenothera 102
Penstemon 103
Physostegia 103
Polemonium 105
Polygonum (some) 105
Prunella 105
Pyrethrum 106
Rudbeckia 106
Scabiosa 106
Sidalcea 107
Sisyrinchium 107
Solidago 107
Stachys 107
Stylophorum 108
Tellima 108
Veronica (dwarf kinds) 110

Full sun with a well-drained soil

Achillea 90
Anchusa 90
Anemone 90
Anthemis 92
Armeria 92
Catananche 94
Centaurea 94
Chrysanthemum 94
Cirsium 94
Coreopsis 94–5
Crepis 95
Delphinium 95
Dianthus 95
Dictamnus 96
Diplarrhena 96
Echinacea 96
Echinops 96
Erigeron 96
Eryngium 96
Euphorbia 96–7
Geum 97–8
Gypsophila 98
Helenium 98
Heliopsis 98
Heuchera 98
Incarvillea 99
Inula 99
Iris 99
Knautia 100
Kniphofia 100
Liatris 100–1
Libertia 101
Limonium 101
Linum 101
Lupinus 101
Lychnis 101–2
Moraea 102
Morina 102
Nepeta 102
Oenothera 102
Origanum 102
Paeonia 102
Papaver 102–3
Penstemon 103
Physostegia 103
Platycodon 103–5
Potentilla 105
Prunella 105
Pulsatilla 106
Pyrethrum 106
Salvia 106
Sanguisorba 106
Satureia 106

Scabiosa 106
Sedum 106–7
Serratula 107
Sidalcea 107
Sisyrinchium 107
Solidago 107
Stachys 107
Stokesia 107
Telekia 108
Thermopsis 109
Tradescantia 109
Verbascum 110
Veronica 110

Annuals and Biennials

For window boxes and other containers

Ageratum 120
Alyssum 113
Bellis 113–14
Calceolaria 127
Calendula 126
Centaurea 115
Cheiranthus 116
Dahlia 114
Lathyrus 114, 116
Limnanthes 114
Lobelia 122
Matricaria 114
Matthiola 114
Myosotis 126
Papaver 118, 126
Petunia 114
Salvia 114
Tropaeolum 114–15, 118

Fragrant annuals and biennials

Alyssum 113
Antirrhinum 126
Asperula 115
Centaurea 115
Cheiranthus 116
Dianthus 116
Exacum 116
Heliotropium 116
Hesperis 119
Humea 116
Lathyrus 114, 116
Tropaeolum 114–15, 118
Viola 120

Climbing annuals

Cobaea 116
Cucurbita 116
Eccremocarpus 116
Humulus 116
Ipomoea 116–17
Maurandya 117
Quamoclit 117
Thunbergia 117–18
Tropaeolum 114–15, 118

Annuals and biennials for drying

Eryngium 118
Gomphrena 118
Gypsophila 118, 120
Helichrysum 118
Helipterum 118
Limonium 118
Lunaria 118
Molucella 118
Nicandra 118
Nigella 118
Papaver 118, 126
Zea 118–19

Shade tolerant annuals and biennials

Aquilegia 119
Begonia 126
Collinsia 119
Cynoglossum 119
Digitalis 119
Hesperis 119
Impatiens 119
Lunaria 118
Meconopsis 119
Mimulus 119–20
Nemophila 120
Tropaeolum 114–15, 118
Viola 120

Annuals for rock gardens and small containers

Adonis 120
Ageratum 120
Brachycome 120
Cotula 120
Dorotheanthus 120
Felicia 120
Gilia 120
Gypsophila 118, 120
Iberis 122
Ionopsidium 122
Layia 122
Linaria 122
Lobelia 122
Nemesia 122
Nierembergia 122
Phlox 122
Portulaca 120
Sedum 122
Silene 122

Annuals and biennials for cutting

Agrostemma 122
Amaranthus 122–3
Calendula 126
Callistephus 123
Centaurea 123
Chrysanthemum 123
Clarkia 123
Cleome 123
Coreopsis 123
Cosmos 123
Dahlia 114
Delphinium 123–4
Dianthus 116
Gaillardia 124
Godetia 124
Lathyrus 114, 116
Rudbeckia 124
Salpiglossis 124
Scabiosa 124–6
Tropaeolum 114–15, 118
Viola 120
Zinnia 126

Long-flowering annuals and biennials

Ageratum 120
Alyssum 113
Antirrhinum 126
Begonia 126
Calendula 126
Chrysanthemum 123
Dahlia 114
Eschscholzia 126
Impatiens 119
Matthiola 114
Myosotis 126
Papaver 118, 126
Primula 126
Tagetes 126
Tropaeolum 114–15, 118
Verbena 126